T0192286

Lecture Notes in Computer Science　14595

Founding Editors

Gerhard Goos
Juris Hartmanis

Editorial Board Members

Elisa Bertino, *Purdue University, West Lafayette, IN, USA*
Wen Gao, *Peking University, Beijing, China*
Bernhard Steffen ⓘ, *TU Dortmund University, Dortmund, Germany*
Moti Yung ⓘ, *Columbia University, New York, NY, USA*

The series Lecture Notes in Computer Science (LNCS), including its subseries Lecture Notes in Artificial Intelligence (LNAI) and Lecture Notes in Bioinformatics (LNBI), has established itself as a medium for the publication of new developments in computer science and information technology research, teaching, and education.

LNCS enjoys close cooperation with the computer science R & D community, the series counts many renowned academics among its volume editors and paper authors, and collaborates with prestigious societies. Its mission is to serve this international community by providing an invaluable service, mainly focused on the publication of conference and workshop proceedings and postproceedings. LNCS commenced publication in 1973.

Romain Wacquez · Naofumi Homma
Editors

Constructive Side-Channel Analysis and Secure Design

15th International Workshop, COSADE 2024
Gardanne, France, April 9–10, 2024
Proceedings

Springer

Editors
Romain Wacquez
CEA LETI
Gardanne, France

Naofumi Homma
Tohoku University
Sendai, Japan

ISSN 0302-9743   ISSN 1611-3349 (electronic)
Lecture Notes in Computer Science
ISBN 978-3-031-57542-6   ISBN 978-3-031-57543-3 (eBook)
https://doi.org/10.1007/978-3-031-57543-3

© The Editor(s) (if applicable) and The Author(s), under exclusive license
to Springer Nature Switzerland AG 2024

This work is subject to copyright. All rights are solely and exclusively licensed by the Publisher, whether the whole or part of the material is concerned, specifically the rights of translation, reprinting, reuse of illustrations, recitation, broadcasting, reproduction on microfilms or in any other physical way, and transmission or information storage and retrieval, electronic adaptation, computer software, or by similar or dissimilar methodology now known or hereafter developed.
The use of general descriptive names, registered names, trademarks, service marks, etc. in this publication does not imply, even in the absence of a specific statement, that such names are exempt from the relevant protective laws and regulations and therefore free for general use.
The publisher, the authors and the editors are safe to assume that the advice and information in this book are believed to be true and accurate at the date of publication. Neither the publisher nor the authors or the editors give a warranty, expressed or implied, with respect to the material contained herein or for any errors or omissions that may have been made. The publisher remains neutral with regard to jurisdictional claims in published maps and institutional affiliations.

This Springer imprint is published by the registered company Springer Nature Switzerland AG
The registered company address is: Gewerbestrasse 11, 6330 Cham, Switzerland

Paper in this product is recyclable.

Preface

The 15th International Workshop on Constructive Side-Channel Analysis and Secure Design (COSADE 2024), was held in Gardanne, France, during April 9–10, 2024. The series of COSADE workshops started in 2010. COSADE provides a well-established international platform for researchers, academics, and industry participants to present current research topics in implementation attacks, efficient and secure HW/SW implementations, attack-resilient architectures and schemes, hardware intrinsic security, secure design and evaluation, practical attacks, test platforms, and open benchmarks.

COSADE 2024 was organized by Mines Saint-Etienne. It was held at the Center of Microelectronics in Provence in Gardanne in-between Marseille and Aix-en-Provence. This year, the workshop received 42 papers from authors of 16 countries. Each of the submissions was reviewed in an anonymous double-blind peer review process by three Program Committee members. Overall, the 35 Program Committee members and the 19 sub-reviewers provided 126 reviews. The Program Committee comprised international experts from academia and industry with strong backgrounds in hardware-related attacks, secure implementations, and secure design, from 15 countries. From the 42 papers, 14 were accepted after the review process, which corresponds to an acceptance rate of approximately 33%. The selected works are contained within these proceedings and were presented as part of the program of COSADE 2024. We thank the Program Committee members as well as the sub-reviewers for their efforts in reviewing, assessing, and discussing the submissions.

In addition to the 14 presentations on regular papers, COSADE 2024 comprised two keynotes. We thank the speakers for their valuable contributions to COSADE 2024.

We would like to thank the Steering Committee, Jean-Luc Danger and Werner Schindler, the General Chair, Jean-Max Dutertre, and the Web Chair, Raphael Viera. In particular, we want to thank the team members from the Mines Saint-Etienne and CEA Leti, for the great preparation and implementation of the conference in Gardanne. We are very grateful for the financial support received from our generous sponsors ST Microelectronics, Riscure, eShard, ALPhANOV, IDEMIA, PQShield, CEA Leti, and Micro-PackS. Last but not least we want to thank the authors: Without your valuable research and submissions, COSADE 2024 would not have been possible.

February 2024   Naofumi Homma
                                                                              Romain Wacquez

Organization

Steering Committee

Jean-Luc Danger   Télécom ParisTech, France
Werner Schindler   Bundesamt für Sicherheit in der
     Informationstechnik (BSI), Germany

General Chair

Jean-Max Dutertre   Ecole des Mines de Saint Etienne, France

Program Chairs

Naofumi Homma   Tohoku University, Japan
Romain Wacquez   CEA Leti, France

Program Committee

Diego F. Aranha   Aarhus University, Denmark
Tolga Arul   University of Passau, Germany
Josep Balasch   Katholieke Universiteit Leuven, Belgium
Alessandro Barenghi   Politecnico di Milano, Italy
Debapriya Basu Roy   IIT Kanpur, India
Noémie Beringuier-Boher   Intrinsic ID, The Netherlands
Shivam Bhasin   Temasek Labs@NTU, Singapore
Jakub Breier   Silicon Austria Labs, Austria
Chitchanok Chuengsatiansup   The University of Melbourne, Australia
Fabrizio De Santis   Siemens AG, Germany
Daniel Dinu   Intel Corporation, USA
Jean-Max Dutertre   Ecole des Mines de Saint-Etienne, France
Wieland Fischer   Infineon Technologies, Germany
Johann Heyszl   Google, Germany
Naofumi Homma   Tohoku University, Japan
Vincent Immler   Oregon State University, USA
Jens-Peter Kaps   George Mason University, USA

Ayesha Khalid	Queen's University Belfast, UK
Juliane Krämer	University of Regensburg, Germany
Victor Lomné	NinjaLab, France
Thorben Moos	Université catholique de Louvain, Belgium
Daniel Page	University of Bristol, UK
Samuel Pagliarini	Carnegie Mellon University, USA
Michael Pehl	Technical University of Munich, Germany
Stjepan Picek	Radboud University, The Netherlands
Simon Pontié	CEA Leti, France
Chester Rebeiro	Indian Institute of Technology Madras, India
Francesco Regazzoni	University of Amsterdam, The Netherlands and Università della Svizzera italiana, Switzerland
Pascal Sasdrich	Horst Görtz Institute for IT-Security, Ruhr-University Bochum, Germany
Tobias Schneider	NXP Semiconductors, Austria
Marc Stöttinger	RheinMain University of Applied Science, Germany
Ruggero Susella	STMicroelectronics, Italy
Rei Ueno	Tohoku University, Japan
Romain Wacquez	CEA Leti, France
Fan Zhang	Zhejiang University, China

Additional Reviewers

Abubakr Abdulgadir	Loïc Masure
Sven Bauer	Philippe Maurine
Marius Eggert	Ugo Mureddu
Niklas Faßbender	Tim Music
Christoph Frisch	Jonas Ruchti
Akira Ito	Patrick Struck
Keerthi K.	Élise Tasso
Caden King	Maximiliane Weishäupl
Kristjane Koleci	Trevor Yap
Suraj Mandal	

Contents

PUF/RNG

Cryptographic Implementations

Analyses and Tools

Characterizing and Modeling Synchronous Clock-Glitch Fault Injection

Amélie Marotta[1]([✉]), Ronan Lashermes[1], Guillaume Bouffard[2],
Olivier Sentieys[1], and Rachid Dafali[3]

[1] University of Rennes, Inria, Rennes, France
{amelie.marotta,ronan.lashermes,olivier.sentieys}@inria.fr
[2] National Cybersecurity Agency of France (ANSSI), Paris, France
guillaume.bouffard@ssi.gouv.fr
[3] DGA-MI, Bruz, France
rachid.dafali@def.gouv.fr

Abstract. In the realm of fault injection (FI), electromagnetic fault injection (EMFI) attacks have garnered significant attention, particularly for their effectiveness against embedded systems with minimal setup. These attacks exploit vulnerabilities with ease, underscoring the importance of comprehensively understanding EMFI. Recent studies have highlighted the impact of EMFI on phase-locked loops (PLLs), uncovering specific clock glitches that induce faults. However, these studies lack a detailed explanation of how these glitches translate into a specific fault model. Addressing this gap, our research investigates the physical fault model of synchronous clock glitches (SCGs), a clock glitch injection mechanism likely to arise from EMFI interactions within the clock network. Through an integrated approach combining experimental and simulation techniques, we critically analyze the adequacy of existing fault models, such as the Timing Fault Model and the Sampling Fault Model, in explaining SCGs. Our findings reveal specific failure modes in D flip-flops (DFFs), contributing to a deeper understanding of EMFI effects and aiding in the development of more robust defensive strategies against such attacks.

Keywords: Fault Injection · Clock Glitch · Physical Fault Model

1 Introduction

The majority of the electronic products used in our daily lives manipulate, store, and transmit sensitive data. The largest part of these products are designed without taking into account the threats generated by fault injection (FI) attacks. To define countermeasures against FI, a full characterization of the fault effects must firstly be conducted. This characterization remains a complex and challenging task because it must be analyzed at various levels (model, microarchitecture, gate and transistor).

© The Author(s), under exclusive license to Springer Nature Switzerland AG 2024
R. Wacquez and N. Homma (Eds.): COSADE 2024, LNCS 14595, pp. 3–21, 2024.
https://doi.org/10.1007/978-3-031-57543-3_1

Various means are used to conduct FI attacks, such as lasers [12] and electro-magnetic [14] injections. However, electromagnetic fault injection (EMFI) [20] is particularly noteworthy as a frequently employed mean due to its minimal setup requirements for targeting a component. In this article, our primary focus is on studying the effects of EMFI attacks. However, EMFI attacks are char-acterized by their lack of precision, resulting in a broad and difficult-to-control impact, potentially affecting a wide range of elements embedded in the targeted component.

Previous studies [5, 25] have shed light on the EMFI impact on phase-locked loops (PLLs). They have brought to attention the generation of clock glitches induced by EMFI, which lead to faults in components. While this research has been pivotal in understanding the effects of EMFI, it falls short of an in-depth explanation of how these clock glitches concretely translate into faults.

Several articles [7–9, 13, 16] have proposed low-level fault models to explain the occurrence of faults induced by EMFI. However, these models focus on the specific case where EMFI interact with power and ground signals.

Consequently, there remains a gap [15] in our comprehension of why EM-induced clock glitches result in specific fault perturbations as it is difficult to isolate them from the predominant effects (power and ground interaction).

Within this context, this article aims at providing a low-level fault model that explain how EM-induced clock glitches lead to faults. However, we use a clock glitching platform and not EMFI to induce faults, allowing us to have only faults of interest. Through physical experimentations and simulations, we highlight the main mechanism of fault as well as influencing factors.

This article is organized as follows. Section 2 reviews the related works con-cerning EM injection and clock glitch attacks and the associated fault models. We conclude that no low level fault model in the literature can be applied to our case. Therefore we state the hypotheses behind our own model dubbed con-trolled synchronous clock glitch in Sect. 3. To verify these hypotheses, we conduct experiments and simulations in Sect. 5, with a setup described in Sect. 4. These experiments allow to develop an understanding of the different factor that may lead to a fault.

2   Related Works

2.1   Overview of Fault Injection Analysis

By utilizing different FI methods and parameters, attackers can achieve various effects. Characterizing these effects aims to develop a fault model that represents what happen at specific abstraction levels. Therefore, understanding the effects of faults is crucial for implementing efficient countermeasures. The fault model is usually characterized at the physical, register-transfer, or microarchitectural levels, as described in [26]. First, the physical fault model analyzes the interaction between FI and transistors and logic gates. At this level, the goal is to understand why the photons injected from a laser pulse can switch a logic gate output, or why a D flip-flop (DFF) samples an incorrect value under EMFI. This level considers the analog nature of electrical current and voltage signals [8,9,16]. Second, at the register-transfer level (RTL), a fault is modeled as a logic signal alteration. Here, the analysis focuses on how a bit flip or a 'stuck at 0' (or 1) propagates through a circuit. Finally, at the microarchitectural level, a fault is analyzed by its impact on the microarchitecture. For instance, a bit-flip on the forwarding control signal can lead to an instruction skip [21]. Microarchitectural fault models include instruction-set architecture (ISA) fault models that represent a fault as an instruction modification. In other words, at the ISA level, the consequence of a fault can be linked to one instruction being transformed into another [22,23]. Some microarchitectural faults cannot be modeled at the ISA level. For example, in [24], faults impact the data cache, but the instructions remain intact.

This paper focuses on analysing the physical fault model arising from a specific EM-induced clock glitch, described in Sect. 2.2. The study intentionally excludes RTL and microarchitectural fault models from its scope.

2.2   EMFI on the PLL

To the best of our knowledge, the first mention of the influence of EMFI on the PLL was in [25]. The PLL is a component that takes a low-frequency clock signal as input and generates a high-frequency, stabilized clock signal. The objective was to use the PLL as a detector for EMFI. The authors consider the booting-up phase of the PLL, where it transitions from an *"unlocked"* state to a *"locked"* one. This transition does not take the same amount of clock cycles with and without EMFI, thus demonstrating the sensitivity of the PLL to EMFI.

Claudepierre *et al.* explain in [5] that EMFI alters the behavior of the PLL and generates clock glitches. More precisely, the injection modifies a clock cycle: the rising edge does not reach the high state because the injection causes a drop in the signal until the next clock cycle. The glitched clock cycle delivers less energy (it has a lower voltage for a shorter duration), but remains synchronous. The authors also show that the injection may eliminate the cycle altogether, suggesting that the characteristics of glitched clock cycles may vary between injections. In this paper, this specific clock glitch is referred to as synchronous clock glitch.

2.3   TRAITOR

To reproduce EMFI clock cycle perturbations, Claudepierre *et al.* introduced an FI tool named TRAITOR [6]. TRAITOR can control the amplitude parameter, which defines the energy level of the synchronous clock glitch. This allows for more precise control over the glitch. For the remainder of this article, this perturbation is referred to as controlled synchronous clock glitch (CSCG). Since there is currently no method to demonstrate equivalence, we refer to EM-induced clock glitches as synchronous clock glitch and TRAITOR-induced clock glitches as CSCG.

In their study, Claudepierre *et al.* targeted a microcontroller to analyze the TRAITOR fault model [6]. The primary induced microarchitectural fault model is an instruction skip. As a result, with its very high success rate and ability to perform a large number of faults, TRAITOR is a suitable FI tool for NOP-oriented programming, as explained in [17]. By carefully replacing selected instructions with a NOP assembly instruction, an attacker can modify a running program, akin to a Returned-Oriented Programming (ROP) attack. As demonstrated by Gicquel *et al.* in [10], without appropriate hardware countermeasures, such an attack is almost guaranteed to succeed.

TRAITOR can be used to simulate the effect of EMFI. Several fault models have been proposed to explain the impact of EMFI on circuits, and these may apply to TRAITOR. However, the physical model of such EM-induced fault has not yet been analyzed, to our best knowledge.

2.4   Known Fault Models

In this paper, an error is defined as an incorrect transient value, for example, when an induced current in a wire modifies its logic state. A fault occurs when an error propagates up to a memory element, allowing the propagation of the incorrect value into the next clock cycle.

For a fault to have a lasting impact on a circuit, an erroneous value must be stored at some specific point. For instance, a current induced by laser FI may create a latch-up, which forms the basis of the stuck-at fault model [18]. In most cases, the storage of an error results from the interaction of transient signals with a positive-edge-triggered DFF. This section discusses the correct behavior of the DFF and known failure modes as described in the literature.

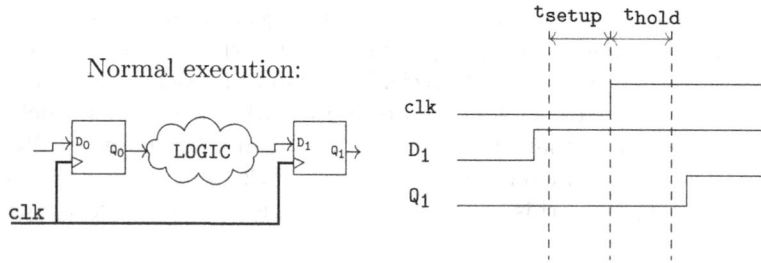

Fig. 1. Normal execution of a simple synchronous circuit.

The DFF's Correct Behavior. Consider a simple circuit composed of two DFFs with some logic in between, as depicted in Fig. 1. For proper sampling (or storage) to occur from D_1 to Q_1 in the second DFF, the data coming from D_1 must be stable during the setup and hold time window, defined by t_{setup} before and t_{hold} after the rising edge of clk, respectively. For the fault models presented in the following sections, this DFF is assumed to be under fault.

Timing Fault Model. The Timing Fault Model was the first of its kind to be proposed. In 2008, Selman *et al.* [19] demonstrated that underpowering a circuit could lead to errors due to setup time violations. Subsequently, in 2010,

Agoyan *et al.* [3] showed that shifting a clock's rising edge in time can trigger similar effects. As illustrated in Fig. 2, D_1 is unstable during the t_{setup} time. This violation of the timing constraint can cause Q_1 to enter a metastable state, potentially leading to a fault. In other words, when the input timing constraints are not met, the value of Q_1 becomes non-deterministic. Metastability refers to the phenomenon where a non-deterministic output is generated if the DFF signal constraints are not adhered to. This setup time violation can occur due to a reduction in the supply voltage of the logic, which extends its execution time (for instance, by underpowering the circuit), or by advancing a clock cycle, resulting in the logic having insufficient time to execute before the next rising edge. This model was initially suggested [7] to explain the effects of EMFI.

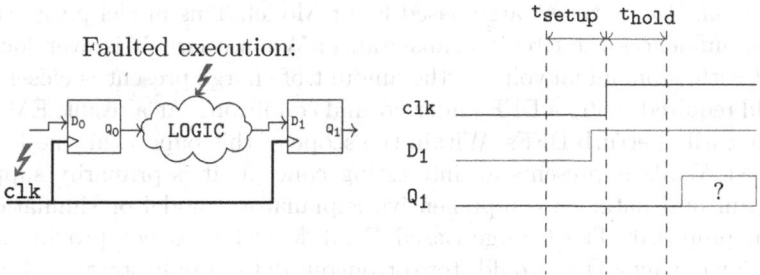

Fig. 2. Timing Fault Model on a simple circuit.

Sampling Fault Model. To the best of our knowledge, the most recent description of the Sampling Fault Model is found in [9]. This article explains that an EM-pulse induces parasitic currents in wire loops located beneath the probe. Consequently, fluctuations occur in the current of affected wires, such as Vdd, Gnd, the clock tree, DFF routing, and others, causing voltage bounces and drops, depending on the injection polarity.

In scenarios where a voltage drop occurs, the pulse causes circuit signals (D_1, Q_1, and clk in Fig. 3) to temporarily decrease, halting circuit operation. These signals eventually return to their nominal values. If the injection occurs just before a rising clock edge (as depicted in Fig. 3), a race ensues between D_1 and clk. A fault occurs if clk returns to its nominal value before D_1.

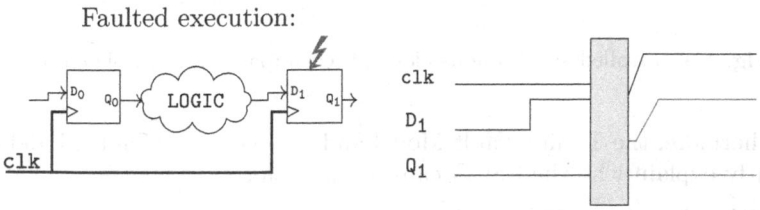

Fig. 3. Sampling Fault Model on a simple circuit. The grey rectangle in the chronogram symbolizes the signal drop.

This model has been further explored and reproduced in [27], with refinements to the coupling model and coverage of cases not previously examined: how to create a fault with a positive pulse when the DFF input is high. A distinctive characteristic of the Sampling Fault Model is the fault sensitivity window which has been experimentally confirmed: a specific timing window relative to the rising edge of the clock, during which faults can be induced. Because of the race condition between clk and D_1, a fault can only occur within a narrowly defined timing window around the clock's rising edge. This sensitivity window remains constant for a given circuit, irrespective of its frequency, but is influenced by the logic situated between the DFFs.

What About the Charge-Based Fault Model? Another model, described by Liao *et al.* [13], is the Charge-based Fault Model. This model posits that an EM-pulse influences the circuit's capacitance. When a circuit is overclocked or powered with subnominal voltage, the amount of charge present is closer to the threshold required to flip a DFF under normal conditions. As a result, EM-pulses can more easily perturb DFFs. Within the scope of this paper, this model is not considered. While it presents an interesting concept, it is primarily supported by experimental data; no comprehensive explanatory model or simulation has yet been proposed. The Charge-Based Fault Model does not provide a clear explanation of why a DFF would store erroneous data, it only states that charges influence this outcome. Instead, it can be viewed as a description of how other factors might aid in the facilitation of EMFI.

Comparison with Controlled Synchronous Clock Glitch. To develop a fault model that explains why the CSCG causes faults, it's essential to identify which component is most susceptible to being impacted. Given that the glitch is carried out by the clock, we hypothesize that DFFs are likely to be affected, as illustrated in Fig. 4.

Faulted execution:

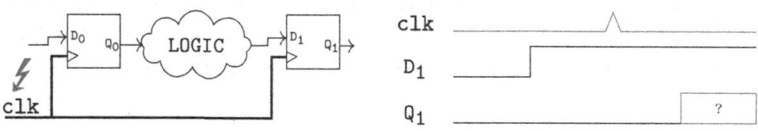

Fig. 4. Controlled synchronous clock glitch impact on a simple circuit.

Furthermore, the Timing Fault Model and the Sampling Fault Model do not sufficiently explain why the CSCG causes faults since:

– Only the clock is modified and other signals, particularly D_1, remain stable, there is no race condition between clk and D_1. Therefore, the Sampling Fault Model is excluded.

– There are no timing variations for either the clock or D_1, thus no setup time violations can occur, ruling out the Timing Fault Model.

Given that the CSCG cannot be accounted for by existing published fault models, further study is necessary to identify a fault model that accurately describes its effects.

3   Understanding the Controlled Synchronous Clock Glitch

Considering the published fault models introduced in Sect. 2, the observed fault model needs to be thoroughly analyzed. In this section, we propose several hypotheses that can explain the CSCG fault model.

Hypothesis 1 (Energy Threshold). *For a DFF to correctly sample a clock's rising edge, the clock signal must meet a certain energy threshold, combination of voltage amplitude and width thresholds.*

The energy of the clock signal determines whether the DFF samples the incoming data. A failure to sample is considered a fault. Depending on the energy of the clock signal, three states of the DFF are observed:

1. When the energy of the clock signal is too low, falling below the required energy threshold, the DFF is in a *always faulted* state.
2. Conversely, when the energy of the clock signal is sufficiently high, surpassing the threshold, the DFF is in an *always unfaulted* state.
3. When the clock signal hovers around the required threshold, the DFF enters a *sometimes unfaulted* state (i.e. when out of X FIs, it has sampled at least once). In this state, the output of the DFF is in a metastable state, influenced by the amount of clock energy. This phenomenon is further explored in 5.1.

This hypothesis alone is insufficient to fully explain the effect of the CSCG. We propose below two additional hypotheses, following the introduction of the *fault sensitivity* concept.

Definition 1 (Fault Sensitivity). *The minimum amplitude at which a DFF becomes sometimes unfaulted is called its fault sensitivity.*

When faulting two DFFs, for instance on a field programmable gate array (FPGA), their behaviors should be similar but not identical, and they may not share the same *fault sensitivity*. This difference can be attributed to variability in the manufacturing process among integrated circuits (ICs) and within individual DFFs of the same IC die. In other words, two identical DFFs, i.e., with the same characteristics and hardware layout, may not share the same *fault sensitivity*. Also, if the two DFFs are from two FPGAs of the same model, they may not share the same *fault sensitivity*.

Hypothesis 2 (Fault Sensitivity Dependency on Intrinsic Properties).
The fault sensitivity of a DFF depends on its intrinsic properties, such as process variability and clock routing up to the DFF among others.

However, the intrinsic properties alone are not sufficient to explain observed variations in fault sensitivity. To add a layer of complexity, we consider the environment surrounding the glitched DFFs, specifically focusing on the wires carrying signals (e.g., `clock`, `Vdd`, `Vss` between DFFs). The energy from neighboring wires may influence the glitched clock, altering the behavior of the target DFFs. This includes both data routing between DFFs and the clock routing on the dedicated clock network.

Hypothesis 3 (Fault Sensitivity Dependency on Extrinsic Properties).
The fault sensitivity of a DFF may also be affected by extrinsic factors, such as the activity in neighboring wires (including routing between DFFs and the routing of the clock tree).

To validate these hypotheses, experiments (either through simulation or on actual hardware) are necessary. In the following sections, the experimental setup is presented.

4   Experimental Setup

The previous section has introduced hypotheses that may explain the effects of the CSCG. In this section, we describe experiments aimed at confirming or refuting these hypotheses. The experimentation is categorized into two types: physical FI and simulated experiments.

4.1   Physical Experiments

Physical FIs are performed using TRAITOR implemented on an Artix-7 FPGA to inject CSCG into our device under test (DUT). To facilitate comprehension, we will begin by elucidating the use of TRAITOR for FI, embedded into our DUT.

In preparation for subsequent discussions, it is imperative to make a clear distinction between logical DFF and physical DFF:

- The logical DFF represents an abstract conceptualization of a DFF in our DUT, with multiple possible mappings onto physical DFFs.
- The physical DFFs are tangible components found on the ICs, such as FPGAs, serving as the foundational element for logical DFF. A logical DFF is mapped onto a given physical DFF.

When logical or physical is not mentionned, then the representation of the DFFs can be either.

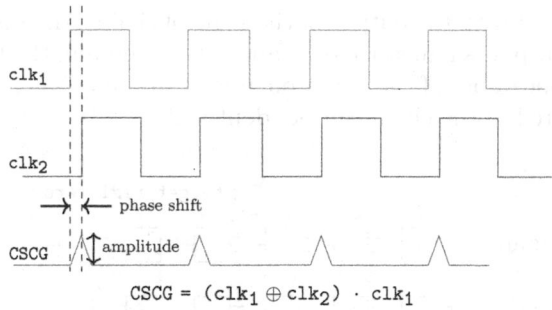

$$\text{CSCG} = (\text{clk}_1 \oplus \text{clk}_2) \cdot \text{clk}_1$$

Fig. 5. The CSCG is generated using two out-of-phase clocks, clk1 and clk2. The TRAITOR user has the capability to replace the regular clock signal with CSCG at their discretion.

How Does TRAITOR Work? To generate a CSCG, we can control the occurrence of the corrupted clock edge in each clock cycle and adjust a single parameter known as the **amplitude**, which shapes the corrupted edge. Figure 5 illustrates the generation of the corrupted edge using two phase-shifted clocks, with the phase under the TRAITOR user's control. Ideally, this method would result in a square pulse. However, the theoretical pulse width, equivalent to the phase shift, is too small relative to the circuit's inductance, preventing the signal from reaching its high value within the available time. Consequently, the **amplitude** of the corrupted edge is determined by the phase shift; a larger phase shift allows the corrupted signal to reach a higher level. Thus, the amplitude parameter influences both the height and the duration (also referred to as width) of the corrupted clock edge.

In our implementation, the phase shift is adjustable in increments of 32 ps. Throughout this paper, the term 'amplitude' applied to TRAITOR will refer to the number of these 32 ps steps in the phase shift.

TRAITOR produces two clocks: a regular clock, referred to as clk_ok, and a clock that incorporates the CSCG, referred to as clk_glitched. Both clocks are synchronous, operating at 16MHz, and are supplied to the DUT.

Composition of the DUT. The DUT, depicted in Fig. 6, comprises several logical DFFs, categorized into two types:

1. Target logical DFFs that receive clk_glitched.
2. Control logical DFFs that receive clk_ok.

These DFFs are organized into groups of 6, with a group consisting of either target logical DFFs (referred to as a target chain) or control logical DFFs (referred to as a control chain). There is one control chain and 32 target chains. Each chain, whether control or target, is fed the same input: a sequence alternating between 0 and 1. This sequence ensures that the content of every DFF, whether logical or physical, changes with each clock cycle. The outputs of the target chains are compared with the output of the control chain. Any discrepancy in at least one target output is indicative of a fault. By examining the timing between the FI and the appearance of the faulty output at the end of a chain, the specific logical DFF affected in the chain can be identified.

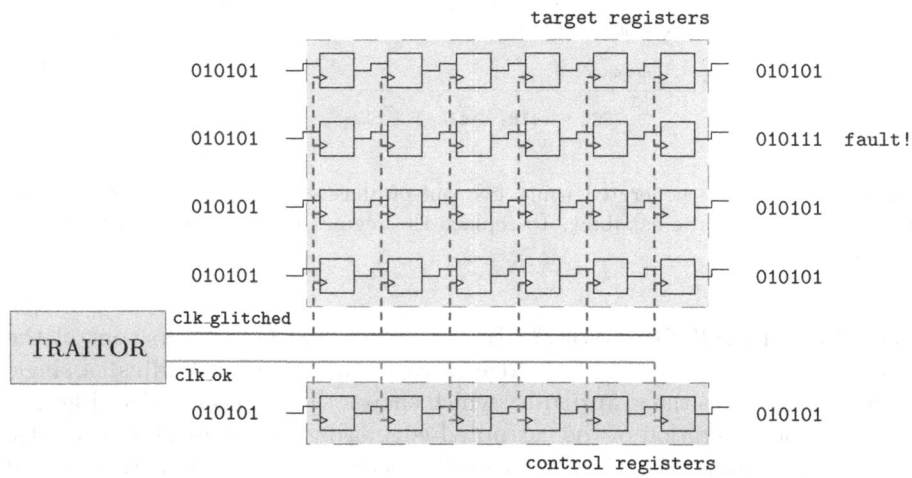

Fig. 6. DUT and TRAITOR on an Artix-7 FPGA.

The logical DFFs are mapped onto the physical DFFs of an Artix-7 FPGA, which are located in slices (8 physical DFFs per slice). Although slices contain other components, for clarity these are not considered in our discussion. Two distinct mappings, as shown in Fig. 7, are used to investigate how these mappings influence our results.

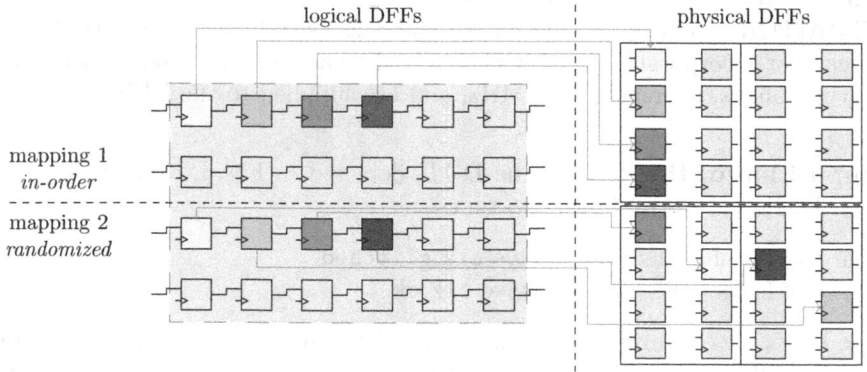

Fig. 7. The two logical-to-hardware mappings: mapping 1 is in-order and mapping 2 is randomized.

Fault Injection Protocol. The physical experiments are detailed in Sect. 5. To conduct these experiments, the following protocol is adhered to:

1. Both TRAITOR and the DUT are implemented on the same Artix-7 FPGA. This setup ensures the shortest and simplest clock paths, avoiding additional hardware components such as IOs or external wiring. To ensure consistency across all experiments, we meticulously determine the placement of TRAITOR and our DUT on the FPGA, aiming for precision. This guarantees that TRAITOR is consistently mapped to the same location for every experiment.
2. The FI process remains constant. Upon receiving a trigger from the target, a CSCG with a specified amplitude is injected. This process is repeated 100 times for each amplitude, ranging from 0 to 29. Subsequently, we analyze which DFF, if any, has been impacted by the FI.
3. Conclusions are drawn based on the observed outcomes and the analysis of results.

4.2 Transistor-Level Simulations

The simulations were carried out using Eldo [2], an ASIC oriented SPICE simulator. Given the proprietary nature of the Artix-7 FPGA design, replicating the exact 28 nm physical DFFs targeted in the physical experiments is not feasible. Instead, the simulations employ DFFs from a similar CMOS technology available in our laboratory, i.e., a 28 nm FDSOI (Fully Depleted Silicon On Insulator) Process Design Kit. These physical DFFs feature three connections: D, Q, and a clock input. However, unlike the physical DFFs used in the Artix-7 experiments, they lack a reset pin. Although the simulated DFFs and the Artix-7 physical DFFs do not have the same implementation, they do not significantly differ since they are designed for similar technology node and tend to behave the same way.

The simulated circuit consists of two DFFs. They first undergo a normal clock cycle, followed by a glitched one. Although a fault is injected into both DFFs, only the first one is considered for analysis; the second DFF is included to more closely mirror our physical experiments by simulating a load. The clock operates at 100 MHz with a voltage amplitude ranging from 0 V to 1 V.

The simulation focuses on a state change in the first DFF, transitioning from 0 to 1. It is important to note that the metastability phenomenon observed in physical experiments is not replicable in simulation. The primary goal of the simulation is to estimate the impact of the voltage and width of the controlled synchronous clock glitch. To achieve this, we independently vary both parameters, incrementally increasing them from low values until the DFF under test samples the input.

5 Hypotheses Validation

In this section, multiple experiments and simulations are conducted to validate the hypotheses presented in Sect. 3.

5.1 Hypothesis 1: Energy Threshold

We examine the behavior of physical DFFs faulted with TRAITOR, observing variations depending on the amplitude parameter. The results of the FI campaign validate Hypothesis 1. The target physical DFFs exhibit the following behaviour, shown on Fig. 8, for 3 distinct DFFs:

1. For amplitudes ranging from 0 to 21, inclusive, all DFFs are in a *always faulted* state.
2. For amplitudes between 22 and 24, inclusive, some DFFs are in a *always faulted* state, while others are in a *sometimes unfaulted* state.
3. Starting from amplitude 25, all DFFs are in a *always unfaulted* state.

The energy threshold is not identified by a single amplitude; instead, it is characterized by a range of 2 to 3 amplitudes in this experiment, with the fault sensitivity as the lower bound. During this transition phase from faulted to unfaulted, a physical DFF progressively experiences fewer faults until it becomes entirely unfaulted. The transition phases of the 192 physical DFFs overlap but are not identical, as illustrated in Fig. 8.

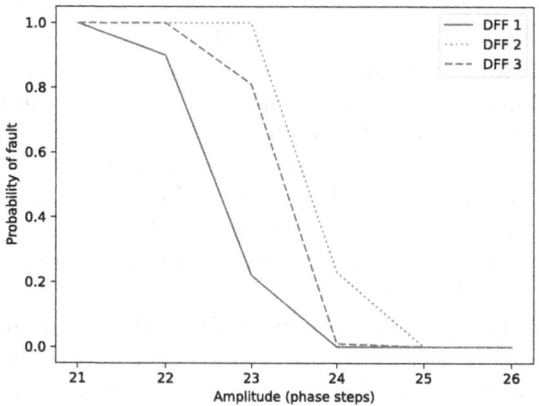

Fig. 8. Transitions phases of three target physical DFFs chosen since they exhibit different characteristics.

Energy Propagation and Metastability. Figure 8 illustrates the variation in fault occurrence probability relative to the glitch amplitude for 3 distinct DFFs, selected for their different characteristics. This figure shows various behaviors.

First, the 3 DFFs exhibit different fault sensitivities (22 for DFF 1, 23 for DFF 3, 24 for DFF 2). DFF 2 remains in a *always faulted* state at a higher amplitude, suggesting more energy loss during clock signal propagation. The causes of this energy loss are examined with Hypotheses 2 and 3. Then, at an amplitude equal to their fault sensitivity, each DFF shows a fraction of samplings being unfaulted and the rest faulted, indicative of metastable behavior. This ratio is consistent and reproducible for each physical DFF.

The standard error of the mean (SEM) is easily calculable: in the worst-case scenario where the fault probability is $p = 0.5$, the standard deviation σ is $\sigma = \sqrt{p \cdot (1 - p)} = 0.5$. Therefore, the SEM is $SEM = \sigma/100 = 0.005$, as we have 100 experiments for each DFF. We can deduce that our fault probability falls within 3 error deviations ($= 0.015$) for approximately 99 % confidence. For instance, our metastability evaluation suggests that at amplitude 23, DFF 1 registers a fault in $22 \pm 1.5\%$ of injection attempts with 99 % confidence.

What we observe in Fig. 8 is a typical S-curve characteristic of metastable behavior due to insufficient energy at the DFF's clock pin [4]. However, only one amplitude per DFF triggers the metastable output.

As a conclusion, each DFF undergoes a transition phase, displaying a limited metastable behavior. The transition phases of different DFFs may overlap but are not identical, attributed to the energy loss during clock signal propagation. This results in a collective transition phase for all DFFs from amplitudes 22 to 24 inclusive.

Simulating the Influence of Glitch Width and Voltage Amplitude Independently. While the previous experiment emphasizes the existence of an energy threshold, TRAITOR's specific design does not allow for independent testing of the influence of the glitch width and voltage amplitude on this threshold. To overcome this limitation, we simulate a small circuit (as described in Sect. 4.2) where we send a glitched clock pulse while varying the glitch width and voltage amplitude independently to observe if the sampling occurs.

The simulation is performed with a glitch width ranging from 0 ns to 5 ns by steps of 0.01 ns and voltage amplitude ranging from 0 V to 1 V by steps of 0.01 V. Figure 9 illustrates the sampling behavior with respect to glitch width and voltage amplitude parameters. The DFF successfully samples above the curve. The plot is constrained to the range from 0 ns to 1 ns, reflecting the fact that the amplitude reaches a lower plateau at 0.46 V.

Remarkably, sampling occurs for very small widths, as long as the voltage amplitude is sufficiently high; the minimum width for this occurrence is 0.03 ns at a voltage of 0.84 V. However, the opposite is not true: the glitch voltage amplitude must be at least 0.46 V for the DFF to sample, regardless of the width. In other words, it is "sufficient" for the DFF to sample that the controlled synchronous clock glitch has a high voltage amplitude for a short width, but not a long width with a low amplitude. Hence, the voltage amplitude threshold appears to be more restrictive than the width threshold.

5.2   Hypothesis 2: Fault Sensitivity Dependency on Intrinsic Properties

In this part of the study, we aim to understand why the transition phase, particularly the fault sensitivity, varies among physical DFF. Our primary focus

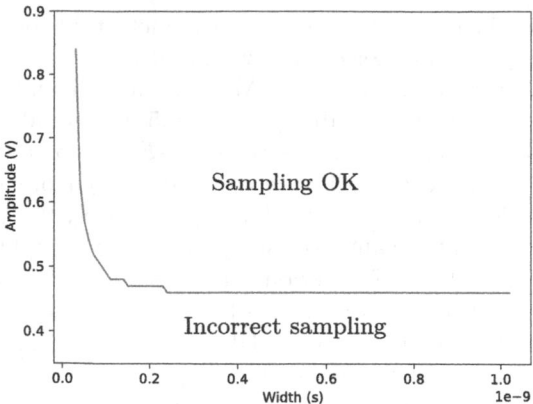

Fig. 9. Simulated sampling results: for a given glitch with voltage amplitude and width above this curve, sampling is correct.

is on the potential dependency of fault sensitivity on the intrinsic properties of physical DFF.

As discussed in Sect. 5.1, each physical DFF exhibits a specific and reproducible fault sensitivity. One primary factor influencing this sensitivity is the layout of clock routing: not all physical DFF on an FPGA share identical clock signal paths. Variations in these paths, potentially due to length differences or coupling with neighboring wires, can introduce disparities in inductance. If the layout of the clock routing was the sole intrinsic factor affecting fault sensitivity, then replicating the same design (with identical mapping) on another FPGA of the same model would result in the same sensitivity for identical logical DFFs.

In the ensuing experiment, the same DUT is mapped onto two Artix-7 FPGAs in the exact same manner. Practically, this involves using the same bitstream FPGA image on both FPGAs. The resulting fault sensitivities are depicted in Figs. 10a and 10b. One can see that while the fault sensitivities of the two FPGAs do show some similarities, notable differences exist. Given that both FPGAs are programmed with the same image and therefore have identical clock routings, the discrepancies observed in Fig. 10 can be attributed to process variations. The individual FPGA dies are not exactly identical, leading to variations in the inductances of clock paths, which in turn result in differing fault sensitivities for placement-equivalent physical DFFs.

Limits to the Intrinsic-Only Fault Model. If we assume that only the intrinsic properties of a physical DFF affect its fault sensitivity, then the mapping of logical DFFs to physical DFFs on a specific FPGA should not influence the fault sensitivities of these physical DFFs. This is because the clock routing is independent of the routing of other signals. Since the glitch is propagated solely by the clock signal, the fault sensitivity, assuming it depends solely on intrinsic properties, would be specific to each physical DFF.

Slice 1	23	23	23	23	23	23	23	23
Slice 2	23	23	23	23	22	22	22	22
Slice 3	23	23	23	23	23	23	23	23
Slice 4	23	23	23	23	23	23	23	23
Slice 5	22	22	22	22	22	22	22	22
Slice 6	22	22	22	22	23	23	23	23
Slice 7	23	23	23	23	23	23	23	23
Slice 8	23	23	23	23	22	22	22	22

(a) Color coded fault sensitivities of the first 64 registers on mapping 1 *in-order* on FPGA 1.

Slice 1	22	22	22	22	21	21	21	21
Slice 2	21	21	21	21	21	21	21	21
Slice 3	22	22	22	22	22	22	22	22
Slice 4	22	22	22	22	21	21	21	21
Slice 5	21	21	21	21	22	22	22	22
Slice 6	22	22	22	22	22	22	22	22
Slice 7	21	21	21	21	21	21	21	21
Slice 8	21	21	21	21	21	21	21	21

(b) Color coded fault sensitivities of the first 64 registers on mapping 1 *in-order* on FPGA 2.

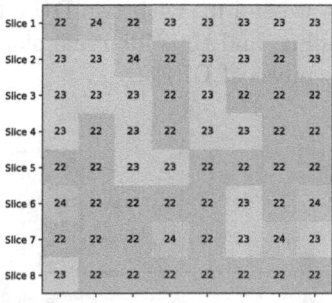

Slice 1	22	24	22	23	23	23	23	23
Slice 2	23	23	24	22	23	23	22	23
Slice 3	23	23	23	22	23	22	22	22
Slice 4	23	22	23	22	23	23	22	22
Slice 5	22	22	23	23	22	22	22	22
Slice 6	24	22	22	22	22	23	22	24
Slice 7	22	22	22	24	22	23	24	23
Slice 8	23	22	22	22	22	22	22	22

(c) Color coded fault sensitivities of the first 64 registers on mapping 2 *randomized* on FPGA 1.

Fig. 10. Comparing fault sensitivities between physical DFFs for various settings.

To test this assumption, we map the same physical DFFs onto the same FPGA in two different configurations (as depicted in the two mappings of Figs. 10a and 10c) and then compare their fault sensitivities. This results in varying fault sensitivities. The clk_glitched signal remains consistent across both mappings since it follows dedicated clock paths, suggesting that the CSCG should be identical in both experiments and consequently result in the same fault sensitivity for each physical DFF independently from the mapping. The two mappings differ in how data signals are routed between physical DFFs which clearly has an impact on the fault sensitivity. This observation leads us to hypothesize that extrinsic properties, such as data signals in this case, may influence CSCG.

5.3 Hypothesis 3: Fault Sensitivity Dependency on Extrinsic Properties

Given that intrinsic properties alone do not account for all variations in fault sensitivity, we now turn our attention to extrinsic properties. Specifically, we examine two types of extrinsic influences:

- Activity on data wires, i.e., the paths linking physical DFFs to each other.
- Activity on clock wires, responsible for carrying clock signals to the physical DFFs.

For each wire type, we conduct a separate experiment to isolate and observe its specific influence.

Impact of Data Wires. The influence of data wires on the `clk_glitched` energy was previously suggested in Sect. 5.2. We delve deeper into this aspect with the following experiment. Figures 10a and 11a illustrate the fault sensitivities of two different routings. Similar to the approach in Sect. 5.1, the target logical DFFs are mapped *in-order*. However, in this case, we alter the routing between two physical DFFs, resulting in a change in the data wire connections between them. Consequently, we end up with two DUT having the same logical DFFs to physical DFFs mapping, and thus identical clock routing, but differing in data wire routing between physical DFFs.

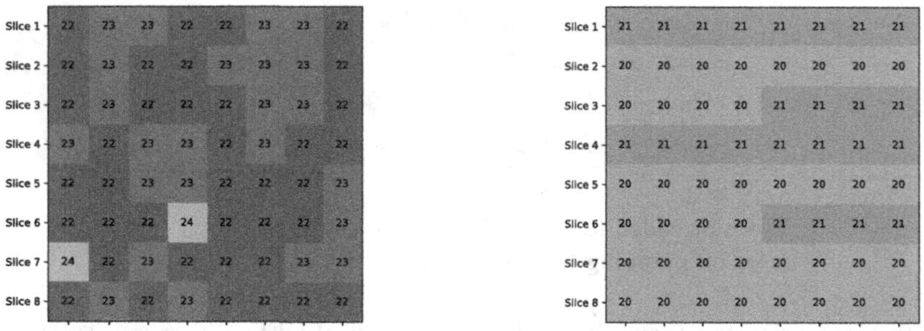

(a) Color-coded fault sensitivities of the first 64 registers on mapping 1 *in-order* with different data routing on FPGA 1, to be compared to Figure 10a.

(b) Color-coded fault sensitivities of the first 64 registers on mapping 1 *in-order* with a forced adjacent path for the clock on FPGA 1, to be compared to Figure 10a.

Fig. 11. Comparing fault sensitivities between physical DFFs for different routing

As a conclusion, the routing of data signals between physical DFFs significantly impacts the energy of the clock signal reaching these physical DFFs, thereby affecting their fault sensitivities.

Impact of Clock Wires. We further hypothesize that the `clk_glitched` signal is influenced by the proximity to the `clk_ok` signal. Previously, the mapping of the DUT and TRAITOR was carefully arranged to avoid any crossing or parallel arrangement of the two clock networks. To assess the impact of clock network interference, we now map some control DFFs on a slice adjacent to the target

DFFs. This setup places both clk_glitched and clk_ok on parallel physical paths, given that the dedicated clock routes are next to each other and originate from nearby sources [1].

Figures 10a and 11b show that the fault sensitivities not only differ but are also notably lower. In all previous experiments on this FPGA, such as on Fig. 10a, fault sensitivities ranged between 22 and 24. However, in this setup, they range between 20 and 21. It appears that positioning the clk_ok signal adjacent to clk_glitched effectively 'adds energy' to the latter, thereby reducing its fault sensitivity.

Interpretation. The observed energy transfers, both data-to-clock and clock-to-clock, are likely the result of cross-talk between these signals. The fault sensitivity of a physical DFF is highly dependent on the energy delivered by the clock's rising edge, so even a small amount of energy added or subtracted through cross-talk can have a noticeable impact [11]. These findings suggest that the fault sensitivity in a DFF is an extremely precise indicator of the activity in the surrounding circuitry.

6   Conclusion

EMFI is a popular yet imprecise method for inducing incorrect behaviors in ICs. Among the various effects caused by EMFI, it triggers a specific clock glitch known as the synchronous clock glitch. We reproduce a similar signal, referred to as the CSCG, directly on the clock network, delivering less energy than a regular clock cycle. This glitch results in faults, but existing physical fault models have not adequately explained it thus far.

To address this knowledge gap, we propose the Energy-threshold Fault Model. This model states that a DFF requires a specific energy level on the clock port to sample correctly. When the energy falls below the required threshold, the DFF fails to sample. When the energy hovers near that threshold, the DFF output enters a metastable state, leading to uncertain sampling. The threshold of each DFF varies based on intrinsic properties, such as process variability and clock network layout. Moreover, it can be influenced by extrinsic factors like the activity of neighboring wires, due to cross-talk. This suggests that measuring the threshold value provides a novel and highly precise means of assessing the activity of a circuit surrounding a specific DFF.

It is worth noting that this model was only tested using the same family of FPGAs. While the relationship between clock energy and sampling should hold true for any IC (as suggested by simulations in Sect. 4.2), the specifics of the cross-talk phenomenon might vary. Additionally, our testing was limited to the use of TRAITOR; future work should focus on recreating CSCG with EMFI as Claudepierre et al. [5] and verify if the Energy-threshold Fault Model requires adjustments.

References

1. 7 Series FPGAs Clocking Resources. https://docs.xilinx.com/v/u/en-US/ug472_7Series_Clocking
2. Eldo Platform. https://eda.sw.siemens.com/en-US/ic/eldo/
3. Agoyan, M., Dutertre, J.-M., Naccache, D., Robisson, B., Tria, A.: When clocks fail: on critical paths and clock faults. In: Gollmann, D., Lanet, J.-L., Iguchi-Cartigny, J. (eds.) CARDIS 2010. LNCS, vol. 6035, pp. 182–193. Springer, Heidelberg (2010). https://doi.org/10.1007/978-3-642-12510-2_13
4. Chen, D., et al.: A comprehensive approach to modeling, characterizing and optimizing for metastability in FPGAs. In: Proceedings of the 18th Annual ACM/SIGDA International Symposium on Field Programmable Gate Arrays (FPGA), pp. 167–176 (2010)
5. Claudepierre, L., Besnier, P.: Microcontroller sensitivity to fault-injection induced by near-field electromagnetic interference. In: APEMC - Asia-Pacific International Symposium on Electromagnetic Compatibility, Sapporo, Japan, pp. 1–4 (2019)
6. Claudepierre, L., Péneau, P.-Y., Hardy, D., Rohou, E.: TRAITOR: a low-cost evaluation platform for multifault injection. In: Meng, W., Li, L. (eds.) ASSS 2021: Proceedings of the 2021 International Symposium on Advanced Security on Software and Systems, Virtual Event, Hong Kong, pp. 51–56. ACM (2021)
7. Dehbaoui, A., Dutertre, J.-M., Robisson, B., Tria, A.: Electromagnetic transient faults injection on a hardware and a software implementations of AES. In: Bertoni, G., Gierlichs, B., (eds.) Workshop on Fault Diagnosis and Tolerance in Cryptography, Leuven, Belgium, pp. 7–15. IEEE Computer Society (2012)
8. Dumont, M., Lisart, M., Maurine, P.: Electromagnetic fault injection: how faults occur. In: Workshop on Fault Diagnosis and Tolerance in Cryptography, FDTC 2019, Atlanta, GA, USA, pp. 9–16. IEEE (2019)
9. Dumont, M., Lisart, M., Maurine, P.: Modeling and simulating electromagnetic fault injection. IEEE Trans. Comput. Aided Des. Integr. Circuits Syst. **40**(4), 680–693 (2021)
10. Gicquel, A., Hardy, D., Heydemann, K., Rohou, E.: SAMVA: static analysis for multi-fault attack paths determination. In: Kavun, E.B., Pehl, M. (eds.) COSADE 2023. LNCS, vol. 13979, pp. 3–22. Springer, Cham (2023). https://doi.org/10.1007/978-3-031-29497-6_1
11. Giechaskiel, I., Rasmussen, K.B., Eguro, K.: Leaky wires: information leakage and covert communication between FPGA long wires. In: Proceedings of the 2018 on Asia Conference on Computer and Communications Security, ASIACCS 2018, pp. 15–27. Association for Computing Machinery, New York (2018)
12. Khuat, V., Danger, J.-L., Dutertre, J.-M.: Laser fault injection in a 32-bit microcontroller: from the flash interface to the execution pipeline. In: 18th Workshop on Fault Detection and Tolerance in Cryptography, FDTC 2021, Milan, Italy, pp. 74–85. IEEE (2021)
13. Liao, H., Gebotys, C.H.: Methodology for EM fault injection: charge-based fault model. In: Teich, J., Fummi, F. (eds.) Design, Automation & Test in Europe Conference & Exhibition, DATE 2019, Florence, Italy, pp. 256–259. IEEE (2019)
14. Maurine, P.: Techniques for EM fault injection: equipments and experimental results. In: Bertoni, G., Gierlichs, B. (eds.) Workshop on Fault Diagnosis and Tolerance in Cryptography, Leuven, Belgium, pp. 3–4. IEEE Computer Society (2012)

15. Nabhan, R., Dutertre, J.-M., Rigaud, J.-B., Danger, J.-L., Sauvage, L.: Highlighting two EM fault models while analyzing a digital sensor limitations. In: 2023 Design, Automation & Test in Europe Conference & Exhibition (DATE), pp. 1–2 (2023)
16. Ordas, S., Guillaume-Sage, L., Maurine, P.: Electromagnetic fault injection: the curse of flip-flops. J. Cryptogr. Eng. **7**(3), 183–197 (2017)
17. Péneau, P.-Y., Claudepierre, L., Hardy, D., Rohou, E.: NOP-oriented programming: should we care? In: IEEE European Symposium on Security and Privacy Workshops, EuroS&P Workshops 2020, Genoa, Italy, pp. 694–703. IEEE (2020)
18. Roscian, C., Dutertre, J.-M., Tria, A.: Frontside laser fault injection on cryptosystems - application to the AES' last round -. In: 2013 IEEE International Symposium on Hardware-Oriented Security and Trust (HOST), pp. 119–124 (2013)
19. Selmane, N., Guilley, S., Danger, J.-L.: Practical setup time violation attacks on AES. In: Seventh European Dependable Computing Conference, EDCC-7 2008, Kaunas, Lithuania, pp. 91–96. IEEE Computer Society (2008)
20. Timmers, N., Spruyt, A., Witteman, M.: Controlling PC on ARM using fault injection. In: Workshop on Fault Diagnosis and Tolerance in Cryptography, FDTC 2016, Santa Barbara, CA, USA, pp. 25–35. IEEE Computer Society (2016)
21. Tollec, S., Asavoae, M., Couroussé, D., Heydemann, K., Jan, M.: Exploration of fault effects on formal RISC-V microarchitecture models. In: Workshop on Fault Detection and Tolerance in Cryptography, FDTC 2022, Virtual Event/Italy, pp. 73–83. IEEE (2022)
22. Trouchkine, T., Bouffard, G., Clédière, J.: Fault injection characterization on modern CPUs. In: Laurent, M., Giannetsos, T. (eds.) WISTP 2019. LNCS, vol. 12024, pp. 123–138. Springer, Cham (2020). https://doi.org/10.1007/978-3-030-41702-4_8
23. Trouchkine, T., Bouffard, G., Clédière, J.: EM fault model characterization on SoCs: from different architectures to the same fault model. In: 18th Workshop on Fault Detection and Tolerance in Cryptography, FDTC 2021, Milan, Italy, pp. 31–38. IEEE (2021)
24. Trouchkine, T., Bukasa, S.K., Escouteloup, M., Lashermes, R., Bouffard, G.: Electromagnetic fault injection against a complex CPU, toward new micro-architectural fault models. J. Cryptogr. Eng. **11**(4), 353–367 (2021)
25. Yuan, S.-Y., Wu, Y.-L., Perdriau, R., Liao, S.-S., Ho, H.-P.:. Electromagnetic interference analysis using an embedded phase-lock loop. In: Asia-Pacific Symposium on Electromagnetic Compatibility, pp. 189–192 (2012)
26. Yuce, B., Schaumont, P., Witteman, M.: Fault attacks on secure embedded software: threats, design, and evaluation. J. Hardw. Syst. Secur. **2**(2), 111–130 (2018)
27. Zhang, M., Li, H., Liu, Q.: Deep exploration on fault model of electromagnetic pulse attack. IEEE Trans. Nanotechnol. **21**, 598–605 (2022)

On-Chip Evaluation of Voltage Drops and Fault Occurrence Induced by Si Backside EM Injection

Rikuu Hasegawa$^{(\boxtimes)}$, Kazuki Monta, Takuya Wadatsumi, Takuji Miki,
and Makoto Nagata

Graduate School of Science, Technology and Innovation, Kobe University, 1-1 Rokkoudai-cho,
Nada-ku, Kobe-shi, Hyogo 657-8501, Japan
{rikuu.hasegawa,kazuki.monta,
takuya.wadatsumi}@it1.stin.kobe-u.ac.jp, miki@port.kobe-u.ac.jp,
nagata@cs.kobe-u.ac.jp

Abstract. Cryptographic modules are vulnerable to fault injection. Electromagnetic fault injection (EMFI) uses electromagnetic (EM) waves as a means of introducing faults into target circuits. These days, EMFI draws attention as a real threat to cryptographic circuits because of its inherent advantages. Although EMFI has become popular, there are only a few works on EMFI at the lowest physical level. In this paper, we experimentally show that EMFI induces negative voltage drops with outstandingly large negative amplitude and with layout-dependent localization on power delivery network (PDN) inside the chip. The drops are very much relevant to failures that occur in digital circuits. A test chip in a 180 nm CMOS technology embeds six crypto cores of 128 bits AES and on-chip voltage waveform monitor. The chip is assembled in flipped-chip packaging and attempted by EMFI from its Si substrate backside. EMFI uses an antenna coil with the diameter of 1 mm, scans and contacts it over the backside chip surface within the area of 3 mm × 4 mm. With our detailed, chip-level and multi-physics exploration of EMFI delivered in this paper, we find the need of more in-depth understandings on EMFI mechanisms from physics viewpoints, toward the design of EMFI resiliency among crypto cores backed with accurate and efficient coupling models from PDN to transistor-level digital circuits.

Keywords: Fault attacks · EM fault injection · power delivery networks · integrated circuit

1 Introduction

Fault analysis attack is a real threat to cryptographic modules. These attacks induce transient or semi-permanent faults in integrated circuits (ICs) first and then extract secret information using several fault results. Bell-core attack was proposed as an attack against RSA [1]. After that, Differential Fault Analysis (DFA) was proposed as an attack against symmetric-key cryptography [2]. With the development of these fault analysis attacks, there have been many works about the means used to induce faults into ICs.

© The Author(s), under exclusive license to Springer Nature Switzerland AG 2024
R. Wacquez and N. Homma (Eds.): COSADE 2024, LNCS 14595, pp. 22–37, 2024.
https://doi.org/10.1007/978-3-031-57543-3_2

Laser [3, 4], voltage/clock glitch [5–7], electromagnetic (EM) waves [8], and body biasing [9, 10] are major injection means. Among the fault injection techniques using these means, electromagnetic fault injection (EMFI) draws attention these days. This can be explained by two advantages of EMFI. The first one is time and spatial resolution. While it is difficult to inject faults in a targeted space by using voltage/clock glitches, EMFI can cause faults in a finely tuned temporal and spatial manner. The second advantage is the ease of attack. This is the biggest reason why EM wave has been drawing attention as a mean for fault injection. EMFI is easier to attack packaged ICs. Since electromagnetic waves penetrate into silicon as well as plastic molds, EM injection directly couples to metal wires and the impact of mounting method of the chip is small. This eliminates the need to remove encapsulation materials and is less sensitive to the method of packaging (face up or flip chip). On the contrary, the presence of metal reduces the attackable area for laser-FI attack from the frontside, and also plastic molds blocks laser illumination from silicon. This reduces the degree of freedom of laser-FI attacks.

There are two types of EM injection techniques. The first one uses continuous EM waves to induce false operations. This is called harmonic EM injection. This technique can disturb the operation of an internal clock generator and can bias the output of a true random number generator [11, 12]. The second technique uses an EM pulse to induce faults into a target chip. This type of EM injection was first reported in [13]. The first analysis of transient faults induced by EM pulse reported that EM pulse induces a timing fault during calculations [14]. After that, [15] experimentally demonstrated that EM pulse can produce not only timing faults but also bit-set and bit-reset faults. One year later, another fault model called the sampling fault model was deduced in [16], and a deeper insight was provided into this fault model in [17]. EMFI detection in [18] uses sampling faults among flip flops but remains also responsive to timing errors [19].

Despite there is much work on logic-level fault evaluation of EMFI as explained above, there are only a few works on EMFI at the lowest physical level. Time to digital converters (TDC) measures voltage fluctuations on power rails [20] which are not related with distributions within IC. Accurate simulation and modeling of EMFI help hardware designers to identify the vulnerability of the device and provide efficient countermeasures. An EMFI simulation technique using an EM coupling model between EM injection coil and on-chip power delivery networks (PDN) was proposed in [21]. The results of this simulation were confronted with experimental results to confirm its soundness. This technique was applicable only to a small design at that time. However, in [22], this technique was improved and became applicable to a larger circuit by splitting the IC surface into segments of a standard-cell row. After that, another work proposed a fast numerical solver to calculate the tile-based effective loop inductance and mutual inductance between the EM injection coil and the on-chip PDN [23]. There are two similarities between these two simulation techniques in [22] and [23]. The first similarity is that both of them focus on the coupling between the EM injection coil and on-chip PDN. The second similarity is that the simulation results of these simulations show that circuits below the EM injection coil are most susceptible to EMFI.

The implications from the measurements in this paper includes the following point. The coupling between the placement of EM injection coil and the location of responded circuits is not necessarily stronger when they are more closely positioned, which had been often assumed in the previous works. It was considered that the size of voltage fluctuations became largest at the node directly under the wires of the EM injection coil. Instead, in this paper, we observed the large voltage fluctuations on the segment of metal wires physically away from the position of an EM coil, even considering the wire thickness or the diameter of windings of the coil. The voltage fluctuations were also reasonably high on the segments nearby the coil. We hope that this paper may contribute to a better understanding of EMFI to support efficient countermeasures development.

The remaining part of this paper is structured as follows. Sect. 2 describes the test chip and measurement flows. In Sect. 3, we evaluate the waveforms at multiple points of the on-chip PDN during EM injection, over different EM injection setup. The same experiments will also be performed during AES operation to analyze faults in AES calculations. Through these results, a discussion on the interaction between physical phenomena and circuits operation will be presented. Finally, Sect. 4 concludes this paper.

2 Experimental Setup

We prepare a test chip employing AES encryption cores and on-chip monitor (OCM) circuits. The detailed of the functionality, power delivery network (PDN) and OCM in the chip is explained in Sect. 2.1 and 2.2. First, power supply dynamic waveforms during EM irradiation are captured and evaluated. And then, we assess the relationship between voltage fluctuations at PDN and the number of AES encryption errors.

2.1 Silicon Demonstrator and Its Power Delivery Networks

A test chip was designed and fabricated in a commercially available 180 nm CMOS technology. Six unprotected AES cores with the key size of 128 bits, an on-chip low-dropout regulator (LDO) and OCM circuits are embodied as shown in Fig. 1.

The VDD side power rail of crypto cores, referred to as V_{DD_CORE} in Fig. 1, is regulated by On-chip LDO while VSS side power rail is directly connected to the VSS IO pads and supplied from off-chip power supply. OCM captures voltage drop, so called current-resistance (IR) drop, at 3 probe points on V_{DD_CORE} wiring, point 1, 2 and 3 depicted in Fig. 1.

The logical function of the six cores is completely identical. First, we made a register-transfer level (RTL) netlist which integrates these six cores along with an interface circuit. And then, the standard-cells constituting these AES cores were physically grouped and respectively packed in placements. During the evaluation of AES faults caused by EM irradiation, 3 cores (AES_a, AES_b and AES_c) close to the three OCM probe points mentioned earlier were selected as targets, for the later evaluation of the relationship between AES faults and local IR drop.

The chip was packaged in a flip-chip ball grid array packaging and was assembled on a printed circuit board (PCB).

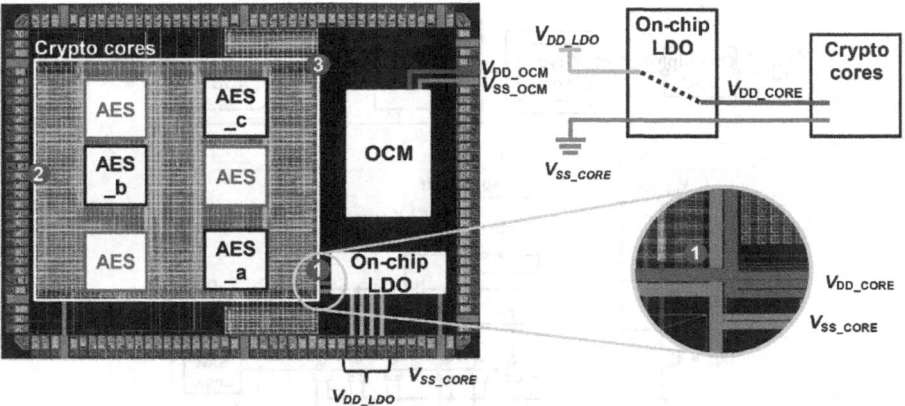

Fig. 1. Test chip layout and its power delivery network structure.

2.2 Architecture of On-Chip Monitor Circuit

The on-chip monitor circuit was developed to observe voltage fluctuations in semiconductor circuits in detail [24, 25]. The power supplies V_{DD_OCM} and V_{SS_OCM} of this OCM circuit are isolated from the crypto circuits, so that the effect of EM injection close to digital circuits on OCM is sufficiently small. And the input of the OCM is connected to any point in the power supply network of the crypto circuits where the V_{DD_CORE} generated by the on-chip LDO is applied. With its wide input bandwidth and high resolution, OCM captures local noise fluctuations in the PDN.

The OCM circuit consists of a buffer circuit with an N-type super source follower (SSF) and a successive approximation resister analog-to-digital converter (SAR ADC), as shown in the Fig. 2, each designed for a wide bandwidth.

The SSF consists of a normal source follower and a feedback transistor that drives the measurement voltage through a low output impedance. The V_{DD_CORE} noise is captured by an N-type SSF with n-MOS input transistors and shifted down to match the input range of the next stage ADC. The input voltage range is defined as 1.0 V.

The sampling structure of the SAR ADC uses a bootstrap switch to reduce the on-resistance. In addition, the capacitive DAC is minimized by introducing a split structure with a series capacitor, which finely reduces the input capacitance of the ADC.

The bandwidth is approximately 1 GHz. The reference voltage V_{REF} is 1.8 V and voltage resolution is 11 bits, so that the minimum quantization unit of the ADC of 1 LSB (least significant bit) is 879 μV.

The equivalent sampling technique, in which the clock CLK_{SAMPLE} synchronized with a reproducible noise source are repeatedly measured with a small delay of one minute, enables digitization with high time resolution.

2.3 Silicon Demonstrator and Its Power Delivery Networks

For EM irradiation, a commercial EM injector, ChipSHOUTER from NewAE Technology Inc. [26], is used in this paper. Figure 3 summarizes parameters of EM injector in

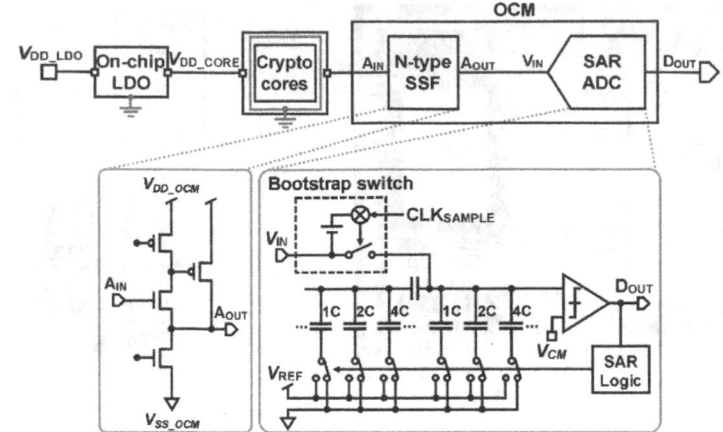

Fig. 2. The test chip PDN and OCM circuits

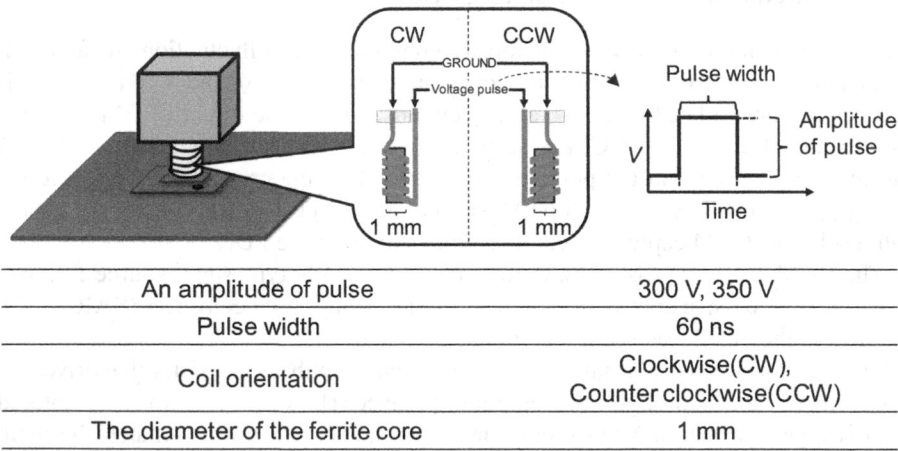

An amplitude of pulse	300 V, 350 V
Pulse width	60 ns
Coil orientation	Clockwise(CW), Counter clockwise(CCW)
The diameter of the ferrite core	1 mm

Fig. 3. EM injection parameter summary.

our measurement setup. A trigger signal to the EM injector controls the timing and the pulse width of EMFI. Also, an amplitude of pulse voltage to the EM injection coil can be controlled by a PC. The amplitude of pulse voltage is set to 300 V or 350 V and the pulse width is set to 60 ns in this paper. A clockwise (CW) ferrite core coil and a counter clockwise (CCW) ferrite coil with a ferrite core diameter of 1 mm are used as the injection tip. This coil is covered by a thin insulating film, so there is no electrical connection between a target device and an EM injection coil even when the coil tip touches the surface of a target device. In this paper, the coil was always in contact with the Si substrate backside of the test chip. It means that EM pulse is injected from the Si substrate backside. The number of EM injection coil placements is 6, as shown in Fig. 4, for both IR drop evaluation and AES faults evaluation. Coil_2, Coil_3 and Coil_6 almost correspond to the position of AES_a, AES_b and AES_c respectively.

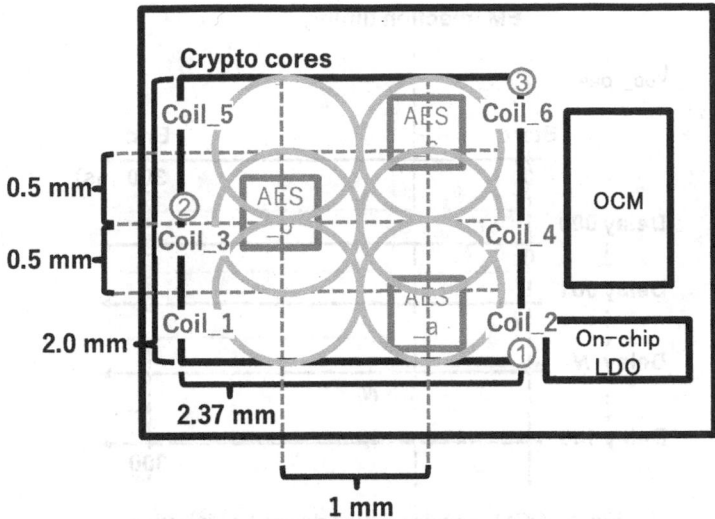

Fig. 4. Placements of EM injection coil and AES cores.

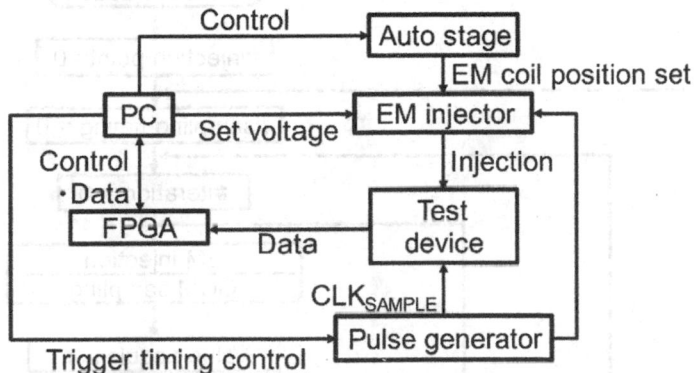

Fig. 5. Block diagram of IR drop evaluation setup.

Figure 5 shows the block diagram of experimental setup for IR drop evaluation using OCM circuits. By synchronizing and controlling the trigger signal to the injector and the input signal, referred to as CLK_{SAMPLE} in Fig. 5, that determines the comparison timing of the OCM circuit with a pulse generator (PG), the OCM circuit can capture the IR drop waveform during EM injection. The timing of a trigger signal for the injector and sampling timing of OCM are depicted in Fig. 6. The evaluation flow is shown in Fig. 7. The number of sampling iteration for each OCM sampling timing is 3 and there are 151 sampling timing for each IR drop waveform.

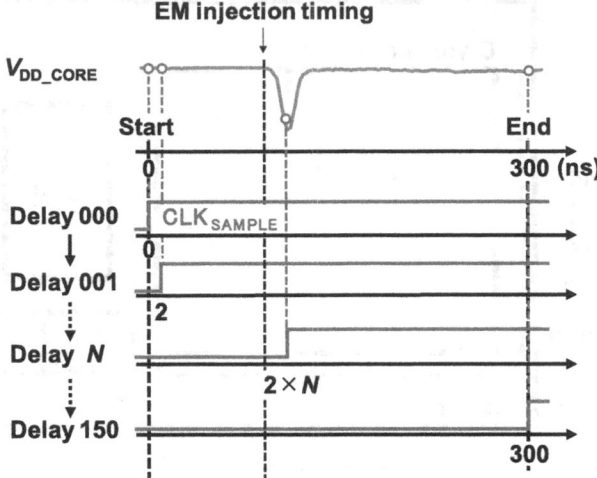

Fig. 6. OCM sampling timing during EM injection.

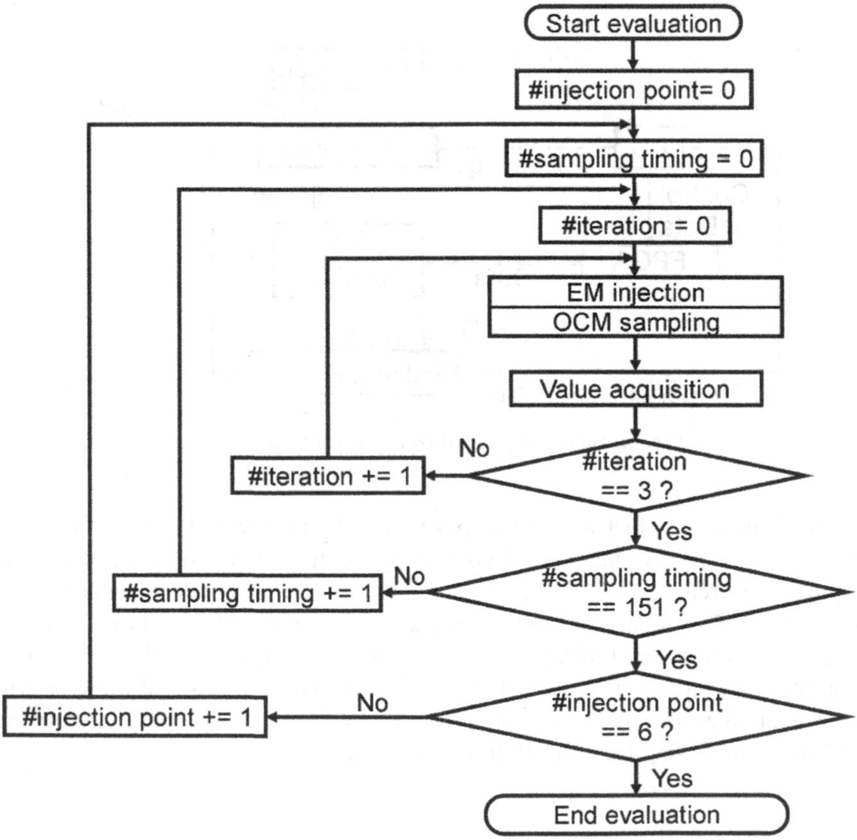

Fig. 7. The flow of IR drop evaluation using OCM circuits.

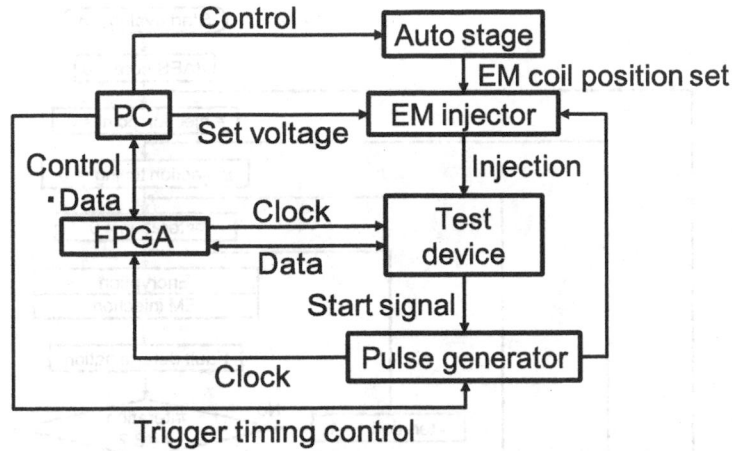

Fig. 8. Block diagram of AES faults evaluation.

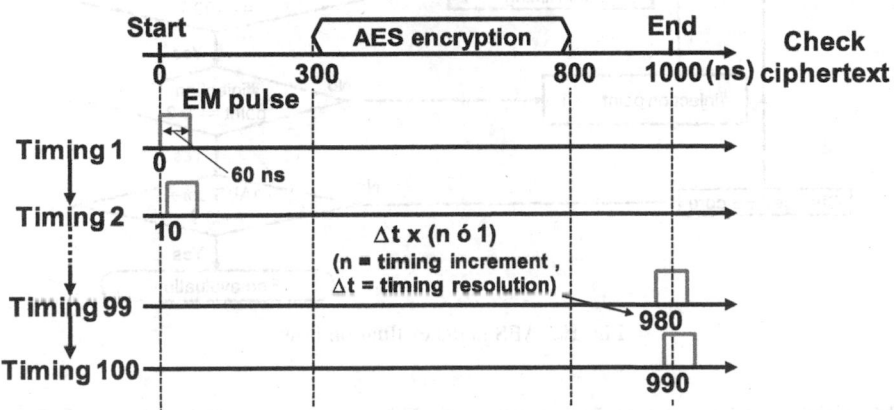

Fig. 9. EM injection timings over AES encryption sequence.

Once the measurement of one waveform is completed, the coil position is changed to start capturing the next waveform. The waveforms at three OCM probe positions, depicted in Fig. 1, are captured in parallel.

The block diagram of measurement setup for evaluating AES faults caused by EM irradiation is depicted in Fig. 8. Input and output data of AES cores are managed by PC via FPGA. The clock signal of AES, the frequency is set to 20 MHz in this paper, is coming from PG through FPGA. This frequency is approximately half of the maximum operating frequency of the AES. The trigger signal to the EM injector is also controlled by the PG and it makes it possible to synchronize AES operation and EM injection. The injection timing was shifted for a total of 1000 ns from 300 ns before AES operation to 200 ns after AES operation in steps of 10 ns as shown in Fig. 9. The evaluation flow is shown in Fig. 10. Reaction of the AES cores to EM injection is assessed with changing conditions such as injection timing, selection of the AES core which operates, and the

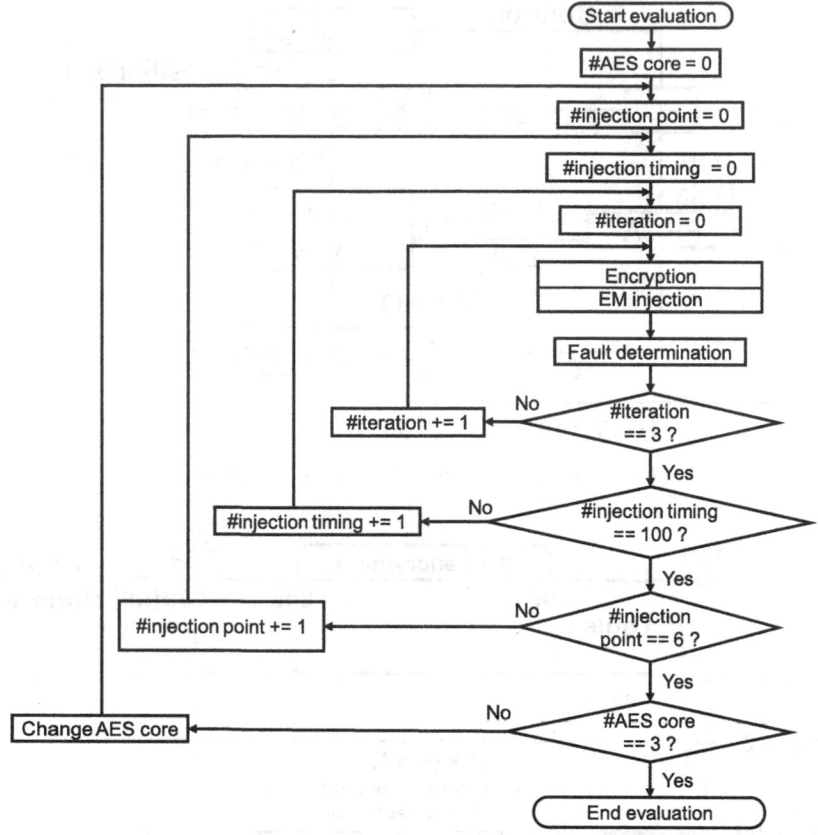

Fig. 10. AES faults evaluation flow.

EM injection coil placement. Initialization of AES, such as writing plain-text and secret-key and fault determination by checking if the generated cipher-text is correct take place for each injection. To ensure a correct evaluation, measurements were repeated three times for each evaluation condition. The number of EM injection coil placements used in this paper is 6 also in this evaluation and the number of AES core evaluated in this evaluation is 3 as shown in Fig. 3.

3 Experimental Results

3.1 On-Chip Voltage Measurements

We have first measured power noise on the core supply voltage, V_{DD_CORE}, nodes over a power delivery network (PDN) shared by crypto cores. The voltage waveforms are given in Fig. 11(a), when the clock-signal networks of all six AES cores are toggling at 24 MHz. In this case, the digital circuit is only supplied with a clock signal and AES is not in operation. We observe the voltage drop, so called IR drop, periodically appears at

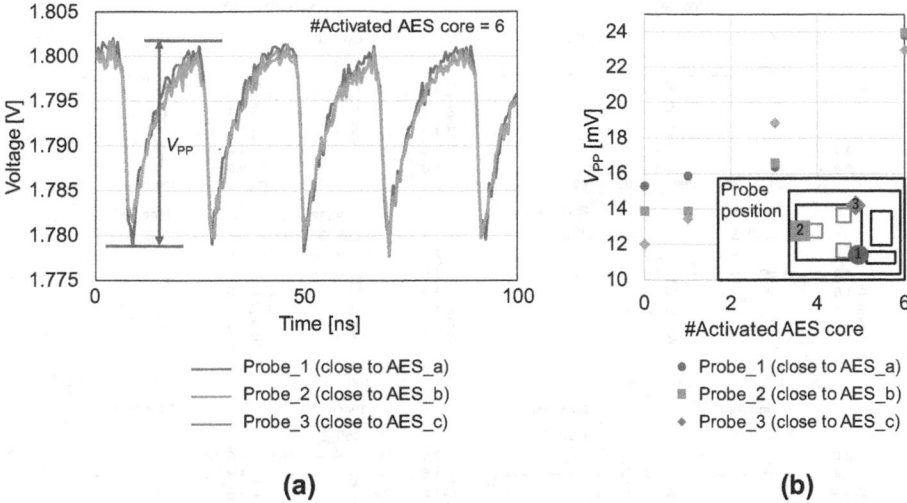

Fig. 11. IR drop waveforms during digital circuits operation.

every 20.8 ns, in response to the power current consumption by an array of clock drivers (typically inverters) synchronously toggled at the rise and fall edge of rectangular signal. The magnitude as large as 24 mV was metered as V_{PP} for PDN noise with six AES cores, while almost linearly responded to the number of AES cores in operation (Fig. 11(b)) The on-chip measurements among the three different OCM probing points exhibit less position dependency of PDN noise, namely, the whole PDN varies as a single voltage plane. This naturally results from the low-impedance nature of V_{DD_CORE} network, and also confirms the proper measurement capability of the OCM. The total number of equivalent 2-input NAND gates reaches 625 in the clock-signal network. The maximum V_{PP} of 24 mV corresponds to 1.3% of the nominal V_{DD_CORE} of 1.8 V, which guarantees the sufficient power supply capability of the PDN.

Figure 12 shows on-chip voltage waveforms measured at the OCM probing points on V_{DD_CORE} nodes; Probe_{1,2,3} when EM injection coil is moved and stably located at one of six different coil positions; Coil_{1,2,3,4,5,6} over the flipped IC chip. The waveforms are compared in each plot for the polarity of EM injection coil; either clockwise (CW) turns or counter clockwise (CCW) turns, with the same applied voltage nominally at 300 V. The location of probing points and coil positions are indicated on the front-side physical layout diagram of Fig. 4. It is noted that their relative placements are carefully hold among the following measurements though the IC chip was assembled in a flipped-chip manner, more precisely, flipped along the X axis (long side.)

At the location of Probe_1, Fig. 12(a), the negative voltage drop is induced by the EM injection with CCW polarity. The drop size reaches as large as 450 mV when the EM injection coil is placed at the Coil_5 and Coil_6, becomes approximately 250 mV at Coil_3 and Coil_4, while insignificant at Coil_1 and Coil_2. The drop time width is approximately equivalent to the pulse width of EM injection.

At the location of Probe_2, Fig. 12(b), in contrast, the negative voltage drop is induced all with CW polarity. The drop size enlarges to the level as high as 1 V, mostly

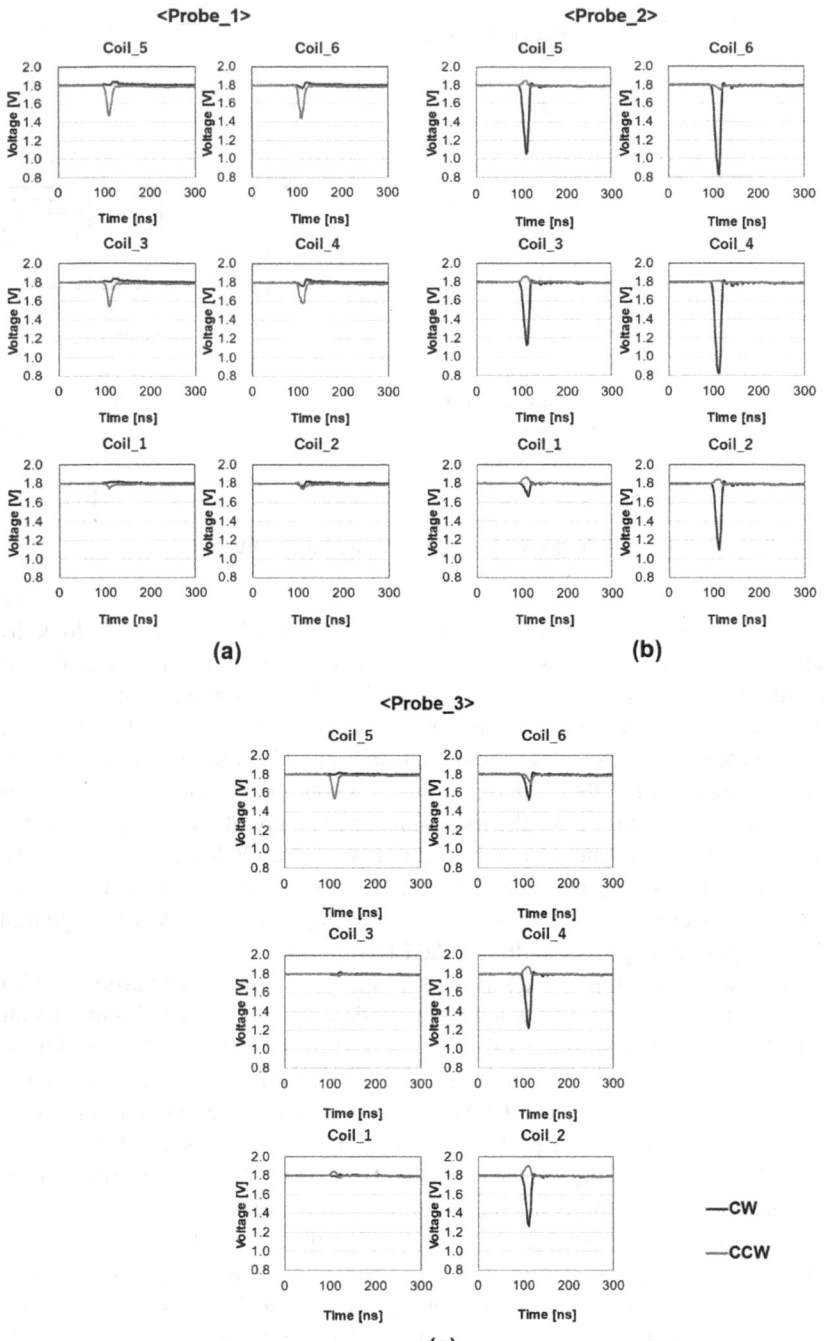

Fig. 12. IR drop waveforms over 3 OCM probe points and 6 EM coil positions.

out of range of the OCM, by the EM injection at Coil_4, Coil_5 and Coil_6. The negative drop is induced with roughly 700 mV similarly at Coil_2 and Coil_3 while becomes insignificant at Coil_1.

At the location of Probe_3, Fig. 12(c), the induced voltage waves differently behave. The negative drop size is as large as 500 mV with CW polarity at Coil_2 and Coil_4. The similar size of roughly 250 mV is observed by the EM injection with CCM polarity at Coil_5 and the CW counterpart at Coil_6, respectively. The drop is almost unseen when EM is injected at Coil_1 and Coil_3.

There are some implications as follows from the measurements, though we have not yet reached the complete explanation from physics viewpoints.

It is very interesting to note that large-amplitude negative voltage induction originates from the EM injection coil located far away from its point of measurements, and therefore does not necessarily arise by the proximately positioned coil. Also, the induction is attributed often by either CW or CCW polarity, not always by both of them, and very dependent on the relative position between the point of measurements and the placement of EM injection coil.

The aforementioned observation suggests the inductive coupling of magnetic flux by EM injection to the closed loops parasitically formed by metal segments among power (VDD) routings. The diameter of EM injection coil, that is associated with its ferrite core in Fig. 3, is 1 mm. This is roughly three times larger than the thickness (350 um) of Si substrate of an IC chip. The coil is contacted on the Si substrate backside and magnetic flux propagates through the Si substrate and reaches metal segments at the surface side of a flipped-down IC chip.

3.2 The Relationship Between AES Faults and IR Drop Waveforms

The operation of AES cores is evaluated under the presence of EM injection. One of three AES cores (AES_{a,b,c}) iteratively encrypts a plain text and outputs a cypher. A checker synchronously compares the output with an expected cypher, and counts when the result is faulty. The measured number of faulty outputs is summarized in Table 1, under the EM injection respectively with the EM injection coil's position and polarity. The number of failure occurrence larger than 5 among 300 iterations is bolded. The number of faulty operations is outstandingly large for AES_b among all the six coil positions, and meaningfully significant for AES_a and AES_c among the specific coil placements.

It is highlighted that the CW EM injection incurs the majority of faults while the CCW counterpart is less impactful in the table, under the provided test conditions. To avoid misunderstanding, it is additionally noted that the CCW EM injection incurs errors if it is with the larger level of applied voltage (Fig. 13).

The number of faulty operations observed for each AES crypto core is plotted against the on-chip measured V_{PP} in Fig. 13. The linear regression calculated among all the plot points roughly indicates that the larger number of faults is deduced by the larger V_{PP}. Once again, the experimental results with the larger voltage applied to CCW EM injection (350 V) are also included in the figure. This also implies the presence of localized, position dependent voltage drops that are induced by EM injection with either polarity and influence nearby digital logic cells.

Table 1. The number of AES faulty operations.

CW				CCW			
AES_c				AES_c			
Coil_5	6	Coil_6	3	Coil_5	1	Coil_6	3
Coil_3	1	Coil_4	7	Coil_3	1	Coil_4	2
Coil_1	2	Coil_2	3	Coil_1	1	Coil_2	2
AES_b				AES_b			
Coil_5	84	Coil_6	74	Coil_5	1	Coil_6	1
Coil_3	75	Coil_4	90	Coil_3	1	Coil_4	0
Coil_1	65	Coil_2	93	Coil_1	1	Coil_2	1
AES_a				AES_a			
Coil_5	9	Coil_6	6	Coil_5	2	Coil_6	1
Coil_3	3	Coil_4	13	Coil_3	2	Coil_4	1
Coil_1	4	Coil_2	2	Coil_1	4	Coil_2	1

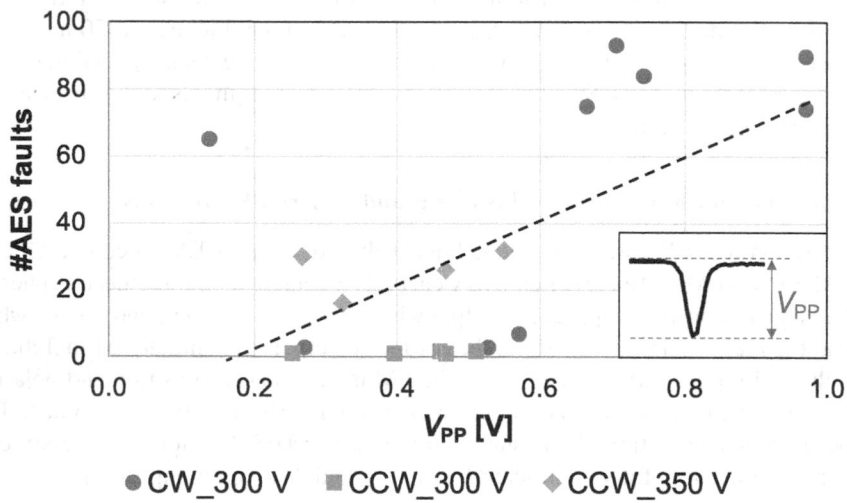

Fig. 13. Faulty operations among the AES crypto cores against the on-chip IR drop.

In summary, the voltage drop induced by EM injection attains the order of magnitude larger than IR drops by regular circuit operation. The drop by EM injection is localized at some points in PDN and dependent on the position of EM injection coil, in contrast to the IR drop that is flattened over PDN. EM injection incurs the voltage drops larger than the implicit threshold and decisively impactful on the operation of AES crypto core. Our experiments relate the observation external to an IC chip and on-chip measurements, for the first time, however, unveil the actual complexity of physics behind the EM injection and its interaction with circuits. The fault mechanisms will be elucidated from further analysis.

4   Conclusion

The fault occurrence by EMFI at different placements of an antenna coil was examined among six AES crypto cores in a 180 nm CMOS test chip. The digital circuits of crypto cores are stably supplied at the nominal voltage of 1.8 V from an on-chip LDO, where the PDN noise due to the continuous toggling among clock signal net-works is much less than 10% of the supply voltage. On the contrary, the voltage drop induced by either CW or CCW EM injection becomes as large as 1 V, reaching two-orders of magnitude larger than PDN noise and exceeding the on-chip voltage monitoring. This incurs erroneous outputs from AES encryption. Further, while the flatness of PDN noise over the entire PDN as found by on-chip measurements, the induced negative drop by EM injection is very much localized and position dependent. This is most probably followed by the distribution of metal wire segments forming parasitic loops that capture magnetic flux of the EM injection. The number of faulty outputs among crypto cores has almost linear response to the size of negative drop, largely irrelevant to the polarity of EM injection coil. All these observations come from on-chip and in-system measurements and describe the multi-physics nature of EMFI.

With these detailed, chip-level and multi-physics exploration of EM injection and fault occurrence, we find the need of more in-depth understandings on EMFI mechanisms from physics viewpoints, including the coupling of EM injection to PDNs, the induction of current and voltage localized among metal wirings of PDNs, and the impact of such induced current and voltage with transistors forming digital circuits. These will help the design of EMFI resiliency among crypto cores backed with accurate and efficient coupling models from PDN to transistor-level digital circuits. Further research efforts will be conducted thoroughly with different chip designs and technologies.

Acknowledgments. This work has been partly supported by JSPS KAKENHI Grant No. JP22H04999 and by SECOM Science and Technology Foundation.

References

1. Boneh, D., DeMillo, R.A., Lipton, R.J.: On the importance of checking cryptographic protocols for faults. In: Fumy, W. (ed.) EUROCRYPT 1997. LNCS, vol. 1233, pp. 37–51. Springer, Heidelberg (1997). https://doi.org/10.1007/3-540-69053-0_4
2. Biham, E., Shamir, A.: Differential fault analysis of secret key cryptosystems. In: Kaliski, B.S. (ed.) CRYPTO 1997. LNCS, vol. 1294, pp. 513–525. Springer, Heidelberg (1997). https://doi.org/10.1007/BFb0052259
3. Skorobogatov, S.P., Anderson, R.J.: Optical fault induction attacks. In: Kaliski, B.S., Koç, K., Paar, C. (eds.) CHES 2002. LNCS, vol. 2523, pp. 2–12. Springer, Heidelberg (2003). https://doi.org/10.1007/3-540-36400-5_2
4. Dutertre, J.-M., et al.: Laser fault injection at the CMOS 28 nm technology node: an analysis of the fault model. In: 2018 Workshop on Fault Diagnosis and Tolerance in Cryptography (FDTC), Amsterdam, Netherlands, pp. 1–6 (2018). https://doi.org/10.1109/FDTC.2018.00009

5. Aumüller, C., Bier, P., Fischer, W., Hofreiter, P., Seifert, J.-P.: Fault attacks on RSA with CRT: concrete results and practical countermeasures. In: Kaliski, B.S., Koç, K., Paar, C. (eds.) CHES 2002. LNCS, vol. 2523, pp. 260–275. Springer, Heidelberg (2003). https://doi.org/10.1007/3-540-36400-5_20

6. Zussa, L., Dutertre, J.-M., Clédière, J., Tria, A.: Power supply glitch induced faults on FPGA: an in-depth analysis of the injection mechanism. In: 2013 IEEE 19th International On-Line Testing Symposium (IOLTS), Chania, Greece, pp. 110–115 (2013). https://doi.org/10.1109/IOLTS.2013.6604060

7. Endo, S., Sugawara, T., Homma, N., et al.: An on-chip glitchy-clock generator for testing fault injection attacks. J. Cryptogr. Eng. 1, 265–270 (2011). https://doi.org/10.1007/s13389-011-0022-y

8. Quisquater, J.-J., Samyde, D.: Eddy current for magnetic analysis with active sensor. In: Proceedings of Esmart, pp. 185–194 (2002)

9. Maurine, P.: Techniques for EM fault injection: equipments and experimental results. In: Bertoni, G., Gierlichs, B. (eds.) 2012 Workshop on Fault Diagnosis and Tolerance in Cryptography, Leuven, Belgium, 9 September 2012, pp. 3–4. IEEE Computer Society (2012)

10. Wadatsumi, T., Kawai, K., Hasegawa, R., Monta, K., Miki, T., Nagata, M.: Characterization of backside ESD impacts on integrated circuits. In: 2023 IEEE International Reliability Physics Symposium (IRPS), Monterey, CA, USA, pp. 1–6 (2023). https://doi.org/10.1109/IRPS48203.2023.10118240

11. Poucheret, F., Tobich, K., Lisarty, M., Chusseauz, L., Robissonx, B., Maurine, P.: Local and direct EM injection of power into CMOS integrated circuits. In: 2011 Workshop on Fault Diagnosis and Tolerance in Cryptography, Nara, Japan, pp. 100–104 (2011). https://doi.org/10.1109/FDTC.2011.18

12. Bayon, P., et al.: Contactless electromagnetic active attack on ring oscillator based true random number generator. In: Schindler, W., Huss, S.A. (eds.) COSADE 2012. LNCS, vol. 7275, pp. 151–166. Springer, Heidelberg (2012). https://doi.org/10.1007/978-3-642-29912-4_12

13. Dehbaoui, A., Dutertre, J.-M., Robisson, B., Orsatelli, P., Maurine, P., Tria, A.: Injection of transient faults using electromagnetic pulses—practical results on a cryptographic system. IACR Cryptology ePrint Archive 2012, 123 (2012)

14. Dehbaoui, A., Dutertre, J.-M., Robisson, B., Tria, A.: Electromagnetic transient faults injection on a hardware and a software implementations of AES. In: 2012 Workshop on Fault Diagnosis and Tolerance in Cryptography, Leuven, Belgium, pp. 7–15 (2012). https://doi.org/10.1109/FDTC.2012.15

15. Ordas, S., Guillaume-Sage, L., Tobich, K., Dutertre, J., Maurine, P.: Evidence of a larger EM-induced fault model. In: Proceedings of the 13th International Conference on Smart Card Research and Advanced Applications (CARDIS), Paris, France, pp. 245–259 (2014)

16. Ordas, S., Guillaume-Sage, L., Maurine, P.: EM injection: fault model and locality. In: Proceedings of the Workshop on Fault Diagnosis and Tolerance in Cryptography (FDTC) Saint Malo, France, pp. 3–13 (2015)

17. Ordas, S., Sage, L.G., Maurine, P.: Electromagnetic fault injection: the curse of flip-flops. J. Cryptograph. Eng. 7(3), 183–197 (2017)

18. El-Baze, D., Rigaud, J.-B., Maurine, P.: A fully-digital EM pulse detector. In: 2016 Design, Automation Test in Europe Conference Exhibition (DATE), pp. 439–444 (2016)

19. Nabhan, R., et al.: A tale of two models: discussing the timing and sampling EM fault injection models. In: Twentieth Workshop on Fault Diagnosis and Tolerance in Cryptography, FDTC 2023 (2023)

20. O'Flynn, C.: PicoEMP: a low-cost EMFI platform compared to BBI and voltage fault injection using TDC and external VCC measurements. Cryptology ePrint Archive (2023)

21. Dumont, M., Lisart, M., Maurine, P.: Electromagnetic fault injection: how faults occur. In: 2019 Workshop on Fault Diagnosis and Tolerance in Cryptography (FDTC), Atlanta, GA, USA, pp. 9–16 (2019). https://doi.org/10.1109/FDTC.2019.00010
22. Dumont, M., Lisart, M., Maurine, P.: Modeling and simulating electromagnetic fault injection. IEEE Trans. Comput. Aided Des. Integr. Circuits Syst. **40**(4), 680–693 (2021). https://doi.org/10.1109/TCAD.2020.3003287
23. Lin, L., et al.: Layout-level vulnerability ranking from electromagnetic fault injection. In: 2022 IEEE International Symposium on Hardware Oriented Security and Trust (HOST), McLean, VA, USA, pp. 17–20 (2022). https://doi.org/10.1109/HOST54066.2022.9840146
24. Nagata, M., Okumoto, T., Taki, K.: A built-in technique for probing power supply and ground noise distribution within large-scale digital integrated circuits. IEEE J. Solid-State Circuits **40**(4), 813–819 (2005). https://doi.org/10.1109/JSSC.2005.845559
25. Wadatsumi, T., Miki, T., Nagata, M.: A dual-mode successive approximation register analog to digital converter to detect malicious off-chip power noise measurement attacks. Jpn. J. Appl. Phys. (JJAP) **60**(SB), SBBL03_1–9 (2021). https://doi.org/10.35848/1347-4065/abde26
26. https://www.newae.com/products/NAE-CW520

EFFLUX-F2: A High Performance Hardware Security Evaluation Board

Arpan Jati[1,2] , Naina Gupta[1(✉)] , Anupam Chattopadhyay[1] ,
and Somitra Kumar Sanadhya[3]

[1] Nanyang Technological University, Singapore, Singapore
{arpan.jati,anupam}@ntu.edu.sg, naina003@e.ntu.edu.sg
[2] Indraprastha Institute of Information Technology Delhi, New Delhi, India
[3] Indian Institute of Technology Jodhpur, Jodhpur, India
somitra@iitj.ac.in

Abstract. Side-channel analysis has become a cornerstone of modern hardware security evaluation for cryptographic accelerators. Recently, these techniques are also being applied in fields such as AI and Machine Learning to investigate possible threats. Security evaluations are reliant on standard test setups including commercial and open-source evaluation boards such as, SASEBO/SAKURA and ChipWhisperer. However, with shrinking design footprints and overlapping tasks on the same platforms, the quality of the side channel information as well as the speed of data capture can significantly influence security assessment.

In this work, we designed EFFLUX-F2, a hardware security evaluation board to improve the quality and speed of side-channel information capture. We also designed a measurement setup to benchmark the signal differences between target boards. Multiple experimental evaluations like noise analysis, CPA and TVLA performed on EFFLUX-F2 and competing evaluation boards showcase the significant superiority of our design in all aspects.

Keywords: SCA · evaluation board · side-channel analysis · CPA · TVLA

1 Introduction

Side channel attacks have been used to attack a wide range of platforms and algorithms. Recently they have also gained importance to attack AI implementations. In order to standardize the side-channel evaluation platforms across different experiments with reproducible results, many works have been reported in literature over the past few years. Katashita et al. started the first project Side-channel Attack Standard Evaluation BOards (SASEBOs) [11,15] in this direction. As part of the project, the authors initially developed four boards SASEBO, SASEBO-G, SASEBO-R and SASEBO-R where SASEBO-R targeted a custom ASIC design and the rest were used to evaluate FPGA based hardware designs. But as the protected cryptographic designs require more resources, the previous platforms did not had sufficient FPGA logic cells. As a result, the authors

© The Author(s), under exclusive license to Springer Nature Switzerland AG 2024
R. Wacquez and N. Homma (Eds.): COSADE 2024, LNCS 14595, pp. 38–56, 2024.
https://doi.org/10.1007/978-3-031-57543-3_3

updated the SASEBO-G design to be more compact, incorporate an FPGA with more logic cells, and support for few other features such as user-controllable configuration. The platform is commonly recognized as SASEBO-GII. This is followed by another platform (SASEBO-W) targeted towards evaluating smart-cards [10]. To further extend the evaluation of more complex and integrated designs, Katashita et al. developed another side-channel board SASEBO-GIII [9] which is equipped with a 28-nm Kintex-7 FPGA. Later, the SASEBO project was terminated and SAKURA boards [8] (successors of SASEBO) were made available in the market.

Apart from these SASEBO/SAKURA boards, another effort by [14] led to the development of a modular platform design. The designers targeted to provide a complete setup which includes target device, measurement setup and trace capture and analysis software. The complete platform design is open-source. Another recent effort by [6] in which the authors designed the platform with Kintex Ultrascale FPGA to allow evaluations of larger designs such as Post-quantum cryptographic (PQC) [1,4] implementations. However, this design is dependent on the type of external power supply provided to the board. Hence, the experiments performed will vary with different power supplies.

In any side-channel attack, the signal-to-noise ratio (SNR) [12] of an SCA setup is a very important and crucial metric. A high SNR allows for cleaner signal and better experimental results. This leads to faster secret recovery or assessments and more confidence in the results. Hence, the main focus of our design is to improve the power circuit to enhance the overall signal quality. The next target is to demonstrate how this improved SNR aids in multiple experiments.

To provide security for constrained devices, smaller footprint or low complexity designs (lightweight cryptography [13]) has gained attention over the past few years. NIST has also started standardizing such designs [16]. But due to the smaller footprint, these designs have very low noise profile. Thus, making it quite difficult to perform side-channel leakage analysis on these designs. Hence, in this work we showcase how our low-noise and high performance EFFLUX-F2 board improves the commonly used Test Vector Leakage Analysis (TVLA) [3] experimental results. We also demonstrate Correlation Power Analysis (CPA) [5] attack differences. For this, we targeted GIFT [2] as it is one of the smallest lightweight cipher.

Further, as the side-channel attacks are becoming more prevalent and sophisticated, so are the countermeasures to protect these designs. The countermeasures if not implemented correctly may still leak information. For this, protected designs are also assessed and analyzed for leakage using TVLA. This analysis is typically performed by capturing and analyzing millions of traces as the designs are protected and may not leak initially. Capturing these many traces usually requires multiple hours. Hence, we also demonstrate how enhanced signal quality improves on the number of required traces and henceforth reduce the time to capture. For this, we used a known GIFT-128 protected implementation with known 1st order leakages. The main contributions can be summarized as follows:

- We designed and developed a high performance and low-noise hardware board for side-channel evaluations. A detailed noise evaluation demonstrates the low-noise characteristics of EFFLUX-F2.
- We performed multiple experimental evaluations (SNR, CPA and TVLA) using a leaky unprotected AES implementation and a very lightweight cipher GIFT, having very low leakage levels compared to the former.
- We also compare EFFLUX-F2 with state-of-the-art commonly employed side-channel evaluation board SAKURA-X.
  - Statistical analysis of the raw noise measurements demonstrate that EFFLUX-F2 has at least 4.5× lower noise levels than SAKURA-X.
  - EFFLUX-F2 achieves almost 8.2× higher SNR than SAKURA-X for AES.
  - For CPA attack on GIFT, we achieve a reduction of at least 5× the required number of traces. We also showcase how EFFLUX-F2 clearly distinguishes between the correct key and wrong keys with high probabilities. Whereas, this is not true for SAKURA-X.
  - Furthermore, we show even though the performance improvement (t-value vs number of traces) for TVLA on an unprotected AES is moderate. It is quite drastic in the case of GIFT. This difference becomes more prominent in case of a partially protected design where the leakage detection is ≈20× better for EFFLUX-F2.

2   EFFLUX-F2

EFFLUX-F2 as shown in Fig. 1 is a high performance FPGA board specifically designed to improve measurement accuracy and noise characteristics. While designing the board we used low-noise power supplies and many low-noise design principles to minimize noise and signal interactions. The board is also designed as a general-purpose FPGA board allowing for many use cases in multiple scenarios. While designing the board we had the following requirements in mind:

- **Low EMI and Noise:** In order to improve measurement quality for both power and EM measurements, keeping the noise low is very important. One normally needs a large number of traces to detect leakage from weakly protected implementations, we aim to improve the SNR significantly in order to make the experiments faster and more reliable.
- **Adjustable Voltages and Fault Injection Support:** Possibility to undervolt the VCCINT rails and voltage glitch fault injection support, with high temporal resolution.
- **FPGA and DRAM measurements:** The current offerings do not support DRAM power measurements. We intend to provide support for the same to make it possible to exploit this avenue in future attacks.
- **Single FPGA design:** To simplify the design and reduce system noise and cost. Two FPGAs are always better, but with careful hardware and software design, we can use a single FPGA in most applications, without much side-effects.

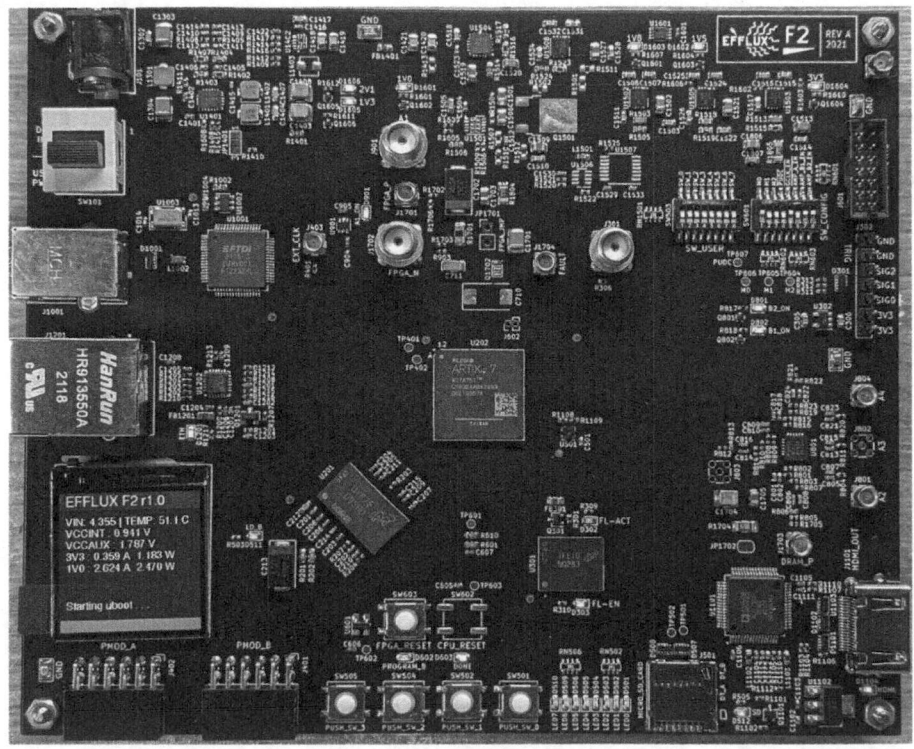

Fig. 1. EFFLUX-F2 Board: LCD showing U-boot starting to load Linux.

- **DRAM, Ethernet, SDIO and HDMI:** To closely replicate real systems and associated noise, DDR3 RAM, Ethernet, SDIO and HDMI output.
- **Built-in amplifiers:** To simplify the trace capture setup, multiple onboard amplifiers are required.
- **General purpose use:** Additional LEDs, LCD display and switches so that the board can be used as a general purpose FPGA development board as well.
- **Compatibility:** By using the same USB-IF chip used in SASEBO/SAKURA boards, the board remains software compatible with existing software setups.

Figure 2 shows the block diagram for the EFFLUX-F2 board. All the devices like RAM, Flash, USB IF, Display interfaces and Ethernet PHY etc., are connected to the FPGA. A specifically designed power supply targeting low noise and EMI emissions is powering all the devices on the board. The power delivery system contains current-sense resistors and sense amplifiers to measure the current in 1.0 V and 3.3 V rails. This allows for precise measurement of FPGA VCCINT current measurement, leading to very precise FPGA core power measurement. In addition to voltage measurement, we have also added a very precise environment sensor with accuracy of $\pm 0.2\,°C$ and $\pm 2\%RH$ temperature and humidity respectively. To keep noise at a minimum, there are no additional microcontroller or CPLD for housekeeping purposes. Further, all the devices other than the FPGA do not contain any additional processing units to avoid noise generation. In addition to this, all noisy peripherals can be power-gated to reduce noise in the captured power traces, this includes high frequency clock generators.

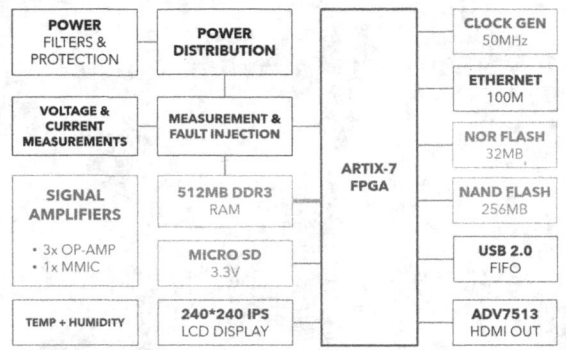

Fig. 2. EFFLUX-F2: Block Diagram

2.1   Choice of FPGA

The board was designed with flexibility and cost in mind. We decided to use Xilinx Artix-7 family of devices. These have wide market adoption and are manufactured using TSMC 28 nm HPL process. On a fundamental design level these devices are very similar to the other 7-series FPGA lines like the Kintex and Virtex. The board is designed to support the CSG324 0.8 mm pitch package. This package supports multiple devices from XC7A15T (16.6K Logic Cells) to XC7A100T (101K Logic Cells). We initially planned on using a 1.0 mm pitch FTG256 package device, but had to migrate to the larger 324-ball package as we quickly ran out of pins during the design phase. Only four pins of the current FPGA are left unused.

Further, having a single FPGA instead of two FPGAs or FPGA + Microcontroller combination has multiple benefits like reduced board complexity and fewer sources of noise. As most of the power leakage comes from switching noise, clock gating the non-cryptographic portion would allow for a design with a single FPGA while having minimal side effects on the noise performance. The clock gating can easily be implemented with small modifications to the hardware.

2.2   Power Supply

Noise sources in any system can vary widely. While designing the board we consider the additional noise generated by the power supply and attempt to keep them at a minimum. The majority of this additional noise comes from the

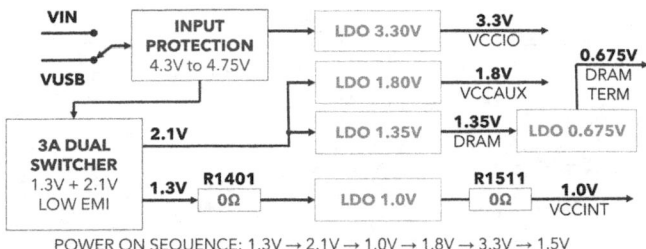

POWER ON SEQUENCE: 1.3V → 2.1V → 1.0V → 1.8V → 3.3V → 1.5V

Fig. 3. Voltage Regulation and Power Delivery

switching noise of power supply components like buck converters. The buck converters are DC-DC power converters which convert a higher voltage to a lower voltage. An inductor is used to temporarily store energy while capacitors are used to reduce ripple. Using such a topology, high efficiencies of around 95% can be achieved, leading to lower power loss through heat and smaller circuits. Unfortunately, these circuits are inherently noisy because the switching activity of the power MOSFETs cause high currents to pass through inductors and capacitors. The inductors store energy in magnetic fields, and rapid switching causes a lot of EM emissions.

In this work, we follow many design techniques, like reducing high current loop areas, appropriately sized and placed capacitors, proper ground planes, protecting sensitive signals from noisy traces and many others during the design optimization process. LDO (Low dropout) linear regulators are known for their low noise, high PSRR (Power Supply Rejection Ratio) and good transient response. We use these devices as post regulators after the initial switching mode power supplies. The switching regulators are also running with spread-spectrum enabled, this distributes the conducted and radiated EM over a wider frequency band. These steps allow us to significantly reduce ripple on the power rails. We also use resistors and components (references, OPAMPs and regulators) with low TCR (Temperature Coefficient of Resistance) of ± 10 ppm/$^\circ$C or better and high accuracy 0.1% wherever applicable for better signal drift characteristics. This helps in experiments that run over a long time and face changing DC levels caused by temperature effects.

Figure 3 shows the voltage regulation and power delivery topology used in the board. The input power first passes through a fuse, a MOSFET based reverse voltage protection circuit and a 5.76 V over-voltage protection circuit. It is then filtered using a wide-band high order power filter with an *insertion loss* of more than 60 dB for frequencies between 100 KHz and 100 MHz. This filtered power then, passes through a 3rd order π type LC EMI filter built using discrete components, before reaching a low EMI switching regulator.

The idea is to convert the 5 V power input (USB or external input) to 1.4 V using a switching regulator and then regulate the 1.4 V to 1.0 V using an LDO for the FPGA VCCINT rail. The LDO input to output voltage difference of 0.4 V is higher than required, but it is intentional as it helps in improving the PSRR

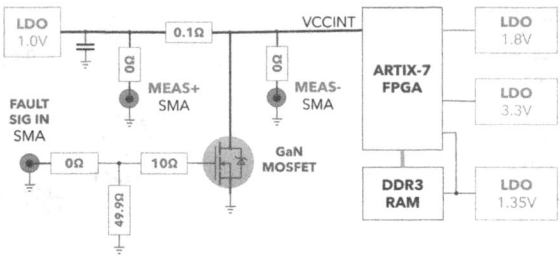

Fig. 4. FPGA Core Power Measurement and Fault Injection

performance of the regulator. The 0.675 V, 1.35 V and 1.8 V rails are generated from a 2.1 V switcher, using three LDOs. The 3.3 V rail is generated directly from the input 5V supply, this is fine as the current demand on this rail is not very high. We use power-sequencing (as shown in the figure) to ensure safe and reliable FPGA power up. We also use a dedicated power on reset chip (with voltage sense) to ensure reliable reset signal to the FPGA, both on power on and manual reset.

2.3 FPGA Power Measurements

Figure 4 shows the FPGA core power measurement setup. The board uses high side current measurement. $0.1\,\Omega$ and $0.36\,\Omega$ resistors are used for the FPGA and DRAM measurement respectively. Measurement points are provided on the board to access these power signals. Multiple amplifier circuits are additionally added to amplify these small signals so that an oscilloscope can be directly connected without inline amplifiers. This simplifies the overall setup. In the figure, the voltage drop through the $0.1\,\Omega$ resistor is amplified by either of the amplifiers and can be used as the leakage signal. An SMA connector also allows for an external amplifier to be used alternatively. Faults can be injected by using an FPGA or pulse generator to generate glitch signals of the required width and then driving it to the gate terminal of the MOSFET. The power supply is designed to handle shorts to the ground for small duration. The MOSFET has a current rating of more than 20A and resistance close to $3\,m\Omega$. As we are using a GaN FET the total gate charge is just 6.6 nC, enabling fast switching performance.

Figure 5a shows the back side of the board with the 5× VCCINT capacitors removed. This is required to improve the captured signal quality.

Onboard Amplifiers. We implemented two amplifiers, a 30 dB MMIC (Monolithic microwave integrated circuit) amplifier and a 3 channel wide-band Low-noise 20 dB op-amp based amplifier as shown in Fig. 5b. Both the amplifiers are 50Ω matched and AC coupled using $0.1\,\mu F$ capacitors. The -3 dB bandwidth for the amplifiers are 2.2 GHz and 446 MHz respectively. These separate amplifiers

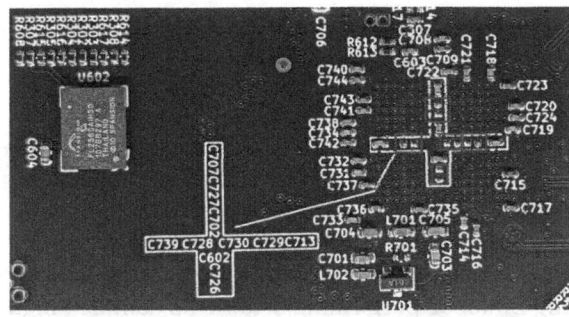 

(a) 5× **VCCINT** rail capacitors removed to improve signal quality.

(b) **AD8003** Op-amp Based Amplifier.

Fig. 5. EFFLUX-F2: PCB under FPGA and Amplifer

provide flexibility in optimizing the measurement setup. The amplifiers can be disabled on a per channel basis to reduce coupled noise when a channel is not needed.

2.4 Clocks Generation

A precise *low-jitter* clock helps SCA measurements. The 50 MHz clock generator SiT9121AI from SiTime is used. **LVDS** version of the chip is employed with 10 ppm stability and 1.2ps RMS (Root Mean Square) period jitter. External clock input and output is also supported.

2.5 Memories

There are four types of supported memories on the board:

- **32 MB Flash:** To store FPGA bitstream or OS images.
- **512 MB DDR3:** 16-bit High speed DRAM (1600 MB/s).
- **NAND Flash:** Large file or OS storage.
- **SDIO:** SD Card.

These memory features allow for testing of countermeasures in realistic scenarios. Further, hardware/software co-design based designs running on Microblaze/RISCV etc. can be tested and verified. Further, the current offerings do not support direct DRAM chip level power measurements. We enable support for the same to enable new avenues of attacks.

2.6 I/O Interfaces

An **FT2232HL** USB 2.0 chip from FTDI is employed for the USB interface. It supports 12 Mbaud (UART) and up-to 40 MB/s (Sync FIFO) using two independent UART/FIFO interfaces. As the interfaces are independent and come with separate 4 KiB TX and RX internal FIFO buffers the chip offers high performance and minimal latency. This allows for fast transfer of data like keys, plain-text, cipher-text etc. The board also has additional protected ports for trigger in and out. To aid in development and debug tasks, multiple devices like LEDs, push switches, slide switches, GPIO pins, and configuration switches are also added. We further implemented 2x Digilent PMOD compatible pin-out and physical connectors so that a variety of extension boards can be used. This is a board primarily designed for side channel attacks, adding Ethernet which may be quite noisy is counter-intuitive. We have added Ethernet as a means of easy data transfer especially while using Linux or performing attacks on complex high throughput AXI peripherals. Power gating is supported to fully disable this unit when performing analysis on low noise or low leakage designs. We use LAN8720A, which is a 10/100 Mbps RMII transceiver. The transceiver supports IEEE 802.3u and Auto-negotiation.

2.7   OS + System Support

Additionally, one of the goals behind designing the board was to allow side-channel trace capture in realistic scenarios with significant background noise for certain experiments. To closely replicate real systems, as discussed above we added the support for 2Gb (256 MB) DDR3 RAM. Further, SDIO was added to support large storage devices to enable booting OSes like Linux. HDMI output was added for display support. All these interfaces can be fully disabled when needed especially while preforming noise sensitive experiments.

2.8   ESD Protection

The board is protected against ESD. We used IEC 61000-4-2 Level 4 compliant ESD Protection ($\pm$12-kV Contact Discharge protection). TVS Diodes with low capacitance are used resulting in negligible distortion to the protected signal lines. All the I/O interfaces like Trigger, PMOD, USB and HDMI pins are protected. The USB and HDMI interfaces are additionally protected using common mode chokes. The protection devices makes the board much more robust against accidental ESD strikes while handling and touching.

2.9   Power Gating

Power-gating is implemented for multiple modules in the board. The SD-Card, Ethernet, Flash, HDMI, individual signal amplifiers etc. can be disabled to reduce noise. The power gating is implemented using P-Channel MOSFETs controlled by signals from the FPGA and individual slide-switches wherever applicable.

2.10   PCB Design and Routing

We used multiple design techniques, including the ones discussed in Sect. 2.2 while placing components and routing the board to improve the performance of the board. The fully routed PCB is shown in Fig. 6. It is evident that a minimum of the traces are routed on the outer layers (red and green), this is done to minimize EMI emissions. Apart from keeping noisy signals away from sensitive ones we also separated critical signals using ground planes. We initially started with an eight layer PCB design, but after routing all the important signals, it was determined that it is possible to have very similar performance and isolation even with six layers; so, the extra layers were removed and the design finished with six layers instead.

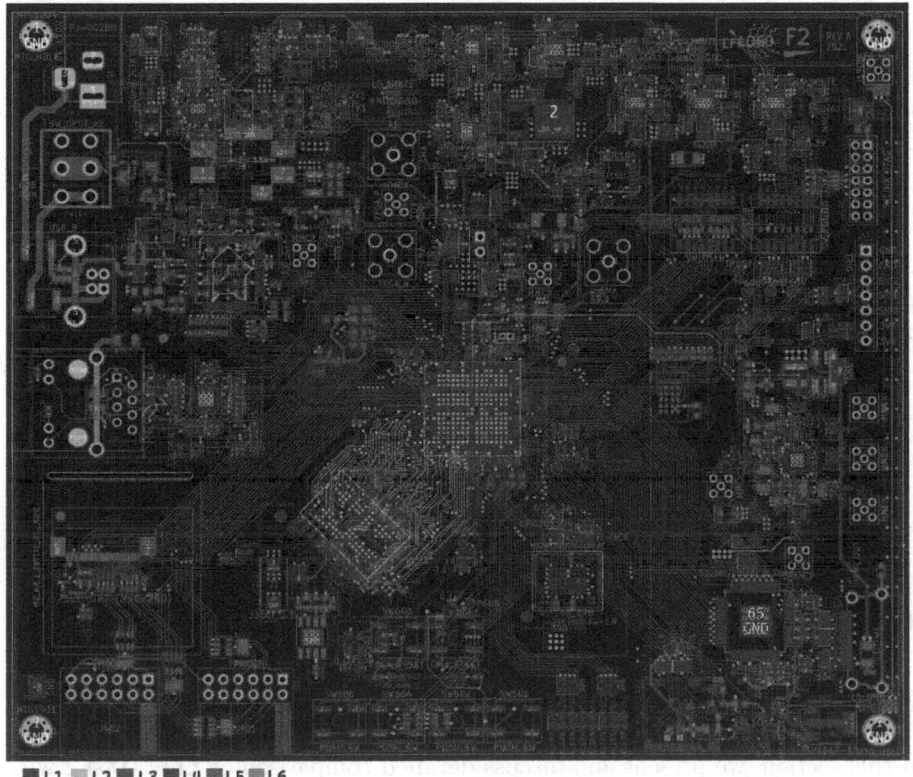

■ L1 ■ L2 ■ L3 ■ L4 ■ L5 ■ L6

Fig. 6. PCB Routing all internal layers. Ground planes not shown for clarity.

3   Experimental Setup

In this work, we present results for multiple experiments using the following metrics:

- Direct Noise Measurements (FPGA VCCINT noise)
- Signal to Noise Ratio (SNR)
- Correlation Power Analysis (CPA)
- Test Vector Leakage Assessment (TVLA)

In order to obtain consistent repeatable results we perform experiments with fixed settings. The SNR, TVLA and CPA experiments use the same setup, Agilent DSO6034A oscilloscope, PA303 Amplifier from Langer EMV-Technik and a 50 MHz Low pass inline SMA filter from Crystek Corporation. All these experiments use traces captured at 2GS/s.

While measuring noise directly, we were faced with many challenges. The first being the fact that we are interested in measuring noise coming from the power supply and not from the FPGA. As the power supplies are designed to be low noise, the voltage levels are very small in the tens to hundreds of μV range. This level is easily below the noise floor of most oscilloscopes as the lowest gain range is often close to $1\,mV$/division. Second, when we tried to measure noise using off-the-shelf amplifiers (from multiple vendors) we quickly ran into the problem that the noise measurement for EFFLUX-F2 was either below or close to the noise floor. Cascading multiple amplifiers did not help as the input noise density (1.5–$2.2\,nV/\sqrt{Hz}$) of the first amplifier in the chain is still quite high. To get around these issues we designed a multi-stage custom amplifier with a differential input section constructed using discrete low-noise transistors (BJTs). The amplifier has an adjustable gain of approx $70\,dB$–$80\,dB$, and an extremely low input voltage noise density of $465\,pV/\sqrt{Hz}$. Further, two separate 2nd order Sallen-Key LPF filters before the output stage allows us to band-limit the signal to 100 kHz and 1 MHz, the unfiltered signal has a bandwidth of around 10 MHz. The performance is enough to measure power supply noise from very clean LDO devices with good accuracy. For noise measurements, the traces are captured at 200 MS/s given the reduced bandwidth.

4   Evaluation Results

In this section, we present and discuss detailed comparison of EFFLUX-F2 with SAKURA-X. Apart from SAKURA-X, CW305 and CW310 boards from NewAE also allows power measurement. Unfortunately, the boards do not use low noise power supplies; the FPGA in the boards are powered directly using noisy switching regulators. This is good enough for many applications, but more that an order of magnitude higher noise levels is measured from CW305 ($\approx$72 μV RMS) compared to EFFLUX-F2. Additionally, as the noise level is too high for our high gain noise measurements setup (without added attenuation) and the measured SNR is lower compared to SAKURA-X, we do not include it in our detailed evaluation.

4.1   Noise Measurements

FPGA core voltage noise measurement allows us to compare multiple boards in a direct manner. For this, we power the board from a fairly noise free power supply, USB or battery and then place the target FPGA under reset. A power trace is then captured using an oscilloscope using the 'single' capture mode to provide the longest possible trace length (4 million points). We use the high-gain low-noise amplifier as discussed above to amplify the power signal by around 76 dB (6300×). Even though we could use a higher gain, we chose to use 76 dB as this limited the peak to peak signal level to around 1V for all experiments, having a higher amplitude would cause other undesirable side effects. For consistency, the same power source is used for both the boards. To transform the time domain results to frequency domain, an FFT is performed on the captured trace points and the results are plotted on a log-log graph. A trace labeled NOISE FLOOR is also added to the graphs. It corresponds to the noise floor of the measurement system, and is obtained by shorting the amplifier input to the ground.

Battery Powered System (Board Generated Noise). This experimental setup captures voltage signal from both the boards powered from two Li-Ion cells in series at a voltage of 8.2 V. The setup is designed to show the inherent noise of the power supplies, and as we do not have any external higher frequency noise sources, we are band-limiting the signals to 1 MHz for this experiment.

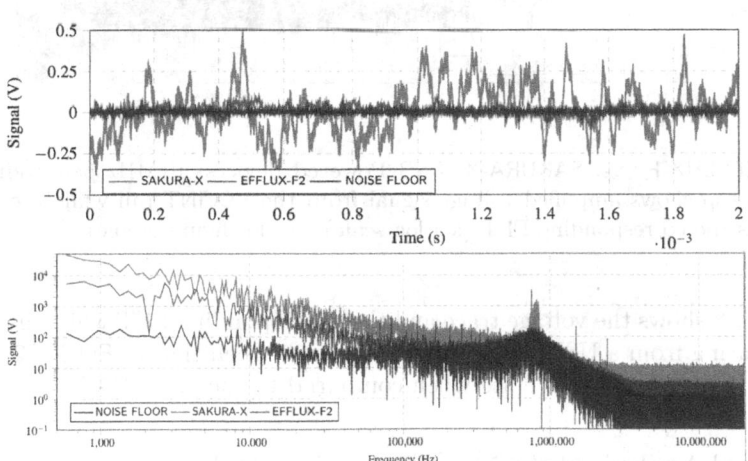

Fig. 7. EFFLUX-F2 vs. SAKURA-X. Battery Powered devices, 1 MHz bandwidth. The graph on top shows amplified voltage signal from the VCCINT rail while the bottom one shows the corresponding FFT (log-log scale). (Color figure online)

It can be seen in Fig. 7 that EFFLUX-F2 (shown in blue) has a much lower noise amplitude when compared to the SAKURA-X board. Noise levels of EFFLUX-F2 is very low, but the even lower noise floor of our measurement setup allows us to demonstrate the accuracy of the results with high confidence. One can also notice the small peak in noise around 800 kHz for SAKURA-X, this is the operating frequency of the switching regulator. Such peaks are not visible in EFFLUX-F2.

USB Powered System (Typical Use Case). This experimental setup captured voltage signal from both the boards, powered from USB (connected to PC) at a voltage of 5.1 V. To show the input power noise filtering, no filter was used and the signal was band limited by the amplifier's bandwidth which is around 10 MHz (Wideband setup).

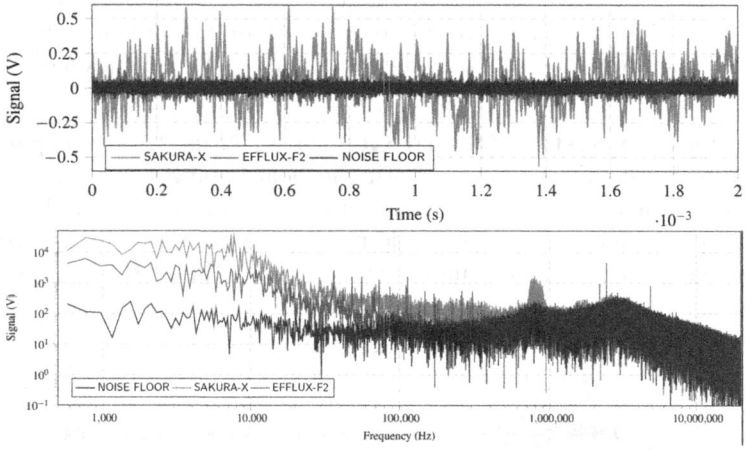

Fig. 8. EFFLUX-F2 vs. SAKURA-X. USB Powered devices, 10 MHz bandwidth. The graph on top shows amplified voltage signal from the VCCINT rail while the bottom one shows the corresponding FFT (log-log scale). (Color figure online)

Figure 8 shows the voltage trace and the corresponding FFT while the boards are operating from a USB power source. It can be seen that EFFLUX-F2 (shown in blue) has a much lower noise when compared to the SAKURA-X.

Statistical Analysis of the Measured Noise. Table 1 shows the noise statistics for the boards. To calculate the voltage at input or the amplifier (or the measurement point of the board) we scale the measured signal with the gain of the amplifier which is set to around 76 dB for the experiments. Under USB powered condition, when directly comparing the two boards, we can see that power measurement noise levels in EFFLUX-F2 is 4.62× lower than SAKURA-X when comparing the RMS noise value. While operation using batteries leads to 5.14× improvement for the same metric.

Table 1. Noise measurement statistics, battery-powered @ 1 MHz B/W, USB-powered @ 10 MHz B/W. The amplifier input is connected to the boards.

Battery-powered	Parameter	Measured at amplifier output			Calculated at amplifier input		
		NOISE FLOOR	SAKURA-X	EFFLUX-F2	NOISE FLOOR	SAKURA-X	EFFLUX-F2
	MEAN	2.504 mV	10.907 mV	12.437 mV	396.838 nV	1.729 µV	1.971 µV
	RMS	5.626 mV	149.032 mV	28.977 mV	891.819 nV	23.622 µV	4.593 µV
	Vpp 6σ	33.759 mV	894.193 mV	173.862 mV	5.351 µV	141.733 µV	27.558 µV
	STDEV	5.039 mV	148.633 mV	26.172 mV	798.662 nV	23.559 µV	4.148 µV
	VARIANCE	25.389 µV	22.092 mV	684.992 µV	0.638 pV	555.018 pV	17.209 pV
USB-powered	Parameter	Measured at amplifier output			Calculated at amplifier input		
		NOISE FLOOR	SAKURA-X	EFFLUX-F2	NOISE FLOOR	SAKURA-X	EFFLUX-F2
	MEAN	3.419 mV	32.492 mV	4.387 mV	541.936 nV	5.150 µV	695.386 nV
	RMS	20.584 mV	176.850 mV	38.207 mV	3.263 µV	28.031 µV	6.056 µV
	Vpp 6σ	123.502 mV	1.061 V	229.241 mV	19.576 µV	168.188 µV	36.335 µV
	STDEV	20.298 mV	173.839 mV	37.954 mV	3.217 µV	27.554 µV	6.016 µV
	VARIANCE	411.998 µV	30.220 mV	1.441 mV	10.351 pV	759.234 pV	36.191 pV

4.2 Signal-to-Noise Ratio (SNR)

The SNR of a side-channel trace is a very important metric as it helps determine the overall quality of the measurement setup. The SNR is the ratio of $\frac{Var(V_{\text{signal}})}{Var(V_{\text{noise}})}$ [12], where V_{signal} is the data-dependent signal component, V_{noise} is the random noise component and Var denotes the variance. The SNR of a side-channel setup is inversely related to the number of traces ($N_{traces} \propto \frac{1}{SNR}$). This means a high SNR setup requires fewer number of traces for attack or analysis compared to a low SNR setup, where the noise dominates. There are many ways of measuring SNR [7,12]. In our experiments we calculate two sets of traces. The $Var(V_{\text{noise}})$ is captured by using random plaintext, whereas for calculating $Var(V_{\text{signal}})$ we captured averaged traces with $N = 100$, in other words, 100 traces with the same plaintext were captured and pointwise averaged. For our evaluation, we captured 10K traces for noise and $10K * 100 = 1M$ traces for the signal. Thus, for final comparison between the two boards, we utilized 10K raw traces for noise and 10K averaged traces for signal.

Figure 9 shows the trace captured using both the boards for AES and also the signal and noise traces for all the sample points. One interesting thing to note from Fig. 9b is that in case of SAKURA-X, the noise trace dominates the signal trace. Whereas in case of EFFLUX-F2, the signal dominates than noise Fig. 9d, which should be the ideal case for any side-channel measurement setup. To further highlight this fact, we also show the comparison of Signal-to-Noise ratio in Fig. 10. One can see that there is a huge difference in the SNR of the captured traces between the two boards. The SNR for EFFLUX-F2 is almost 8.2× better than SAKURA-X for the same settings. This clearly demonstrates that even for a highly leaky design such as unprotected AES, EFFLUX-F2 captured signal quality is much better than currently used SAKURA-X.

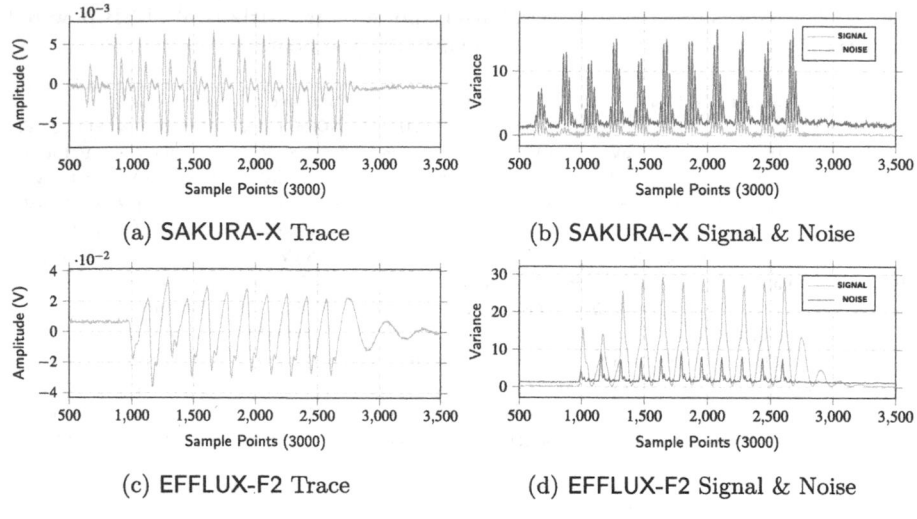

(a) SAKURA-X Trace (b) SAKURA-X Signal & Noise

(c) EFFLUX-F2 Trace (d) EFFLUX-F2 Signal & Noise

Fig. 9. Signal and noise traces for all the sample points.

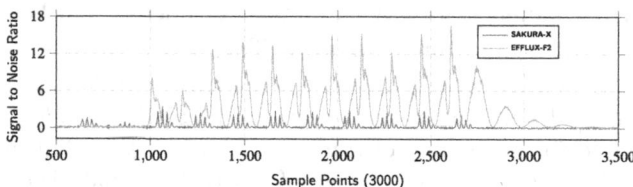

Fig. 10. Signal-to-Noise Ratio Comparison. The maximum SNR in the points of interest (last round of AES) for SAKURA-X is measured at sample point 2664 and is 2.020. Whereas, for EFFLUX-F2, the maximum SNR is measured at sample point 2609 and is 16.562.

4.3   Correlation Power Analysis (CPA)

CPA is a well-known side-channel attack which exploits the correlation of the power with the data to extract secret key. We performed CPA attack on an unprotected implementation of lightweight cipher GIFT. We intentionally chose this as the target design for demonstrating the comparison between the two boards as the power consumption for GIFT is close to the noise floor. We targeted the last round of the cipher and considered hamming distance model for our attack.

Figure 11 shows results for correlation values for all possible keys corresponding to number of traces. Due to space constraint, the results are shown corresponding to key bytes 0, 1 and 2 for both the boards. Similar trends are observed for other keys as well. One can see that for key byte 0, almost 60K traces are required using SAKURA-X to distinguish it from other possible key values. Whereas, the same key can be recovered using only 12K traces from EFFLUX-F2 achieving a reduction of almost 5×. Similarly, EFFLUX-F2 requires

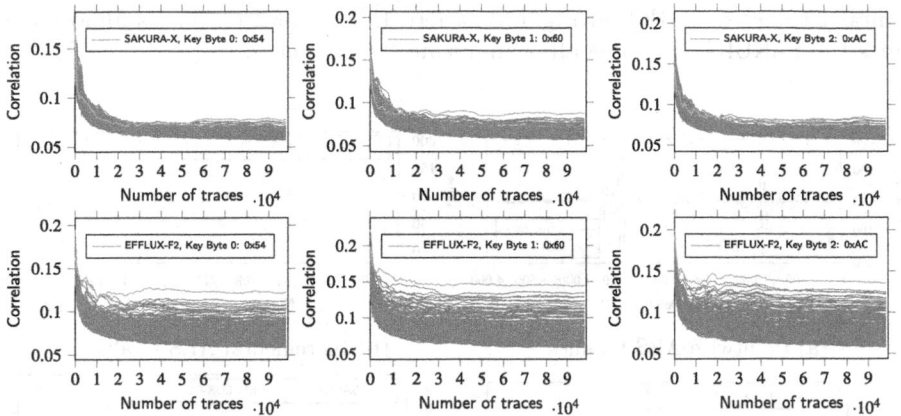

Fig. 11. CPA results for unprotected GIFT

5× and 17× less traces than **SAKURA-X** to recover key byte 1 and 2 respectively. One should also note that in case of **SAKURA-X**, the correlation values between top two-three values are quite close. Whereas, in case of **EFFLUX-F2**, it is quite consistent and clearly distinguishable for all the three key bytes. Thus, providing high confidence towards key recovery. We would also like to highlight the fact that this huge reduction in required number of traces is quite significant in terms of time required to collect these many traces.

4.4 Test Vector Leakage Assessment (TVLA)

TVLA is a commonly used technique to detect any type of leakage (source may be unknown) rather than exploit the leakage in any system. If the t-value crosses a certain threshold (commonly used threshold ±4.5), then it is considered that the leakage is detected. We used incremental formulae for our calculations.

To present comparison between the two boards, we performed our evaluation around two cryptographic ciphers; an unprotected AES implementation (composite implementation) and a lightweight low noise implementation of GIFT-128. We first performed non-specific TVLA analysis on unprotected implementations of both AES and GIFT. The results are shown in Fig. 12. We show pointwise t-values as well as incremental t-values in the graph. As the AES implementation leaks significantly, the threshold value easily crosses 50 just after 2000 traces for both the boards. EFFLUX-F2 shows more leakage (higher t-value) than SAKURA-X. This fact is more evident when comparing the results for GIFT. GIFT is a lightweight cipher and consumes power within noise floor level. Hence, it becomes difficult to analyse leakage of such a design. As can be seen from Fig. 12c, the t-values obtained from traces captured by SAKURA-X is barely crossing the threshold ±4.5. Whereas, using EFFLUX-F2, it is quite evident the design is highly leaky as an unprotected design will be. This is also visible from the incremental t-values for GIFT in Fig. 12d, where EFFLUX-F2 t-value is almost five times the SAKURA-X t-value after analyzing 20000 traces.

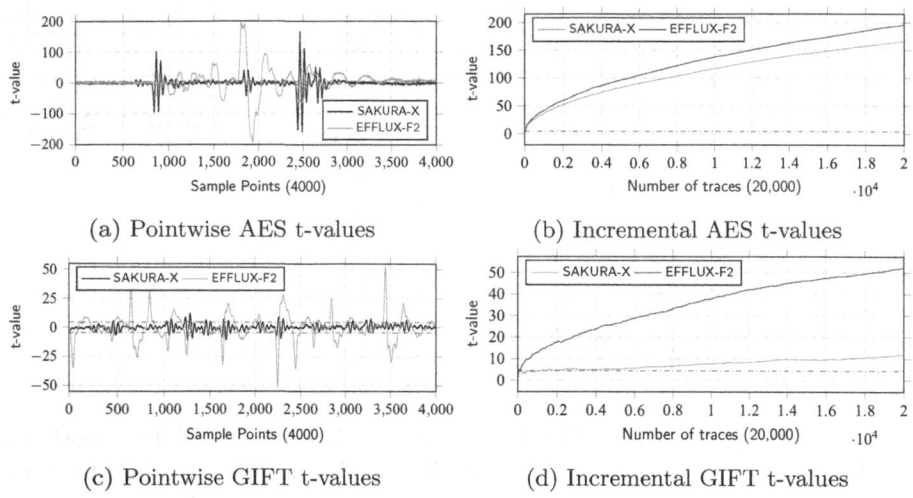

(a) Pointwise AES t-values

(b) Incremental AES t-values

(c) Pointwise GIFT t-values

(d) Incremental GIFT t-values

Fig. 12. TVLA results for unprotected implementations

In order to protect designs from side-channel attack, it has become common to integrate side-channel countermeasure such as masking, threshold implementation, etc. There has also been an effort towards development of side-channel resistant cryptographic ciphers. As TVLA analysis can detect leakage from any source, it is also used to evaluate whether a design is indeed side-channel resistant. If the countermeasures are not properly implemented then the design may still leak but at a much later point in time. Hence, it is a common practice to capture and analyze millions of traces for a protected design which typically requires few hours.

We also performed TVLA analysis of GIFT protected using a threshold countermeasure. To show the significance and performance characteristics of our low-noise board design, we utilized a known partially protected design of GIFT. This is done by intentionally removing a register layer between the decomposed S-boxes. The results are presented in Fig. 13. The t-values in the case of SAKURA-X at different sample points is mostly within the threshold as is expected from a fully protected design, but not from a partially protected design. It shows that the threshold has crossed only at a few sample points (somewhere around 250). Whereas, using EFFLUX-F2, it is quite prominent from multiple sample points that the design still leaks. One should also note the comparison results of incremental TVLA values from Fig. 13b. In case of SAKURA-X, the threshold is crossed only after 100,000 traces are captured and analyzed. Whereas, EFFLUX-F2 shows leakage even before 5000 traces have been analyzed, and the t-value increasing steadily. Thus, significantly reducing the leakage analysis time

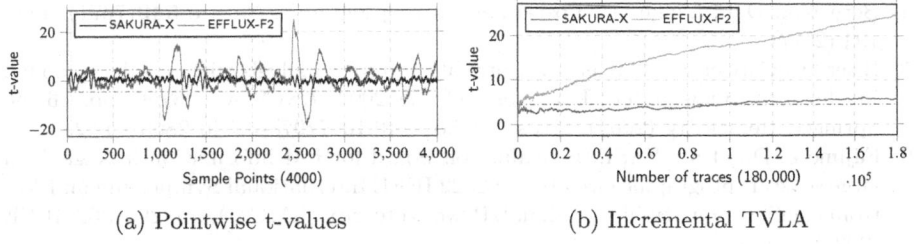

(a) Pointwise t-values   (b) Incremental TVLA

Fig. 13. TVLA results for partially protected GIFT

of a partially protected design from a few hours to a few minutes or less. The comparison results clearly shows that EFFLUX-F2 outshines SAKURA-X.

5   Conclusion

In this work, we present EFFLUX-F2 a SCA evaluation board designed with the targets of low noise and high SNR. These features leads to the reduction in the number of power traces required for experiments. With detailed experiments we show that the board provides significantly improved performance compared to the current platforms. Apart from the PCB design details, we also delve into the factors involved in achieving high SNR and discuss the reasoning behind the design choices. We show that EFFLUX-F2 has 4.5× lower noise and 8.2× higher SNR compared to SAKURA-X. We also show that EFFLUX-F2 required ≈20× fewer traces compared to the latter when analysing a protected leaky lightweight cipher implementation using TVLA.

Acknowledgement. This research is partially supported by the National Research Foundation, Singapore, and Cyber Security Agency of Singapore under its National Cybersecurity Research & Development Programme (Cyber-Hardware Forensic & Assurance Evaluation R&D Programme NRF2018NCRNCR009-0001). Any opinions, findings and conclusions or recommendations expressed in this material are those of the author(s) and do not reflect the view of National Research Foundation, Singapore and Cyber Security Agency of Singapore.

References

1. Alagic, G., et al.: Status report on the third round of the NIST post-quantum cryptography standardization process. US Department of Commerce, NIST (2022)
2. Banik, S., Pandey, S.K., Peyrin, T., Sasaki, Yu., Sim, S.M., Todo, Y.: GIFT: a small present: towards reaching the limit of lightweight encryption. In: Fischer, W., Homma, N. (eds.) CHES 2017. LNCS, vol. 10529, pp. 321–345. Springer, Cham (2017). https://doi.org/10.1007/978-3-319-66787-4_16
3. Becker, G., et al.: Test vector leakage assessment (TVLA) methodology in practice. In: International Cryptographic Module Conference, vol. 1001, p. 13. sn (2013)

4. Bernstein, D.J., Lange, T.: Post-quantum cryptography. Nature **549**(7671), 188–194 (2017)
5. Brier, E., Clavier, C., Olivier, F.: Correlation power analysis with a leakage model. In: Joye, M., Quisquater, J.-J. (eds.) CHES 2004. LNCS, vol. 3156, pp. 16–29. Springer, Heidelberg (2004). https://doi.org/10.1007/978-3-540-28632-5_2
6. Fujimoto, D., et al.: SASIMI: Evaluation board for EM information leakage from large scale cryptographic circuits. In: 2022 IEEE International Symposium on Electromagnetic Compatibility & Signal/Power Integrity (EMCSI), pp. 299–302. IEEE (2022)
7. Guilley, S., Maghrebi, H., Souissi, Y., Sauvage, L., Danger, J.L.: Quantifying the quality of side channel acquisitions. COSADE (2011)
8. Guntur, H., Ishii, J., Satoh, A.: Side-channel attack user reference architecture board SAKURA-G. In: 2014 IEEE 3rd Global Conference on Consumer Electronics (GCCE), pp. 271–274. IEEE (2014)
9. Hori, Y., Katashita, T., Sasaki, A., Satoh, A.: SASEBO-GIII: a hardware security evaluation board equipped with a 28-nm FPGA. In: The 1st IEEE Global Conference on Consumer Electronics 2012, pp. 657–660. IEEE (2012)
10. Katashita, T., Hori, Y., Sakane, H., Satoh, A.: Side-channel attack standard evaluation board SASEBO-W for smartcard testing. Power **3**(2012), 400 (2012)
11. Katashita, T., Satoh, A., Sugawara, T., Homma, N., Aoki, T.: Development of side-channel attack standard evaluation environment. In: 2009 European Conference on Circuit Theory and Design, pp. 403–408. IEEE (2009)
12. Mangard, S., Oswald, E., Popp, T.: Power Analysis Attacks: Revealing the Secrets of Smart Cards, vol. 31. Springer, Heidelberg (2008). https://doi.org/10.1007/978-0-387-38162-6
13. McKay, K., Bassham, L., Sönmez Turan, M., Mouha, N.: Report on lightweight cryptography. Technical report, National Institute of Standards and Technology (2016)
14. O'Flynn, C., Chen, Z.D.: ChipWhisperer: an open-source platform for hardware embedded security research. In: Prouff, E. (ed.) COSADE 2014. LNCS, vol. 8622, pp. 243–260. Springer, Cham (2014). https://doi.org/10.1007/978-3-319-10175-0_17
15. Satoh, A., Katashita, T., Sakane, H.: Secure implementation of cryptographic modules-development of a standard evaluation environment for side channel attacks. Synthesiol. Engl. Edn. **3**(1), 86–95 (2010)
16. Turan, M.S., et al.: Status report on the final round of the NIST lightweight cryptography standardization process (2023)

Attack Methods

Practical Improvements to Statistical Ineffective Fault Attacks

Barış Ege[1] , Bob Swinkels[1] , Dilara Toprakhisar[2(✉)] ,
and Praveen Kumar Vadnala[1]

[1] Riscure B.V., Delft, The Netherlands
{ege,swinkels,vadnala}@riscure.com
[2] COSIC, KU Leuven, Leuven, Belgium
dilara.toprakhisar@esat.kuleuven.be

Abstract. Statistical Fault Attacks (SFA), introduced by Fuhr *et al.*, exploit the statistical bias resulting from injected faults. Unlike prior fault analysis attacks, which require both faulty and correct ciphertexts under the same key, SFA leverages only faulty ciphertexts. In CHES 2018, more powerful attacks called Statistical Ineffective Fault Attacks (SIFA) have been proposed. In contrast to the previous fault attacks that utilize faulty ciphertexts, SIFA exploits the distribution of the intermediate values leading to fault-free ciphertexts. As a result, the SIFA attacks were shown to be effective even in the presence of widely used fault injection countermeasures based on detection and infection. In this work, we build upon the core idea of SIFA, and provide two main practical improvements over the previously proposed analysis methods. Firstly, we show how to perform SIFA from the input side, which in contrast to the original SIFA, requires injecting faults in the earlier rounds of an encryption or decryption operation. If we consider the start of the operation as the trigger for fault injection, the cumulative jitter in the first few rounds of a cipher is much lower than the last rounds. Hence, performing the attack in the first or second round requires a narrower parameter range for fault injection and hence less fault injection attempts to recover the secret key. Secondly, in comparison to the straightforward SIFA approach of guessing 32-bits at a time, we propose a chosen input approach that reduces the guessing effort to 16-bits at a time. This decreases the key search space for full key recovery of an AES-128 implementation from 2^{34} to 2^{19}.

Keywords: Fault attacks · SIFA · AES · Chosen plaintext attack

1 Introduction

Since the seminal work of Boneh et al. [7], which introduced fault attacks on RSA, numerous publications highlighted the susceptibility of the implementations of cryptographic algorithms to such active attacks exploiting their physical characteristics. Fault attacks involve deliberately injecting faults during the

© The Author(s), under exclusive license to Springer Nature Switzerland AG 2024
R. Wacquez and N. Homma (Eds.): COSADE 2024, LNCS 14595, pp. 59–75, 2024.
https://doi.org/10.1007/978-3-031-57543-3_4

execution of a cryptographic algorithm through physical means, followed by an analysis of the reaction of the device under attack. These faults can be injected through various methods, including voltage/clock glitching [2], temperature manipulation [22], white light [29], electromagnetic waves [16], or laser injections [1,3,12,21,23,31], as well as software-based faults [26,30].

Since Biham and Shamir [5] have extended Differential Fault Analysis (DFA), the work of Boneh *et al.*, on symmetric key algorithms, numerous techniques improving DFA have been published [4,6,14,18,20,24,25,27]. In general, DFA-like analysis techniques retrieve the secret key by utilizing the characteristics of the induced fault and the faulty ciphertexts, which use the value of the faulty and the corresponding correct ciphertexts to retrieve the key. In a different vein, Fuhr *et al.* [19] introduced Statistical Fault Attacks (SFA), exploiting the statistical distributions of the targeted intermediate values derived from the faulty ciphertexts. In contrast to DFA-like attacks, SFA only requires access to the faulty ciphertexts, and exploits the non-uniform distribution of a state byte value caused by the fault injection.

DFA and SFA involve modifying the value of an intermediate variable during the computation, and exploiting the faulty output. However, Ineffective Fault Analysis (IFA), as introduced by Clavier *et al.* [13], takes a different approach. IFA exploits the fault-free ciphertexts by using ineffective faults to probe the intermediate value. In other words, IFA exploits the cases where the injected fault does not affect the output, utilizing only correct ciphertexts. Building upon the core ideas of SFA and IFA, Dobraunig *et al.* proposed Statistical Ineffective Fault Attacks (SIFA) [17] in CHES 2018. SIFA exploits the non-uniform distributions of the intermediate values targeted by ineffective faults derived from correct ciphertexts. SIFA is akin to IFA in that both exploit faults that do not alter the output. As with SFA, they both exploit the bias in the statistical distribution of an intermediate value. Notably, SIFA exploiting the correct ciphertexts circumvents simple redundancy based countermeasures that protect against SFA and DFA-like attacks. Moreover, it does not require an adversary to know the injected fault, enhancing its practical applicability. In this regard, SIFA has more relaxed requirements compared to IFA, and it can utilize various fault models creating bias in the targeted variable. However, this attack requires analysis of 2^{32} key candidates to perform the analysis on AES, which imposes practical limitations especially when a large number of ciphertexts need to be analyzed per key candidate. When analyzing an AES-128 implementation for instance, this leads to a total of 2^{34} analysis steps for full key recovery. In this work, we adopt the chosen input approach in SIFA as an attempt to decrease the computational complexity of the SIFA analysis.

Contributions. First, we show how to perform SIFA from the input side. This involves injecting biased faults early in the encryption or decryption operation, and analyzing the distribution of the targeted intermediate value computed from the collected plaintexts corresponding to fault-free ciphertexts, where the injected fault is ineffective. Performing SIFA from the input side has an advantage in practice due to less jitter introduced. As the cumulative jitter in the first few rounds is expected to be lower than the last few rounds, this attack has the advantage of narrower fault injection parameter range, thus, less number of fault injection attempts to recover the secret key.

Secondly, we propose a chosen-input SIFA, which requires only two key bytes to be guessed, as opposed to the four byte key guesses in the original attack, decreasing the size of the key search space to 2^{16} from 2^{32}. This reduces the total number of key guesses from 2^{34} to 2^{19} when applied to AES-128.

Outline. In Sect. 2, we discuss SFA, IFA, and SIFA which our work is based on. Then, in Sect. 3, we describe our first contribution, performing SIFA from the input side. We first present the attack description, then, the results of the simulations evaluating the presented attack. In Sect. 4, we present the attack description of the chosen input SIFA, and the simulation results. Then, we evaluate both attacks in practice, and present the practical experiment results in Sect. 5. Finally, in Sect. 6, we discuss the impacts of the proposed techniques that improve SIFA in practice, and pose open questions regarding future work.

2 Preliminaries

In this section, we recall Statistical Fault Attacks (SFA) and Ineffective Fault Attacks (IFA). Next, we describe how both these ideas were combined and extended in Statistical Ineffective Fault Attacks (SIFA).

2.1 Statistical Fault Attacks

SFA was introduced by Fuhr *et al.* [19] as a technique to recover the secret key in AES. SFA exploits the bias in the distribution of an intermediate value obtained from the faulty ciphertexts. For symmetric key algorithms, the intermediate values computed during the execution are expected to be uniformly distributed. However, if the distribution of intermediates changes due to the injected faults, then it is possible to exploit these biases to recover the secret key. To perform SFA, an attacker needs to collect faulty ciphertexts and follow an appropriate key recovery strategy depending on the targeted round. The same idea applies to all key recovery strategies: the attacker is required to decrypt the faulty ciphertexts back to the intermediate value targeted by the induced fault with the key hypotheses, and apply a distinguisher to recover the secret key.

The working principle of SFA depends on changing an intermediate value and obtaining faulty ciphertexts. Therefore, SFA can be prevented with the existing countermeasures as the output is suppressed (in case of detection) or randomized (in case of infection) in the presence of a fault.

2.2 Ineffective Fault Attacks

IFA [13] uses fault injection as a probing tool on the targeted intermediate value by comparing the value of this variable with the expected value (*i.e.,* when no fault was injected). These values are equal when the fault has no effect on the targeted intermediate value. The goal here is to find a fault model that does not cause a change in the intermediate value and yields the correct output. Therefore, detection-based countermeasures are not effective against IFA as they work only with the existence of faulty ciphertexts.

IFA works as follows: the attacker induces a stuck-at-x fault to an intermediate value in one execution where the other execution is fault-free. If the attacker receives the same output regardless of the induced fault, the targeted intermediate value must have been x already. The secret key can be recovered by performing the cipher operations in reverse up to the targeted operation. Correct guess of the corresponding byte of the key should lead to the value x in the intermediate value. However, one of the problems of this attack is determining if the fault was actually successful or not. Moreover, in practice, stuck-at faults occur less frequently compared to other faults, *e.g.,* bit-flips.

2.3   Statistical Ineffective Fault Attacks

SIFA [17] was proposed as a novel fault attack technique that works under detection-based and infective countermeasures. It extends the ideas of SFA and IFA so as to overcome the limitations of both. It exploits the bias in the distribution of an intermediate value that is targeted by fault injection leading to a fault-free ciphertext.

For the SIFA attack to be successful, the only requirement is the existence of a bias in the distribution of the intermediate value. The probability of changing an intermediate value by a fault is not the same for all possible values of a byte. Table 1 shows the non-uniformity in the probability distribution when a random-and fault model, where each bit has a 50% probability of being reset, is applied to two-bit values. When the fault is injected, the possibility of an intermediate value 00 staying the same is 1, whereas the value 11 staying the same is $1/4$. The bias in this probability distribution makes a cryptographic implementation susceptible to SIFA.

Table 1. Fault distribution table for random-and fault model

	x'			
	00	01	10	11
00	1	0	0	0
01	$\frac{1}{2}$	$\frac{1}{2}$	0	0
10	$\frac{1}{2}$	0	$\frac{1}{2}$	0
11	$\frac{1}{4}$	$\frac{1}{4}$	$\frac{1}{4}$	$\frac{1}{4}$

In the original paper, the faults were injected to one byte before the last Mix-Columns operation. Then, the distribution of the targeted byte value obtained from collected fault-free ciphertexts will be non-uniformly distributed. This non-uniformity can be exploited by using a key revealing technique similar to the one used in SFA [19] to recover four bytes of the last round key. To obtain the partial state S_9, the collected ciphertexts need to be partially decrypted:

$$S_9 = MC^{-1} \circ SB^{-1} \circ SR^{-1}(C \oplus K_{10}) \tag{1}$$

Next, the distribution of the partial state S_9 obtained from the collected ciphertexts is evaluated by computing χ^2 statistic (or SEI) for each key hypothesis (using the formula in Eq. 2). If enough successful faults were injected around the target operation, the key hypothesis leading to the highest χ^2 statistic will be the correct key.

$$\chi^2(\hat{p}, \theta) = N \sum_{x \in \mathcal{X}} \frac{(\hat{p_k}(x) - \theta(x))^2}{\theta(x)} \tag{2}$$

Here $\theta(x) = 1/256$ is the probability distribution of the byte values in the uniform distribution, and $\hat{p_k}(x)$ is the probability distribution of the byte values in the observed distribution using the key hypothesis k.

This attack allows an attacker to exploit any ineffective fault that causes a non-uniform distribution in the targeted value. The SIFA is robust against dummy rounds or unsuccessful fault injections and the attacker does not necessarily need to know the distribution of the injected faults.

If the AES implementation is protected with detection-based countermeasures, only the fault-free ciphertexts will be collected. In case of infective countermeasures, the fault-free ciphertexts need to be filtered by performing encryption or decryption operations without injecting fault, comparing the results, and keeping the ciphertexts that are same as the non-faulty ones.

3   Performing SIFA on the Inputs

In this section, we describe how to perform SIFA from the input side on AES. Fundamentally, the fault analysis strategy remains the same as the original attack. However, in this approach, faults are injected very early in the AES encryption/decryption. Subsequently, the fault analysis is performed on the inputs corresponding to the fault-free outputs. Our simulations demonstrate that bias introduced to the distribution of the targeted intermediate value can be exploited, which facilitates the key recovery when the attack is executed from the input side. Moreover, with the increasing cumulative jitter during the encryption or decryption operation, injecting faults in the early rounds demands fewer fault injection attempts, thanks to the narrower parameter range. We first outline the assumptions related to the capabilities of the adversary performing the fault injection. Subsequently, we describe how the injected fault is exploited. Then, we present the simulation results of the attack.

Adversarial Model. The adversary is capable of injecting a biased fault with precise control on the timing of the injection (*i.e.,* targets a specific operation). Moreover, the adversary has some control over the location of the injected fault, *i.e.,* allowing the injection of the fault affecting any set of bits within the target byte value.

Attack Description. Considering the encryption operation, to perform SIFA on the plaintexts, an adversary with the described capabilities injects a fault between the first and second MixColumns operations. This differs from the original SIFA approach, which requires a fault to be injected before the last MixColumns operation. We assume an adversary injects a fault after the second SubBytes operation as shown in Fig. 1. As a result of the fault injection, the adversary obtains a set of filtered plaintext-ciphertext pairs under the detection-based countermeasures, where the targeted intermediate value after the first MixColumns exhibits a non-uniform distribution.

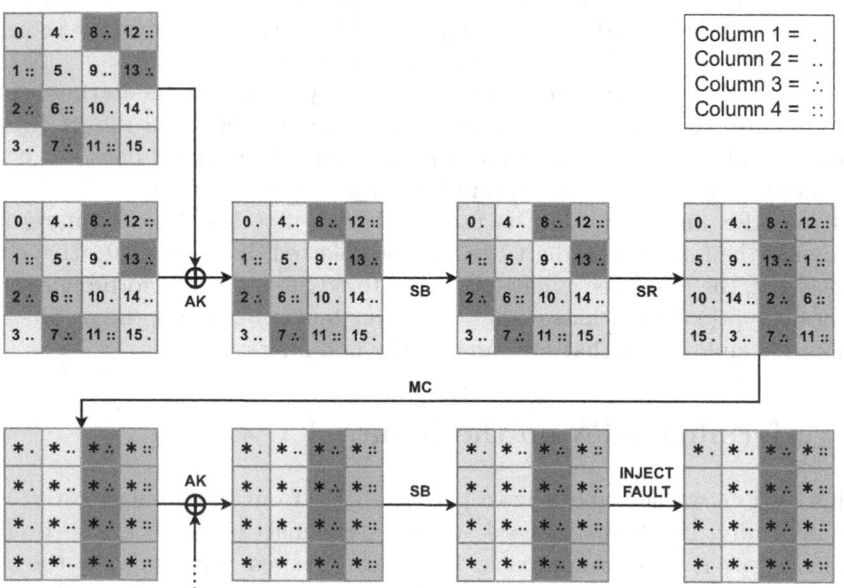

Fig. 1. Sketch of the attack on round 2 using a fault injection after the second SubBytes operation.

The key recovery also follows the same strategy as the original attack. Specifically, the adversary guesses four bytes of the first round key, aligning with the bytes of the plaintext that influence the distribution of the targeted intermediate value (*i.e.,* bytes in Column 1 in Fig. 1). Subsequently, the adversary partially computes the first and second round operations of AES encryption for each plaintext corresponding to a correct ciphertext, resulting in the derivation of the partial state denoted as S_1:

$$S_1 = ((PT \oplus K_0) \circ SB \circ SR \circ MC \tag{3}$$

Then, for each key guess, the adversary analyzes the distribution of the targeted byte within the state S_1, and computes an χ^2 statistic. The highest χ^2 statistic value serves as the indicator of the correct key guess.

Practical Benefits. For AES implementations with clock-jitter, clock randomization countermeasures, or random delays, it is beneficial to target an operation that is performed early in the encryption/decryption operation. This is because the cumulative jitter during the encryption or decryption operation is smaller, which improves the precision of the fault injection. Moreover, the number of fault injection attempts needed to inject a fault repeatedly at the same location is reduced.

For instance, consider the clock randomization countermeasure proposed in [8], where the randomized clock implementation can generate pulses of at least 403 different frequencies ($n = 403$) with one fixed base frequency ($m = 1$). When attacking the 2nd round ($r = 2$) rather than the 9th round ($r = 9$), of an AES encryption operation that takes 10 clock cycles to complete, the number of different times to complete the operation gets reduced from $_{r+n-1}C_r{\cdot}m =_{9+403-1} C_9 \cdot 1 \approx 8.44 \cdot 10^{17}$ to $_{r+n-1}C_r \cdot m =_{2+403-1} C_2 \cdot 1 = 81.4 \cdot 10^3$. This substantial reduction minimizes the number of fault injection attempts needed to repeatedly inject a fault that targets the same operation.

Simulations. To simulate the attack from the input side, a four-bit random-AND fault model is used. In this model, each of the four least significant bits in the targeted byte has a probability of 50% to be reset. In the simulations, an AES implementation protected with a detection countermeasure was used which implements various degrees of dummy rounds; namely no dummy rounds, 10 dummy rounds and 40 dummy rounds.

When attacking an implementation with no dummy rounds, four key bytes can be recovered by collecting approximately 325 plaintexts corresponding to correct ciphertexts (*i.e.,* ineffective faults), as shown in Fig. 2a. When 10 dummy rounds are used, four key bytes can be recovered by collecting approximately 13,500 plaintexts corresponding to correct ciphertexts, as shown in Fig. 2b. When 40 dummy rounds are used, four key bytes can be recovered by collecting approximately 212,500 plaintexts corresponding to correct ciphertexts, as shown in Fig. 2c.

These simulations show that it is possible to perform SIFA from the input side on AES. The number of traces required to recover the secret key is comparable to the number of traces required to perform SIFA from the output side. Note that the actual benefit of our approach is seen in practical evaluation, when there is clock jitter during the execution as explained above.

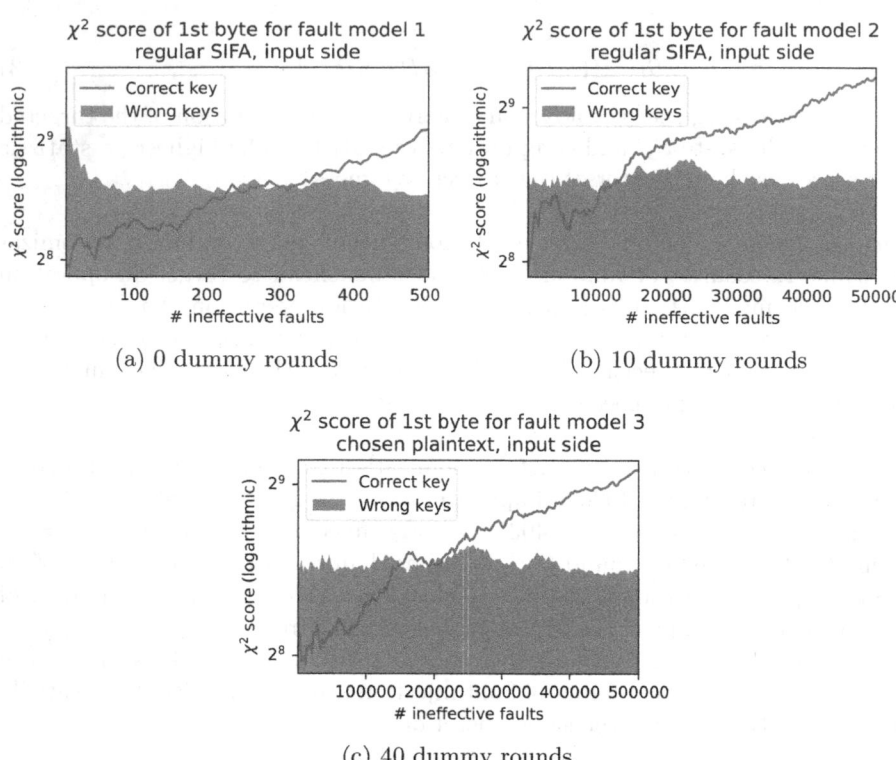

(a) 0 dummy rounds   (b) 10 dummy rounds

(c) 40 dummy rounds

Fig. 2. Comparison of χ^2 score for actual key and wrong keys with detection counter-measure

4   Chosen Input SIFA

In this section, we describe the working principle of the chosen input SIFA. Essentially, the attack follows the process described in Sect. 3, except with a notable difference that, in this attack, the inputs are explicitly chosen by the adversary. In addition to the adversarial capabilities detailed in Sect. 3, the adversary has the capability to feed the encryption or decryption algorithm with inputs of their choosing.

Attack Description. We consider the encryption operation to describe the attack. Similar to the described attack from the input side, the adversary injects a fault between the first and second MixColumns operations, where we assume a byte after the second SubBytes is targeted as depicted in Fig. 1. However, in this attack, two out of the four bytes of the plaintext inputs that influence the distribution of the targeted byte are held constant, while the other two bytes are generated randomly. Then, instead of attempting to guess four bytes of the key corresponding to these four bytes of the plaintext at a time, the adversary guesses only two bytes of the key corresponding to the random bytes of the plaintext. Subsequently, the adversary applies the first round operations for the chosen plaintexts corresponding to a correct ciphertext, resulting in the partial state S_1 as described in Eq. 3. Then, the same key recovery strategy described in Sect. 3 is followed to determine the correct key. This improvement reduces the key search space to 2^{16} (*i.e.*, two bytes) from 2^{32} (*i.e.*, four bytes) for a single guess, utilizing an equal or fewer number of traces depending on the fault capabilities of the fault injection adversary.

It's essential to note that utilizing a statistical test-based distinguisher (*e.g.*, SEI) does not allow reducing the search space for a single guess to 2^8. Achieving a size of 2^8 may be possible by holding only one of the four bytes influencing the distribution of the targeted byte as random, and only guessing the corresponding key byte, while keeping the others constant. Among the operations shown in Eq. 3 that the adversary applies to obtain the partial state S_1, only the MixColumns operation changes the probability distribution of the targeted byte. That is, until the MixColumns operation, the random plaintext byte retains a random value, while the other constant bytes retain constant values across a number of chosen plaintexts. Let r denote this random byte value. Then, the MixColumn operation applied to this state results in a state where r becomes $r + c$ with c being a constant. The operations applied after MixColumns, likewise, do not change the probability distribution of the targeted byte, making the distribution obtained by the key guesses indistinguishable. Hence, it is not possible to reduce the search space further.

Attack Method. By using a methodical approach, the above described analysis can be performed on all columns simultaneously. This is desirable in practice since the specific column targeted by the fault injection is often unknown beforehand. To achieve simultaneous analysis of all columns, we generate the crafted plaintext inputs in two steps as follows:

1. Attack the key bytes with even indices (Fig. 3).
2. Attack the key bytes with odd indices (Fig. 4).

First, every odd byte of plaintext input is set to a fixed value, *e.g.*, zero, while keeping the other bytes random. Then, a fault is injected after the second SubBytes operation during the encryption operation. The crafted plaintexts corresponding to correct ciphertexts are collected (*i.e.*, when the injected fault is ineffective). As shown in Fig. 3, for the key recovery, if a key hypothesis for the first column outranks the other key guesses by a large margin, it indicates the correct guess for the key bytes with the indices 0 and 10. Then, if a key hypothesis for the second, third, and the last column, outranks the other guesses by a large margin, it also indicates the correct guess for the key bytes with indices 4 and 14, 2 and 8, and 6 and 12, respectively.

This process is then repeated for the second step where every even byte of the plaintext input is set to a fixed value. As shown in Fig. 4, for the key recovery, if a key hypothesis for the first column outranks the other key guesses by a large margin, it indicates the correct guess for the key bytes with the indices 5 and 15.

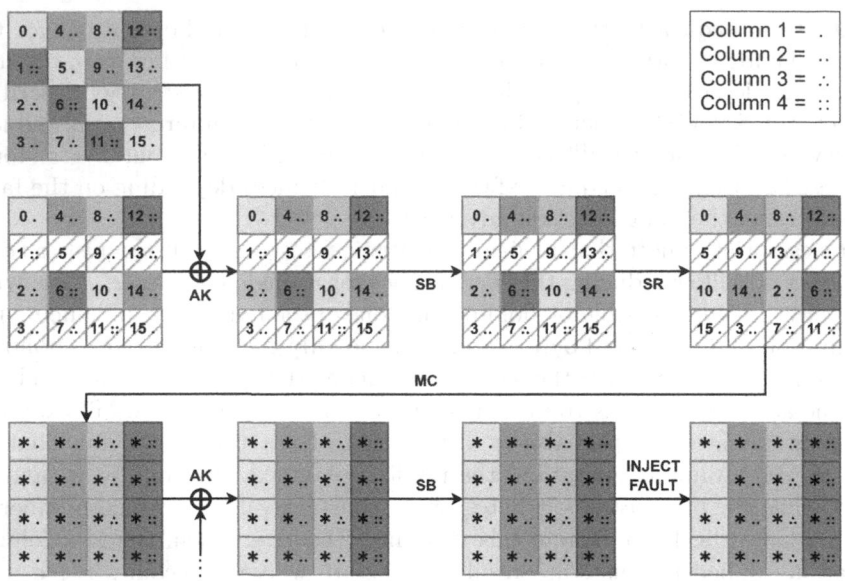

Fig. 3. Sketch of the chosen plaintext attack on round 1 using a fault injection after the second substitute bytes operation and every odd byte set to zero

Then, if a key hypothesis for the second, third, and the last column, outranks the other guesses by a large margin, it indicates the correct guess for the key bytes with indices 3 and 9, 7 and 13, and 1 and 11, respectively.

If no key hypothesis significantly outranks the other key guesses, it indicates that key recovery is not possible. This can be attributed to factors such as insufficient fault injection attempts, the fault model not being effective enough, or unsuccessful fault injection.

Simulations. To simulate the chosen input SIFA, a four-bit random-AND fault model is used. In this model, each of the four least significant bits of the targeted byte has a probability of 50% to be reset. Similar to the simulations of SIFA from the input side, an AES implementation protected with a detection countermeasure was used which implements various degrees of dummy rounds; namely no dummy rounds, 10 dummy rounds, and 40 dummy rounds.

When attacking an implementation with no dummy rounds, two key bytes can be recovered by collecting approximately 235 chosen plaintexts corresponding to correct ciphertexts, as shown in Fig. 5a. When 10 dummy rounds are used, two key bytes can be recovered by collecting approximately 25,750 chosen plaintexts corresponding to correct ciphertexts, as shown in Fig. 5b. When 40 dummy rounds are used, two key bytes can be recovered by collecting approximately 240,000 chosen plaintexts corresponding to correct ciphertexts, as shown in Fig. 5c.

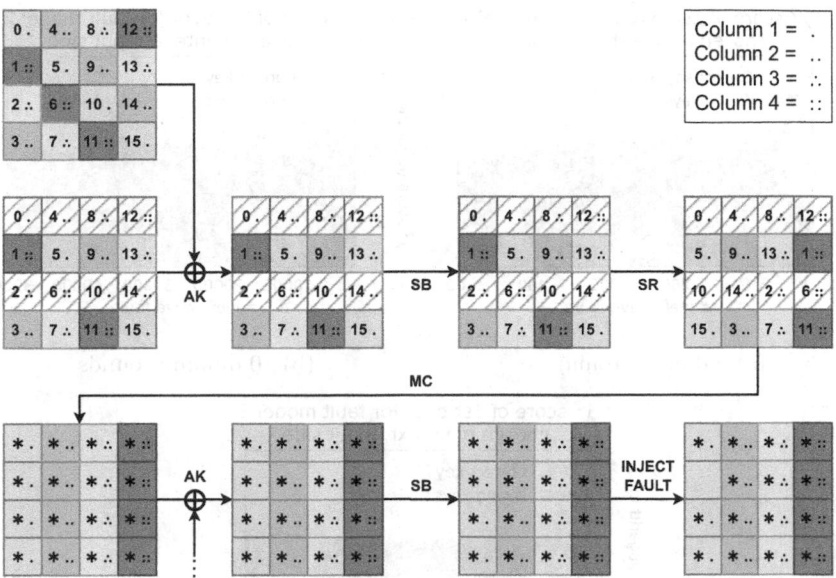

Fig. 4. Sketch of the chosen plaintext attack on round 1 using a fault injection after the second substitute bytes operation and every even byte set to zero

These simulations show that it is possible to perform the chosen input SIFA on AES. The number of traces required to recover the secret key is comparable to the number of traces required to perform SIFA from the input side. However the search space to recover four key bytes is decreased by a factor of $2^{15} = 32\ 768$, therefore the brute force attack takes significantly less time.

5   Practical Evaluation

SIFA from the input side and the chosen input SIFA were evaluated using an 8-bit software AES implementation (as described in Sect. 4.1 of [15]) and a 32-bit t-table software AES implementation (as described in Sect. 4.2 of [15]) running on an STM32F407IG Arm Cortex-M4 core. For this, a Piñata development board [10] was used, which has been physically modified by removing the decoupling capacitors to make it more susceptible to voltage glitches. The board is shown in Fig. 6.

Fault Setup. To inject faults into the target device, voltage glitches were used. For this, a device called Spider [11] was used to control the glitch timing and the glitch voltage, and a device called Glitch Amplifier [9] was used to amplify the glitches and inject the fault into the target device. Communication with the target device was realized through the use of an FTDI FT232RL USB to serial UART interface. To determine a range for the parameters, side channel profiling was performed. The parameters used for the voltage glitching experiments are shown in Table 2.

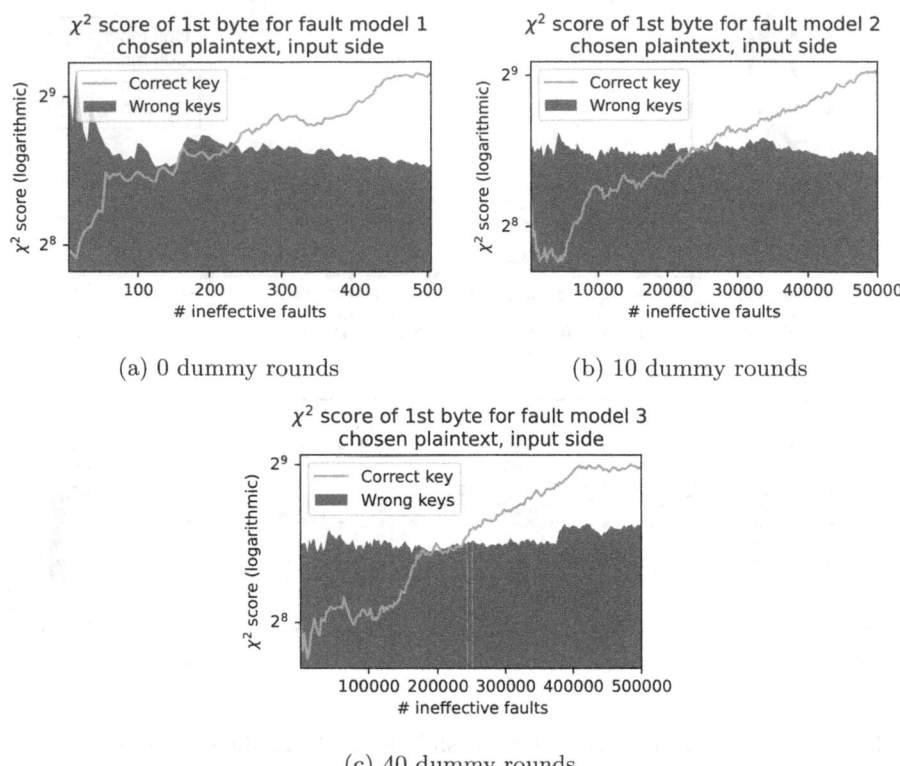

(a) 0 dummy rounds   (b) 10 dummy rounds

(c) 40 dummy rounds

Fig. 5. Comparison of χ^2 score for actual key and wrong keys with detection counter-measure

Four different experiments were carried out evaluating the SIFA from the input side and the chosen input SIFA on both a textbook software AES and a t-table software AES implementation. For the experiments performing SIFA from the input side, the χ^2 distributions of the correct key and 100,000 wrong keys were compared. For the experiments performing chosen input SIFA, the χ^2 distributions of the correct key and all possible $2^{16} - 1$ wrong keys were compared. Analysis was performed on a Debian system with an AMD Ryzen Threadripper 3970X 32-Core processor and 256 GB RAM. Using a pure python implementation we can iterate over 135 key candidates per second. This leads to an estimated running time of about a year for SIFA from the input side and about 16 min for chosen input SIFA to recover 32 bits of the secret key.

In the experiment evaluating SIFA from the input side on a textbook AES implementation, 76% of the glitches were successful. After 8278 glitches, 1150 ineffective faults were observed, and the χ^2 score of the correct key exceeded the χ^2 score of the wrong keys, as shown in Fig. 7a. Similarly, when attacking the t-table implementation with SIFA from the input side, 73% of the glitches were successful. After 4366 glitches, 865 ineffective faults were observed, and the χ^2

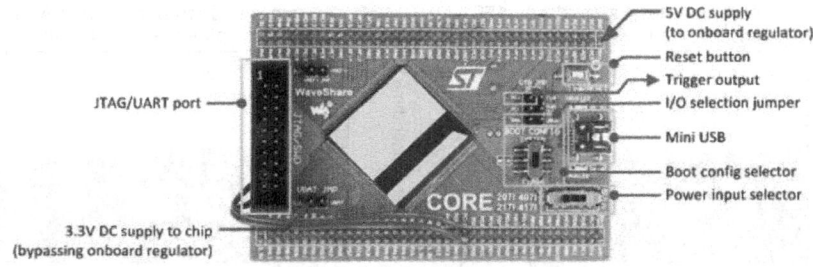

Fig. 6. Piñata board

Table 2. Parameters used in the experiments

Parameters	Input side SIFA		Chosen Input SIFA	
	Textbook	T-Table	Textbook	T-Table
Normal voltage	3.3 V	3.3 V	3.3 V	3.3 V
Glitch voltage	1.0 V	1.0 V	1.0 V	1.0 V
Glitch length	123 ns	123 ns	123 ns	123 ns
Glitch delay	32500 ns	5550 ns	32500 ns	5550 ns

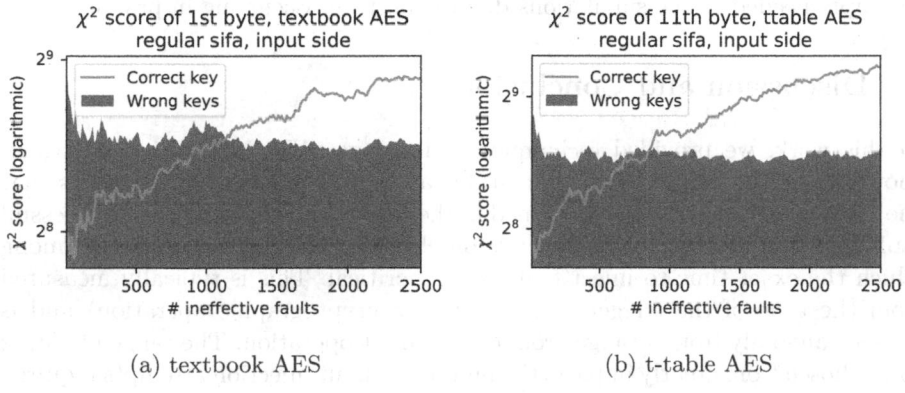

(a) textbook AES   (b) t-table AES

Fig. 7. Evaluation of SIFA from input side

score of the correct key exceeded the χ^2 score of the wrong keys, as shown in Fig. 7b. Even though these results are quite similar to the results obtained from the simulations, the number of fault injection attempts needed to recover the key is higher than the number of attempts needed in the simulations. This is due to the jitter that occurs when performing fault injection in practice.

In the experiment evaluating the chosen plaintext attack on a textbook AES implementation, the successful fault rate was 89%. After 17706 glitches, 1085 ineffective faults were observed, and the χ^2 score of the correct key exceeded the χ^2 score of the wrong keys, as shown in Fig. 8a. Similarly, when attacking

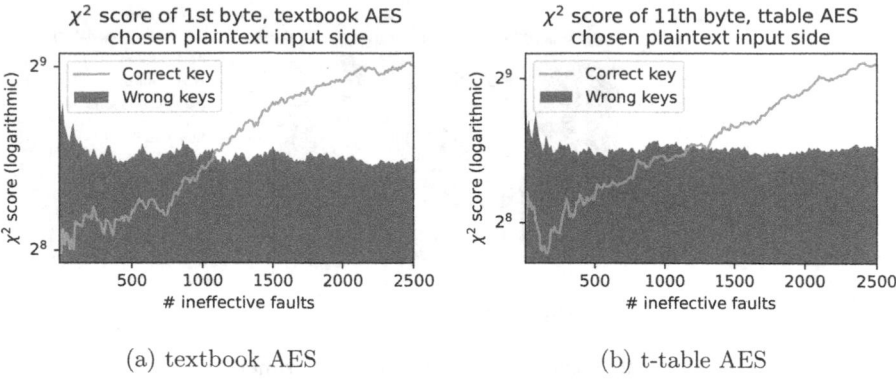

(a) textbook AES   (b) t-table AES

Fig. 8. Evaluation of chosen plaintext SIFA

the t-table implementation with the chosen plaintext attack, 65% of the glitches were successful. After 5390 glitches, 1310 ineffective faults were observed, and the χ^2 score of the correct key exceeded the χ^2 score of the wrong keys, as shown in Fig. 8b. Similar to the experiments evaluating SIFA from the input side, the number of attempts needed to recover the key was higher than the number of attempts needed in the simulations due to the jitter occurring in practice.

6 Discussion and Conclusion

In this work, we provided techniques to improve SIFA in practice. First, we showed with the help of both simulations as well as practical experiments that the SIFA attack can also be performed in the first rounds of a cipher. A successful fault injection attack greatly depends on choosing the right parameters among which the exact time to inject fault is very critical. This is typically measured from the time of the trigger (*e.g.,* start of a cryptographic operation) and is chosen randomly from a range around the target operation. The range of values to be chosen from greatly impacts the number of fault injection attempts required to get a successful fault. The bigger the range, the higher the number of required attempts. This range depends on the time jitter from the trigger point to the target operation. This jitter could be natural or artificially induced, *e.g.,* due to a countermeasure. Naturally, the farther the operation is from the trigger, the higher is the jitter and hence the range for glitch offset is also higher. As a result, the ability to inject faults in the first few rounds of a cipher operation leads to a better success rate in practice than injecting in the last few rounds as we discussed in the paper.

Secondly, the SIFA attack requires brute force on a part of the key, which is 32 bits in case of AES. For recovering a full AES-128 key, we needed to perform this 4 times which leads to brute force complexity of 2^{34}. We showed that by using chosen inputs we can reduce the key search space to 16-bits a time. This is only possible because, as we showed in this paper, the SIFA works also when we inject faults in the first round. As a result, it requires 2^{16} key guess for a 16-bit subkey and improves the overall complexity to 2^{19} for full key recovery of AES-128. Using this technique, we could reduce the estimated attack time to recover 32 bits of the secret key from around a year to about 16 min. Note that this implementation was not fully optimized for performance but gives an indication of the speed up that can be achieved even for optimized implementations.

One promising avenue for future research involves investigating the applicability of the Statistical Ineffective Fault Injection (SIFA) methods to other symmetric cryptographic implementations. While our current work has primarily focused on AES, it is crucial to assess the effectiveness and adaptability of SIFA across a broader spectrum of symmetric ciphers. This could involve examining different algorithms with varying design principles, key sizes, or modes of operation.

While our current study has shown that SIFA can be performed using voltage glitching on certain software implementations of AES, an important direction for future work is to reproduce the practical results with AES hardware implementations. By extending our investigation to AES hardware implementations, we can deepen our understanding of the robustness of SIFA across different platforms.

Furthermore, a valuable area for future investigation lies in enhancing the input-side and chosen plaintext attack methods through the utilization of advanced statistical fault analysis techniques, such as Fault Intensity Map Analysis (FIMA) [28], instead of SIFA. This approach holds the potential to further diminish the number of required traces for key retrieval, thereby enhancing the efficiency and practicality of the proposed attacks.

Acknowledgements. This work was partially supported by CyberSecurity Research Flanders with reference number VR20192203.

References

1. Agoyan, M., Dutertre, J.-M., Mirbaha, A.-P., Naccache, D., Ribotta, A.-L., Tria, A.: How to flip a bit? In: 16th IEEE International On-Line Testing Symposium (IOLTS 2010), 5–7 July 2010, Corfu, Greece, pp. 235–239. IEEE Computer Society (2010)

2. Anderson, R., Kuhn, M.: Low cost attacks on tamper resistant devices. In: Christianson, B., Crispo, B., Lomas, M., Roe, M. (eds.) Security Protocols 1997. LNCS, vol. 1361, pp. 125–136. Springer, Berlin, Heidelberg (1998). https://doi.org/10.1007/bfb0028165

3. Bar-El, H., Choukri, H., Naccache, D., Tunstall, M., Whelan, C.: The sorcerer's apprentice guide to fault attacks. IACR Cryptol. ePrint Arch. **2004**, 100 (2004)

4. Biham, E., Granboulan, L., Nguyen, P.Q.: Impossible fault analysis of RC4 and differential fault analysis of RC4. In: Gilbert, H., Handschuh, H. (eds.) FSE 2005. LNCS, vol. 3557, pp. 359–367. Springer, Heidelberg (2005). https://doi.org/10.1007/11502760_24

5. Biham, E., Shamir, A.: Differential fault analysis of secret key cryptosystems. In: Kaliski, B.S. (ed.) CRYPTO 1997. LNCS, vol. 1294, pp. 513–525. Springer, Heidelberg (1997). https://doi.org/10.1007/BFb0052259

6. Blömer, J., Seifert, J.-P.: Fault based cryptanalysis of the advanced encryption standard (AES). In: Wright, R.N. (ed.) FC 2003. LNCS, vol. 2742, pp. 162–181. Springer, Heidelberg (2003). https://doi.org/10.1007/978-3-540-45126-6_12

7. Boneh, D., DeMillo, R.A., Lipton, R.J.: On the importance of checking cryptographic protocols for faults. In: Fumy, W. (ed.) EUROCRYPT 1997. LNCS, vol. 1233, pp. 37–51. Springer, Heidelberg (1997). https://doi.org/10.1007/3-540-69053-0_4

8. Brisfors, M., Moraitis, M., Dubrova, E.: Do not rely on clock randomization: a side-channel attack on a protected hardware implementation of AES. In: Jourdan, G.V., Mounier, L., Adams, C., Sédes, F., Garcia-Alfaro, J. (eds.) Foundations and Practice of Security. Lecture Notes in Computer Science, vol. 13877, pp. 38–53. Springer, Cham (2023)

9. Riscure B.V. Glitch amplifier. https://getquote.riscure.com/en/quote/2101070/glitch-amplifier.htm. Accessed 01 Dec 2023

10. Riscure B.V. Pinata S (software crypto). https://getquote.riscure.com/en/quote/2101127/pinata-s-software-crypto.htm. Accessed 01 Dec 2023

11. Riscure B.V. Spider. https://getquote.riscure.com/en/quote/2492015/spider.htm. Accessed 01 Dec 2023

12. Canivet, G., Maistri, P., Leveugle, R., Clédière, J., Valette, F., Renaudin, M.: Glitch and laser fault attacks onto a secure AES implementation on a SRAM-based FPGA. J. Cryptol. **24**(2), 247–268 (2011)

13. Clavier, C.: Secret external encodings do not prevent transient fault analysis. In: Paillier, P., Verbauwhede, I. (eds.) CHES 2007. LNCS, vol. 4727, pp. 181–194. Springer, Heidelberg (2007). https://doi.org/10.1007/978-3-540-74735-2_13

14. Courtois, N.T., Ware, D., Jackson, K.M.: Fault-algebraic attacks on inner rounds of DES. In: The eSmart 2010 European Smart Card Security Conference (2010)

15. Daemen, J., Rijmen, V.: The Design of Rijndael: AES - The Advanced Encryption Standard. Information Security and Cryptography. Springer, Hidelberg (2002). https://doi.org/10.1007/978-3-662-04722-4

16. Dehbaoui, A., Dutertre, J.-M., Robisson, B., Tria, A.: Electromagnetic transient faults injection on a hardware and a software implementations of AES. In: Bertoni, G., Gierlichs, B. (eds.) 2012 Workshop on Fault Diagnosis and Tolerance in Cryptography, Leuven, Belgium, 9 September 2012, pp. 7–15. IEEE Computer Society (2012)

17. Dobraunig, C., Eichlseder, M., Korak, T., Mangard, S., Mendel, F., Primas, R.: SIFA: exploiting ineffective fault inductions on symmetric cryptography. IACR Trans. Cryptogr. Hardw. Embed. Syst. **2018**(3), 547–572 (2018)

18. Dusart, P., Letourneux, G., Vivolo, O.: Differential fault analysis on A.E.S. IACR Cryptol. ePrint Arch. **2003**, 10 (2003)

19. Fuhr, T., Jaulmes, É., Lomné, V., Thillard, A.: Fault attacks on AES with faulty ciphertexts only. In: Fischer, W., Schmidt, J.-M. (eds.) 2013 Workshop on Fault Diagnosis and Tolerance in Cryptography, Los Alamitos, CA, USA, 20 August 2013, pp. 108–118. IEEE Computer Society (2013)

20. Giraud, C.: DFA on AES. IACR Cryptol. ePrint Arch. **2003**, 8 (2003)

21. Habing, D.H.: The use of lasers to simulate radiation-induced transients in semiconductor devices and circuits. IEEE Trans. Nucl. Sci. **12**(5), 91–100 (1965)

22. Hutter, M., Schmidt, J.-M.: The temperature side channel and heating fault attacks. IACR Cryptol. ePrint Arch. **2014**, 190 (2014)

23. Kömmerling, O., Kuhn, M.G.: Design principles for tamper-resistant smartcard processors. In: Guthery, S.B., Honeyman, P. (eds.) Proceedings of the 1st Workshop

on Smartcard Technology, Smartcard 1999, Chicago, Illinois, USA, 10–11 May 1999. USENIX Association (1999)

24. Li, Y., Gomisawa, S., Sakiyama, K., Ohta, K.: An information theoretic perspective on the differential fault analysis against AES. IACR Cryptol. ePrint Arch. **2010**, 32 (2010)

25. Moradi, A., Shalmani, M.T.M., Salmasizadeh, M.: A generalized method of differential fault attack against AES cryptosystem. In: Goubin, L., Matsui, M. (eds.) CHES 2006. LNCS, vol. 4249, pp. 91–100. Springer, Heidelberg (2006). https://doi.org/10.1007/11894063_8

26. Murdock, K., Oswald, D.F., Garcia, F.D., Van Bulck, J., Gruss, D., Piessens, F.: Plundervolt: Software-based fault injection attacks against intel SGX. In: 2020 IEEE Symposium on Security and Privacy, SP 2020, San Francisco, CA, USA, 18–21 May 2020, pp. 1466–1482. IEEE (2020)

27. Piret, G., Quisquater, J.-J.: A differential fault attack technique against SPN structures, with application to the AES and KHAZAD. In: Walter, C.D., Koç, Ç.K., Paar, C. (eds.) CHES 2003. LNCS, vol. 2779, pp. 77–88. Springer, Heidelberg (2003). https://doi.org/10.1007/978-3-540-45238-6_7

28. Ramezanpour, K., Ampadu, P., Diehl, W.: FIMA: fault intensity map analysis. In: Polian, I., Stöttinger, M. (eds.) COSADE 2019. LNCS, vol. 11421, pp. 63–79. Springer, Cham (2019). https://doi.org/10.1007/978-3-030-16350-1_5

29. Skorobogatov, S.P., Anderson, R.J.: Optical fault induction attacks. In: Kaliski, B.S., Koç, K., Paar, C. (eds.) CHES 2002. LNCS, vol. 2523, pp. 2–12. Springer, Heidelberg (2003). https://doi.org/10.1007/3-540-36400-5_2

30. Tang, A., Sethumadhavan, S., Stolfo, S.J.: CLKSCREW: exposing the perils of security-oblivious energy management. In: Kirda, E., Ristenpart, T. (eds.) 26th USENIX Security Symposium, USENIX Security 2017, Vancouver, BC, Canada, 16–18 August 2017, pp. 1057–1074. USENIX Association (2017)

31. Zhang, F., Zhang, Y., Jiang, H., Zhu, X., Bhasin, S., Zhao, X., Liu, Z., Dawu, G., Ren, K.: Persistent fault attack in practice. IACR Trans. Cryptogr. Hardw. Embed. Syst. **2020**(2), 172–195 (2020)

CAPABARA: A Combined Attack on CAPA

Dilara Toprakhisar[1]([✉]) [iD], Svetla Nikova[1] [iD], and Ventzislav Nikov[2]

[1] COSIC, KU Leuven, Leuven, Belgium
{dilara.toprakhisar,svetla.nikova}@esat.kuleuven.be
[2] NXP Semiconductors, Leuven, Belgium

Abstract. Physical attacks pose a substantial threat to the secure implementation of cryptographic algorithms. While considerable research efforts are dedicated to protecting against passive physical attacks (*e.g.,* side-channel analysis (SCA)), the landscape of protection against other types of physical attacks remains a challenge. Fault attacks (FA), though attracting growing attention in research, still lack the prevalence of provably secure designs when compared to SCA. The realm of combined attacks, which leverage the capabilities of both SCA and FA adversaries, introduces powerful adversarial models, rendering protection against them challenging. This challenge has consequently led to a relatively unexplored area of research, resulting in a notable gap in understanding and efficiently protecting against combined attacks. The CAPA countermeasure, published at CRYPTO 2018, addresses this challenge with a robust adversarial model that goes beyond conventional SCA and FA adversarial models. Drawing inspiration from the principles of Multiparty Computation (MPC), CAPA claims security against higher-order SCA, higher-order fault attacks, and their combination. In this work, we present a combined attack that breaks CAPA within the constraints of its assumed adversarial model. In response, we propose potential fixes to the design of CAPA that increase the complexity of the proposed attack, although not provably thwarting it. With this presented combined attack, we highlight the difficulty of effectively protecting against combined attacks.

Keywords: Fault attacks · Combined attacks · CAPA

1 Introduction

Cryptographic algorithms are designed to have certain properties to withstand cryptanalytic attacks. Nevertheless, devices running the implementations of these cryptographic algorithms in practice are susceptible to physical attacks that observe or disrupt their physical characteristics. Side-Channel Analysis (SCA), being a passive physical attack, exploits the observable leakage arising from physical effects, such as power consumption [17], timing [16], or electromagnetic emanation [10]. Masking [4,12,15,19] stands out as a prominent and widely

© The Author(s), under exclusive license to Springer Nature Switzerland AG 2024
R. Wacquez and N. Homma (Eds.): COSADE 2024, LNCS 14595, pp. 76–89, 2024.
https://doi.org/10.1007/978-3-031-57543-3_5

established countermeasure against SCA. The working principle of masking is to split the secret variable into a number of statistically independent random shares. Consequently, observing all but one share does not reveal information related to the secret variable. Boolean masking [4], being a well-understood countermeasure against SCA, replaces each secret variable $x \in \mathbb{F}_2$ by a vector of s shares $\bar{x} = (x_0, x_1, ..., x_{s-1})$ such that $x = \sum_{i=0}^{s-1} x_i$ over $\mathbb{F}_2$, where each x_i is uniformly random.

Unlike SCA, fault attacks (FA) are active attacks that deliberately disrupt computations through physical means, such as clock/voltage glitching [1], electromagnetic waves [7], and laser injections [14]. Consequently, they extract information from the device's response to the induced errors. Since the seminal work of Boneh *et al.* [3], introducing Differential Fault Attacks (DFA) on RSA, numerous fault analysis methods have emerged, focusing on exploiting incorrect outputs. A commonly employed countermeasure against such attacks involves introducing redundancy in time, area, or information to detect if a fault is injected into the computation. Upon fault detection, these countermeasures either suppress or infect the output, rendering it non-exploitable by the adversaries. Nevertheless, Statistical Ineffective Faults Attacks (SIFA) [9], also referred to as SIFA-1, exploit the dependency between fault propagation and secret values, effectively utilizing correct ciphertexts. This characteristic enables SIFA to circumvent the countermeasures based on straightforward redundancy.

Another prevalent approach combines masking and redundancy to protect against fault attacks. In addition to protecting implementations against SCA through masking, these countermeasures offer protection against SIFA-1-like attacks by introducing randomness to the computation. Nevertheless, Dobraunig *et al.* [8] exploited SIFA-1 (which is then referred to as SIFA-2), circumventing most of the masking combined with redundancy based countermeasures. This underscores the need for more intricate countermeasures, such as fine-grained error detection [5] or error correction, in the landscape of protecting against fault attacks.

In addition to examining the capabilities of SCA and FA adversaries individually, combined attacks that leverage both capabilities simultaneously have attracted attention. However, relying solely on the integration of SCA and FA countermeasures alone is insufficient to protect against such combined attacks. Even advanced countermeasures designed with intricate protection mechanisms may still prove ineffective against these sophisticated attacks [21]. One of the few countermeasures that is designed to protect against combined attacks is the CAPA countermeasure by Reparaz *et al.* [20], published in CRYPTO 2018. CAPA leverages the principles of the Multiparty Computation (MPC) protocol SPDZ [6] that adopts a full threshold setting where all but one party can be corrupted. It performs computations on shared variables and shared information-theoretic MAC tags associated with the secret variables, combining masking and fine-grained redundancy. CAPA claims provable security against higher-order SCA, higher-order (*i.e.*, multiple shot) FA, and their combination. Unlike common SCA and FA adversary models that assume the t-probing model [15] and faulting up to a limited number of gates/registers, CAPA introduces a unique adversary model: *The Tile-Probe-and-Fault Model*. This model assumes that the chip under attack is partitioned into tiles with their own combinational and control logic, and PRNGs, connected to each other by wires. The tile-probe-and-fault model assumes an adversary capable of probing a bounded number of tiles with all their possessed intermediate values, which is an extension of the t-probing model. Simultaneously, the adversary is assumed to have the capability to inject known-value faults to any variable within a bounded number of tiles, which generalizes the bounded gate/register faulting model, or inject random-value faults to an unbounded number of tiles.

The design of CAPA consists of two stages: an evaluation stage to compute the cryptographic algorithms and a preprocessing stage to generate auxiliary data that is used in the evaluation stage, where the two stages can be interleaved. While the evaluation stage adheres to SPDZ principles, the preprocessing stage diverges by utilizing a passively secure shared multiplier to generate auxiliary data. This design choice enhances the efficiency of CAPA compared to SPDZ, where the corresponding offline phase employs somewhat homomorphic encryption for the generation of auxiliary data.

Contributions. In this work, we introduce the first known attack, a combined attack, targeting the CAPA countermeasure within the assumed adversary model, the tile-probe-and-fault model. The proposed attack necessitates an ineffective fault to be injected during the preprocessing stage, resulting in a secret variable in the evaluation stage to be masked by a zero value. Subsequently, this unmasked value is probed to recover the secret. The proposed attack capitalizes on the divergence in the preprocessing stage of CAPA from SPDZ, exploiting an ineffective fault passing to the evaluation stage undetected. This exploitation leads to the breaking of CRYPTO 2018's work within its own adversarial model. In response, we propose fixes for the CAPA countermeasure. Although these fixes do not entirely prevent the proposed attack, they do contribute to an increase in attack complexity.

2   CAPA

Before delving into the proposed attack, we provide an overview of the CAPA countermeasure. We first describe its associated adversarial model, the *tile-probe-and-fault model*, and then its design.

2.1   The Tile-Probe-and-Fault-Model

In this section, we introduce the adversarial model of the CAPA countermeasure along with the security guarantees based on this model. The tile-probe-and-fault model extends the t-probing model as introduced by Ishai *et al.* [15], where an adversary is limited to observe at most t predetermined wires of the Boolean circuit. In the CAPA countermeasure, an integrated circuit is assumed to be separated into tiles, each consisting of wires as well as combinational and sequential logic. This structural arrangement aligns with the MPC setting, where each tile can be viewed as an independent party.

Each tile in the partitioned integrated circuit is denoted with T_i, where wires are running between each pair of tiles as depicted in Fig. 1. Each tile encompasses its own combinational logic, control logic, and pseudo-random number generator. The leakage from each tile being local, does not disclose information about other tiles. An adversary with probing and faulting capabilities can obtain information about *all* variables in the probed tile, or inject faults to *all* variables within the targeted tile. The CAPA countermeasure employs Boolean masking, where each secret variable is split into d shares. This implies that the integrated circuit is partitioned into d tiles, where each tile stores and manipulates at most one share of each intermediate variable. The wires running between the tiles carry only the blinded versions of the shares of the secret variables, and faults happening on these wires are confined to affecting only the receiving tiles.

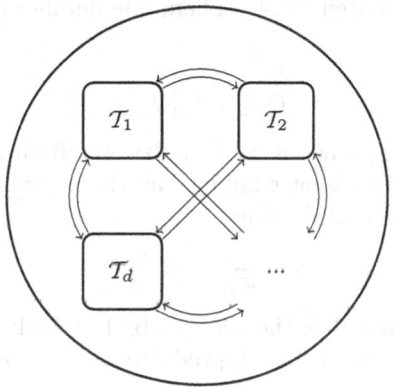

Fig. 1. Tile architecture of an integrated circuit

Probing Capabilities. The CAPA countermeasure assumes an adversary with d_p-probing capabilities, where they are given information about all intermediate variables within the specified d_p tiles from the beginning to the end of the computation with a probability of one. This contrasts with the commonly assumed t-probing model, where an adversary can access only t intermediate values. CAPA's assumption of a more potent probing adversary aligns with real-world scenarios, accommodating, for instance, EM probes that enable the observation of multiple intermediate values in the target area.

Faulting Capabilities. CAPA assumes two types of fault capabilities under the tile-probe-and-fault model: d_f-faulting and ϵ-faulting. In d_f-faulting, an adversary can inject chosen-value faults to any number of precisely chosen intermediate variables within the specified d_f tiles. On the other hand, ϵ-faulting allows an adversary to inject random-value faults following some distribution to any variable within any tile, for example, flipping each bit with a certain probability. However, the adversary cannot set all variables to a chosen fixed value.

Adversarial Models. CAPA assumes two adversarial models: $\mathcal{A}_1$ with both d_p-probing and d_f-faulting capabilities, and $\mathcal{A}_2$ with both d_p-probing and ϵ-faulting capabilities. Let $\mathcal{P}_1$ denote the set of up to d_p tiles that can be probed, and $\mathcal{F}_1$ denote the set of up to d_f tiles that can be faulted by $\mathcal{A}_1$, ensuring that at least one share/tile remains unaccessed with the following constraint:

$$(\mathcal{F}_1 \cup \mathcal{P}_1) \subseteq \cup_{j=1}^{d-1} \mathcal{T}_{i_j}.$$

Furthermore, a chosen-value fault injected by the adversary $\mathcal{A}_1$ cannot be preceded by a probe within the same clock cycle; it can only depend on the probes from previous clock cycles.

Let $\mathcal{P}_2$ denote the set of up to d_p tiles that can be probed and $\mathcal{F}_2$ denote the set of tiles that can be faulted by $\mathcal{A}_2$. Then, the number of probed tiles remains limited to $d - 1$:

$$\mathcal{P}_2 \subseteq \cup_{j=1}^{d-1} \mathcal{T}_{i_j}.$$

However, for $\mathcal{A}_2$ injecting random-value faults, the limitation on the number of tiles that can be faulted no longer applies, as the injected faults do not set the unshared values to chosen fixed values:

$$\mathcal{F}_2 \subseteq \mathcal{T}.$$

It is important to note that the tiles probed or faulted by both adversaries are predetermined, and cannot be adapted during the computation.

2.2 The CAPA Design

The CAPA design consists of two stages: the preprocessing step and the evaluation step. During the preprocessing step, auxiliary data is generated, which is subsequently used in the evaluation step to blind the sensitive variables.

All computations in the design are performed over $\mathbb{F}_{2^k}$. The preprocessing stage variables are denoted by a, b, c, and the evaluation stage variables (*i.e.,* secret variables) are denoted by lowercase letters x, y, z. The bold versions of these letters indicate that the variables are shared (*e.g.,* $\mathbf{a} = (a_0, ..., a_{d-1})$ where $\sum_{i=0}^{d-1} a_i = a$). The MAC key is denoted by α, which is also shared among the tiles such that $\boldsymbol{\alpha} = (\alpha_0, ..., \alpha_{d-1})$. Then, a value $a \in \mathbb{F}_{2^k}$ is represented as a pair $\langle a \rangle = (\mathbf{a}, \boldsymbol{\tau_a})$ consisting of the data and the associated tag shares in the masked domain, where $\tau_a = \alpha a$. In the CAPA design, there can be multiple independent MAC keys, associating multiple tags with each variable. However, for the sake of simplicity, we assume that the design employs only a single MAC key in this work. The Kronecker delta function is denoted by $\delta_{i,j}$, returning 1 if $i = j$, and 0 otherwise.

We first describe the multiplication as a building block in the evaluation stage, which is the focal point of interest in the proposed attack. Subsequently, we delve into the preprocessing components.

Evaluation Stage

Each tile T_i stores the ith share of each sensitive and auxiliary variable, along with the ith share of the associated MAC tags and the MAC key. Linear operations, such as addition, do not necessitate communication between tiles, unlike nonlinear operations like multiplication which also require auxiliary data.

Multiplication. To compute the multiplication of (x, τ_x) and (y, τ_y), a Beaver triple $(\langle a \rangle, \langle b \rangle, \langle c \rangle)$ satisfying $c = ab$, generated during the preprocessing stage, is utilized. The multiplication then proceeds as follows:

Step 1: blinding. Each tile T_i locally randomizes its share of the secrets x and y: $\varepsilon_i = x_i + a_i$ and $\eta_i = y_i + b_i$. Likewise, the associated MAC tag shares are computed: $\tau_{\varepsilon_i} = \tau_{x_i} + \tau_{a_i}$ and $\tau_{\eta_i} = \tau_{y_i} + \tau_{b_i}$.

Step 2: partial unmasking. Each tile T_i broadcasts ε_i and η_i computed in Step 1 to the other tiles. Then, each tile locally computes and stores the values $\varepsilon = \sum_{i=0}^{d-1} \varepsilon_i$ and $\eta = \sum_{i=0}^{d-1} \eta_i$. ε and η (*i.e.*, blinded versions of the secrets) are partially unmasked as their MAC tags τ_ε and τ_η remain shared among the tiles.

Step 3: checking the MAC tags of the partially unmasked values. The tiles check whether the tags τ_ε and τ_η are consistent with the unmasked public values ε and η using a method described below.

Step 4: Beaver computation. Each tile locally computes the following:

$$z_i = c_i + \varepsilon b_i + \eta a_i + \varepsilon \eta \delta_{i,1},$$
$$\tau_{z_i} = \tau_{c_i} + \varepsilon \tau_{b_i} + \eta \tau_{a_i} + \alpha_i \varepsilon \eta. \tag{1}$$

One can verify that the shared output (z, τ_z) of the above protocol corresponds to $z = xy$ given that no faults are present.

Checking the MAC Tags of Partially Unmasked Values. The CAPA multiplication continues its computation only if both of the partially unmasked values are consistent with their associated MAC tags. Consider a partially unmasked value $\varepsilon = x + a$, then, each tile has its own share of the corresponding MAC tag which is computed in the first step of the multiplication as $\tau_{\varepsilon_i} = \tau_{x_i} + \tau_{a_i}$. Then, to verify the correctness of the MAC tag, each tile locally computes and broadcasts the value $\alpha_i \varepsilon + \tau_{\varepsilon_i}$ to the other tiles. Ensuring the correctness of the tag, where $\sum_{i=0}^{d-1} \tau_{\varepsilon_i} = \alpha \varepsilon$ holds, involves each tile computing $\sum_{i=0}^{d-1} (\alpha_i \varepsilon + \tau_{\varepsilon_i})$ and proceeding only if the result is zero.

Preprocessing Stage

The Beaver triples $(\langle a \rangle, \langle b \rangle, \langle c \rangle)$, satisfying $c = ab$, used in the multiplication, are generated in the preprocessing stage of the CAPA design.

Auxiliary Data Generation. The Beaver triple $(\langle a \rangle, \langle b \rangle, \langle c \rangle)$ is generated through a process where each tile $\mathcal{T}_i$ independently draws random shares a_i and b_i such that $a = (a_0, ..., a_{d-1})$ and $b = (b_0, ..., b_{d-1})$, where $a = \sum_{i=0}^{d-1} a_i$ and $b = \sum_{i=0}^{d-1} b_i$. Subsequently, a passively secure multiplier (*e.g.,* [2,11,13,18,19]) is employed to compute $c = (c_0, ..., c_{d-1})$, where $c = \sum_{i=0}^{d-1} c_i$ such that $c = ab$. Simultaneously, shared MAC tags τ_a, τ_b, τ_c are computed using a passively secure multiplier and the shared MAC key α.

Relation Verification of Auxiliary Data. The faults injected during the evaluation stage in CAPA are detected through the MAC tag check performed in Step 3 of the CAPA multiplication. In contrast, similar to SPDZ, to detect the faults injected during the preprocessing stage, a relation verification is executed for each Beaver triple transitioning from the preprocessing stage to the evaluation stage. This verification ensures the correctness of the triple, specifically validating that $c = ab$. The verification of the correctness of $(\langle a \rangle, \langle b \rangle, \langle c \rangle)$ is executed by employing another Beaver triple $(\langle d \rangle, \langle e \rangle, \langle f \rangle)$:

1. A random $r_1 \in \mathbb{F}_{2^k}$ is drawn.
2. Utilizing the second triple $(\langle d \rangle, \langle e \rangle, \langle f \rangle)$, the multiplication of $r_1 \langle a \rangle$ and $\langle b \rangle$, and the associated MAC tag are computed. This involves a constant multiplication with r_1, which is performed locally as it is a linear operation, and an actively secure multiplication executed as described in Eq. 1. Then, the outcome $\langle \tilde{c} \rangle$ is a shared representation of $\tilde{c} = r_1 ab$.
3. Each tile $\mathcal{T}_i$ locally computes and broadcasts the differences of the shares of $r_1 c$ and $\tilde{c}$, and their corresponding tags: $\Theta_i = r_1 c_i + \tilde{c}_i$ and $\tau_{\Theta_i} = r_1 \tau_{c_i} + \tau_{\tilde{c}_i}$. Then, $\Theta = \sum_{i=0}^{d-1} \Theta_i$ and $\tau_\Theta = \sum_{i=0}^{d-1} \tau_{\Theta_i}$ are unmasked.
4. If at least one of the unmasked differences, Θ and τ_Θ, is nonzero, $(\langle a \rangle, \langle b \rangle, \langle c \rangle)$ is rejected as a valid triple.
5. Else, another $r_2 \in \mathbb{F}_{2^k}$ is drawn such that $r_1 \neq r_2$, and the described procedure is repeated for a second time.

While this stage corresponds to the offline phase of the MPC protocol, SPDZ, there are notable distinctions rendering the CAPA preprocessing stage more lightweight. In CAPA, Beaver triples are generated on the fly, as needed, resulting in reduced storage requirements. Moreover, these triples are generated using a passively secure multiplier, in contrast to SPDZ's use of a somewhat homomorphic encryption scheme. This choice is motivated by somewhat homomorphic encryption exceeding any efficiency requirements for deployment in hardware devices. Unlike SPDZ, where each party proves the correctness of the generated randoms (a_i, b_i) that are shares of the Beaver triple elements (a, b), CAPA does not error check the generated Beaver triple elements which are then fed into a passively secure multiplier. The proposed attack leverages this distinction in CAPA's design from SPDZ, specifically the absence of error checks of the generated Beaver triples. CAPA solely verifies $c = ab$, overlooking ineffective faults.

3   The Combined Attack Description

In this section, we describe the proposed combined attack targeting CAPA. The attack assumes an adversarial model that stays within the adversarial model of CAPA, namely, the tile-probe-and-fault model. The adversary in the proposed attack is assumed to have both faulting and probing capabilities. Importantly, the attack does not rely on any strong assumptions inherent in the tile-and-probe-fault model, such as probing or faulting all variables within a tile. Specifically, the attack demonstrates effectiveness by faulting a single variable and probing another one, which retains the feasibility even under conventional adversarial models like t-probing and a bounded number of gate/register faulting. The attack necessitates only a single fault injected during the preprocessing step, which may take the form of a random fault (*i.e.*, randomly chosen set, reset, or bit flip fault). This fault is complemented by a probing event during the evaluation stage, where the probed value is subsequently unmasked due to the injected fault becoming ineffective.

For readability, we consider the attack scenario where the CAPA countermeasure is instantiated with $d = 2$ (*i.e.*, 2 shares/tiles). It is important to highlight that the attack scenario is independent of the number of shares, and can be generalized for any arbitrary order d as it only requires faulting a single share/tile. Additionally, the adversary can probe the same faulted tile, where the probed variable is unmasked, making it adaptable for different values of d.

3.1   The Attack Scenario

The combined attack scenario consists of two steps: the fault injection step, and the subsequent probing step that exploits the manifestation of the injected fault. We first describe the assumptions regarding the faulting and probing capabilities of the adversary, then, describe the fault injection step targeting the preprocessing stage. Following the fault injection step, we describe the probing step exploiting the injected fault, and outline the success conditions for the attack.

Capabilities
We describe the faulting capabilities of the assumed adversary performing the fault injection step as follows:

- The adversary injects a single-shot fault to a variable in $\mathbb{F}_{2^k}$, potentially affecting a random number of bits within the targeted variable.
- The fault location is loose, allowing the injection of a fault affecting any set of bits within any share of the target secret variable.
- Precise timing is crucial for the injected fault, necessitating its occurrence before the tag computation of the targeted secret variable.
- The effectiveness period of the fault is transient.
- The fault is required to be injected to a registered value, and can be of a random type.

Additionally, the adversary is assumed to be capable of probing a variable of their choosing.

Fault Injection Step

The fault injection in the preprocessing stage is formalized as follows:

(1) Each tile draws randoms $\mathcal{T}_0 \rightarrow a_0, b_0 \in \mathbb{F}_{2^k}$, $\mathcal{T}_1 \rightarrow a_1, b_1 \in \mathbb{F}_{2^k}$, such that $\boldsymbol{a} = (a_0, a_1)$ where $a = a_0 + a_1$ and $\boldsymbol{b} = (b_0, b_1)$ where $b = b_0 + b_1$.

(2) The tiles compute $\boldsymbol{c} = (c_0, c_1)$ where $c = c_0 + c_1$ such that $c = ab$ using a passively secure shared multiplier.

(3) The tiles compute the corresponding MAC tags $\boldsymbol{\tau_a}, \boldsymbol{\tau_b}, \boldsymbol{\tau_c}$ using a passively secure shared multiplier (*i.e.*, $\tau_x = \alpha x$).

  (3.1) Before the computation of $\boldsymbol{\tau_a}$, a fault is injected to a share of $\boldsymbol{a}$. Assuming a_0 is the targeted share, $\mathcal{T}_0$ now stores the faulty value $a_0' = a_0 + \Delta$, and uses it in the subsequent computations.

  (3.2) Then, the incorrect MAC tag $\boldsymbol{\tau_{a'}}$ consistent with a' is computed, where $\tau_{a'} = \alpha a'$ and $a' = a + \Delta$, while $\boldsymbol{\tau_b}, \boldsymbol{\tau_c}$ are correct and consistent with $\boldsymbol{b}, \boldsymbol{c}$, respectively.

(4) Relation verification for the triple $(\langle \boldsymbol{a'} \rangle, \langle \boldsymbol{b} \rangle, \langle \boldsymbol{c} \rangle)$ is performed utilizing another triple $(\langle \boldsymbol{d} \rangle, \langle \boldsymbol{e} \rangle, \langle \boldsymbol{f} \rangle)$ that is assumed to be correct:

  (4.1) A random $r_1 \in \mathbb{F}_{2^k}$ is drawn.

  (4.2) $(\langle \boldsymbol{d} \rangle, \langle \boldsymbol{e} \rangle, \langle \boldsymbol{f} \rangle)$ is used to compute $\langle \tilde{c} \rangle$ where $\tilde{c} = r_1 a'b$. As $\boldsymbol{\tau_{a'}}$ and $\boldsymbol{\tau_b}$ are consistent with the values $\boldsymbol{a'}$ and $\boldsymbol{b}$, the actively secure multiplication is executed with a successful MAC tag check step.

  (4.3) Each tile locally computes and broadcasts $\mathcal{T}_0 \rightarrow \Theta_0 = r_1 c_0 + \tilde{c}_0, \tau_{\Theta_0} = r_1 \tau_{c_0} + \tau_{\tilde{c}_0}, \mathcal{T}_1 \rightarrow \Theta_1 = r_1 c_1 + \tilde{c}_1, \tau_{\Theta_1} = r_1 \tau_{c_1} + \tau_{\tilde{c}_1}$. $\Theta = \Theta_0 + \Theta_1$ and $\tau_\Theta = \tau_{\Theta_0} + \tau_{\Theta_1}$ are then unmasked.

  (4.4) Then, the relation verification checks whether at least one of unmasked Θ and τ_Θ is non-zero. If one of them is non-zero, then the triple is rejected as it is not valid. That is, if b is non-zero, the faulty triple $(\langle \boldsymbol{a'} \rangle, \langle \boldsymbol{b} \rangle, \langle \boldsymbol{c} \rangle)$ will not pass the check as the fault injected to $\boldsymbol{a}$ is effective (*i.e.*, $a'b = c + \Delta b \neq c$), making the triple invalid. However, the faulty triple will pass the check if $b = 0$ as the injected fault is ineffective due to b nullifying it (*i.e.*, $a'b = c + \Delta 0 = c$), maintaining the validity of the triple.

Probing Step

In this step of the attack, the adversary exploits the injected fault by probing to deduce information about the secrets. Considering that $b = 0$ and $c = 0$, the triple $(\langle \boldsymbol{a'} \rangle, \langle \boldsymbol{b} \rangle, \langle \boldsymbol{c} \rangle)$ successfully passes the relation verification for $a' = a + \Delta$. This triple is then employed in the multiplication (Eq. 1) to blind the shares of the secret inputs. As a result, one of the secret variables (consider y in our example) in the multiplication $z = xy$ is blinded by a zero value: $\eta = y + b = y$. Subsequently, the adversary probes the unmasked variable $\eta = y$ to reveal the secret value y.

This described attack involves a single fault injection in one of the randoms (*i.e.*, a) of a Beaver triple, coupled with a single probe. The attack is successful if and only if the injected fault to a (where any of the shares can be faulted) is ineffective due to the value of $b = 0$, occurring with a probability of 2^{-k}. Consequently, the leakage results from an unmasked byte value, which is not directly targeted by the fault. In essence, as long as the fault injection step is successful, i.e., the injected fault is ineffective, an unmasked variable occurs in the subsequent multiplication some cycles after the fault injection event. It is crucial to note that the fault does not need to be repeatable for a successful attack. The ineffectiveness of the fault injected into a is solely contingent on the value of b, and the fault can take any random fault type.

It is essential to highlight that, in the CAPA countermeasure, faults are undetected only if both the value and its corresponding MAC tag are altered such that they are consistent, which requires two faults to be injected. For an $\mathcal{A}_1$ adversary to successfully obtain a pair of a faulty value and a consistent MAC tag, knowledge of the MAC key (α) is required. Due to the MAC key being secret, the adversary is limited to probabilistic guessing, which is successful with a probability of 2^{-k}. For an $\mathcal{A}_2$ adversary, the faults go undetected only when the value and the corresponding tag happen to be consistent, occurring with a probability of 2^{-k}. In this context, the success probability of the proposed attack, conditioned on $b = 0$, remains the same at 2^{-k}. Nevertheless, it exploits a specific vulnerability that arises in the preprocessing stage, requiring a single fault and a subsequent probe, in contrast to the need for two faults. Moreover, employing multiple MAC tags for each variable reduces the success probability of obtaining consistent variable and MAC tags to 2^{-lk}, where l denotes the number of tags. However, this does not impact the success probability of the proposed attack, as the tags are computed based on the faulty value.

4   Fixes Against the Proposed Attack

In this section, we propose a few fixes against the aforementioned attack. It is important to emphasize that while the proposed fixes do not completely eliminate the vulnerability, they do increase the complexity of the attack.

Computing the Tags of a and b Prior to Forming the Triple

In response to this attack, one proposed fix involves precomputing the tags of a and b before forming the triple in the preprocessing stage, prior to the computation of c such that $c = ab$. As the proposed attack requires the fault to be injected after c is computed, this fix aims to prevent faults injected to a and b from going undetected by computing the associated MAC tags based on their non-faulty values. Then, the faults injected to a and b will be detected in the MAC tag check step of the actively secure multiplication of the relation verification step, thus circumventing the proposed attack.

However, it is crucial to note that an adversary can still execute the described attack, albeit with multiple faults. Specifically, the adversary needs to inject three faults. First, the adversary injects a fault to a to obtain $a' = a + \Delta$ before computing τ_a to get a faulty tag associated with a'. Then, they inject the same fault to a' to revert it to a, allowing c to be computed using the correct a and *b*. Lastly, they inject one more fault to a after computing c as in the original attack. We formalize this fault injection step as follows:

(1) Each tile draws randoms $\mathcal{T}_0 \rightarrow a_0, b_0 \in \mathbb{F}_{2^k}$, $\mathcal{T}_1 \rightarrow a_1, b_1 \in \mathbb{F}_{2^k}$, such that $\boldsymbol{a} = (a_0, a_1)$ where $a = a_0 + a_1$ and $\boldsymbol{b} = (b_0, b_1)$ where $b = b_0 + b_1$.
(2) The tiles compute the corresponding MAC tags $\boldsymbol{\tau}_a, \boldsymbol{\tau}_b$.
 (2.1) Before the computation of $\boldsymbol{\tau}_a$, a fault is injected to a share of $\boldsymbol{a}$. Assuming a_0 is the targeted share, $\mathcal{T}_0$ now stores the faulty value $a_0' = a_0 + \Delta$, and uses it in subsequent computations.
 (2.2) Then, the incorrect MAC tag $\boldsymbol{\tau}_{a'}$ consistent with a' is computed, where $\tau_{a'} = \alpha a'$ and $a' = a + \Delta$, while $\boldsymbol{\tau}_b$ is correct and consistent with $\boldsymbol{b}$.
 (2.3) After the computation of $\boldsymbol{\tau}_a'$, the same fault Δ is injected to a share of $\boldsymbol{a}'$ to obtain the initial value a (*i.e.* $a = a' + \Delta$).
(3) The tiles compute $\boldsymbol{c} = (c_0, c_1)$ where $c = c_0 + c_1$ such that $c = ab$, and the corresponding MAC tag $\boldsymbol{\tau}_c$.
(4) The same fault Δ is injected to any share of a once more, obtaining $a' = a + \Delta$.
(5) Relation verification for the triple $(\langle \boldsymbol{a}' \rangle, \langle \boldsymbol{b} \rangle, \langle \boldsymbol{c} \rangle)$ is executed utilizing another triple $(\langle \boldsymbol{d} \rangle, \langle \boldsymbol{e} \rangle, \langle \boldsymbol{f} \rangle)$ that is assumed to be correct:
 (5.1) A random $r_1 \in \mathbb{F}_{2^k}$ is drawn.
 (5.2) $(\langle \boldsymbol{d} \rangle, \langle \boldsymbol{e} \rangle, \langle \boldsymbol{f} \rangle)$ is used to compute $\langle \tilde{c} \rangle$ where $\tilde{c} = r_1 a' b$. As $\boldsymbol{\tau}_{a'}$ and $\boldsymbol{\tau}_b$ are consistent with the values a' and b, the actively secure multiplication is executed with a successful MAC tag check step.
 (5.3) Each tile locally computes and broadcasts $\mathcal{T}_0 \rightarrow \Theta_0 = r_1 c_0 + \tilde{c}_0, \tau_{\Theta_0} = r_1 \tau_{c_0} + \tau_{\tilde{c}_0}, \mathcal{T}_1 \rightarrow \Theta_1 = r_1 c_1 + \tilde{c}_1, \tau_{\Theta_1} = r_1 \tau_{c_1} + \tau_{\tilde{c}_1}$. $\Theta = \Theta_0 + \Theta_1$ and $\tau_\Theta = \tau_{\Theta_0} + \tau_{\Theta_1}$ are then unmasked.
 (5.4) Then, the relation verification checks whether at least one of unmasked Θ and τ_Θ is non-zero. If one of them is non-zero, then the triple is rejected as it is not valid. That is, the triple is rejected if b is non-zero, and the triple is used for blinding if $b = 0$.

We note that, in certain cases, a copy of a rather than the value itself may be used to compute c (step 3). In such instances, step 4 becomes unnecessary, given that a' is already stored and utilized in subsequent computations.

The probing step follows the same process described in the original attack which is conditioned on the injected fault to a being ineffective (*i.e.*, $b = 0$), occurring with a probability of 2^{-k}. In both adversarial models, $\mathcal{A}_1$ and $\mathcal{A}_2$, the adversary is able to inject the same additive fault (Δ) repeatedly, as it is independent of the value a. Although this attack maintains the success probability of the original attack, the proposed fix increases the complexity by necessitating three faults to be injected.

Randomly Choosing the Beaver Triple to Be Used in the Multiplication

In a manner similar to SPDZ, the CAPA countermeasure can exert control over the selection of the Beaver triple used for blinding secrets in the multiplication (Eq. 1). That is, the CAPA countermeasure can choose between the two Beaver triples $(\langle a \rangle, \langle b \rangle, \langle c \rangle)$, $(\langle d \rangle, \langle e \rangle, \langle f \rangle)$ to be used for blinding in the multiplication (Eq. 1) or to be sacrificed. Consequently, for an adversary to execute the same attack with equivalent success probability 2^{-k}, faults must be injected to both Beaver triples $(1/2 \cdot 2^{-k} + 1/2 \cdot 2^{-k} = 2^{-k})$. The injected faults do not need to be identical, as achieving an ineffective fault hinges solely on the value of b (*i.e.*, the fault-free variable of the Beaver triple inputs). Therefore, akin to the first proposed fix, this one also increases the complexity of the attack, requiring a total of two fault injections, albeit maintaining the same success probability. It is essential to highlight that an alternative attack strategy still incorporates a single fault injection, as assumed in the proposed attack. In this scenario, the adversary can still be successful, albeit with half of the initial success rate (2^{-k-1}), when the faulty Beaver triple is chosen with a probability of 2^{-1}.

Another fix involves the generalization of the above described fix. During the preprocessing stage, the countermeasure can generate multiple Beaver triples. To be used in the evaluation phase, two of the triples can be randomly selected for the relation verification, and consequently, for blinding the secrets. This further increases the complexity of the attack, meaning that more faults (*i.e.*, the number of Beaver triples) must be injected to execute the same attack with the same success rate. Alternatively, the adversary can still execute the attack with a single fault, albeit with a probability of $(1/m \cdot 2^{-k})$, where m is the number of Beaver triples available to be selected for blinding in the multiplication (Eq. 1). If the number of used Beaver triples for the selection is less than $2^{(l-1)k}$, this alternative attack still proves more efficient than the straightforward attack of injecting two faults to achieve a consistent value and a tag, when more than one MAC tag is employed.

Zero-Check on c

The CAPA countermeasure can implement a zero-check on c, indirectly checking whether either a or b is zero, as $c = ab$, constituting the condition for the ineffectiveness of the injected fault. In this way, the countermeasure selectively forms the Beaver triple (a, b, c) only for non-zero inputs. While implementing a zero-check on masked values is not inherently efficient, this fix does serve as a preventive measure against the proposed attack, assuming the zero-check protocol and its result remain unaffected by the faults.

Nevertheless, it is important to note that excluding zero inputs from the Beaver triple generation process will compromise the uniformity of the partially unmasked multiplication inputs. The potential impact of this strategy on the susceptibility of the non-uniformly blinded values to exploitation by a probing adversary should be carefully considered.

5   Conclusion

Our work presents the first known attack, CAPABARA, targeting the CAPA countermeasure within its own adversarial model, the tile-probe-and-fault model. We highlight the distinct preprocessing stage of CAPA that differs from the offline phase of SPDZ, as discussed in Sect. 2.2. While these distinctions render the CAPA preprocessing stage more lightweight, it sacrifices certain security properties provided by somewhat homomorphic encryption utilized in SPDZ.

Our proposed attack exploits the lack of error checks of the generated randoms (a_i, b_i) forming the Beaver triples after they are fed to the passively secure multiplier. Despite CAPA's assumption of a robust adversary model, CAPABARA exploits only a single fault injected during the preprocessing stage and a probe performed during the evaluation stage, where the probed value is unmasked due to the ineffective fault.

In response to the proposed attack, we also propose a few fixes to the CAPA design. While these fixes do not fully eliminate the exploited vulnerability, they enhance the attack complexity. The task of eliminating this vulnerability while meeting efficiency requirements for deployment is left as a future work that merits further investigation.

Acknowledgements. This work was supported by CyberSecurity Research Flanders with reference number VR20192203.

References

1. Anderson, R., Kuhn, M.: Low cost attacks on tamper resistant devices. In: Christianson, B., Crispo, B., Lomas, M., Roe, M. (eds.) Security Protocols 1997. LNCS, vol. 1361, pp. 125–136. Springer, Heidelberg (1998). https://doi.org/10.1007/BFb0028165

2. Bilgin, B., Gierlichs, B., Nikova, S., Nikov, V., Rijmen, V.: Higher-order threshold implementations. In: Sarkar, P., Iwata, T. (eds.) ASIACRYPT 2014. LNCS, vol. 8874, pp. 326–343. Springer, Heidelberg (2014). https://doi.org/10.1007/978-3-662-45608-8_18

3. Boneh, D., DeMillo, R.A., Lipton, R.J.: On the importance of checking cryptographic protocols for faults. In: Fumy, W. (ed.) EUROCRYPT 1997. LNCS, vol. 1233, pp. 37–51. Springer, Heidelberg (1997). https://doi.org/10.1007/3-540-69053-0_4

4. Chari, S., Jutla, C.S., Rao, J.R., Rohatgi, P.: Towards sound approaches to counteract power-analysis attacks. In: Wiener, M. (ed.) CRYPTO 1999. LNCS, vol. 1666, pp. 398–412. Springer, Heidelberg (1999). https://doi.org/10.1007/3-540-48405-1_26

5. Daemen, J., Dobraunig, C., Eichlseder, M., Groß, H., Mendel, F., Primas, R.: Protecting against statistical ineffective fault attacks. IACR Trans. Cryptogr. Hardw. Embed. Syst. **2020**(3), 508–543 (2020)

6. Damgård, I., Pastro, V., Smart, N., Zakarias, S.: Multiparty computation from somewhat homomorphic encryption. In: Safavi-Naini, R., Canetti, R. (eds.) CRYPTO 2012. LNCS, vol. 7417, pp. 643–662. Springer, Heidelberg (2012). https://doi.org/10.1007/978-3-642-32009-5_38

7. Dehbaoui, A., Dutertre, J.-M., Robisson, B., Tria, A.: Electromagnetic transient faults injection on a hardware and a software implementations of AES. In: Bertoni, G., Gierlichs, B. (eds.) 2012 Workshop on Fault Diagnosis and Tolerance in Cryptography, Leuven, Belgium, 9 September 2012, pp. 7–15. IEEE Computer Society (2012)

8. Dobraunig, C., Eichlseder, M., Gross, H., Mangard, S., Mendel, F., Primas, R.: Statistical ineffective fault attacks on masked AES with fault countermeasures. In: Peyrin, T., Galbraith, S. (eds.) ASIACRYPT 2018. LNCS, vol. 11273, pp. 315–342. Springer, Cham (2018). https://doi.org/10.1007/978-3-030-03329-3_11

9. Dobraunig, C., Eichlseder, M., Korak, T., Mangard, S., Mendel, F., Primas, R.: SIFA: exploiting ineffective fault inductions on symmetric cryptography. IACR Trans. Cryptogr. Hardw. Embed. Syst. **2018**(3), 547–572 (2018)

10. Gandolfi, K., Mourtel, C., Olivier, F.: Electromagnetic analysis: concrete results. In: Koç, Ç.K., Naccache, D., Paar, C. (eds.) CHES 2001. LNCS, vol. 2162, pp. 251–261. Springer, Heidelberg (2001). https://doi.org/10.1007/3-540-44709-1_21

11. Gross, H., Mangard, S.: Reconciling $d + 1$ masking in hardware and software. In: Fischer, W., Homma, N. (eds.) CHES 2017. LNCS, vol. 10529, pp. 115–136. Springer, Cham (2017). https://doi.org/10.1007/978-3-319-66787-4_6

12. Groß, H., Mangard, S., Korak, T.: Domain-oriented masking: compact masked hardware implementations with arbitrary protection order. In: Bilgin, B., Nikova, S., Rijmen, V. (eds.) Proceedings of the ACM Workshop on Theory of Implementation Security, TIS@CCS 2016 Vienna, Austria, October 2016, p. 3. ACM (2016)

13. Gross, H., Mangard, S., Korak, T.: An efficient side-channel protected AES implementation with arbitrary protection order. In: Handschuh, H. (ed.) CT-RSA 2017. LNCS, vol. 10159, pp. 95–112. Springer, Cham (2017). https://doi.org/10.1007/978-3-319-52153-4_6

14. Habing, D.H.: The use of lasers to simulate radiation-induced transients in semiconductor devices and circuits. IEEE Trans. Nucl. Sci. **12**(5), 91–100 (1965)

15. Ishai, Y., Sahai, A., Wagner, D.: Private circuits: securing hardware against probing attacks. In: Boneh, D. (ed.) CRYPTO 2003. LNCS, vol. 2729, pp. 463–481. Springer, Heidelberg (2003). https://doi.org/10.1007/978-3-540-45146-4_27

16. Kocher, P.C.: Timing attacks on implementations of Diffie-Hellman, RSA, DSS, and other systems. In: Koblitz, N. (ed.) CRYPTO 1996. LNCS, vol. 1109, pp. 104–113. Springer, Heidelberg (1996). https://doi.org/10.1007/3-540-68697-5_9

17. Kocher, P., Jaffe, J., Jun, B.: Differential power analysis. In: Wiener, M. (ed.) CRYPTO 1999. LNCS, vol. 1666, pp. 388–397. Springer, Heidelberg (1999). https://doi.org/10.1007/3-540-48405-1_25

18. Nikova, S., Rechberger, C., Rijmen, V.: Threshold implementations against side-channel attacks and glitches. In: Ning, P., Qing, S., Li, N. (eds.) ICICS 2006. LNCS, vol. 4307, pp. 529–545. Springer, Heidelberg (2006). https://doi.org/10.1007/11935308_38

19. Reparaz, O., Bilgin, B., Nikova, S., Gierlichs, B., Verbauwhede, I.: Consolidating masking schemes. In: Gennaro, R., Robshaw, M. (eds.) CRYPTO 2015. LNCS, vol. 9215, pp. 764–783. Springer, Heidelberg (2015). https://doi.org/10.1007/978-3-662-47989-6_37

20. Reparaz, O., et al.: CAPA: the spirit of beaver against physical attacks. In: Shacham, H., Boldyreva, A. (eds.) CRYPTO 2018. LNCS, vol. 10991, pp. 121–151. Springer, Cham (2018). https://doi.org/10.1007/978-3-319-96884-1_5

21. Saha, S., Bag, A., Jap, D., Mukhopadhyay, D., Bhasin, S.: Divided we stand, united we fall: security analysis of some SCA+SIFA countermeasures against SCA-enhanced fault template attacks. In: Tibouchi, M., Wang, H. (eds.) ASIACRYPT 2021. LNCS, vol. 13091, pp. 62–94. Springer, Cham (2021). https://doi.org/10.1007/978-3-030-92075-3_3

Deep-learning-based Side-channel Attacks

Exploring Multi-task Learning in the Context of Masked AES Implementations

Thomas Marquet[1(✉)] and Elisabeth Oswald[1,2]

[1] Digital Age Research Center (D!ARC), University of Klagenfurt,
Klagenfurt, Austria
{thomas.marquet,elisabeth.oswald}@aau.at
[2] University of Birmingham, Birmingham, UK

Abstract. Deep learning is very efficient at breaking masked implementations even when the attacker does not assume knowledge of the masks. However, recent works pointed out a significant challenge: overcoming the initial learning plateau. This paper discusses the advantages of multi-task learning to break through the initial plateau consistently. We investigate different ways of applying multi-task learning against masked AES implementations (via the ASCAD-r, ASCAD-v2, and CHESCTF-2023 datasets) under the assumption that the attacker cannot access masks during training. We offer evidence that multi-task learning significantly increases the consistency of convergence and performance of deep neural networks. Our work provides a wide range of experiments to understand the benefits of multi-task strategies over the current single-task state-of-the-art. Furthermore, such strategies achieve novel milestones against protected implementations as we propose models that defeat all masks of the affine masking on ASCAD-v2 for the first time.

Keywords: Side Channel Attacks · Masking · Deep Learning · Multi-Task Learning

1 Introduction

Deep learning techniques have quickly become an alternative to classical statistics in the context of profiled side-channel attacks because of their unrivaled ability to utilise information across many tracepoints efficiently. The approach taken by many deep learning architectures still somewhat depends on the thinking found in traditional statistics-based attacks: a single intermediate target is learned at a time (thus, a network is trained for each intermediate).

Recent publications have begun to move beyond this single-task learning paradigm towards a multi-task learning approach: Mahgrebi [6] explores a deep learning architecture to learn two intermediate values (bit-wise) on an AES implementation simultaneously; Masure and Strullu [9] revisit Mahgrebi's idea and learn many intermediate values simultaneously. They set a new record for a

© The Author(s), under exclusive license to Springer Nature Switzerland AG 2024
R. Wacquez and N. Homma (Eds.): COSADE 2024, LNCS 14595, pp. 93–112, 2024.
https://doi.org/10.1007/978-3-031-57543-3_6

"non-dissecting" approach for the ASCAD-v2 dataset and successfully recovered the key bytes with 60 traces when assuming knowledge of the masks during profiling. Their paper concludes by reflecting on the potential power of multi-task learning: "A further study of the advantages and drawbacks of such paradigm is yet to be done. Still, this could lead the SCA practitioner towards new milestones against protected implementations." (p. 21, [9]). Marquet et Oswald [7] further explore this multi-task learning and provide evidence that multi-task learning models have an edge over single-task models in a scenario where knowledge of the masks during training is not assumed.

1.1 Breaking Free of the "Plateau"

The "plateau" effect is a common problem when training deep learning models. This situation happens when the network encounters challenging topographies during the gradient descent, for example, being stuck in a local minimum. Masure et al. [8] discuss this problem in a side-channel context in the presence of masking. The authors link related works reporting similar learning curves. During the first epochs, the loss function marginally decreases until a sudden exponential drop happens for a few epochs before returning to "linear" learning. The authors interpret this phenomenon using the stochastic nature of deep learning. The gradient descent is stuck at the beginning, as no single point in the trace gives up information about the target in a straightforward manner (no first-order leakage), and the weights are initialised at random. This leads to very weak feedback from the back-propagation and indicates that a certain amount of luck on the initial starting point is involved.

Masure et al. [8] empirically demonstrate that the complexity of passing the plateau is exponential with the number of shares, as the feedback signal given by the labels is less and less related to the given inputs. Backed with classical deep learning literature, the authors hypothesize that the complexity of passing the plateau does not come from the choice of hyperparameters but rather the number of steps needed by the gradient descent to reach sufficient learning. This leaves the deep learning practitioners hints on how to improve model design.

1.2 Summary of Contributions and Outline

We discuss the ability of multi-task learning to break through the initial plateau consistently regardless of the initialization. We propose a novel idea for improving multi-task designs to focus the gradient flow and further improve deep learning models in a side-channel context. We focus on the application of multi-task learning in the context of the masked AES-128 implementations that are the basis of the ASCAD-r and ASCAD-v2 databases introduced in Prouff et al. [14] and Masure et Strullu [9]. We continue those experiments on the new CHESCTF-2023 dataset [16]. After providing some notation and background in Sect. 2, we introduce multi-task learning in Sect. 3, and our multi-task designs in Sect. 4. Finally, we present our experimental results in Sect. 5 on both datasets. Our innovations can be succinctly listed as follows:

Contributions

- We show that multi-task models reduce the variance introduced by the initialisation of the weights in the convergence of models.
- We propose to leverage multi-task learning to enable collaboration between different intermediates and/or different bytes of the same intermediates.
- We provide evidence that multi-task learning allows an attacker to leverage constraints to "guide" the learning of the model.
- We provide experimental evidence that such constraints are beneficial to the overall performance of the model but also its convergence speed.
- We compare novel multi-task architectures against state-of-the-art single-task designs.

With profiled attacks, the most challenging setting is the one where knowledge of the countermeasures is not assumed. In the context of masked implementations, we would then assume that—because of a lack of access to internal randomness—the training data cannot be labeled with masks or masked values, but only the (unmasked) intermediate values. Again, due to the absence of randomness information, a point of interest selection might not be feasible. Given that the application of multi-task learning to masked implementations is based on designing branches that learn masks and masked values, it is non-trivial to come up with a way to apply multi-task learning when masks are unknown. For this reason, we target multiple bytes at the same time to leverage common features between the masks of the targets. For example, a mask might be shared across bytes, but also, in the case of a state mask, the leakage of each byte of the mask might depend on the same underlying operations.

Reproducing Experiments. In order to make our experiments reproducible, we provide our code via a git repository (see link below). For convenience, we provide links to all utilsed data below as well.

- ASCAD-r
- ASCAD-v2
- Github

1.3   Related Works

Hu et al. [5] explains that it can be beneficial to use the data from the processing of the AES state bytes to train a single model representing an intermediate value. This is possible in the case of many software implementations because each state byte undergoes the same operations (the same sequence of Assembly instructions), which means that their leakage is very similar. Ngo et al. [10,11] shows a similar technique to reduce the size of the dataset to attack a masked Saber implementation.

Ngo et al. [10] and later on, Masure et al. [8] consider the possibility of assuming the presence of masking during the training of two models and propagating a loss on the combined probabilities from both outputs. Such training relieves the network by giving it a better understanding of what it should learn. The first authors, however, present bit-wise designs, while the latter's designs are over one hot encoded byte.

In the side-channel community, Mahgrebi [6] was the first to pick up on the idea of multi-task learning. Followed by Masure and Strullu [9] along with the first attacks on the ASCAD-v2 database. The core idea behind the existing architectures in these two previous works is that each intermediate value is learned by an independent branch of the deep net and that all branches are connected to several shared layers dealing with the higher-level features. This is the canonical design of multi-task networks, as summarised in [15]. Even though the work Masure and Strullu [9] introduces multi-task learning in a scenario where randomness is not known, their designs do not take advantage of the idea of Masure et al. [8], which demonstrate the benefits of layers that perform combined probabilities between two branches of a network to encode the masking scheme in the architecture. Marquet et Oswald. [7] showcase the benefits of said principles in a multi-task architecture. In a scenario where masks are unknown but shared, they demonstrate the superiority of multi-task learning over single-task learning. Finally, Bursztein et al. [1] presents SCANET, a multi-task architecture defeating multiple countermeasures against protected implementations of ECC. They also complete their investigation by discussing the performance of their architecture on the ASCAD-v2 dataset with full knowledge of the countermeasures during profiling.

2   Preliminaries

We stick to as simple notation as possible and stay with the variable naming conventions of the ASCAD databases: upper case letters denote sets (which we overload and simultaneously use as random variables), and lower case letters denote realisations of the random variables (and equivalently elements of a set). All variable/set names are taken (without renaming) from the original papers (implementations/data sets), such that "matching up" of our work with these original implementations is straightforward. The index i refers to the ith state byte, and we generally drop any indexing referring to points within a trace from our notation.

2.1   Profiling Based on Deep Learning

We consider side-channel attacks that operate in two stages: a leakage identification stage, where (if necessary) points of interest are selected and deep neural networks are trained, and a leakage exploitation stage, where the trained nets are used as classifiers in the context of differential side-channel attacks. During the leakage identification stage, traces are collected from a clone of the target device using random keys and plaintexts. After a variable amount of pre-processing, depending on the dataset, a model m_{θ_z} with hyperparameters θ_z is trained to recover the intermediate information $Z = \varphi(P, K)$ about one or multiple 8-bit key chunks (single-task or multi-task). Once the classifiers are trained, an attack dataset of N_a traces is collected on the target device, but this time with an unknown fixed key k^* and random plaintexts p. The i-th trace l_i is fed to the classifiers in order to recover the predictions $g_i = m_\theta(l_i)$. Finally the key guesses $d[k]$ is recovered using:

$$d[k] = \sum_{i=1}^{N_a} \log(g_i[z_i]), \text{ where } z_i = \varphi(p_i, k)$$

Training Methodology. We use the same methodology across all datasets. To enable meaningful comparisons, we train each approach with the same learning rate and optimizer. We compare each approach's abilities to learn a given task x with a given set of hyperparameters θ_x, initialized with the same weight values. This means that regardless of whether it is a single-task or a multi-task, each task x_i is learned using the same amount of weights and biases. The only difference between models is how the branches are connected.

As per good practice, we divide the available data into training data, validation data, and attack data. All training happens on the training data set. We validate a learned model on a validation set of size N_v. During this validation phase, we monitor the validation accuracy. Our best training model is selected based on the best validation loss, and we use a Tensorflow callback to retrieve this model.

2.2   Data Sets and Corresponding Notation

Our work is based on the ASCAD datasets as well as the new CHESCTF-2023 dataset, which are all based on masked AES implementations. We assume familiarity with low-order masking, as we keep the following text as short as possible.

ASCAD-r. The original ASCAD database (v1) features one data set of a masked AES implementation (on a simple 8-bit microcontroller) with varying keys, which we utilize in our work. The database is generous; each side channel trace offers many data points for inclusion in training. The dataset contains the information that relates to the masked computation of the AES SubBytes operation. The masking scheme is a simple two-share scheme, which precomputes a masked AES S-Box Table $SubBytes^*$ prior to encryption. The accompanying write-up for the database already performs an analysis to highlight the leakiest intermediate variables, which are the masked input and output of the SubBytes operation $(t_i \oplus r_{in}, s_i \oplus r_i)$ as well as the two involved masks r_i and r_{in} respectively the state mask, and the SubBytes input mask. We select in the dataset 60k traces from the random key split for training ($N_t = 50k$ traces) and validation ($N_v = 10k$ traces), and 10k from the fixed key split for the attack dataset ($N_a = 10k$ traces).

Several papers have reported results for this database for a variety of network architectures and approaches. Our approach is to work with the raw traces (thus no points of interest selection take place). With this setting in mind, the best previous work is Perin et al. [13], which reached single trace success for some key bytes—culminating in 3 traces for the most resilient key bytes.

ASCAD-v2. The ASCAD-v2 dataset contains traces from a masked and shuffled AES implementation (on a more complex 32-bit architecture); however, **the shuffling is disabled in this work**. The full dataset contains 800k traces with random keys and inputs. Each trace has 1 million sample points. The masking scheme is slightly more complex. It uses both a non-zero multiplicative mask β, as well as a Boolean mask α, i.e., each intermediate value x is represented by three shares: $(x \otimes \beta \oplus \alpha, \beta, \alpha)$ (the multiplication must be understood over the appropriate finite field). We take a special interest in the masked SubBytes inputs $r_m \otimes t_j \oplus r_{in}$, outputs $r_m \otimes s_j \oplus r_{out}$, the multiplicative mask r_m, and the corresponding additive masks r_{in} and r_{out}. We craft our dataset with a subsampling using a moving average in the way of Perin et al. [13] on ASCAD-r. This divides the number of total samples by 4. We extract from the traces the points of interest of the masks using SnR analysis and the samples related to the first round of SubBytes operation. After shuffling all traces, we split the available data into training ($N_t = 450$k traces), validation ($N_v = 45$k traces), and attack ($N_a = 5$k traces) data sets.

This dataset has successful attacks in two situations where the countermeasures are toned down. The first one by Masure et Strullu. [9] has a successful attack without requiring the knowledge of the permutations but also without requiring the knowledge of the multiplicative mask. The paper Marquet et Oswald. [7] provides successful attacks when the additive mask r_{in} is unknown. The best results for a full key recovery attack depend on the scenario. For a scenario where knowledge of masks and permutations is assumed during profiling but not during an attack, the best attack of Masure et Strullu. [9] takes 60 traces. In the same scenario, Bursztein et al. [1] reach full key recovery with around 80 traces. Wu et al. [21] present two non-profiled attacks on the dataset. The first utilises the fact that each byte shares the same masks to perform collision attacks and recover most of the key bytes with around 70k traces. The second attack takes advantage of the fact that an intermediate value of 0 effectively removes the multiplicative mask. Using correlations between the SubBytes patterns and the pattern of the additive mask, they show decreasing key ranks with around 500k attack traces. Finally, the best attacks of Marquet et Oswald. [7] take 21 traces, assuming knowledge of permutations and the multiplicative mask r_m during attack and profiling.

CHESCTF-2023 (Spartan-6). The CHESCTF-2023 contained two datasets. Both are based on an AES implementation, using a 32-bit datapath with state-of-the-art Hardware Private Circuits (HPC) masking [3] (two shares). We elect to use the dataset that was released without information about the masks: this requires training without the knowledge of masks (thus, the situation is akin to what we have in the selected ASCAD datasets). This dataset was sampled from a Spartan-6 FPGA. Adopting the notation from the ASCAD datasets, the S-box inputs can be represented as $t_i \oplus r_i$ for each 8-bit chunk. We do not pre-process the traces, but we extract the samples related to the clock cycles of the S-box computation. The winning strategy on this target is taking advantage of the transition leakages on the S-box input wires. On the last column bytes (1,6,11,12), the transitions leak the full value of the bytes since they transition to zero. Therefore, those specific bytes leak significantly stronger than the others, and our discussion will be limited to those bytes. There is no state of the art on this dataset besides the challenge participants, with the winner reaching a full key rank of 2^{68} with 901k traces [16].

2.3   Custom Layers: Xor and Inverse multGF256

Masure et al. [8] introduced the idea of using custom layers. They calculate the conditional probabilities using FFTs between the softmax layers of two models trained during the same process. Our implementation calculates the conditional probabilities directly using a parallelized version of the following computations. Given two vectors x and y of size 256:

$$f_\oplus(x,y)[i] = \sum_{j=0}^{255} x[j] \times y[i \oplus j] \ \ \forall \ i \ \in \ [0, 255] \tag{1}$$

$$f_\otimes(x,y)[i] = x[0] + \sum_{j=1}^{255} x[j] \times y[i \otimes j] \ \ \forall \ i \ \in \ [0, 255] \tag{2}$$

The function $f_\otimes$ has to discriminate the first case where $j = 0$, being a null element. We decided that, in this case, the probabilities of x should be unchanged.

2.4   Single-Task Designs

We define *a single-task model as a model that is trained using the knowledge of only one label*. In our scenario, where access to internal randomness is not assumed, this means that we have a model labeled with the unmasked value of an intermediate. State-of-the-art single-task designs against masked implementations are composed of d-branches networks in the like of Masure et al. [9] and Ngo et al. [10], one for each share. We note each branch's hyperparameters $\theta_1, ..., \theta_d$. If points of interest from each share cannot be extracted and fed directly to the respective branch, the same trace points are fed to all the branches after passing through a shared part of the network used to process the inputs θ_Y. Examples of such architectures are given in Fig. 1.

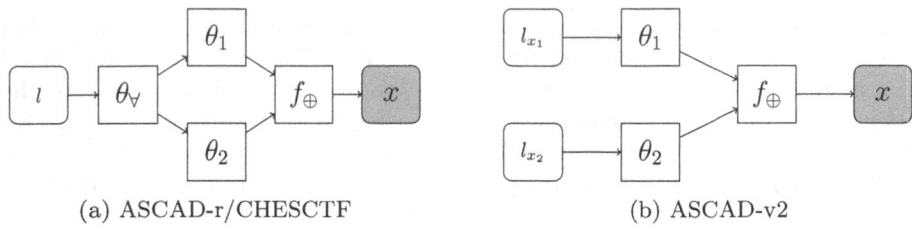

(a) ASCAD-r/CHESCTF   (b) ASCAD-v2

Fig. 1. Single-task architectures using $d = 2$ branches.

3   Multi-task Learning

Multi-task learning has been introduced by Caruana [2] and has become state-of-the-art in many pattern recognition domains. Multi-task models benefit from the knowledge of multiple labels during training through collaboration among all tasks. Given N tasks x_i, the respective set of hyperparameters θ_{x_i}, the resulting loss $\mathcal{L}_{x_i}$ and the associated weight λ_i, the multi-task learning objective can be defined as the weighted sum:

$$\mathcal{L}_{mtl}(\theta) = \sum_{i=1}^{N} \lambda_i \mathcal{L}_{x_i}(\theta_{x_i})$$

Hard-Parameter Sharing. To enable collaboration of tasks within the network, one must introduce relationships between each task's hyperparameters. One way to achieve this is through hard-parameter sharing. Considering two tasks x_1 and x_2, with the underlying hyperparameters θ_{x_1}, θ_{x_2} related to their respective tasks, hard-parameter sharing can be defined as the requirement that at least some hyperparameters are shared between the tasks: $\theta_{x_1} \cap \theta_{x_2} \neq \emptyset$. By this logic, sharing convolutions or layers at the beginning of the network is already hard-parameter sharing. However, sharing layers close to the input is usually made to share higher-level features. Going further down the network with shared layers means, on the contrary, sharing lower-level features. The difficulty of sharing the latter comes from the fact that the output must be different but obtained with similar inputs and the same weights. Once relationships are established between the hyperparameters of different tasks, according to Caruana [2] and Ruder [15], multi-task learning brings potential benefits such as:

- **Input explainability:** Assuming two tasks x_1 and x_2, the inputs l given to the network could be explained using $l = f(x_1, x_2) + \epsilon_{noise}$. Approximating the function f through the weights of the network is expected to be easier if it has knowledge of x_1 and x_2.
- **Noise cancellation:** If x_1 and x_2 share features, the gradient will be averaged over both tasks, therefore reducing the noise.
- **Eavesdropping:** If x_1 has a stronger signal-to-noise ratio than x_2 and both share features. Then, training both at the same time is beneficial for x_2, as the shared features will be highlighted by x_1.

– **Representation bias:** Constraining the network by encoding relationships between tasks prevents the gradient from falling into local minima that do not benefit all tasks. This reduces the search problem by removing unfitting weight representations.

4   Multi-task Designs

4.1   Competition or Collaboration

One of the main drawbacks of multi-task learning is the possibility of two tasks competing against each other. Understanding the potential collaboration between tasks is key to successful multi-task design. It is not clear if straight-forward multi-task learning using high-level parameter sharing as presented in Caruana [2], and then applied to the side-channel domain [1,6,9,19] is beneficial. The potential competition between multiple gradients can damage the learning of one or multiple tasks, as explained in Standley et al. [17] or in Yu et al. [22]. Special care has to be ensured so that tasks are effectively collaborating with each other. Marquet et Oswald [7] introduce the idea that one can utilise the knowledge of a shared mask between multiple bytes of a targeted intermediate. It is by encoding known relationships into the network that the superiority of multi-task learning can be leveraged. With this philosophy in mind, we expand on the idea of masks that are not shared.

4.2   Parameter Sharing

The idea of using d-branch networks can be utilized in the context of multi-task learning. If we call n_t the number of tasks, then the corresponding multi-task network has $n_t \times d$ branches. In this section, we explain three different ways to connect the different tasks through hard-parameter sharing, with the aim of enabling positive collaboration between the tasks.

To compare these multi-task designs with a suitable single-task reference design, we proceed as follows: if leakages are extracted, and no shared layer $\theta_\forall$ is introduced in the network, then parts related to each task are completely independent of each other. Training the resulting network is equivalent to training n_t single-task models in parallel, and we will use this strategy to train suitable single-task reference networks.

High-Level Parameter Sharing. The classical use of multi-task learning introduced by Caruana [2] is based on the utilization of shared layers to process the input. In our designs, we use a set of layers $\theta_\forall$ close to the inputs to perform extraction of interesting information and propagate this information to each branch of the network. The intuition is that the multiple tasks will collaborate to explain the given inputs and share their knowledge at this level. In the case of the ASCAD-v2 dataset, those layers are not used because the inputs are extracted manually, like in Fig. 1b.

Shared Randomness. In a single-task context, regardless of whether (or not) a mask is shared between multiple intermediates, the information gained about the common randomness cannot be transmitted to the other classifiers. In a multi-task context where all intermediates share the same randomness, one can design a network with $n_t + (d-1)$ branches. Each task x_i, will benefit from the individual hyperparameters θ_i, while sharing the common randomness hyperparameters such that $\theta_{x_i} = \{\theta_i, \theta_{n_t+1}, \dots, \theta_{n_t+d-1}\}$ and $\theta_{x_1} \cap \dots \cap \theta_{x_{n_t}} = \{\theta_{n_t+1}, \dots, \theta_{n_t+d-1}\}$. For the shared randomness, each branch connects the tasks to allow collaboration. The $f_\oplus$ layer acts as a constraint, forcing each branch to take a very specific representation (conditional probabilities). The cumulative effect of those constraints, thanks to multi-task learning, is a natural improvement.

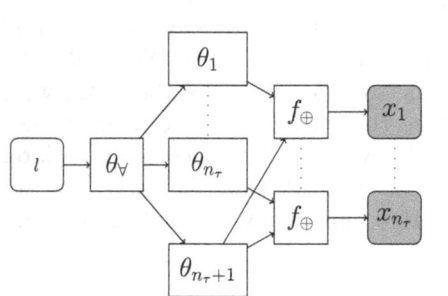
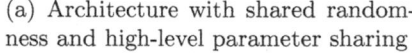
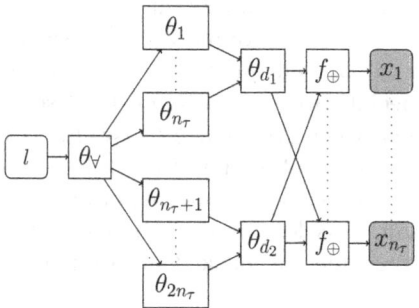

(a) Architecture with shared random-ness and high-level parameter sharing

(b) Architecture with high-level and low-level parameter sharing

Fig. 2. Examples of multi-task architectures using different parameter sharing with d = 2 shares

Low-Level Parameter Sharing. To maximize the sharing of weights for all tasks, we design models that share the same weights for the resp. prediction head leading to the introduction of θ_{d_i} in Fig. 2b. The resulting network possesses d-branches even though it is learning n_t tasks. This additional layer encourages the preceding layers to agree on weights that are consistent across all bytes. This strategy may help, especially initially, when the network is initialized to a random initial state, which may, in turn, enable it to overcome the initial "plateau".

Strategies, where one leverages the common features between bytes, are very successful in a single-task scenario [4,5,10,11]. Our strategy is an adaptation of such a technique in a multi-task learning scenario. Since a single-task scenario requires extraction and alignment of the related samples, a direct adaptation would also require such a constraint. However, we can design models in case such extraction is not possible. At least $n_t \times d$ individual layers have to be introduced in order to create n_t channels that will be fed to the shared layers. Therefore, our modeling does not need the extraction and alignment of each byte leakage in the trace, as it is done by the network instead of being a pre-processing step.

5   Results

Overcoming the initial plateau is the main interest of this paper. With this in mind, we take a special interest in which epoch the model converges. Throughout our experiments, we wish to discuss the performance of our designs against single-task learning but also the improvement from sharing weights at a lower level of the network. To do so, we train our designs ten times using a different seed for the initialization of each weight. We then observe the properties of the different architectures with respect to multiple starting points. Initialisation of the training procedure has a significant impact on the potential convergence of a deep learning architecture, especially in SCA, as showed in Wu et al. [20]. Each design possesses the same number of weights for each task; the difference is the total amount of weights, as some weights are used multiple times. This technique aims to efficiently utilize all the information available in one trace to maximize the chances of breaking through the initial plateau. We take a special interest in the following metrics: the number of traces T_{win} to recover the key, ratio of seeds $n_{\text{win}}/n_{\text{seeds}}$ leading to a full recovery of the key and finally the epoch of convergence e_c. The epoch e_c can be clearly identified manually on the ASCAD datasets, as the learning slope drastically changes when the model reaches convergence. Examples of such slopes are given in Masure et al. [8], Timon [18], Perin and Picek [12]. To automate the process, we regress the next epoch loss value based on the previous epochs and observe when the squared difference between the regressed loss and the real value is above a threshold. We give an example of such a process in Fig. 3, where we plot the losses and the selected epochs of convergence for each seed of one model type. However, the loss changes on the CHESCTF are minimal because of the low learning rate used to capture the weak signal. Therefore, on this dataset, we note the epoch of convergence e_c as the first epoch where the validation loss is under the random guess of cross entropy. This method of acquisition is less meaningful as a model can converge and not immediately generalise to the validation split.

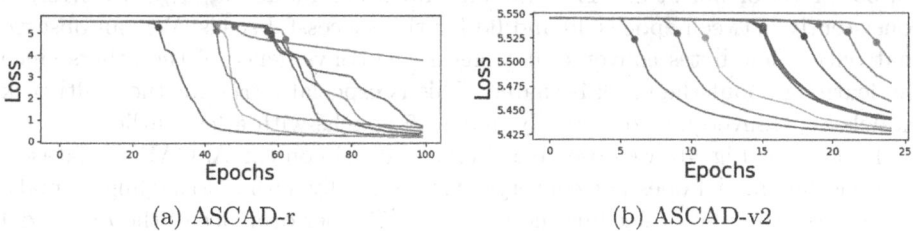

(a) ASCAD-r   (b) ASCAD-v2

Fig. 3. Examples of the acquisition of the epoch of convergence for all seeds of one model type.

5.1 Leveraging Common Masks with a Shared Branch

In the special case where each byte of an intermediate shares a mask, we can take advantage of architectures with a shared branch. Such weaknesses are found in both ASCAD datasets. On ASCAD-r, all bytes of the SubBytes inputs share a strongly leaking mask r_{in}, and on ASCAD-v2, all bytes share r_m and r_{in} for the S-box inputs, and r_m and r_{out} for the S-box outputs.

ASCAD-r. The targeted leakage pair is $(t \oplus r_{in}, r_{in})$. Using the raw traces, we train a baseline multi-task model in the likes of Fig. 2a noted $m_{n_t+(d-1)}$ which posses high-level parameter sharing, and share the mask branch across all intermediates. We extend this design with low-level parameter sharing that we note m_d. Finally, we train 14 single-task models m_s according to the design in Fig. 1a. We show a scatter plot of the epochs of convergence for each target byte and all approaches in Fig. 4a. Then, we perform a full key recovery attack, 1000 times over 100 randomly picked raw traces from the attack dataset, and note the results in Table 1.

ASCAD-v2. To further investigate the impact of constraints on multi-task models, we experiment with a scenario where only the additive mask r_{out} is unknown. Knowledge of r_m is given to the network during profiling and attack, reducing the masking scheme's complexity. The targets are the S-box outputs, $r_m \otimes s \oplus r_{out}$, and the mask r_{out}. To increase the difference in performance between each approach, we reduce the size of the training dataset to only 225k traces. The architectures used in this experiment are the same as in the previous one, with a multi-input design in the likes of Fig. 1b since the dataset is extracted. Again, we show a scatter plot of the epochs of convergence for each target byte and all approaches in Fig. 4b and note the performance metrics of an attack with 200 traces over 1000 experiments in Table 1.

On the ASCAD-r dataset Fig. 4a, we first see that the learning of single-task models varies greatly. Depending on the seed, the st converges around the epoch 20, 30, or 70, or not at all. The baseline multi-task model $m_{n_t+(d-1)}$ converges consistently between epochs 40 and 60 for the successful seeds. We can observe that once a few bytes converge, it triggers the convergence of the others since the learning about the mask is shared. This is especially true for the multi-task models m_d, converging consistently under 35 epochs with a few outliers.

Looking at Fig. 4b, we observe a similar scenario on the ASCAD-v2 dataset. The baseline model does not converge systematically, either struggling to make sense of the samples or needing more epochs. The performance of the m_d model also coincides with the previous dataset, as it consistently outperforms the baseline model and manages to converge on all seeds. Finally, on this intermediate, only one single-task model managed to learn its target byte. This is another example of the superiority of multi-task approaches, especially in this scenario where masks are shared among different intermediates.

No seed allowed the single-task models to recover all bytes on both datasets. The baseline multi-task model $m_{n_t+(d-1)}$ recovers the full key with six seeds also

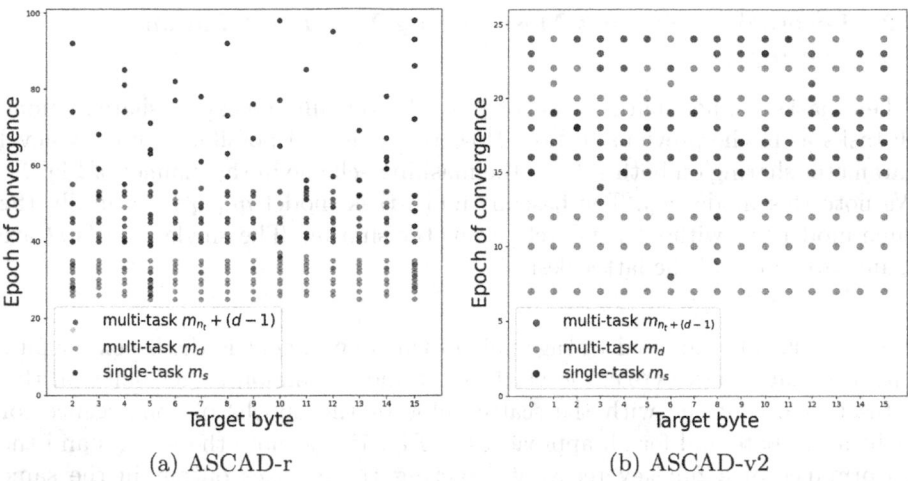

(a) ASCAD-r   (b) ASCAD-v2

Fig. 4. Epoch of convergence for all seeds and targeted bytes in the scenario where the mask is shared across them.

Table 1. Performance metrics for the experiment leveraging a shared mask

Model type	ASCAD-r				ASCAD-v2			
	f_r	$n_{\mathrm{win}}/n_{\mathrm{seeds}}$	$\overline{T_{\mathrm{win}}}$	$best\ T_{\mathrm{win}}$	f_r	$n_{\mathrm{win}}/n_{\mathrm{seeds}}$	$\overline{T_{\mathrm{win}}}$	$best\ T_{\mathrm{win}}$
m_s	0.56	0.0	>100	>100	0.99	0.0	>200	>200
$m_{n_t+(d-1)}$	0.4	0.6	**4.33**	4	0.4	0.6	134	98
m_d	**0.0**	**1.0**	5.8	**2**	**0.0**	**1.0**	118.1	**92**

on both datasets, while the multi-task model with low-level parameter sharing m_d is successful on all seeds. Trace-wise, the baseline multi-task model is, on average, more performant than the m_d model on the ASCAD-r dataset. This is a bias in the mean calculation from more difficult seeds that are excluded since they are not successful with the baseline multi-task model. The baseline multi-task model is also outperformed by the model with low-level parameter sharing.

We can observe in that scenario that multi-task learning is vastly superior to single-task learning in terms of consistency. Moreover, the more the multi-task models are constrained through parameter sharing, the more consistent they are. Many multi-task-induced effects can be the cause of this improvement in consistency. The first one is the regularisation from the shared mask. All bytes collaborate to learn the mask, and therefore, the branch of the mask benefits from multiple gradients. In addition, the weights from individual bytes are not free to explore representations that do not benefit others. This effect is further reinforced by the sharing of low-level weights. As the model mt_{2d} improves significantly, the baseline model m_0, in convergence speed, but also in the success of convergence.

5.2   Leveraging Different Masks Using Low-Level Parameter Sharing

When masks are not shared, it is not possible to train one expert shared among all tasks as in the previous section. However, it is still possible to use low-level parameter sharing on both sides of the masking scheme in the manner of Fig. 2b. We note this model m_d. The baseline multi-task model $m_{n_t.d}$ is naturally the same model but without low-level parameter sharing. The single models st are again submodels of the latter design.

ASCAD-r. The targeted leakage pair in this experiment is the S-box outputs with the state mask $(s \oplus r, r)$, which is the most common target point on this dataset. We continue with the scatter plot of the epochs of convergence for each target byte and for all approaches in Fig. 5a and note the metrics and the performance of a full key recovery targeting the S-boxes output in the same setup as the previous experiment in Table 2.

CHESCTF. The targeted leakage pair can be noted as $(t \oplus r, r)$, corresponding to the S-box inputs with the state mask. The specificity of this dataset is that both share leaks at the same samples, and all targeted bytes are within the same 32-bit word. Since each 8-bit chunk is not a "repetition" of the same piece of code or wire, their leakage features are different. This allows us to observe the impact of low-level parameter sharing in a case where it is not optimal. Moreover, since we are only targeting four tasks at a time, we benefit less from multi-tasking than in the previous experiments. We plot the epoch where the validation loss crosses the random guess threshold in Fig. 5b and the rank evolution of each targeted byte over 100 iterations of an attack using 102400 traces in Fig. 6.

Figure 5a shows similar results to those in the previous scenario on ASCAD-r. Single-task models m_s are inconsistent and mostly converge after the multi-task models. Looking closely, one can see that some bytes do not possess even one successful seed in this experiment. Moving on to the multi-task models, we can see, overall, the epoch of convergence being a lot more inconsistent than in the previous experiments where the mask was shared by all bytes. This indicates that the shared mask strongly benefits the training process. While for the single-task models, the number of successful convergences is inferior to the previous experiment, the baseline model $m_{n_t.d}$ learns overall seeds, more bytes. This can be explained by the highest signal-to-noise ratio. The design m_d successfully converges on all seeds. The sharing of weights managed to force collaboration between each byte, leading to consistent learning. We also observe a faster convergence for the latter model than any other one, once again hinting at its superior learning ability.

From Table 2, we observe that no seed led to successful key recovery using the single-task models m_s. Furthermore, no seed allowed byte 12 to converge, and therefore, even by picking the best models across all seeds, a successful attack would not have been possible. The baseline model $m_{n_t.d}$ succeeded on four

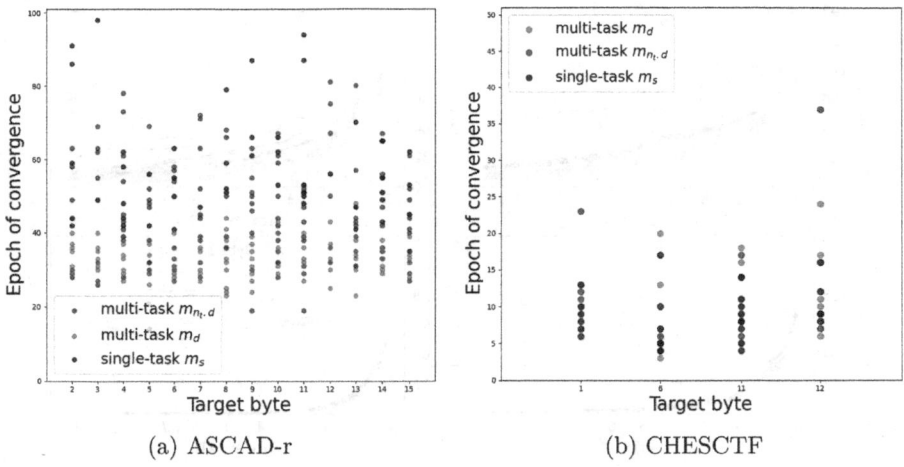

(a) ASCAD-r (b) CHESCTF

Fig. 5. Epoch of convergence for all seeds and targeted bytes, in a scenario where randomness is not shared

Table 2. Performance metrics for the experiment leveraging a shared mask

Model type	ASCAD-r			
	f_r	$n_{\text{win}}/n_{\text{seeds}}$	$\overline{T}_{\text{win}}$	$best\ T_{\text{win}}$
m_s	0.69	0.0	>100	>100
$m_{n_t.d}$	0.21	0.4	**6**	5
m_d	**0.0**	**1.0**	2.13	**2**

seeds to recover the key, with an average performance of 6 traces. Finally, hard-parameter sharing successfully improved the success rate of multi-task models, as m_d recovers the full key with around two traces on average. However, even though all seeds led to convergence, 100 traces were not enough for two seeds, as the learning suffered from too much overfitting.

On the CHESCTF dataset Fig. 5b, we observe when the model generalizes enough to be better than a random guess. All approaches generalise enough, if they do, around the same epochs, with a slight advantage for multi-task learning. This is due to the relatively high number of traces and low number of tasks. Additionally, said tasks are not expected to collaborate at a low level since they are different chunks from the same 32-bit word. Still, the model m_d, benefiting from the regularization induced by having to share more weights, generalize over all seeds, while 21% of the time, the model $m_{n_t.d}$ fail to gather enough information. This failure rate is even more considerable for single-task models with 69%.

Looking at the key ranking Fig. 6, we can observe first that the two lower bytes in the word, bytes 12 and 1, are harder to learn and recover than the two higher bytes, 6 and 11. We can observe a clear ranking of the designs, the

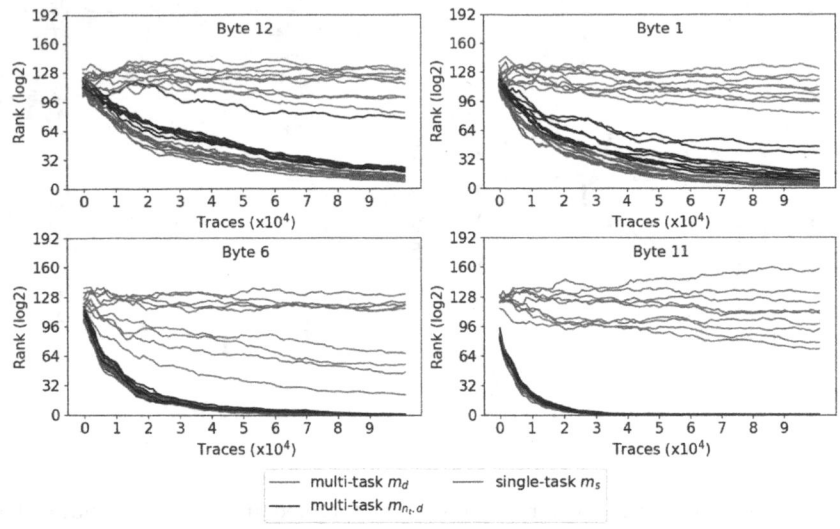

Fig. 6. Key rank evolution for all targeted bytes and for each seed

best being the model with low-level parameter sharing m_d, which takes full advantage of the regularization induced by having fewer weights. Second, the baseline multi-task model $m_{n_t.d}$, struggling to recover the designated key byte only on a couple of seeds. Finally, the single-task model is able to reduce the key ranks. The difference between the two multi-task models is small; however, as they learn the full word and not a single 8-bit chunk, they clearly outperform the single-task approach thanks to the high-level shared parameters.

5.3   Leveraging Different Targets Masked by the Same Randomness

On the ASCAD-v2 dataset, the affine masking scheme shares the multiplicative mask between $r_m \otimes s_j \oplus r_{out}$ and $r_m \otimes t_j \oplus r_{in}$. We design multi-target models that learn the unmasked S-box input and output at the same time, allowing us to take advantage of the shared multiplicative mask. We expect branches learning the different intermediates to collaborate on how to fit r_m. Based on this idea, we train the two usual models, $m_{n_t+(d-1)}$ and its counterpart m_d using low-level parameter sharing. Finally, to understand the impact of training multiple intermediates, we additionally train a model without this "multi-target" approach. **In this section, only multi-task models are trained.** We note this model m_{st-d}, as it learns only t_j through the triplet $(r_m \otimes t_j \oplus r_{in}\ ,\ r_m\ ,\ r_{in})$, using low-level parameter sharing. We note the main performance metrics after performing the usual full key recovery in Table 3 and plot the evolution of the losses in Fig. 7b.

The single-target model m_{st-d}, trained using only the labels from the unmasked S-box inputs, fails to converge consistently, even though the leakage from the S-box inputs triplet is considerably higher than the second triplet

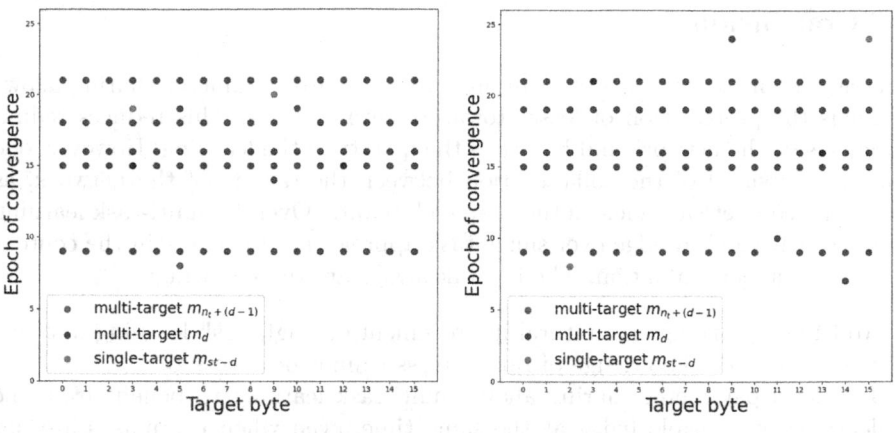

(a) Convergences related to the S-box inputs t_j

(b) Convergences related to the S-box outputs s_j

Fig. 7. Epoch of convergence for all seeds and targeted intermediates

linked to the S-box outputs. Moreover, the model $m_{n_t+(d-1)}$, using a multi-target strategy during training but no low-level parameter sharing, also fails to converge consistently. Only the model m_d leveraging a multi-target strategy **during training** and low-level hard-parameter sharing converge multiple times. This feat, repeated five times while the other model never converges, is a testimony to the importance of linking potential collaboration between intermediates even during training.

Table 3. Performance metrics against the full affine masking on ASCAD-v2

Model type	$n_{\text{win}}/n_{\text{seeds}}$	$\overline{T_{\text{win}}}$	$best\ T_{\text{win}}$
m_{st-d}	0.0	>200	>200
$m_{n_t+(d-1)}$	0.0	>200	>200
m_d	**0.5**	**17.6**	**16**

Observing the performances of the different models on a full key recovery attack, we see that every seed leading to convergence during training also leads to successful attacks with good performances. Our best model recovers the full key in only 16 traces and is, to the best of our knowledge, the best attack on ASCAD-v2, even in this simplified scenario, where PoIs from the masks are assumed and permutations are disabled.

6   Conclusion

Among all our experiments, we can observe that hard-parameter sharing allows to focus the propagation of losses towards fewer weights. This reduces redundancy inside the network and increases the quality of the learning. However, one has to be assured of the collaboration between the targets of the network, as losses can compete as much as they can collaborate. Overall, multi-task learning seems to have a clear edge over single-task approaches, especially in the context of a side-channel evaluation. The key takeaways are the following:

– Multi-task learning is a natural improvement of single-task learning in a scenario where the knowledge of randomness cannot be accessed.
– Low-level parameter sharing allows multi-task learning to benefit from the learning of multiple bytes at the same time, even when the masks are not shared.
– Multi-task learning breaks through the initial plateau more consistently
– Constraints on the network further increase the previous point.
– Multi-task learning allows an attacker to take advantage of multi-target strategies even during profiling.

Our results contribute to the research of multi-task deep learning models in the context of side-channel key recovery attacks. We extend previous results from Marquet et Oswald [7] to more challenging scenarios where masks are not shared by multiple potential targets but also show positive interaction between intermediates. We show that linking potential common features and accumulating constraints on the network benefits the network by reducing overfitting and further enables models to lead successful attacks. In addition, we target the multiple masks of the ASCAD-v2 and successfully build an attack using the previously introduced concepts. We suggest that more complex architectures, adding helpful constraints on the network, would further improve the chances of an attacker finding successful attacks.

Acknowledgments. Thomas Marquet and Elisabeth Oswald have been supported in part by the European Research Council (ERC) under the European Union's Horizon 2020 research and innovation program (grant agreement No 725042).

References

1. Bursztein, E., Invernizzi, L., Král, K., Moghimi, D., Picod, J.M., Zhang, M.: Generic attacks against cryptographic hardware through long-range deep learning (2023)
2. Caruana, R.: Multitask learning. In: Thrun, S., Pratt, L.Y. (eds.) Learning to Learn, pp. 95–133. Springer, Boston (1998). https://doi.org/10.1007/978-1-4615-5529-2_5
3. Cassiers, G., Grégoire, B., Levi, I., Standaert, F.X.: Hardware private circuits: from trivial composition to full verification. IEEE Trans. Comput. (2020). https://doi.org/10.1109/tc.2020.3022979. https://inria.hal.science/hal-03133227

4. Dubrova, E., Ngo, K., Gärtner, J., Wang, R.: Breaking a fifth-order masked implementation of crystals-kyber by copy-paste. In: Proceedings of the 10th ACM Asia Public-Key Cryptography Workshop, APKC 2023, pp. 10–20. Association for Computing Machinery, New York (2023). https://doi.org/10.1145/3591866.3593072
5. Hu, F., Wang, H., Wang, J.: Cross-subkey deep-learning side-channel analysis. Cryptology ePrint Archive, Report 2021/1328 (2021). https://eprint.iacr.org/2021/1328
6. Maghrebi, H.: Deep learning based side-channel attack: a new profiling methodology based on multi-label classification. Cryptology ePrint Archive, Report 2020/436 (2020). https://eprint.iacr.org/2020/436
7. Marquet, T., Oswald, E.: A comparison of multi-task learning and single-task learning approaches. Cryptology ePrint Archive, Paper 2023/611 (2023). https://doi.org/10.1007/978-3-031-16815-4. https://eprint.iacr.org/2023/611
8. Masure, L., Cristiani, V., Lecomte, M., Standaert, F.X.: Don't learn what you already know: scheme-aware modeling for profiling side-channel analysis against masking. IACR Trans. Cryptographic Hardware Embed. Syst. **2023**(1), 32–59 (2022). https://doi.org/10.46586/tches.v2023.i1.32-59. https://tches.iacr.org/index.php/TCHES/article/view/9946
9. Masure, L., Strullu, R.: Side-channel analysis against Anssi's protected AES implementation on arm: end-to-end attacks with multi-task learning. J. Cryptographic Eng. **13**, 1–19 (2023). https://doi.org/10.1007/s13389-023-00311-7
10. Ngo, K., Dubrova, E., Guo, Q., Johansson, T.: A side-channel attack on a masked IND-CCA secure saber KEM implementation. IACR Trans. Cryptographic Hardware Embed. Syst. **2021**(4), 676–707 (2021). https://doi.org/10.46586/tches.v2021.i4.676-707. https://tches.iacr.org/index.php/TCHES/article/view/9079
11. Ngo, K., Wang, R., Dubrova, E., Paulsrud, N.: Higher-order Boolean masking does not prevent side-channel attacks on LWE/LWR-based PKE/KEMs. In: 2023 IEEE 53rd International Symposium on Multiple-Valued Logic (ISMVL), pp. 190–195 (2023). https://doi.org/10.1109/ISMVL57333.2023.00044
12. Perin, G., Picek, S.: On the influence of optimizers in deep learning-based side-channel analysis. In: Dunkelman, O., Jacobson, M.J., Jr., O'Flynn, C. (eds.) Selected Areas in Cryptography, pp. 615–636. Springer, Cham (2021). https://doi.org/10.1007/978-3-030-81652-0_24
13. Perin, G., Wu, L., Picek, S.: Exploring feature selection scenarios for deep learning-based side-channel analysis. IACR Trans. Cryptographic Hardware Embed. Syst. **2022**(4), 828–861 (2022). https://doi.org/10.46586/tches.v2022.i4.828-861. https://tches.iacr.org/index.php/TCHES/article/view/9842
14. Prouff, E., Strullu, R., Benadjila, R., Cagli, E., Canovas, C.: Study of deep learning techniques for side-channel analysis and introduction to ascad database. IACR Cryptology ePrint Archive **2018**, 53 (2018). https://api.semanticscholar.org/CorpusID:41991837
15. Ruder, S.: An overview of multi-task learning in deep neural networks. CoRR abs/1706.05098 (2017)
16. SIMPLE-Crypto: Smaesh-challenge leaderboard (2023/2023). https://smaesh-challenge.simple-crypto.org/leaderboard.html
17. Standley, T., Zamir, A., Chen, D., Guibas, L.J., Malik, J., Savarese, S.: Which tasks should be learned together in multi-task learning? CoRR abs/1905.07553 (2019). http://arxiv.org/abs/1905.07553
18. Timon, B.: Non-profiled deep learning-based side-channel attacks with sensitivity analysis. IACR Trans. Cryptographic Hardware Embed. Syst. **2019**(2),

107–131 (2019). https://doi.org/10.13154/tches.v2019.i2.107-131. https://tches.iacr.org/index.php/TCHES/article/view/7387

19. Weissbart, L., Picek, S.: Lightweight but not easy: side-channel analysis of the ascon authenticated cipher on a 32-bit microcontroller. Cryptology ePrint Archive, Paper 2023/1598 (2023). https://eprint.iacr.org/2023/1598

20. Wu, L., Perin, G., Picek, S.: On the evaluation of deep learning-based side-channel analysis. In: Balasch, J., O'Flynn, C. (eds.) Constructive Side-Channel Analysis and Secure Design, pp. 49–71. Springer, Cham (2022). https://doi.org/10.1007/978-3-030-99766-3_3

21. Wu, L., Perin, G., Picek, S.: Not so difficult in the end: breaking the ASCADv2 dataset. Cryptology ePrint Archive (2023)

22. Yu, T., Kumar, S., Gupta, A., Levine, S., Hausman, K., Finn, C.: Gradient surgery for multi-task learning. CoRR abs/2001.06782 (2020). https://arxiv.org/abs/2001.06782

The Need for MORE: Unsupervised Side-Channel Analysis with Single Network Training and Multi-output Regression

Ioana Savu[1], Marina Krček[2], Guilherme Perin[3], Lichao Wu[4],
and Stjepan Picek[4]([✉])

[1] NXP Semiconductors, Eindhoven, The Netherlands
[2] Delft University of Technology, Delft, The Netherlands
[3] Leiden University, Leiden, The Netherlands
[4] Radboud University, Nijmegen, The Netherlands
picek.stjepan@gmail.com

Abstract. This work explores the performance of multi-output regression models in side-channel analysis. We start with the recently proposed multi-output regression (MOR) approach for non-profiling side-channel analysis. Then, we significantly improve its performance by updating the loss function and distinguisher, then employing a novel concept of validation set to reduce overfitting. We denote our approach as MORE - Multi-Output Regression Enhanced, which emphasizes significantly better attack performance than MOR. Our results demonstrate that combining the MORE methodology, ensembles, and data augmentation presents a potent strategy for enhancing non-profiling side-channel attack performance and improving the reliability of distinguishing key candidates.

Keywords: Side-channel Analysis · Deep learning · Non-profiling · Regression

1 Introduction

Side-channel attacks (SCAs) explore unintended leakage of information from secure devices. To evaluate the threats from such attacks, security certification methods are commonly applied to secure devices during the design and pre-market phases. This process usually considers two main types of side-channel attacks: profiling [7] and non-profiling attacks [5,14]. From the security evaluator's perspective, applying profiling attacks allows a more formal security assessment as it follows a threat model in which the attacker has full access to the clone version of the target device. On the other hand, non-profiling attacks directly use the side-channel measurements from the target device. While profiling attacks are more potent and considered the worst-case attack assumption [6], non-profiling attacks are more realistic from a practical point of view.

In recent years, the application of deep learning to side-channel analysis (DLSCA) has received significant attention from the academic community in

© The Author(s), under exclusive license to Springer Nature Switzerland AG 2024
R. Wacquez and N. Homma (Eds.): COSADE 2024, LNCS 14595, pp. 113–132, 2024.
https://doi.org/10.1007/978-3-031-57543-3_7

the profiling SCA setting [19]. The research has predominantly concentrated on profiling SCA, whereas non-profiling techniques received less attention. Non-profiling deep learning-based SCA was first proposed by B. Timon in 2019 [21], with an approach called Differential Deep Learning Analysis (DDLA). Although its performance is better than conventional non-profiling attacks such as CPA, it is mainly criticized for practical limitations. Indeed, to attack one key byte, DDLA needs to train a deep neural network 256 times (one network for each key hypothesis for commonly attacked byte-oriented cipher like AES) to brute force all possible key bytes. Such an attack may easily become impractical, considering a dataset with millions of measurements. From the adversary's perspective, this also means that the cost of a DDLA attack may easily become higher than the benefit of the attack itself. In [16], the authors proposed several solutions to mitigate observed issues with DDLA. They presented a parallel network architecture to decrease time consumption. However, that increased the memory consumption, which the authors resolved using shared layers. Recently, the authors of [11] proposed using multi-output learning (MOL) [27], where the model is trained to predict multiple outputs from a single input simultaneously. Their work considered multi-output classification (MOC) and multi-output regression (MOR) [3] architectures for non-profiling SCA. These models reduce the complexity of Timon's attack as they require a single neural network training. Moreover, the authors achieved lower execution time and better performance. Still, the performance remains mediocre and is far from profiling DLSCA.

Identifying these pitfalls, we propose MORE - Multi-Output Regressions Enhanced, which significantly improves the attack performance compared with the state-of-the-art MOR strategy [11]. Additionally, we investigate techniques like data augmentation and ensembles to enhance MORE's attack performance further. We provide the source code of MORE implementation[1].

2   Preliminaries

2.1   Machine Learning and SCA

Machine learning algorithms can be classified into several categories based on their learning approach. Supervised learning algorithms utilize labeled training data. These algorithms train a model f to predict labels for previously unseen data by analyzing the data and labels. Most supervised learning methods follow the Empirical Risk Minimization framework, where the model parameters θ are obtained by solving the following optimization problem:

$$\arg\min_{\theta} \frac{1}{n} \sum_{i}^{n} \mathcal{L}(f_{\theta}(t_i), y_i), \tag{1}$$

where $\mathcal{L}$ represents the loss function and n is the size of the dataset T. Supervised machine learning occurs in two phases: training and testing. Classification and regression are two common problem types in supervised machine learning that differ primarily in the nature of their output.

---

[1] https://github.com/AISyLab/MORE-for-Unsupervised-SCA.

– **Classification** problems involve categorizing input data into discrete classes or categories. In these problems, the output is a discrete value representing the class or category that an input data point belongs to. Various algorithms can be used for classification, such as logistic regression, decision trees, support vector machines, and neural networks.
– **Regression** problems involve predicting continuous output values based on input data. In these problems, the output is a continuous numeric value, often representing a measurement or quantity. Common regression algorithms include linear regression, polynomial regression, ridge regression, and support vector regression.

There is a natural relationship between machine learning algorithms based on learning style and side-channel analysis. Profiling attacks depend on a labeling function that utilizes secret information from a device under the adversary's control. Since supervised machine learning involves a labeling function with secret information, it falls within the profiling attack setting. Similarly, although the true label is unknown, non-profiling attacks hypothesize labels without knowing the secret information. Thus, supervised learning can also be applied to this type of attack using the measurements and the hypothesized labels.

Common Regression Loss Functions. We define common loss functions for regression tasks [22] that we use in this work. As mentioned, we hypothesize the labels in non-profiling attacks by calculating them from the key byte hypothesized values. The following definitions refer to those hypothesized labels as actual, true, or correct. However, these are not correct labels as used in profiling SCA as we do not know the correct key, but we use all possible key bytes and obtain what the labels would be given a specific key value.

Mean Squared Error (MSE). MSE is a commonly used measure of the difference between actual and predicted values. It measures the average of the square of the differences between the actual and predicted values according to the following expression:

$$\mathcal{L}_{MSE} = \frac{1}{n} \sum_{i=1}^{n} (y_i - \hat{y}_i)^2, \tag{2}$$

where n is the size of the dataset, while true and predicted labels are represented with y_i and $\hat{y}_i$, respectively. MSE is used in regression problems, where the goal is to predict a continuous value based on input variables. Lower MSE values indicate a better fit between the actual and predicted values.

Mean Absolute Error (MAE). MAE calculates the average of the absolute differences between the actual and predicted values as follows:

$$\mathcal{L}_{MAE} = \frac{1}{n} \sum_{i=1}^{n} |y_i - \hat{y}_i|. \tag{3}$$

Unlike MSE, MAE does not square the differences and is more robust to outliers. Thus, MAE tends to be a less efficient loss function than MSE for our non-profiling attack. We evaluate MAE to show empirically that our assumptions are valid.

Huber Error. Huber Error is a loss function used in regression problems that balances the mean squared error and the mean absolute error. This loss function is defined as:

$$\mathcal{L}_{Huber} = \begin{cases} \frac{1}{2n}\sum_{i=1}^{n}(y_i - \hat{y}_i)^2 & \text{if } |y_i - \hat{y}_i| \leq \delta \\ \frac{\delta}{n}\sum_{i=1}^{n}(|y_i - \hat{y}_i| - 0.5\delta) & \text{otherwise,} \end{cases} \tag{4}$$

where the δ parameter specifies the transition point between the quadratic and linear regions of the loss function. Larger δ values make the function more robust to outliers, which we want to avoid. In our experiments, δ is set to 1 based on the preliminary investigations, and it makes a good balance between MAE and MSE, where it should be less robust to outliers but also sensitive to small errors.

2.2   Non-profiling Multi-output Regression-Based SCA

Do et al. developed a novel method called Multi-output regression (MOR) DLSCA to decrease the computational efforts of DDLA [11]. Rather than training 256 models, where each aims to classify hypothetical labels with probabilities accurately, MOR utilizes the concept of multi-output regression, which seeks to *regress* the prediction outputs to the actual label values. A model is trained to map input leakage traces to the actual values of all possible $y_i(k)$, which denotes the key-related intermediate data (label) given a specific key byte k. The most likely key k^* is determined by identifying the smallest loss measured by MSE.

$$k^* = \arg\min_{k} \frac{1}{n} \sum_{i}^{n} (y_i(k) - f_{\theta}^{k}(\mathbf{t_i}))^2, \; k \in \mathcal{K}, \tag{5}$$

where $f_{\theta}^{k}(\mathbf{t_i})$ represents the model's prediction value to approximate $y_i(k)$. In SCA, the regression output is a key-related intermediate data, e.g., the output of $\mathsf{Sbox}(d_i \oplus k)$, and can be parameterized by the leakage models such as the Identity (ID) or Hamming Weight (HW).

2.3   Datasets

ASCADf [2]. This dataset consists of the trimmed interval of 700 features that includes the second-order leakages of the third S-box in the first encryption round We also run experiments with the raw measurements from the NOPOI scenario presented in [18], which contains 10 000 features, and we refer to it as `ASCADf_nopoi_10000` dataset.[2]

ASCADr [2]. For non-profiling attacks, we use the part of this dataset commonly used as the attack set in DLSCA, where all plaintexts are encrypted

---

[2] Raw measurements contain 100 000 sample points. We resampled it into 10 000 to reduce the input dimension, significantly impacting the profiling model size.

with the same key, while for profiling setup, a training dataset with randomized keys is used. The first version consists of the trimmed interval of 1 400 features that includes the second-order leakages of the third S-box in the first encryption round, which we refer to as ASCADr. We also run experiments with the raw measurements from the NOPOI scenario from [18], which contains 25 000 features, and we refer to it as ASCADr_nopoi_25000 dataset.[3]

AES_RD [8]. The plaintexts are encrypted using the same fixed key, and the collected traces have 3 500 features each. This dataset has random delay as a countermeasure.

AES_HD [13]. The same key is used for all collected traces, which consist of 1 250 features.

3 Related Work

The DDLA method involves training a neural network for each key guess and selecting the one with the best result as the correct key guess [21]. While effective, DDLA is computationally expensive and requires a non-bijective leakage function. Kuroda et al. conducted a follow-up study on DDLA, examining neural network structures and attack points, and concluded that simpler architectures and a broader range of points of interest were preferable [15]. Alipour et al. investigated DDLA's performance against a hiding-based AES countermeasure using correlated noise generation and found DDLA was less effective than CPA in this context [1]. Kwon et al. proposed improvements to DDLA to increase its speed and enhance neural network architectures' performance [16]. Do et al. further analyzed DDLA to understand its behavior in more complex scenarios and explored different data preparation techniques and neural network architectures to improve performance [10]. Hoang et al. introduced a non-profiling SCA technique using multi-output classification, achieving up to 30× faster and 20% better results than DDLA [12]. Do et al. investigated multi-output classification (MOC) and multi-output regression (MOR) models for non-profiling SCA [11]. They concluded that MOC reduced execution time compared to DDLA and showed that MOR, although slower than MOC, worked for the Identity leakage model. Both MOC and MOR outperformed DDLA by at least 25%. Finally, Do et al. further improved the MOR concept by using identity labeling [9]. The authors reported results up to 40× faster than DDLA and at least 30% better success rate. Wu et al. recently proposed a non-profiling deep learning-based attack called PLDL based on the bijective relationship between plaintext/ciphertext and secret information [24]. The authors reported the attack as powerful and easily rivaling the performance of profiling deep learning-based SCA. Note that multiple works use unsupervised deep learning techniques like autoencoders, see, e.g. [20,25]. Still, since such methods are used as preprocessing for profiling SCA, we do not consider them further. Since MOR is already shown to perform much better than DDLA, we do not compare our MORE approach with

---

[3] Raw measurements contain 250 000 sample points. For the same reason as ASCADf, they are resampled into 25 000.

DDLA but only with MOR. Finally, since PLDL is a two-stage classification-based attack (more similar to a profiling attack as there is still a notion of the labeling function), we do not consider it in this work.

4   MOR Enhanced (MORE)

4.1   Loss Functions and Distinguishers

The learning process implemented by a multi-output regression model should minimize the empirical error for all outputs. For the application to non-profiling SCA, the MOR model should minimize the empirical error for only one of the outputs because only one output is related to the correct key candidate. Thus, it is important to find the most efficient loss function that is also more sensitive (i.e., less robust) to *outliers*. Outliers are usually variables whose characteristics are distant from the mean of the data group. This characteristic is desirable from an adversary's perspective because the outlier is the attacker's best guess for the correct key candidate. In this case, if we consider a loss function, the wrong keys would have a similar loss value, where the correct key should be an outlier having a lower loss value than the rest.

The loss functions outlined in Sect. 2.1 are typically employed in regression models. As mentioned, a learning process would benefit from a loss function that is highly sensitive to outliers. A functional model should produce significantly larger prediction errors for all incorrect key candidates than those for the correct key. To this end, we propose to use the Z-Score normalization [17] to build the loss function. Specifically, Z-Score normalization aids outlier detection by making it easier to identify data points that deviate significantly from the mean. In the context of our learning process, normalizing the predictions before computing the loss function accentuates the differences between data points. The increased sensitivity can help the learning process focus more on the correct key candidate, considered an outlier, than the incorrect key candidates, potentially leading to improved performance in MOR-based non-profiling attacks. As such, we propose combining the aforementioned loss functions with the Z-Score normalization. For instance, we can rewrite MSE defined in Eq. (2) to Eq. (6):

$$\mathcal{L}_{Z-scoreMSE} = \frac{1}{n} \sum_{i=1}^{n} \left(\frac{y_i - \mu(\mathbf{y})}{\sigma(\mathbf{y})} - \frac{\hat{y}_i - \mu(\hat{\mathbf{y}})}{\sigma(\hat{\mathbf{y}})} \right)^2, \qquad (6)$$

where the original y_i and $\hat{y}_i$ are normalized and MSE is calculated with normalized values. μ and σ denote the mean and standard deviation functions, respectively, and n is the size of the dataset.

Additionally to the three common regression loss functions and their normalized versions, we propose another loss function, **Pearson Correlation loss**, for which we also test its normalized version. Wu et al. [26] show that assessing the correlation between key distribution[4] and guessing vector can considerably

---

[4] Key distribution measures differences between key candidates based on label distance.

enhance the convergence rate of the profiling model. We do not use label distance in our case, as we can directly utilize the hypothesized labels. Thus, we introduce a novel loss function that aims to maximize the linear correlation between the hypothesized (actual) and predicted labels for all possible keys, defined as:

$$\mathcal{L}_{Pearson} = 1 - |\rho(\mathbf{y}(k), \hat{\mathbf{y}}(k))|, \ k \in \mathcal{K}, \tag{7}$$

where ρ represents the Pearson correlation. $\mathbf{y}(k)$ and $\hat{\mathbf{y}}(k)$ represent vectors of the actual and predicted labels for all n traces given a key byte k. Compared with other loss functions, $\mathcal{L}_{Pearson}$ considers the correlation, leveraging inter-key dependence that could lead to more efficient learning. Thus, this paper benchmarks eight loss functions where, in figures, we differentiate between the non-normalized and normalized ones by adding a prefix 'z_score' or 'z' before the loss function names 'mse', 'mae', 'huber', and 'corr'.

Since we defined different loss functions that we evaluated in our experiments, we also considered key distinguishers. In a non-profiling attack, the most likely key is commonly obtained by sorting the key candidates according to a distinguisher. First, we propose a novel key distinguisher, **Pearson correlation distinguisher**, based on the Pearson correlation coefficient between the true labels vector for each key candidate $\mathbf{y}(k)$ and its predicted labels $\hat{\mathbf{y}}(k)$. The most likely key k^* has the maximum correlation coefficient among all key candidates, defined with Eq. (8).

$$k^* = \arg\max_k \rho(\mathbf{y}(k), \hat{\mathbf{y}}(k)), \ k \in \mathcal{K}. \tag{8}$$

The Pearson correlation distinguisher and Pearson loss function use the same function to calculate the correlation. However, when used as the loss function, the correlation function is inverted for training. Besides, we consider a **loss function distinguisher**. Indeed, MOR models leverage the loss value for each key candidate k. The most likely key k^* is the one with minimum loss function value among all key candidates, defined in Eq. (9).

$$k^* = \arg\min_k \mathcal{L}(k), \ k \in \mathcal{K}. \tag{9}$$

Note that in the case where we use the loss function for the distinguisher, and the loss function for training the model was the Pearson correlation loss function, the distinguisher minimizes the inverted correlation function, which converges to maximizing correlation as is done using the Pearson correlation distinguisher.

4.2   Objective Function for Hyperparameter Tuning

Our MOR models are deep neural networks, so hyperparameter tuning is necessary, especially when attacking datasets with low signal-to-noise ratio (SNR). Hyperparameter tuning is already a complex problem in profiling SCA where an objective function can be defined (i.e., with metrics extracted from a labeled validation set) [23]. In profiling SCA, the main goal is to find a deep neural network that provides better generalization, which implies a more efficient attack.

That requires computing SCA metrics, such as guessing entropy, which assumes a known secret key for the clone device, for selecting the model that requires fewer validation traces to recover the correct key candidate. Unfortunately, the secret key is unknown in a non-profiling setting. Thus, finding a model that provides the best SCA metrics is impossible.

Section 4.1 considers two distinguishers, based on Pearson correlation and loss function, to rank the key candidates. In our experiments, we verified that the first approach based on correlation provides faster convergence, which means that a MOR model may require fewer training epochs to recover the correct key candidate. Therefore, we consider all key candidates' maximum Pearson correlation value as the objective function for hyperparameter tuning for our approach - MORE.

4.3   Validation Set to Mitigate Overfitting

It is essential to realize that MOR models also show overfitting, meaning they do not generalize well on the previously unseen data. As a result, the training loss for every key candidate may decrease, increasing the difficulty of distinguishing the correct key as the outlier. The same occurs when we compute the Pearson correlation between predicted and true labels from training traces. To avoid selecting the wrong key byte as the correct one (minimum loss value or maximum Pearson correlation from all key byte candidates), one can compute the objective function from a separate set of traces not considered during training. The idea is similar to using *validation* traces in a profiling SCA setting. Still, the concept differs, as a validation set, in this case, does not have known labels. Typically, in non-profiling SCA, as is done in MOR, the model is trained on all collected traces, and the same dataset is used to obtain the most likely correct key byte using a distinguisher objective function (such as the loss function). We propose a different approach, dividing the collected traces into two datasets for training and validation. Just like in supervised learning, these two datasets are distinct. Once the model is trained on the training dataset, we select the most likely key byte from the validation set. To the best of our knowledge, this concept was not used in other deep learning non-profiling SCA methods.

4.4   Experimental Results

Loss Function Benchmark. The experiments in this section aim to identify the best loss function for a MOR model using the ASCAD datasets. We consider the trimmed and resampled versions of ASCADf and ASCADr datasets to improve generality, which we evaluate later on two additional datasets. While these datasets are considered representative for our current analysis, future work could expand dataset variety to enhance our findings' generalizability. First, we consider the trimmed ASCAD datasets. We investigate the success rate of the MOR approach by considering all loss functions: MSE, MAE, Huber, correlation (Corr), and their Z-score normalized variants. We randomly drew 1 000 models from the hyperparameter search space defined in Table 1 using only MLP models as the datasets are not desynchronized. We computed the success rate (SR) based on whether these models could find the correct key byte.

Table 1. Hyperparameter search space for finding the best MLP and CNN models. Symbol | separates the range values for MLP and CNN models.

Hyperparameter	MLP			CNN	
	Min		Max		Step
Learning Rate	0.00005		0.005		0.00025
Mini-batch	50		200		50
Dense Layers	1	4	1	|1	2	1
Neurons	200		1 000		100
Convolutional Layers	/		1	4	1
Filters	/			4, 8, 12, 16 or 32	
Kernel Size	/			5, 10, 20, 30 or 40	
Pool Type	/			Average or Max	
Activation			ReLU, ELU, or SELU		
Optimizer			Adam or RMSprop		
Weight Initializer		random_uniform, he_uniform, glorot_uniform, random_normal, he_normal, or glorot_normal				

Table 2 shows the success rate of the MOR approach for the ASCADf dataset using both distinguishers (loss and Pearson correlation). Moreover, we also report the results using both leakage models. We show the results using the training and validation set for distinguishing between the correct and the other key candidates. Z-score MSE, denoted by z-MSE, achieves excellent performance and is the best-performing loss function regardless of the key distinguisher, dataset used, or leakage model. z-MSE results are followed by the Z-score correlation (z-Corr) loss functions. z-MSE has at least ≈19% higher success rate than all other loss functions. On the other hand, compared to the standard loss functions and their Z-score variants, z-MSE has at least ≈65% higher success rate. The success rate with the ID leakage model is lower than when the HW model is utilized. Thus, we further increased the number of training traces to 40 000, with 10 000 validation traces, and obtained 85% SR for z-MSE on training and 86% for validation data.

We conduct the same experiments for the ASCADr dataset and provide the results in Table 3. As before, z-MSE achieves the best success rate in all tested scenarios. Considering the ASCADr datasets, z-MSE achieves at least ≈74% higher success rate than other standard loss functions and their Z-score variants. Compared to correlation losses, it achieves a minimum 36% higher SR. The validation set concept improved SR for the z-MSE loss function in almost all cases. Other loss functions did not attain the same improvement using the validation set. However, using the Pearson correlation as the key distinguisher for the ASCADr dataset, using the validation set improved the SR for six out of eight tested functions. We mentioned that we achieve faster convergence using this key distinguisher so we could observe overfitting to the training data in these cases. Therefore, using a validation set mitigates this effect and selects the correct key byte, leading to better SR. We obtain the same SR when using the correlation loss function with both distinguishers because, in this scenario, distinguishers essentially use the same function. The loss distinguisher minimizes inverted correlation, while the correlation distinguisher maximizes correlation function, ending in the same results. The functions of the loss and correlation distinguisher for when the z-Corr loss is used differ only in the Z-score normalization. Here, the SR results stay the same, as the relations remain unchanged with and without the normalization.

The Z-score MSE performs the best since it creates the most significant numerical gap between loss values for the correct and wrong key candidate bytes.

Table 2. Success rate of MOR for the ASCADf dataset using both leakage models and different loss functions. The training set is 16 000, while the validation set is 4 000 when the HW leakage model (LM) is used, and 32 000 and 8 000, respectively, for the ID leakage model. We considered the loss and Pearson Correlation (Pearson) of validation (Vl) and training (Tr) set for the distinguishers.

Dstgh	LM	Set	MSE	z-MSE	MAE	z-MAE	Huber	z-Huber	Corr	z-Corr
loss	HW	Vl	15.68%	**94.95%**	8.14%	3.75%	16.29%	18.46%	72.8%	77.1%
		Tr	27.31%	**92.5%**	9.21%	6.25%	18.35%	8.54%	75.3%	77.5%
	ID	Vl	0%	**74.1%**	0.6%	0.3%	0%	0.8%	41.2%	44.0%
		Tr	25.7%	**77.6%**	35.8%	14%	36.1%	10.4%	45.4%	50.0%
Pearson	HW	Vl	45.9%	**94.9%**	37.7%	6.7%	48.5%	29%	72.8%	77.1%
		Tr	51%	**92.5%**	43.3%	10.1%	55.9%	35.7%	75.3%	77.5%
	ID	Vl	25.7%	**73.9%**	29.2%	22.8%	29.0%	13.7%	41.2%	44.0%
		Tr	37.5%	**77.6%**	43.4%	26.1%	44.5%	16.1%	45.4%	50.0%

Table 3. Success rate of MOR for the ASCADr dataset using both leakage models (LM) and different loss functions. The training set is 32 000, while the validation set is 8 000. We considered the loss and Pearson Correlation (Pearson) of validation (Vl) and training (Tr) set for the distinguishers.

Dstgh	LM	Set	MSE	z-MSE	MAE	z-MAE	Huber	z-Huber	Corr	z-Corr
loss	HW	Vl	3.9%	**91.2%**	1.5%	1.0%	2.2%	8.2%	44.7%	50.0%
		Tr	30.9%	**77.2%**	15.9%	9.0%	20.8%	12.2%	42.9%	44.6%
	ID	Vl	1.2%	**22.2%**	1.3%	0%	0%	0.4%	14.7%	13.8%
		Tr	4.5%	**9.4%**	2.6%	3.6%	0%	2.2%	6.9%	3.4%
Pearson	HW	Vl	36.6%	**90.2%**	28.4%	8.7%	39.0%	18.4%	44.7%	50.0%
		Tr	31.5%	**77.2%**	27.5%	8.7%	33.4%	21.6%	42.9%	44.6%
	ID	Vl	10.8%	**20.5%**	8.8%	3.9%	10%	3.5%	14.7%	13.8%
		Tr	4.3%	**9.4%**	3.5%	4.8%	2%	5.4%	6.9%	3.4%

In terms of the success rate (see Tables 2 and 3), z-MAE performed worse than z-Huber. Loss function z-Corr performs worse than z-MSE but significantly better than the other loss functions. We observed that the SR was better as the difference between the loss values of correct and wrong key bytes is larger.

Considering the significant improvement in the observed success rate of the MOR-based SCA using z-MSE, we further test the adaptability of the functions using the following strategy:

1. We run random hyperparameter search processes for both ASCADf_nopoi_10000 and ASCADr_nopoi_25000 datasets. The hyperparameter search space is shown in Table 1. A separate random search is launched for each leakage model (ID or HW), model type (MLP or CNN), and loss function (defined in Sect. 4.1) combination. In total, we deploy 64 random search processes. In each of these searches, we try 100 different hyperparameter combinations, which sum up to 6 400 models. We conduct this search to assess the performance of diverse options properly.[5]
2. For each random search process, we select the best MOR model by sorting the models according to the objective function defined in Sect. 4.2. Experiments were executed using both distinguishers (loss function and Pearson correlation). This sorting procedure is done for each dataset, leakage model, model type, and loss function combination.
3. We retrain each of the best models with all other loss functions. The main idea is to see which loss function performs better across different hyperparameter configurations. The reported key rank is computed from a validation set described in Sect. 4.3, which are measurements not used during training. We opted to use the validation set as it improved the results for the best-performing loss function and the ASCADr dataset with the correlation distinguisher.

Figure 1 illustrates the *key rank* outcomes, derived using loss distinguisher defined with Eq. (9), of the top-performing model obtained with various loss functions represented on the y-axis. The optimal model is retrained with other loss functions depicted on the x-axis, and the key rank is presented in each cell. The darker colors in the graphs indicate better performance with lower key ranks. In these experiments, we use 40 000 traces for training and 10 000 for validation in the case of ASCADf, and 80 000 traces for training and 20 000 for validation in the case of ASCADr. The columns show that Z-Score MSE demonstrates superior adaptability across different hyperparameter configurations for various MOR models trained with other loss functions. Overall, the Z-score versions of the loss functions show greater adaptability than the standard loss functions.

Figure 2 presents the key rank outcomes determined using a correlation distinguisher defined with Eq. (8), in which key candidates are ranked based on the highest correlation coefficient. We used the same number of training and validation traces as for the previous experiment. These findings emphasize that

---

[5] The attack commonly skips this procedure by selecting the loss function based on experience or shared knowledge and focuses on tuning other hyperparameters.

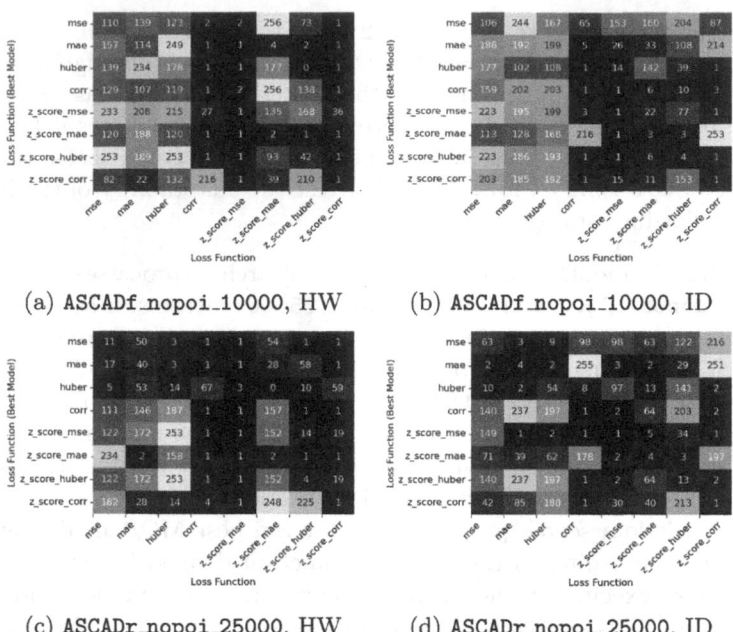

(a) `ASCADf_nopoi_10000`, HW   (b) `ASCADf_nopoi_10000`, ID

(c) `ASCADr_nopoi_25000`, HW   (d) `ASCADr_nopoi_25000`, ID

Fig. 1. Loss function adaptation to different models. Each grid cell is the key rank result obtained with loss function distinguisher (Eq. (9)). The y-axis indicates the loss function set for finding the best model in a random search, while the x-axis indicates loss functions used during retraining.

Z-Score MSE exhibits better adaptability to varying hyperparameter configurations when the HW leakage model is employed for both datasets. Conversely, when utilizing the ID leakage model with the `ASCADf_nopoi_10000` dataset, the performance of correlation and Z-Score MSE loss is comparable. The median and mean for correlation loss are 2 and 36.63, respectively, while for Z-Score MSE, the median is 8, and the mean is 38.13. For the `ASCADr_nopoi_25000` dataset with the ID leakage model, MSE, MAE, and Huber demonstrate slightly better results when averaged than Z-Score MSE. However, MORE adopts the Z-score MSE as its preferred loss function due to its significantly higher SR when compared to other loss functions and its remarkable adaptability to various models.

MORE vs. MOR. The main aspects of MORE that improve performance over the MOR models are

- Pearson correlation for the key distinguisher.
- Z-score normalized MSE as loss function.
- Validation set for finding the correct secret information.

We compare MOR and MORE methods using success rate calculated based on randomly chosen MLP models from the hyperparameter space presented in

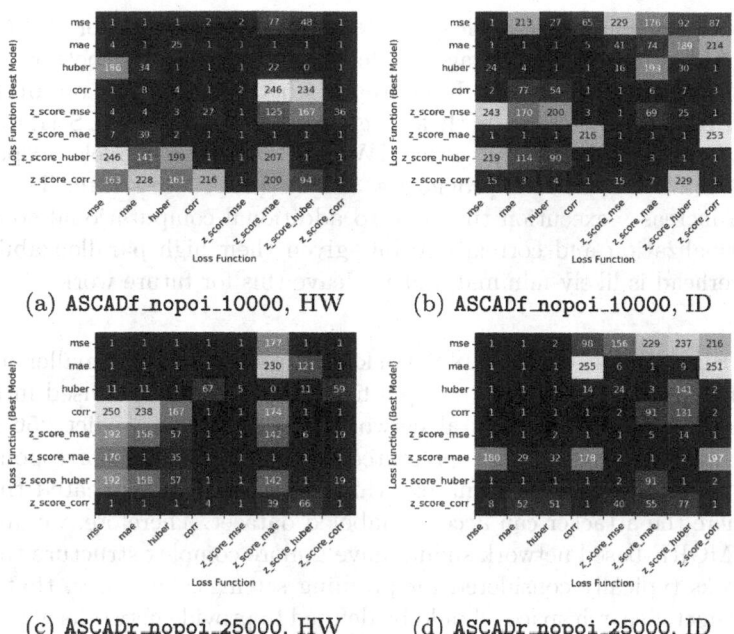

(a) ASCADf_nopoi_10000, HW   (b) ASCADf_nopoi_10000, ID

(c) ASCADr_nopoi_25000, HW   (d) ASCADr_nopoi_25000, ID

Fig. 2. Loss function adaptation to different models. Each grid cell is the key rank results obtained with Pearson Correlation distinguisher (Eq. (8)). The y-axis indicates the loss function set for finding the best model in a random search, while the x-axis indicates loss functions used during retraining.

Table 4. Average success rate comparison between MOR and MORE. For ASCADf and ASCADr, we used 16 000 training and 4 000 validation traces with the HW (HD) leakage model, and 32 000 training and 8 000 validation with ID. For AES_HD and AES_RD, we used 16 000 training and 4 000 validation traces for both leakage models.

Dataset	HW/HD		ID	
	MOR	MORE	MOR	MORE
ASCADf	27.3%	92.5%	25.7%	74.1%
ASCADr	33.9%	77.2%	4.5%	22.2%
AES_HD	10.2%	77.3%	11.3%	58.0%
AES_RD	22.01%	75.8%	0.7%	1.1%

Table 1, where the optimizer is set to Adam optimizer, and the weight initialization method is fixed to *he_uniform*. Thus, the search space for MLP is reduced from 51 840 possible combinations compared to 4 320 by fixing the optimizer and weight initialization method. This is still a significantly larger search space than the one introduced in [9] (192 possible combinations). Table 4 shows the success rate for both models on ASCADf, ASCADr, AES_HD, and AES_RD datasets with the ID and HW (HD) leakage models. Considering the HW (HD) leakage model, MORE presents at least 2.3× higher SR obtained for the ASCADr dataset, and, with the ID leakage model, it is at least 1.6× better, which is the result obtained on the AES_RD dataset, where both models obtain low SR. The best improvement with both leakage models is on the AES_HD dataset, with 7.6× and 5.1× higher SR using HW and ID leakage models, respectively. Overall, on average, MORE provides a 3.9× higher success rate. The MORE approach increases execution time due to additional computational steps of Z-score normalization and correlation, but given their high parallelizability, the added overhead is likely minimal, but we leave this for future work.

On the Size of the MORE Networks. In profiling SCA, smaller networks commonly work well enough on the public datasets most often used in DLSCA literature. A MORE-based neural network is designed to predict 256 distinct outputs simultaneously (each represented by a set of labels corresponding to each key byte candidate). Ultimately, this task is more complicated than profiling, where the attacker can access a labeled dataset. Therefore, we anticipate that the MORE-based network should have a more complex structure than neural networks typically considered for profiling settings. Moreover, that implies hyperparameter search spaces should be defined to provide networks with enough capacity to learn a more challenging task of non-profiling SCA.

We experimentally compare the performance of various neural networks for MORE (non-profiling) and profiling attacks. For each leakage model and model type (MLP or CNN), we randomly generate up to 3 000 neural network architectures, with trainable parameters ranging from 10 000 to 1 000 000, since the complexity (size) of neural network models can be measured in the number of trainable parameters when the same type of networks are compared, such as MLPs. The hyperparameter search space is defined in Table 1, with fixed Adam optimizer and *he_uniform* initializer. The search space also increases the number of fully connected layers to eight for MLPs and four for CNNs to enable large networks. Each randomly generated architecture is trained as both MORE and a profiling model. The comparison criterion is the final guessing entropy (key rank) relative to the number of trainable parameters. For this analysis, we consider the ASCADf and ASCADr datasets. In the case of the ASCADf dataset in the profiling setup, 50 000 traces are considered for training, while 100 000 are utilized for the ASCADr dataset. For the attack, we used 5 000 attack traces. In the non-profiling case, for ASCADf, we use 40 000 for training and 10 000 traces for validation, while for ASCADr, we have 80 000 for training and 20 000 traces for validation.

Due to the page limit, we omit the figures, but the results suggest that MORE-based models generally exhibit better performance when they include more trainable parameters. In contrast, the profiling task demonstrates an optimal range with enhanced key recovery performance. As models become excessively large for a profiling task, overfitting signs emerge for the two examined datasets, which is not observed for MORE-based models. Thus, employing larger models for MORE tasks could be an appropriate choice requiring careful consideration of the network size. On the contrary, successful models in a profiling attack were smaller, indicating that the structure can be more straightforward to define and more time can be spent fine-tuning other hyperparameters.

5 Getting More from MORE

5.1 MORE Ensembles for SCA

Bootstrap aggregating (also known as bagging) [4] is an ensemble technique in machine learning that combines multiple models to improve performance and reduce overfitting. The idea is to create multiple sub-samples (bootstraps) of the original dataset chosen randomly, train a separate model on each sub-sample, and then combine the predictions of the individual models. We consider the ID and the HW/HD leakage models for ASCADf, ASCADr, AES_RD, and AES_HD datasets. Based on the preliminary tuning phase, we set the number of epochs to 40 and varied the number of available traces for the MORE model. From the available traces, 80% are training traces, while the remaining 20% are validation traces. The key rank is calculated based on the different number of input traces and shown in the graphs. We test a single best MORE model and ensembles comprising 50 models. Each model is randomly selected from the same hyperparameter space detailed in Table 1, except for the optimizer being set to Adam and the weight initialization set to *he_uniform*. The number of models in an ensemble is decided based on the preliminary experiments with different numbers of models for the ensemble. We do not show results for CNN ensembles as we could not observe any significant improvements when using more than one model. We compare the ensemble's key rank to the key rank of the best model.

In Fig. 3a, we plot the key rank for ASCADf with the HW leakage model while varying the number of traces. The best model chosen according to the Pearson correlation distinguisher displays higher key ranks with fewer traces than the ensemble. However, both methods perform similarly when the number of traces exceeds 5 000. Figure 3b demonstrates the key rank for the ID leakage model. In this case, the ensemble recovers the secret key more quickly, using fewer traces, than the single best model. Similarly to the results on ASCADf, ensembles on ASCADr for the HW leakage model show slightly better performance when less than 10 000 traces are used, while with more traces, the single best model and ensemble consistently retrieve the correct key. We observed no improvement for the ID leakage model using ensembles due to the low success rate we obtained. We omit these results due to lack of space and similar results.

Figure 4 shows the key rank of the ensemble and the best model for AES_RD. As seen in Fig. 4a, the ensemble performs slightly better than the best model using fewer traces. Figure 4b shows that overfitting for ID is not entirely avoided, not even when using ensembles. In this case, there was no significant benefit when employing the ensembles. The performance based on the key rank is similar between the two setups.

Figure 5 considers MORE experimental setup for AES_HD and plots the key ranks for the HD and ID leakage models varying the number of traces. Compared

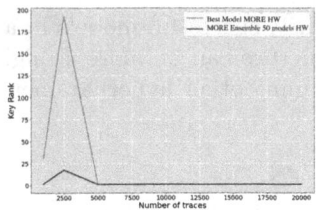 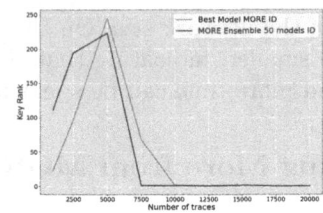

(a) ASCADf, Key rank, HW leakage (b) ASCADf, Key rank, ID leakage

Fig. 3. Key rank for ASCADf for the HW and ID leakage models.

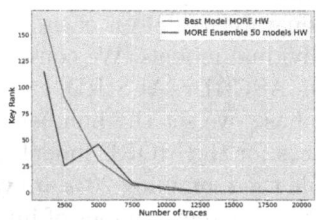 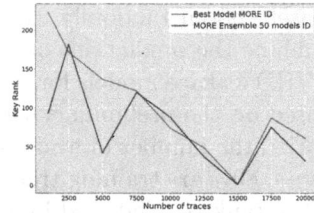

(a) AES_RD, Key rank, HW leakage (b) AES_RD, Key rank, ID leakage

Fig. 4. Key rank for AES_RD for the HW and ID leakage models.

to the best model, the MORE ensemble shows improvement for both leakage models. It reaches the minimum key rank faster in the case of the HD leakage model and decreases the key rank with the ID leakage model when less than 15 000 traces are used. The effect visible with the ID leakage model comes from retraining the models for the different number of available traces we tested and a rather noisy data.

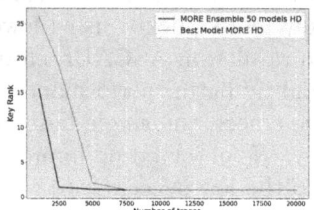 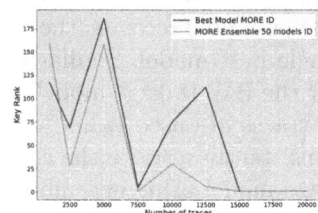

(a) AES_HD, Key rank, HD leakage (b) AES_HD, Key rank, ID leakage

Fig. 5. Key rank for AES_HD for the HD and ID leakage models.

5.2 Data Augmentation with MORE-Based SCA

Insufficient data in a non-profiling side-channel analysis setting can lead to an unsuccessful attack. A possible reason is the overfitting that can easily occur, resulting in an unreliable distinguishing phase between key candidates. This section presents results for the MORE methodology with data augmentation (DA). We employ data augmentation with the best MORE model. We utilized random shifting as the first data augmentation technique, which involves applying a random time shift to each trace. The shift amount can be positive or negative and can be drawn from a uniform or normal distribution. In this work, we opted for a shift of five samples and a uniform distribution. The second data augmentation approach we employed is Gaussian noise, which applies a small perturbation to each trace sample. The perturbation value is drawn from a standard normal distribution (mean 0 and standard deviation 1). For both approaches, we augment the original traces by adding 10 000 more or double the number of traces if the original set is smaller than 10 000. This setting is selected based on the preliminary experiments. Figure 6a displays SR for ASCADf, AES_HD, and AES_RD with and without data augmentation for 500 randomly chosen neural networks from the hyperparameter space defined in Table 1 (optimizer set to Adam, and initialization method to *he_uniform*) with MORE methodology. We observe that Gaussian noise DA slightly helps the success rate, especially when the number of traces before augmentation is less than 10 000. However, when shifting DA is employed, the success rate for all initial numbers of traces is rather low. On the other hand, in the case of AES_HD, we see that both approaches show a significant SR increase, especially for Gaussian noise, as can be seen in Fig. 6b. For AES_RD, results in Fig. 6c show that both techniques can help when the number of input traces is smaller than 10 000. We notice that SR can significantly decrease when using MORE with data augmentation. We believe this is because data augmentation reduces overfitting, which can quickly happen in the MORE context. Although we try to minimize this effect for MORE by using a validation set rather than the training set, as in the case of MOR, MORE is still susceptible to overfitting.

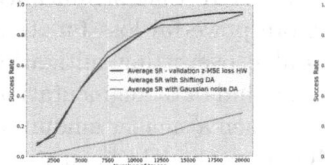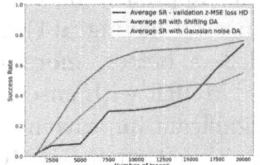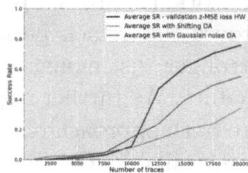

(a) **ASCADf**, SR varying the number of traces before augmentation

(b) **AES_HD**, SR varying the number of traces before augmentation

(c) **AES_RD**, SR varying the number of traces before augmentation

Fig. 6. Success rate for MORE on ASCADf, AES_HD, and AES_RD for the HW/HD leakage model.

Although there is no substantial improvement in the success rate of MORE with the application of data augmentation, it is worth noting that the average guessing entropy can significantly decrease when DA is employed for the best MORE model. We trained the best MORE model 100 times with 5 000 traces before augmentation and compared the average GE with the average GE of the same model when using data augmentation. Figure 7a illustrates that Gaussian noise data augmentation yields better results compared to shifting, leading to a slight reduction in the overall guessing entropy across 40 training epochs. It is worth noting that this DA technique also yields the best results for AES_HD where after just five training epochs, the guessing entropy drops below ten, as indicated in Fig. 7b. In the case of AES_RD, shifting DA appears to be even more effective in reducing GE, as seen in Fig. 7c, but again, both DA techniques provide improvement. We note that DA methods on ASCADr obtained lower SR than without using DA for both HW and ID leakage models. As explained here, the experiments comparing the GE of the best model with and without DA show that GE within the first 40 epochs is the lowest without using DA methods. We omit the figures with results due to space.

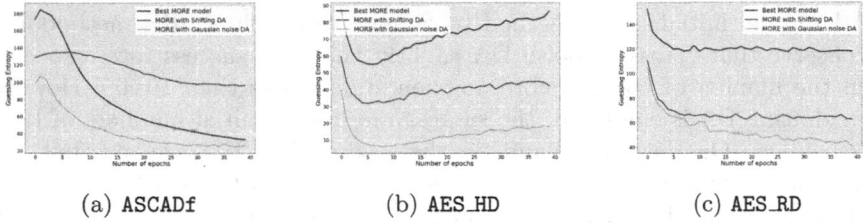

    (a) ASCADf   (b) AES_HD   (c) AES_RD

Fig. 7. Guessing entropy for MORE on ASCADf, AES_HD, and AES_RD, varying the number of epochs for the HW/HD leakage model with data augmentation.

6   Conclusions and Future Work

This work proposes MORE, an approach based on MOR that significantly improves the attack performance by having a 1) more powerful loss function, 2) stronger distinguisher, and 3) a better, more stable overfitting mitigation procedure. We further improved MORE with ensembles and data augmentation, where both approaches show significant improvements when a smaller amount of data is available. Overall, the combination of the MORE methodology, ensemble methods, and data augmentation presents a promising approach for enhancing non-profiling DLSCA performance and improving the reliability of distinguishing between key candidates. Future research could explore other data augmentation techniques and ensemble strategies to optimize the performance of MORE-based models further. Additionally, incorporating advanced regularization techniques may help address overfitting and improve the generalization capabilities of the models.

References

1. Alipour, A., Papadimitriou, A., Beroulle, V., Aerabi, E., Hély, D.: On the performance of non-profiled differential deep learning attacks against an AES encryption algorithm protected using a correlated noise generation based hiding countermeasure. In: Proceedings of the 23rd Conference on Design, Automation and Test in Europe, DATE 2020, pp. 614–617. EDA Consortium, San Jose (2020)
2. Benadjila, R., Prouff, E., Strullu, R., Cagli, E., Dumas, C.: Deep learning for side-channel analysis and introduction to ASCAD database. J. Cryptographic Eng. **10**(2), 163–188 (2020). https://doi.org/10.1007/s13389-019-00220-8
3. Borchani, H., Varando, G., Bielza, C., Larranaga, P.: A survey on multi-output regression. Wiley Interdisc. Rev. Data Min. Knowl. Discov. **5**(5), 216–233 (2015)
4. Breiman, L.: Bagging predictors. Mach. Learn. **24**(2), 123–140 (1996)
5. Brier, E., Clavier, C., Olivier, F.: Correlation power analysis with a leakage model. In: Joye, M., Quisquater, J.J. (eds.) CHES 2004. LNCS, vol. 3156, pp. 16–29. Springer, Heidelberg (2004). https://doi.org/10.1007/978-3-540-28632-5_2
6. Bronchain, O., Durvaux, F., Masure, L., Standaert, F.: Efficient profiled side-channel analysis of masked implementations, extended. IEEE Trans. Inf. Forensics Secur. **17**, 574–584 (2022). https://doi.org/10.1109/TIFS.2022.3144871
7. Chari, S., Rao, J.R., Rohatgi, P.: Template attacks. In: Kaliski, B.S., Koc, K., Paar, C. (eds.) CHES 2002. LNCS, vol. 2523, pp. 13–28. Springer, Heidelberg (2003). https://doi.org/10.1007/3-540-36400-5_3
8. Coron, J.S., Kizhvatov, I.: An efficient method for random delay generation in embedded software. In: Clavier, C., Gaj, K. (eds.) CHES 2009. LNCS, vol. 5747, pp. 156–170. Springer, Heidelberg (2009). https://doi.org/10.1007/978-3-642-04138-9_12
9. Do, N.T., Hoang, V.P., Doan, V.S.: A novel non-profiled side channel attack based on multi-output regression neural network. J. Cryptographic Eng. 1–13 (2023)
10. Do, N.T., Hoang, V.P., Doan, V.S., Pham, C.K.: On the performance of non-profiled side channel attacks based on deep learning techniques. IET Inf. Secur. (2022).https://doi.org/10.1049/ise2.12102. https://ietresearch.onlinelibrary.wiley.com/doi/abs/10.1049/ise2.12102
11. Do, N.T., Le, P.C., Hoang, V.P., Doan, V.S., Nguyen, H.G., Pham, C.K.: MODLSCA: deep learning based non-profiled side channel analysis using multi-output neural networks. In: 2022 International Conference on Advanced Technologies for Communications (ATC), pp. 245–250 (2022). https://doi.org/10.1109/ATC55345.2022.9943024
12. Hoang, V.P., Do, N.T., Doan, V.S.: Efficient non-profiled side channel attack using multi-output classification neural network. IEEE Embed. Syst. Lett. 1 (2022). https://doi.org/10.1109/LES.2022.3213443
13. Kim, J., Picek, S., Heuser, A., Bhasin, S., Hanjalic, A.: Make some noise. Unleashing the power of convolutional neural networks for profiled side-channel analysis. IACR Trans. Cryptographic Hardware Embed. Syst. 148–179 (2019)
14. Kocher, P., Jaffe, J., Jun, B.: Differential power analysis. In: Wiener, M. (ed.) CRYPTO 1999. LNCS, vol. 1666, pp. 388–397. Springer, Heidelberg (1999). https://doi.org/10.1007/3-540-48405-1_25
15. Kuroda, K., Fukuda, Y., Yoshida, K., Fujino, T.: Practical aspects on non-profiled deep-learning side-channel attacks against AES software implementation with two types of masking countermeasures including RSM. In: Proceedings of the 5th Workshop on Attacks and Solutions in Hardware Security, ASHES 2021, pp. 29–40.

Association for Computing Machinery, New York (2021). https://doi.org/10.1145/3474376.3487285

16. Kwon, D., Hong, S., Kim, H.: Optimizing implementations of non-profiled deep learning-based side-channel attacks. IEEE Access **10**, 5957–5967 (2022)

17. Patro, S., Sahu, K.K.: Normalization: a preprocessing stage. arXiv preprint arXiv:1503.06462 (2015)

18. Perin, G., Wu, L., Picek, S.: Exploring feature selection scenarios for deep learning-based side-channel analysis. IACR Trans. Cryptographic Hardware Embed. Syst. **2022**(4), 828–861 (2022). https://doi.org/10.46586/tches.v2022.i4.828-861. https://tches.iacr.org/index.php/TCHES/article/view/9842

19. Picek, S., Perin, G., Mariot, L., Wu, L., Batina, L.: SoK: deep learning-based physical side-channel analysis. ACM Comput. Surv. (2022). https://doi.org/10.1145/3569577

20. Ramezanpour, K., Ampadu, P., Diehl, W.: SCARL: side-channel analysis with reinforcement learning on the ascon authenticated cipher. CoRR abs/2006.03995 (2020). https://arxiv.org/abs/2006.03995

21. Timon, B.: Non-profiled deep learning-based side-channel attacks with sensitivity analysis. IACR Trans. Cryptogr. Hardw. Embed. Syst. **2019**(2), 107–131 (2019). https://doi.org/10.13154/tches.v2019.i2.107-131

22. Wang, Q., Ma, Y., Zhao, K., Tian, Y.: A comprehensive survey of loss functions in machine learning. Ann. Data Sci. 1–26 (2020)

23. Wu, L., Perin, G., Picek, S.: I choose you: automated hyperparameter tuning for deep learning-based side-channel analysis. IEEE Trans. Emerg. Top. Comput. 1–12 (2022). https://doi.org/10.1109/TETC.2022.3218372

24. Wu, L., Perin, G., Picek, S.: Hiding in plain sight: non-profiling deep learning-based side-channel analysis with plaintext/ciphertext. Cryptology ePrint Archive, Paper 2023/209 (2023). https://eprint.iacr.org/2023/209

25. Wu, L., Picek, S.: Remove some noise: on pre-processing of side-channel measurements with autoencoders. IACR Trans. Cryptogr. Hardw. Embed. Syst. **2020**(4), 389–415 (2020). https://doi.org/10.13154/tches.v2020.i4.389-415

26. Wu, L., et al.: Label correlation in deep learning-based side-channel analysis. IEEE Trans. Inf. Forensics Secur. **18**, 3849–3861 (2023). https://doi.org/10.1109/TIFS.2023.3287728

27. Xu, D., Shi, Y., Tsang, I.W., Ong, Y.S., Gong, C., Shen, X.: Survey on multi-output learning. IEEE Trans. Neural Netw. Learn. Syst. **31**(7), 2409–2429 (2019)

Towards Private Deep Learning-Based Side-Channel Analysis Using Homomorphic Encryption
Opportunities and Limitations

Fabian Schmid[1]([✉]), Shibam Mukherjee[1,5], Stjepan Picek[2], Marc Stöttinger[3], Fabrizio De Santis[4], and Christian Rechberger[1]

[1] Graz University of Technology, Graz, Austria
fabian.schmid@iaik.tugraz.at
[2] Radboud University, Nijmegen, The Netherlands
[3] RheinMain University of Applied Science, Wiesbaden, Germany
[4] Siemens AG, Munich, Germany
[5] Know-Center GmbH, Graz, Austria

Abstract. This work investigates using Homomorphic Encryption (HE) to assist the security evaluation of cryptographic devices without revealing side-channel information. For the first time, we evaluate the feasibility of execution of deep learning-based side-channel analysis on standard server equipment using an adapted HE protocol. By examining accuracy and execution time, it demonstrates the successful application of private SCA on both unprotected and protected cryptographic implementations. This contribution is a first step towards confidential side-channel analysis. Our study is limited to the honest-but-curious trust model, where we could reconstruct the secret of an unprotected AES implementation in seconds and of a masked AES implementation in under 17 min.

Keywords: Side-channel Analysis · Deep Learning · Neural Networks · Homomorphic Encryption · Private AI

1 Introduction

Side-channel analysis represents one of the pillars for security evaluations of security products. In particular, profiling side-channel attacks represent a de-facto standard evaluation technique, and deep learning is a powerful tool in this context [40]. Deep learning (DL) is commonly considered data-hungry and power-hungry. As such, it makes sense to consider obtaining data from multiple sources to train more powerful deep learning models. Moreover, outsourcing the heavy computations to third parties, like various Machine Learning as a Service (MLaaS), becomes not only feasible but common [22].

We can notice a similar trend in the context of deep learning-based SCA (DLSCA), see, e.g., [8]. There, while the requirements on computational power do not increase as fast as in some other domains like computer vision or text

© The Author(s), under exclusive license to Springer Nature Switzerland AG 2024
R. Wacquez and N. Homma (Eds.): COSADE 2024, LNCS 14595, pp. 133–154, 2024.
https://doi.org/10.1007/978-3-031-57543-3_8

processing, we still see more elaborate approaches and larger datasets.[1] Thus, it opens a question of how to outsource the computationally heavy DLSCA to third parties (e.g., certification labs in the case of the certification process or any MLaaS in the case of a preliminary evaluation) while not disclosing sensitive information or abuse of the side-channel information to reverse engineer the device under evaluation cf. [15,43]. Indeed, interacting with a third party involves a noticeable exchange of confidential information. The client has a "prepared" device under test and a set of measurements collected under precise conditions. Those measurements are necessary to conduct the analysis, but will leak information to the third party.

Homomorphic encryption is a cryptographic tool that enables computation on encrypted data without decrypting it. With such a tool, a third-party evaluator can privately interact with a customer desiring a side-channel security evaluation for a device under test. The evaluator receives the HE traces from the customer, analyses them in encrypted form homomorphically, and reports for any possible leakage to the customer without learning anything about the traces or the final results. Once the customer is confident about the security of its device, it can send it to the certifying authority for final security certification.[2]

Related Work. Artificial intelligence techniques have recently gained significant attention from the side-channel community, owing to their success in various domains where data analysis is used. In particular, the applicability of deep learning to side-channel analysis has spurred numerous investigations into its performance and effectiveness, showing excellent results. For instance, deep neural networks (DNNs) outperformed traditional profiling attacks such as template attacks in practice [10] and were proven highly successful even on devices protected with various countermeasures. In 2016, Maghrebi et al. showcased how deep learning (deep neural networks) can break various targets [30]. This work started a series of research on DLSCA, where most of the works explored how to conduct such attacks as efficiently as possible. Zaid et al. provided the first methodology to build convolutional neural networks for SCA [48]. Rijsdijk et al. [42] and Wu et al. [47] discussed how to improve the hyperparameter tuning phase with reinforcement learning and Bayesian optimization, respectively. These works considered targets protected with both masking and hiding countermeasures but also required more computation power than previous works due to complex tuning mechanisms.

HE has already been successfully tested in various real-world applications, including energy forecasting predictions, healthcare, and financial services, showing that it is a viable solution for safeguarding privacy of AI computations. While HE schemes are semantically secure, they do not provide chosen-ciphertext attack (CCA) security or data integrity protection. Therefore, these schemes

---

[1] For instance, the first version of the ASCAD dataset commonly used in SCA has 60 000 traces, while the latest one has 810 000 traces.

[2] The process of pre-certification and its costs can be amortized across more trials executed through a cloud service where homomorphically encrypted traces can be uploaded to the cloud for preliminary testing.

require a semi-honest adversarial model where all parties must adhere to the protocol specification. Further, the computational overhead of encrypted computations has decreased tremendously since its inception in 2009 but is nevertheless substantial.

There are many works in the literature regarding classification based on homomorphic encryption. Among the first was Cryptonets [21], with an HE scheme working over integer polynomials and later improved upon by Chou et al. [14]. Independently, there have been works on HE neural network compilers. First, CHET [16] proposed a compiler optimizing parameter selection for network encoding. Next, Concrete-ML [33] is a compiler to the torus-based HE scheme. Besides these fundamental works, there are several improvements to the setup. In Gazelle [25], the authors proposed a runtime-communication trade-off to improve accuracy by involving the client in the computation of non-linear functions.

Further, two works showcased pure HE networks with high multiplicative depth. In Privft [4], the authors practically showcased encrypted learning using more significant parameters and hardware acceleration. Next, Lee et al. [28] implemented bootstrapping with significant HE parameters. Both approaches managed to solve their computation tasks but with high computational complexity. The first takes about five days to train a network for text classification, while the latter takes around three hours for one classification in a 20-layer neural network. While these works brought many improvements and dedicated optimizations, they all face the trade-off between limited neural network depth and computational overhead. While this limits the use cases for private ML, these works show the practicability of applying privacy-preserving methods to neural networks.

Contributions. The main goal of this work is to investigate the technical feasibility of HE-assisted side-channel analysis using deep neural networks to highlight strengths and understand limitations in terms of performance. Given state-of-the-art DNN models for side-channel analysis, we outline the challenges for HE and provide a guideline for adoption with practical performance results. We evaluate our approach using standard public datasets from the SCA literature, including unprotected and protected software implementations of AES-128, showing that both datasets can be successfully analyzed with standard server equipment and modern HE protocols/libraries. Next, we evaluate the advantages and constraints of HE-assisted DLSCA. Although current DNN models are not directly applicable to HE, we outline the required steps for adaptation and achieving "HE-friendliness". We demonstrate that this adaptation yields highly accurate classification results similar to plain classification while aligning with expected performance metrics for HE applications (i.e., four to six orders of magnitude runtime overhead). Our system operates under the semi-honest trust model, ensuring the privacy of computation inputs, with adherence to the protocol being necessary for validity.

This is the first attempt in the open literature to evaluate the feasibility of HE-assisted side-channel analysis using DNNs to establish the basis and pave the way for future studies and advancements in this emerging area.

2   Background

2.1   Neural Network-Based Side-Channel Analysis

Side-channel analysis represents an attack method that targets the implementation rather than the cryptographic algorithm. Among SCA techniques, profiling side-channel attacks are considered the most powerful because they make worst-case security assumptions [39]. In these attacks, the attacker has access to a copy of a device that is used to build a profile, which can be then used to obtain the secret information from the target device [31].

The SCA community has recently focused on deep learning techniques due to their success in various domains. The potential applicability of deep learning to SCA has triggered investigations into its performance. The results are promising: deep learning outperforms traditional profiling attacks [10].

Profiling side-channel analysis happens in two phases: profiling and attack. Let $\mathcal{X}^{tr} \in \mathbb{X}^{N \times P}$ be a 2D array (training input dataset) with N rows (side-channel traces) and P columns (point-of-interest (PoI)), where $\mathbb{X}$ represents the set of available side-channel traces. Let $\mathcal{Y}^{tr} \in \mathbb{Y}^N$ be an array of N rows (training labels), where $\mathbb{Y}$ contains the set of all possible classification labels, such that there exists a function $f : \mathcal{X}^{tr} \mapsto \mathcal{Y}^{tr}$. The goal of the profiling phase is to find the parameters θ $g_\theta(\mathcal{X}^{tr})$ that maximize the chance of outputting the expected value $\mathcal{Y}^{tr}$. In the attack phase, the goal is to predict the labels $\mathcal{Y}^{pr} \in \mathbb{Y}^N$ based on the attack traces $\mathcal{P}^{pr} \in \mathbb{P}^{Q \times C}$ and the trained model g_θ, where $\mathbb{P} \in [0,1]$ (probability), Q is the number of attack traces and C is the number of labels (that depends on the cryptographic algorithm and the leakage model). Here, each value $\mathbf{p_i} \in \mathcal{P}^{pr}$, denotes the probability of obtaining $\mathbf{y_i} \in \mathcal{Y}^{pr}$ for a specific key $\mathbf{k}$ and some input $\mathbf{a} \in \mathcal{M}$, where $\mathcal{M}$ is the message space.

Finally, the cumulative sum $S(\mathbf{k})$ for any key byte candidate $\mathbf{k}$ is a side-channel distinguisher with a common maximum log-likelihood principle: $S(\mathbf{k}) = \sum_{i=1}^{Q} \log(\mathbf{p}_{i,\mathbf{y}})$. The cumulative sums for each possible key value from a key guessing vector are ordered per the probability of the key being correct (the first position in the vector is the most likely key, and the last position is the least likely key). The position of the correct key is called the key rank, and it denotes the remaining effort the attacker requires to break the target. To reduce the effects of a random choice of test measurements, it is common to assess the average behavior over many randomly selected traces, called guessing entropy (i.e., average key rank) [45]. Besides considering the attack performance, one often also considers the complexity of the obtained models by assessing the number of trainable parameters [37].

Commonly used neural networks in the profiling SCA are multilayer perceptron (MLP) and convolutional neural network (CNN) [26]. Both neural networks are feed-forward neural networks, but CNNs consist of more types of layers - convolutional layer, pooling layer, and fully connected layer - while MLP consists of fully connected layers only. While both neural network types work well when considering SCA, CNNs have the potential advantage of being shift-invariant, giving them more advantage when dealing with desynchronization countermeasure [9].

2.2   Homomorphic Encryption (HE)

With homomorphic encryption (HE), we refer to encryption schemes that allow operations on encrypted data that directly carry over to the underlying plaintext domain. Without decryption, a server can execute some algorithm on encrypted data without leaking any information of the processed data. Encryption schemes allowing additions *and* multiplications of ciphertexts rely on noise to secure the secret. This inherent noise increases with the number of homomorphic operations and thus limits the maximum number of operations. We refer to such schemes as *Somewhat* HE (SHE) schemes. Allowing unlimited operations was an open problem until 2009 when Gentry introduced the first *Fully* HE (FHE) scheme [20]. The key step to FHE is the bootstrapping procedure, which allows resetting the noise of a ciphertext for unbounded depth in the evaluation circuit.

Today, FHE schemes can be divided into binary [17] and arithmetic [7,13,19], depending on the types of operations supported. Binary FHE schemes have a bootstrapping step after each computation, naturally giving them an unbounded number of operations. However, decomposing inputs for binary encryption gives a substantial ciphertext expansion and runtime penalty when working with integers and integer arithmetic. Arithmetic FHE schemes, on the other hand, provide several optimizations for computations on integers (in the case of BGV [7] and BFV [6]) or fixed precision approximate numbers (in the case of CKKS [13]). In contrast to binary schemes, bootstrapping is expensive. In general, one can boost the number of operations one can perform before the noise grows too large by increasing the parameters of HE. Multiplication is the primary driver of noise growth. In practice, one counts the required multiplications and tunes the parameters to fit the specific use case. We refer to such an instantiation as *Levelled* HE (LHE), as we can perform exactly "L" levels of multiplications. In theory, one can compute any circuit with such a scheme. However, as additional levels increase the parameter size and thus the ciphertext expansion, the overhead soon reaches prohibitive levels. Next to the noise problem, these LHE schemes only allow homomorphic addition and multiplication in all settings and vector rotations when using special encoding. For every non-linear function, such as typical activation functions in neural networks, it is, therefore, necessary to work with approximations such as Taylor approximation or Chebyshev approximation [27].

When considering the HE scheme as a black box for secure computation, one could instantiate our use case with any of the described methods above. However, we do want to motivate our use of the CKKS scheme. The main driving factor of multiplicative depth in neural network inference tasks is the number of layers and degree of the approximation polynomials. Since our task can be achieved with only a few layers (see, e.g., [38] where the authors required neural networks with only a few layers to break the targets protected even with masking and hiding countermeasures) and a low degree of the approximation polynomial gives us good results, the multiplicative depth is not prohibitive. Thus, we can select an arithmetic LHE scheme. Contrary to other LHE schemes, CKKS is built to work directly with approximate numbers. This property makes it a natural fit for neural network tasks. Finally, CKKS allows for batching of ciphertexts. This optimization allows encrypting multiple data points into a single ciphertext and performing operations in a *single instruction multiple data* (SIMD) fashion. This encoding lets us encrypt the entire input (traces) vector into one ciphertext, amortizing the encrypted inference evaluation. In summary, the optimizations of LHE schemes outweigh their noise limitation. Finally, within the arithmetic schemes, only the CKKS scheme naturally supports approximate numbers, making it a better fit for application in machine learning. We will discuss further implications of using CKKS for evaluating neural networks in Sect. 2.3.

CKKS: Approximate Homomorphic Encryption. In this section, we will describe the specifics of the CKKS [12,13] cryptosystem. Fundamentally, CKKS provides an encoding strategy that allows us to encrypt complex vectors in integer-polynomial-based encryption schemes. While this approach can be instantiated with different methods, our discussion revolves around the BFV [6,19] cryptosystem with CKKS encoding.

Encoding. In BFV-like HE schemes, we operate on polynomial rings denoted as $R_q = \mathbb{Z}_q[X]/(X^n + 1)$, for some large q and a power of two n. More precisely, public and private keys and ciphertexts are represented as integer polynomials with fixed degree n and coefficient modulus q. The individual polynomial coefficients are centered around zero. They lie within $(-q/2, q/2]$. Additions and multiplications of an encoded plaintext polynomial lead to element-wise operations on the underlying vector of complex numbers. Next, to element-wise operations, this encoding strategy preserves the Galois automorphisms, enabling vector rotations in the encrypted domain. In CKKS, the input numbers are multiplied with the scale parameter Δ to avoid substantial accuracy loss in the encoding function. Typically, this scale is in a limited range $\Delta \in \{2^{20}, \ldots, 2^{60}\}$. The inherent noise required for the security of the encryption is then added in the least significant bits of the encoded numbers. Thus, increasing the Δ parameter decreases the noise impact. Ultimately, choosing the correct value for Δ is use-case specific and can be done empirically. In practical implementations, we set the integer precision γ as part of the parameters.

In summary, we have the capabilities of SIMD addition, multiplication, and vector rotation. Thus, all algorithms that can be evaluated with addition, subtraction, multiplication, and rotation of vectors can be performed in SIMD fashion. Next, we will discuss the adaptations necessary to make algorithms compliant with these restrictions and, thus, HE-friendly.

2.3 Adoption of HE-Friendliness

The concept of HE-friendliness in neural networks pertains to how a model can be effectively employed in the encrypted domain by applying HE. An in-depth evaluation of HE-friendliness necessitates careful analysis of each layer within the network. Notably, the definition of HE-friendliness varies depending on the specific HE schemes under consideration. For instance, binary schemes provide highly efficient lookup tables (LUT) that facilitate precise evaluation of nonlinear functions. Nevertheless, their efficiency remains limited to low degrees of numerical precision. In contrast, HE schemes employing arithmetic operations and SIMD encoding demand the consideration of different metrics. With such schemes, layers representable as arithmetic circuits are inherently compatible, while non-linear layers must be approximated or bypassed using hybrid approaches. Further, multiplicative depth is the primary driver of parameter size in such schemes. Hence, wider networks are more amenable than deeper ones.

Here, we give an overview of different techniques to achieve HE-friendliness for the CKKS approximate HE scheme. Generally, there are two main points when discussing these adaptations. First, non-linear functions cannot be evaluated directly and must be approximated. Second, linear functions can be implemented; however, some can be implemented more efficiently than others. The second property directly relates to the SIMD encoding of the CKKS scheme.

Linear Functions. Linear functions can be implemented in HE. However, using the CKKS encryption scheme imposes limitations that must be considered when dimensioning the parameters. Here, we give an overview of widely used linear layers in neural networks and considerations for their application in HE. We will distinguish between a known and unknown model for all functions involving trained parameters. This distinction determines whether the computing party operates with a plain trained model and solely an encrypted query or with both an encrypted model and an encrypted query.

Dense Layer. In all our networks, we employ fully connected layers, also called dense layers. These layers are implemented as a matrix-vector multiplication. For the known model approach, the optimized baby-step-giant-step (BSGS) method by Halevi and Shoup [23] is used. This strategy allows for the efficient implementation of plain-matrix, encrypted-vector multiplication. We elaborate on our implementation of this method in Sect. 3.4.

For unknown models, there are several improvements to the BSGS method [24]. Since the matrix is also encrypted in this scenario, operations cannot be performed as freely. Optimizations rely on intelligent packing methods to reduce multiplications and rotations. Generally, these algorithms achieve maximum amortized performance when the matrix dimensions align with the CKKS encoding capacity.

Convolutional Layer. In a convolution layer, we perform a convolution between the input and a filter. With different filter dimensions, the input can be correlated across axes. In the known model setting (i.e., the filter is known to the computing party), the convolutional layer can be efficiently implemented in HE, as shown first in Gazelle [25]. This approach can naturally be expanded to higher dimensions, diverse filter sizes, and varying numbers of filters. However, the stride parameter is inherently costly to support in HE. With a stride parameter of one, the filter kernel is applied to all input elements, with a stride of two, it is applied to every second, and so on. The algorithm mentioned above uses the SIMD encoding to apply the filter simultaneously to all input elements.

A stride larger than one renders this improvement impossible and produces a significant performance penalty. In the unknown model setting, convolutions are directly applicable, given the efficient packing of the filter kernel. However, while the multiplicative depth stays the same (i.e., both plaintext-ciphertext and ciphertext-ciphertext multiplications consume a modulus level), ciphertext multiplication incurs the costly relinearization operation.

Pooling Layer. In neural networks, many types of pooling layers are used for multiple reasons. Pooling aggregates input values to create the output, allowing dimensionality reduction and preventing overfitting. Further, these layers are often combined with convolutional layers for feature extraction. While numerous pooling methods exist, we will discuss the most prominent ones in the HE context. *Max Pooling* considers a pooling window as input and outputs the maximum value of this window. This pooling type should be avoided since comparisons are inherently expensive or inaccurate in CKKS. Next, *Lp Pooling* computes the p-norm of the pooling window. This type of pooling is even less compatible, as it implies a high multiplicative depth and an approximation error for the p-th root. Further, *Stochastic Pooling*, which selects a random element in the window, can be realized by masking the selected values and shifting them. However, since the selected position within the window may differ for each output element, it is expensive to compute in SIMD fashion. Finally, *Global Pooling* and *Average Pooling* compute the average of the input vector and the pooling window, respectively. These types are inherently HE-friendly as they can be efficiently realized with rotations, additions, and one plaintext-ciphertext multiplication. As the pooling methods described above do not have trainable parameters, there is no distinction between known and unknown models.

Non-linear Functions. In neural networks, non-linear layers play crucial roles in learning non-linear relations, preventing overfitting or dimensioning outputs for classification. Here, we overview some important non-linear functions and potential approaches to using them in the HE context.

Activation Layers. In neural networks, activation functions introduce non-linearity into the model. While this property is necessary for complex behavior, it is inherently not HE-friendly. Typically, polynomial approximations such as least-squares, Taylor series, or Chebyshev approximation are used in the literature [27]. All approximation methods achieve the best results within a given range and increase accuracy with the degree of the approximation polynomial. In the context of the CKKS scheme, it is necessary to find low-degree approximations that do not diverge in the input range.

Softmax Layer. In classification tasks, the last neural network layer is usually a Softmax function. This function re-scales all inputs between 0 and 1 such that they sum up to 1. When each output neuron corresponds to one class, the output after the Softmax function can be interpreted as the probability of the input belonging to a specific class. In our use case, this probability can be directly used in accumulating each key candidate's log-likelihood. In the context of private classification, it is unnecessary to compute this function in the encrypted domain. The Softmax function does not change ordering or require pre-trained parameters. If the output of Softmax can be disclosed, so can the input.

Next to the obvious computational benefit of executing the Softmax in plain, approximating the Softmax function comes with additional problems. Approximations work best in pre-defined ranges, as for the last layer in a neural network, depending on the network depth, it is more likely that inputs are out of bounds. In HETAL [29], the authors presented an accurate approximation by normalizing the inputs into the approximation range by approximated comparisons [27] and then computed their Softmax function. While they pushed the approximate error down, their implementation requires a costly bootstrapping procedure to work with reasonable parameters.

Batch Normalization Layers. Normalization functions map the input values to a given, typically smaller, region. This procedure reduces overfitting, avoids blowup of intermediate values, and has several advantages for training neural networks. The calculation of the mean and covariance are comparably cheap. However, the inverse square root necessary for this type of normalization is hard to approximate, and good results in the literature require more than 30 multiplications for the least accurate approximations [35].

Given an unknown model, the scale and shift operation that uses trained parameters introduces another ciphertext multiplication and addition. However, this is negligible compared to the inverse square root approximation. Ideally, Batch normalization layers should be avoided when using CKKS.

3   HE-Assisted DL-Based Side-Channel Analysis

Ideally, we would possess an agnostic cloud capable of training and evaluating encrypted traces. In the present study, we offer an encrypted trace inference implementation, thereby demonstrating a practical solution for the initial aspect of the problem. We base our implementation on the homomorphic encryption library SEAL [44]. We provide an implementation of the neural network layers and approximated non-linear functions relevant to our use case. Our implementation has a flexible setup that allows us to combine neural network layers more freely for different setups. In the following section, we give insights into the general setup of our HE-assisted DL-based SCA.

On a high level, our design is divided into two sections: plain training and HE classification. First, we perform the profiling phase of the device under test (DUT) with access to corresponding key and plaintext data with measured traces. Given this data, the server trains a network with state-of-the-art machine learning libraries. We will elaborate on the implementation specifics in Sect. 3.4. In the HE classification phase, only the client can access the DUT and the acquired traces. This client encrypts the relevant traces and sends them to the server. Given the encrypted traces and the pre-trained model, the server homomorphically classifies the query and returns the encrypted result. At no point does the server have access to the unencrypted query or intermediate results. Ultimately, the client decrypts the classification result and updates its key prediction. Based on the results, the client analyses and improves the required protection of its cryptographic implementation on the target device. The same machine learning model must be used for profiling and classification.

3.1 Profiling Phase

In the profiling phase (or training phase), the server has physical access to the DUT. First, the server measures traces $\mathcal{X}^{tr} \in \mathbb{X}^{N \times P}$ of the device and stores the corresponding key and input data. Before using the traces for profiling or classifying, as a preprocessing phase, we need to select points of interest (PoIs), i.e., reduce the columns of the traces matrix to contain relevant data. These points are the measurements that correlate most strongly with the key or a derived value. If no statistical analysis is feasible, we work with the entire trace matrix of the underlying dataset. The following sections will refer to the number of selected PoIs as P. We can reduce P for each trace in case of statistical leakage.

As a case study, we analyze encrypted traces of the first round of AES. We use either an unprotected implementation or measurements recorded with the masking countermeasure enabled. Thus, we aim to detect correlations between our traces and the targeted intermediate values. Generally, our attacks only target individual key bytes (but the extension to the whole key is straightforward). Given the key k and the plaintext p as an array of 16 bytes, we attack the ith byte by targeting the AES S-box output. More specifically, we target the intermediate result of the S-box in the first round of AES.

Given the trace matrix and the labels from the associated data, we train a deep learning classifier. For the unprotected AES implementation, simple network architectures suffice. There, we directly build models with HE in mind and showcase the impacts of different parameters. In our implementation, we present the feasibility of such a setting with both CNN and MLP. Given the protected AES implementations, we adopted a different strategy. We used a model from the literature [48] to demonstrate the use of the ideas from Sect. 2.3 to make it HE-friendly.

3.2 Private Classification Phase

In the classification phase, the server classifies the encrypted traces of the client. First, both parties agree on CKKS parameters that support the trained network. For our implementation, we give the following considerations on the choice of parameters. We need to dimension the parameters $\{n, q, \Delta, \gamma\}$. See Sect. 2.2 for an overview of CKKS and its parameters. For Δ, γ, the fixed-point scale, and the integer scale, it is sufficient to evaluate the correct setting empirically. In practice, depending on the multiplicative depth of the evaluation circuit (depending on the network), we scale our coefficient modulus to $\log_2 q = L \cdot \log_2 \Delta + 2(\log_2 \Delta + \gamma)$.

In other words, we have L primes $q_i \approx \Delta$, and two distinct special primes $\log_2 q_s = \log_2 \Delta + \gamma$. For further insights into the selection of q we refer the reader to the original paper [12] and the documentation of SEAL [44]. Next, we set n according to either the recommendations of the homomorphic encryption standard [2] or the lattice hardness estimator [3]. For different levels of security, they provide the limit of q for a given n. Remember that a larger q has a negative impact on security and must be compensated with a larger n. Depending on the respective multiplicative depth and the resulting bit size in q, we set our n to the minimum required value with 128-bit security. Given our models, we work with $n = 16\,384$. Increasing security to 256-bit is achieved by doubling n, which roughly translates to doubling the runtime of HE computations. This level lies well in the NIST recommendation with a minimum of 80-bit security [5].

Once the client and the server agree on the CKKS parameters, the client sends the encrypted traces to the server. The server uses the HE-friendly network to classify the traces in the encrypted domain and returns the encrypted output of the last layer before the Softmax function.

3.3   Analysis Strategy

Following the generic introduction in Sect. 2.1, we now specify how we analyze our homomorphic predictions to reconstruct a key. We train our model to specific target labels in one-hot encoded form depending on the scenario. For an unmasked implementation, it is sufficient to set the label of an input trace to the Hamming weight of the S-box output $y_{i,j} = HW(\text{S-box}(p_j \oplus k_j))$, where i is the trace index and j is the attacked byte of the key. Given a masked implementation, we do not apply the Hamming weight as this would make our model dependent on the specific mask in the unknown mask scenario. Thus, our labels are the byte values of the S-box output $y_{i,j} = \text{S-box}(p_j \oplus k_j)$, and the classification results of the model are 256 probabilities, one for each potential S-box output value.

We obtain a prediction matrix with 9 (in the unmasked scenario with the Hamming weight leakage model) or 256 probabilities (in the masked scenario with the Identity leakage model) for each attacked trace and compute the element-wise natural logarithm.[3] Then, we calculate the S-box output for each key hypothesis with the plaintext corresponding to the attacked trace. We create a hypothesis vector, storing the probability of the S-box output to the index of the corresponding key hypothesis. We sum up the log-likelihoods in this hypothesis vector for multiple attacked traces. Finally, we compute the rank, i.e., the index of the correct key in the hypothesis list sorted by its prediction probabilities. The key rank indicates the difficulty of recovering the key byte after classifying a specific number of traces. When the key rank converges to zero, an attacker can read off the key byte directly.

---

[3] The number of probabilities is decided based on the leakage model and the cryptographic function.

3.4   Layer Implementation

We discussed the implications of different neural network layers in the HE context in Sect. 2.3. Here, we state the concrete parameters we used in our instantiations and provide an overview of the implementation specifics.

Dense Layer. We evaluate this type of layer as an encrypted vector plain matrix multiplication, with the Baby-Step Giant-Step method (BSGS). As a precondition asymmetric matrices must be padded with zeroes in the shorter dimension. Given the square weight-matrix W with size $t = t_1 \cdot t_2$ and the encrypted trace vector x, the BSGS method calculates

$$ W \cdot x = \sum_{i=0}^{t_1-1} \mathrm{rot}_{(i \cdot t_2)} \left(\sum_{j=0}^{t_2-1} \mathrm{rot}_{(k)} \left(\mathrm{diag}_{(k+j)}(W) \right) \circ \mathrm{rot}_{(i)}(x) \right), $$

where diag_i is the i-th diagonal of the matrix represented as a vector, rot_i is the ciphertext rotated by i slots to the left, and $\circ$ represents the Hadamard product of the vectors. Given a negative value i, the ciphertext is rotated to the right. Further, $k = (-\lfloor (i \cdot t_2 + j)/t_2 \rfloor \cdot t_2)$. This optimization requires a total number of $t_1 + t_2 - 2$ rotations, t multiplications, and $t - 1$ additions in the encrypted domain. Thus, the closer the factors t_1 and t_2 are, the higher the performance improvement. In total, we see that two factors improve performance. First, Square matrices improve amortized performance as no padding is necessary. Second, we need a matrix dimension t, with close factors $t_1 \cdot t_2 = t$. Thus, matrices with a square size $t_1 = t_2 = \sqrt{t}$ yield optimal performance.

Convolution Layer. We implemented the convolutional layer with a stride of 1 and the option to apply multiple filters sequentially. The output is flattened into the ciphertext vector by default when using multiple filters. In other words, a multi-dimensional tensor is mapped into a single vector within the ciphertext. This flattening requires one rotation per filter dimension. Given each filter with size f, we require $f - 1$ rotations, $f - 1$ plaintext-ciphertext multiplications, and additions. This network layer consumes one modulus layer.

Pooling Layer. We apply average-pooling layers as they are particularly HE-friendly. Given a stride of $s = 1$, where the average is applied to all elements within the filter size f, we compute $\mathbf{x}_p = \frac{1}{f} \sum_{i=0}^{f} \mathrm{rot}_{-i}(\mathbf{x})$. This procedure computes the average filter for all elements in the SIMD-encoded ciphertext. Given a flattened input vector, we must not pool elements of different channels. We accommodate by combining the division with a masking step, saving a plaintext-ciphertext multiplication. Then, we compute the sum for each channel and shift it to the new position. As each channel shrinks by $f - 1$ elements, we must rotate the $j - th$ channel by $j \cdot (f - 1)$ to the left to uphold the flattened encoding. Ultimately, the required operations increase linearly in the number of channels. Thus, the pooling layer's complexity relies on the number of input elements and channels.

Approximated ReLU. As an activation function in the encrypted domain, we use a polynomial approximation of the ReLU function. We applied the Chebychev approximation, which provided fast convergence. More precisely, we had satisfying results with a degree three approximation defined as:

$$ReLU_{approx}(x) = -0.0061728x^3 + 0.092593x^2 + 0.59259x + 0.49383. \qquad (1)$$

4 Experiments and Evaluation

Given the general description of our approach, we apply it to different models and datasets to evaluate the performance. Our experiments focus on two settings: first, we assess models designed explicitly with HE in mind, with power traces of an unprotected AES implementation obtained with the aid of a ChipWhisperer device[4]. Second, we apply our setup to a state-of-the-art approach using CNNs to attack protected AES implementations [41]. The second experiment gives us insights into performance in real-world applications and the adaptation strategies to make neural networks HE-friendly. Refer to Sect. 2.3 for further information about HE-friendliness. Finally, we evaluate our experiments regarding runtime, memory usage, accuracy, and key recovery speed. The latter is the required number of traces to recover the attacked key byte reliably.

4.1 Experiment Setup

Environment. We run our experiments on a Linux server with an AMD Ryzen 9 7900X 12-core Processor, 4.7 GHz clock speed, and 128 GB Memory. Regarding implementation, we use TensorFlow v2.13[5] and scikit-learn v1.3 [36] for the plain deep learning Python implementations to train and test our networks. We use SEAL v4.1 [44] for their CKKS homomorphic encryption implementation. We demonstrate our attacks using two datasets containing the side-channel traces of AES-128 implementations.

Datasets. The ChipWhisperer dataset gives a standard comparison base for evaluating different algorithms [34]. The dataset is obtained from an unprotected AES-128 implementation on the Chipwhisperer CW308 Target. The dataset contains 3 000 traces, each consisting of up to 5 000 PoIs for the same key. As discussed in Sect. 3, the pre-processing phase selects the 20–2 500 best-fitting PoIs for the training dataset for each trace. Additionally, we use the entire dataset with 5 000 PoIs (without pre-processing) to train our classification model.

The ASCAD dataset is generated by taking measurements from an ATMega8515 running masked AES-128 and is proposed as a benchmark dataset for SCA [41]. The dataset consists of 50 000 profiling traces and 10 000 attack traces, each with 700 features. In this paper, we use 45 000 profiling traces as training data and 5 000 as test data. The profiling and attacking sets both use

---

[4] https://www.newae.com/chipwhisperer.
[5] https://www.tensorflow.org/.

the same fixed key.[6] We follow the common naming convention for this dataset and denote it as `ASCADf`. We attack the third key byte as that is the first masked byte, and we consider the Identity (ID) leakage model. The dataset is provided on the `ASCADf` GitHub repository.[7]

Training. As stated, we train networks for the unprotected ChipWhisperer and the protected `ASCADf` datasets. We analyze the first dataset with two neural networks. The MLP has two dense layers. The CNN has convolutional, dense, and average pooling layers. The kernel size of the convolutional layer is set to 9, the average-pooling layer has a pool size of 3, and the last dense layer has nine outputs for each output label. Both networks use the approximated ReLU and Softmax as activation functions. We discuss implementation specifics in Sect. 3.4.

Regarding `ASCADf`, we adopt the model architecture of [48] for HE. While their model is optimized for training and classification runtime, it naturally does not consider HE-friendliness. Contrary to the ChipWhisperer dataset, where we designed a model directly, we adapted an existing model to HE needs. We used the approximate ReLU function from Eq. (1) for the activation functions in the hidden layers. We removed the batch normalization layer, which boosts learning speed and prevents overfitting next to other aspects. Our experiments found that a dropout layer was sufficient to compensate for the overfitting control. Further, a stride parameter of size s leads to an output ciphertext where only every s'th value is relevant. One can shift the relevant elements to their new position. However, this approach would take $c_{out} - 1$ homomorphic rotations, where c_{out} is the flattened output size of the average pooling layer. Ultimately, we set the stride parameter to one, as this did not impact the classification performance. In more complex networks, where the stride is more relevant, it is possible to implement the average pooling as a matrix-vector multiplication and enjoy the optimizations of the BSGS algorithm. In summary, all our experiments with the `ASCADf` dataset run with the network consisting of a convolutional layer, an average pooling layer, and three dense layers. The convolutional layer has four filters with a size of 1. The average pool has a stride of one and a kernel size of two. The three dense layers start with an input dimension of $d = 4 \cdot P - 4$ (i.e., factor 4 expansion by the convolutional filter and reduction of 4 by the pooling layers), have ten neurons each, and output 256 key probabilities.

4.2 Evaluation

Table 1 shows our MLP and CNN encrypted classification results. The memory and time columns report the results for a single client query containing one trace. MLP and CNN achieve a somewhat quadratic memory and time complexity regarding the number of PoIs used during the model training. However, contrary

---

[6] Current state-of-the-art results indicate that the ASCAD version with random keys is not significantly more complex than the fixed key version [38].

[7] https://github.com/ANSSI-FR/ASCAD/tree/master/ATMEGA_AES_v1/ATM_ AES_v1_fixed_key.

Table 1. Classification results.

Model	PoIs	Accuracy	Memory Usage (Private SCA)	Avg. Query Time (Private SCA)	Avg. Query Time (Plain SCA)	Avg. Query Time Overhead
MLP	20	0.3	721 MB	310 ms	0.001 ms	$31 \cdot 10^4$
	500	1.0	2.7 GB	2.4 s	0.237 ms	$1.0 \cdot 10^4$
	2500	0.9	20.1 GB	12 s	13 ms	$0.09 \cdot 10^4$
	5000	0.7	16.3 GB	39 s	72 ms	$0.05 \cdot 10^4$
CNN	20	0.5	210 MB	141 ms	0.001 ms	$14 \cdot 10^4$
	500	0.8	790 MB	1 s	0.019 ms	$53 \cdot 10^4$
	2500	1.0	2.4 GB	4.7 s	0.1 ms	$4.7 \cdot 10^4$
	5000	0.2	12.3 GB	25 s	0.2 ms	$12.5 \cdot 10^4$

to this trend, some input dimensions lead to unexpectedly good metrics (e.g., $P = 5\,000$ for MLP or $P = 2\,500$ for CNN). This non-linear behavior stems from the matrix-vector product in the dense layer using the BSGS optimization as discussed in Sect. 3.

Additionally, we compare the runtime overhead between private and non-private classifications, offering a perspective on the efficiency of our private SCA versus a non-private SCA. While the private implementation is observed to be up to five orders of magnitude slower than the plain network evaluation, we argue that the modest time requirement for private SCA, particularly with PoIs up to $2\,500$, brings significantly enhanced privacy advantages at a minimal cost. The accuracy column in the table shows the probability of predicting the correct Hamming weight during key byte identification. Note that this is an iterative attack. Next to the actual prediction, the probability value of each class matters. Even though the accuracy with $P = 5\,000$ is low, the key recovery converges after less than five trace queries. Regarding scaling, the performance for the entire key scales *linear* time w.r.t. the security parameter of AES.

ASCAD Evaluation. After testing our implementation on the ChipWhisperer dataset, we focused on analyzing the masked implementation. For comparability, we set up the optimized model [48] to have a baseline for our implementation. Then, we applied our adaptations to make the model HE-friendly as described in Sects. 2.3 and 3.4. We evaluated our model in plain to have a baseline for the impact of our changes. Finally, we ran the encrypted classifications with 128-bit and 256-bit security. We refer the reader to Sect. 3.2 for more information on the security level or the classification procedure. A comprehensive description of the key recovery process can be found in Sect. 3.3. Table 3 shows the concrete CKKS parameters for each setting.

In Fig. 1, we show the development of the key rank, averaged over 100 runs (i.e., guessing entropy). The private and plain classifications yielded reasonably similar results. This fact shows the feasibility of our approach in terms of accuracy. We see a similar convergence speed when comparing our model to the unadapted version. For each attack run, a different subset of 300 traces is selected from $1\,000$ classifications of the test set. The correct key byte is among the top

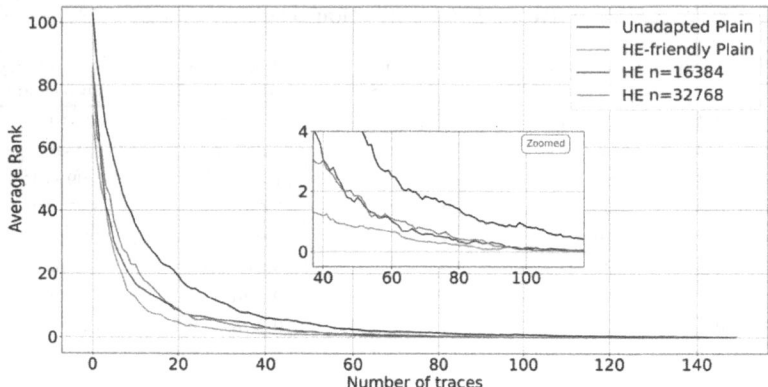

Fig. 1. Comparison of key recovery attack on the `ASCADf` dataset with different approaches. Unadapted Plain uses the optimized model from [48] and performs classification in plain. HE-friendly Plain uses the adapted model but executes the classification in plain, while HE applies private classification with different polynomial degrees n and different security levels. All attacks use the same training data and classification data.

two candidates after 75 encrypted classifications in under 17 min. Nevertheless, we can see in Table 2 that the accuracy of our model is very close to the original one. Again, it is worth noting that the accuracy describes the relation between traces and accurate key byte predictions. However, our side-channel distinguisher is built by summing the log-likelihoods. Thus, on average, high probabilities matter more than correct classifications. The higher accuracy with 256-bit security is best understood with Table 3. This table shows the different CKKS parameters we used for our models. There are the two settings used in the ChipWhisperer attacks. Then, the settings that are used for our `ASCADf` model. The choice of $n = 32\,768$, as seen in the 4th row, gave us a little more budget for our q, so we could increase the integer precision γ. Recall that the maximum size of q depends on the security level and the polynomial degree n. It seems reasonable that doubling the security level leads to roughly twice the runtime and memory costs.

Table 2. Benchmark data for the `ASCADf` dataset. We tested the state-of-the-art model against our adapted HE-friendly version. All runs evaluated the same attack traces. We ran the adapted model in plain and HE with 128 and 256 bit security levels.

Model	Security Level	Accuracy	Memory Usage (Private SCA)	Avg. Query Time	Avg. Query Time Overhead
Reference [48]	None	0.013	2 GB	0.03 ms	–
Our Model	None	0.010	2 GB	0.03 ms	–
	128 bit	0.003	14 GB	13.3 s	$4.5 \cdot 10^5$
	256 bit	0.010	27 GB	27.4 s	$9.4 \cdot 10^5$

Table 3. CKKS parameters for our HE classifications. We see the results for both datasets we tested and both security levels evaluated. Further, we have the polynomial degree n, the bit size of the coefficient modulus q, the required multiplicative depth L, the fixed-point precision Δ, and the integer precision γ.

Dataset	Security Level	n	$\log_2 q$	L	Δ	γ
CW dataset	128 bit	16 384	360	6	40	20
	256 bit	32 768	360	6	40	20
ASCADf	128 bit	16 384	430	11	30	20
	256 bit	32 768	450	11	30	30

5   Discussion

Performance and Accuracy. The results of Sect. 4.2 demonstrate that private SCA and state-of-the-art DL-based SCA exhibit similar performance in terms of accuracy and convergence speed. As shown in Fig. 1, HE does not limit the convergence speed. More precisely, given an HE-friendly neural network, we can select parameters that incur no performance penalty compared to plain evaluations. Of course, the adaptation to HE-friendliness might cost precision.

Contrary to accuracy, the primary distinction lies in the computational runtime needed to obtain these results. The private SCA requires a significantly longer computation time than the simple SCA, with a difference of four to six orders of magnitude, depending on the network architecture. It has been demonstrated in [4] that GPUs can be employed to expedite HE-related computations by one or two orders of magnitude, thereby substantially mitigating the additional overhead. Similarly, there have been dedicated hardware optimizations for HE computation. In [32], the authors presented a successful port of CKKS to the FPGA platform. They achieved similar speedups with a single FPGA running at 200 MHz. Considering the boundaries in neural network depth, we have seen several studies tackling this issue with more significant parameter settings [4] or the costly bootstrapping operation [28]. Recall that the parameter choices of the papers above increase the computational overhead of HE. The overhead factor between HE and plain evaluations scales linearly with the multiplicative depth. Another option is to integrate interactive procedures, where the client has an increased network cost to reduce complexity on the server side, as in [25]. Given all these costly approaches, the first goal should always be the reduction of the network depth.

Trust Model. Homomorphic encryption paves the way for data protection during computation. However, discussing the trust assumptions more precisely is necessary to understand its security guarantees. Our system works in the semi-honest trust model. We assume parties that want to obtain input from the other parties but will never actively deviate from the protocol. In other words, given the correct use of the CKKS algorithms for key generation, encryption, decryption, and encrypted operations, input privacy is guaranteed up to the specified security parameter. If one party deviates from the protocol, several potential problems arise. A malicious client can send random traces, so the final result will never identify any key leakage. Further, a client might send specifically crafted input traces to leak the private model parameters of the server [1]. Targeting the former issue requires verification of the measured traces, which is a challenging problem when combined with privacy. The privacy of the model can be boosted with differential privacy (DP) [18], a method to add fine-tuned noise to a dataset to limit the privacy loss caused by publishing (output) data. Given a malicious server, a client cannot verify whether the correct model was executed. However, verifiable computations are a very active line of research [46]. We acknowledge that these concerns are crucial for enabling the feasibility of HE-assisted DLSCA. However, addressing these issues falls beyond the current research scope. Further analysis and research are necessary to explore and resolve these challenges.

Limitations and Conditions. Our work shows the general feasibility of HE-assisted DL-based SCA. Evaluating state-of-the-art models for side-channel leakage in the encrypted domain is possible. However, our approach requires a server with access to training data. Without this precondition, multiple problems arise. First, we require encrypted learning when preventing the server from learning the model. Then, the model is encrypted under the key of the data provider. If just the training data but not the model is private, the model parameters can be decrypted. If the model should remain private as well, we need to employ multi-key HE [11] settings that allow operations on ciphertexts encrypted by different parties. Such an approach would make it necessary for the data provider to play an active role in the classification part, which might be unrealistic depending on the setting. Finally, HE classification would get much more expensive if the model weights and biases were encrypted. We extensively discussed the impacts of the unknown model setting in Sect. 2.3.

6   Conclusions and Future Work

This work delved into the practicality of integrating homomorphic encryption with neural networks for private side-channel analysis. Its primary aim was to assess the strengths and limitations of this method. Further, it highlights the associated constraints, including the need to trust the data sources. Our evaluation of modern HE protocols and libraries suggests that unprotected and protected implementations can be attacked while traces remain encrypted. For further scaling towards larger use cases, we also identify high-level strategies to remain "HE-friendly". Avoiding the increase in the depth of the neural network too much while allowing for "wider" neural networks is an approach that will work well with the current most suitable CKKS homomorphic encryption scheme. We have seen that shallow networks of traces with 5 000 PoIs can be classified in 40 s. Exploring SCA applications that test these boundaries with private classifications is an open challenge.

In future work, it would be interesting to consider further the impact of hiding countermeasures (e.g., desynchronization) or noisy datasets (e.g., hardware implementations and/or software implementation with increased noise levels) on HE-encrypted data analysis to assess how well HE handles various noise sources. These problems are conventionally investigated with deeper neural networks.

References

1. Abadi, M., Chu, A., Goodfellow, I.J., McMahan, H.B., Mironov, I., Talwar, K., Zhang, L.: Deep learning with differential privacy. In: Weippl, E.R., Katzenbeisser, S., Kruegel, C., Myers, A.C., Halevi, S. (eds.) ACM CCS 2016: 23rd Conference on Computer and Communications Security, pp. 308–318. ACM Press, Vienna (2016). https://doi.org/10.1145/2976749.2978318
2. Albrecht, M.R., et al.: Homomorphic encryption standard. IACR Cryptol. ePrint Arch., p. 939 (2019)
3. Albrecht, M.R., Player, R., Scott, S.: On the concrete hardness of learning with errors. J. Math. Cryptol. **9**(3), 169–203 (2015)
4. Badawi, A.A., Hoang, L., Mun, C.F., Laine, K., Aung, K.M.M.: Privft: private and fast text classification with homomorphic encryption. CoRR arxiv:1908.06972 (2019)
5. Barker, E.: Recommendation for key management, part 1: General (2016). https://doi.org/10.6028/NIST.SP.800-57pt1r4
6. Brakerski, Z.: Fully homomorphic encryption without modulus switching from classical GapSVP. In: Safavi-Naini, R., Canetti, R. (eds.) CRYPTO 2012. LNCS, vol. 7417, pp. 868–886. Springer, Heidelberg (2012). https://doi.org/10.1007/978-3-642-32009-5_50
7. Brakerski, Z., Gentry, C., Vaikuntanathan, V.: (leveled) fully homomorphic encryption without bootstrapping. In: ITCS, pp. 309–325. ACM (2012)
8. Bursztein, E., Invernizzi, L., Král, K., Moghimi, D., Picod, J.M., Zhang, M.: Generic attacks against cryptographic hardware through long-range deep learning (2023)
9. Cagli, E., Dumas, C., Prouff, E.: Convolutional neural networks with data augmentation against jitter-based countermeasures. In: Fischer, W., Homma, N. (eds.) CHES 2017. LNCS, vol. 10529, pp. 45–68. Springer, Cham (2017). https://doi.org/10.1007/978-3-319-66787-4_3
10. Chari, S., Rao, J.R., Rohatgi, P.: Template attacks. In: Kaliski, B.S., Koç, K., Paar, C. (eds.) CHES 2002. LNCS, vol. 2523, pp. 13–28. Springer, Heidelberg (2003). https://doi.org/10.1007/3-540-36400-5_3
11. Chen, H., Dai, W., Kim, M., Song, Y.: Efficient multi-key homomorphic encryption with packed ciphertexts with application to oblivious neural network inference. In: Cavallaro, L., Kinder, J., Wang, X., Katz, J. (eds.) ACM CCS 2019: 26th Conference on Computer and Communications Security, pp. 395–412. ACM Press, London (2019). https://doi.org/10.1145/3319535.3363207
12. Cheon, J.H., Han, K., Kim, A., Kim, M., Song, Y.: A full RNS variant of approximate homomorphic encryption. In: Cid, C., Jacobson, M., Jr. (eds.) SAC 2018. LNCS, vol. 11349, pp. 347–368. Springer, Heidelberg (2018). https://doi.org/10.1007/978-3-030-10970-7_16

13. Cheon, J.H., Kim, A., Kim, M., Song, Y.: Homomorphic encryption for arithmetic of approximate numbers. In: Takagi, T., Peyrin, T. (eds.) ASIACRYPT 2017. LNCS, vol. 10624, pp. 409–437. Springer, Cham (2017). https://doi.org/10.1007/978-3-319-70694-8_15
14. Chou, E., Beal, J., Levy, D., Yeung, S., Haque, A., Fei-Fei, L.: Faster cryptonets: leveraging sparsity for real-world encrypted inference. CoRR arxiv:1811.09953 (2018)
15. Clavier, C., Isorez, Q., Wurcker, A.: Complete SCARE of AES-like block ciphers by chosen plaintext collision power analysis. In: Paul, G., Vaudenay, S. (eds.) INDOCRYPT 2013. LNCS, vol. 8250, pp. 116–135. Springer, Cham (2013). https://doi.org/10.1007/978-3-319-03515-4_8
16. Dathathri, R., et al.: CHET: an optimizing compiler for fully-homomorphic neural-network inferencing. In: Proceedings of the 40th ACM SIGPLAN Conference on Programming Language Design and Implementation, pp. 142–156. PLDI 2019, Association for Computing Machinery, New York (2019). https://doi.org/10.1145/3314221.3314628
17. Ducas, L., Micciancio, D.: FHEW: bootstrapping homomorphic encryption in less than a second. In: Oswald, E., Fischlin, M. (eds.) EUROCRYPT 2015. LNCS, vol. 9056, pp. 617–640. Springer, Heidelberg (2015). https://doi.org/10.1007/978-3-662-46800-5_24
18. Dwork, C., McSherry, F., Nissim, K., Smith, A.: Calibrating noise to sensitivity in private data analysis. In: Halevi, S., Rabin, T. (eds.) TCC 2006. LNCS, vol. 3876, pp. 265–284. Springer, Heidelberg (2006). https://doi.org/10.1007/11681878_14
19. Fan, J., Vercauteren, F.: Somewhat practical fully homomorphic encryption. IACR Cryptol. ePrint Arch., p. 144 (2012)
20. Gentry, C.: Fully homomorphic encryption using ideal lattices. In: STOC, pp. 169–178. ACM (2009)
21. Gilad-Bachrach, R., Dowlin, N., Laine, K., Lauter, K.E., Naehrig, M., Wernsing, J.: Cryptonets: applying neural networks to encrypted data with high throughput and accuracy. In: ICML. JMLR Workshop and Conference Proceedings, vol. 48, pp. 201–210. JMLR.org (2016)
22. Google: Google cloud (2018). https://cloud.google.com/
23. Halevi, S., Shoup, V.: Faster homomorphic linear transformations in HElib. In: Shacham, H., Boldyreva, A. (eds.) CRYPTO 2018. LNCS, vol. 10991, pp. 93–120. Springer, Cham (2018). https://doi.org/10.1007/978-3-319-96884-1_4
24. Jiang, X., Kim, M., Lauter, K.E., Song, Y.: Secure outsourced matrix computation and application to neural networks. In: Lie, D., Mannan, M., Backes, M., Wang, X. (eds.) Proceedings of the 2018 ACM SIGSAC Conference on Computer and Communications Security, CCS 2018, Toronto, ON, Canada, 15–19 October 2018, pp. 1209–1222. ACM (2018). https://doi.org/10.1145/3243734.3243837
25. Juvekar, C., Vaikuntanathan, V., Chandrakasan, A.: GAZELLE: a low latency framework for secure neural network inference. In: Enck, W., Felt, A.P. (eds.) USENIX Security 2018: 27th USENIX Security Symposium, pp. 1651–1669. USENIX Association, Baltimore (2018)
26. LeCun, Y., Bottou, L., Bengio, Y., Haffner, P.: Gradient-based learning applied to document recognition. Proc. IEEE 86(11), 2278–2324 (1998)
27. Lee, E., Lee, J., No, J., Kim, Y.: Minimax approximation of sign function by composite polynomial for homomorphic comparison. IEEE Trans. Dependable Secur. Comput. 19(6), 3711–3727 (2022). https://doi.org/10.1109/TDSC.2021.3105111
28. Lee, J., et al.: Privacy-preserving machine learning with fully homomorphic encryption for deep neural network. IEEE Access 10, 30039–30054 (2022)

29. Lee, S., Lee, G., Kim, J.W., Shin, J., Lee, M.: HETAL: efficient privacy-preserving transfer learning with homomorphic encryption. In: Krause, A., Brunskill, E., Cho, K., Engelhardt, B., Sabato, S., Scarlett, J. (eds.) International Conference on Machine Learning, ICML 2023, Honolulu, Hawaii, USA, 23–29 July 2023. Proceedings of Machine Learning Research, vol. 202, pp. 19010–19035. PMLR (2023). https://proceedings.mlr.press/v202/lee23m.html

30. Maghrebi, H., Portigliatti, T., Prouff, E.: Breaking cryptographic implementations using deep learning techniques. In: Carlet, C., Hasan, M.A., Saraswat, V. (eds.) SPACE 2016. LNCS, vol. 10076, pp. 3–26. Springer, Cham (2016). https://doi.org/10.1007/978-3-319-49445-6_1

31. Mangard, S., Oswald, E., Popp, T.: Power Analysis Attacks - Revealing the Secrets of Smart Cards. Springer, Heidelberg (2007). https://doi.org/10.1007/978-0-387-38162-6

32. Mert, A.C., Aikata, Kwon, S., Shin, Y., Yoo, D., Lee, Y., Roy, S.S.: Medha: microcoded hardware accelerator for computing on encrypted data. IACR Trans. Cryptogr. Hardw. Embed. Syst. **2023**(1), 463–500 (2023). https://doi.org/10.46586/tches.v2023.i1.463-500

33. Meyre, A., et al.: Concrete ML: a privacy-preserving machine learning library using fully homomorphic encryption for data scientists (2022). https://github.com/zama-ai/concrete-ml

34. O'Flynn, C., Chen, Z.D.: ChipWhisperer: an open-source platform for hardware embedded security research. In: International Workshop on Constructive Side-Channel Analysis and Secure Design (2014)

35. Panda, S.: Polynomial approximation of inverse sqrt function for FHE. In: Dolev, S., Katz, J., Meisels, A. (eds.) CSCML 2022, vol. 13301, pp. 366–376. Springer, Heidelberg (2022). https://doi.org/10.1007/978-3-031-07689-3_27

36. Pedregosa, F., et al.: Scikit-learn: machine learning in python. J. Mach. Learn. Res. **12**, 2825–2830 (2011)

37. Perin, G., Chmielewski, L., Picek, S.: Strength in numbers: improving generalization with ensembles in machine learning-based profiled side-channel analysis. IACR Trans. Cryptogr. Hardware Embed. Syst. **2020**(4), 337–364 (2020). https://doi.org/10.13154/tches.v2020.i4.337-364. https://tches.iacr.org/index.php/TCHES/article/view/8686

38. Perin, G., Wu, L., Picek, S.: Exploring feature selection scenarios for deep learning-based side-channel analysis. IACR Trans. Cryptogr. Hardw. Embed. Syst. 828–861 (2022)

39. Picek, S., Heuser, A., Perin, G., Guilley, S.: Profiled side-channel analysis in the efficient attacker framework. In: Grosso, V., Poppelmann, T. (eds.) CARDIS 2021. LNCS, vol. 13173, pp. 44–63. Springer, Heidelberg (2021). https://doi.org/10.1007/978-3-030-97348-3_3

40. Picek, S., Perin, G., Mariot, L., Wu, L., Batina, L.: Sok: deep learning-based physical side-channel analysis. ACM Comput. Surv. **55**(11) (2023). https://doi.org/10.1145/3569577

41. Prouff, E., Strullu, R., Benadjila, R., Cagli, E., Dumas, C.: Study of deep learning techniques for side-channel analysis and introduction to ASCAD database. Cryptology ePrint Archive, Report 2018/053 (2018). https://eprint.iacr.org/2018/053

42. Rijsdijk, J., Wu, L., Perin, G., Picek, S.: Reinforcement learning for hyperparameter tuning in deep learning-based side-channel analysis. IACR Trans. Cryptogr. Hardw. Embed. Syst. **2021**(3), 677–707 (2021). https://doi.org/10.46586/tches.v2021.i3.677-707. https://tches.iacr.org/index.php/TCHES/article/view/8989

43. Rivain, M., Roche, T.: SCARE of secret ciphers with SPN structures. In: Sako, K., Sarkar, P. (eds.) ASIACRYPT 2013. LNCS, vol. 8269, pp. 526–544. Springer, Heidelberg (2013). https://doi.org/10.1007/978-3-642-42033-7_27

44. Microsoft SEAL (release 4.1). Microsoft Research, Redmond (2023). https://github.com/Microsoft/SEAL

45. Standaert, F.-X., Malkin, T.G., Yung, M.: A unified framework for the analysis of side-channel key recovery attacks. In: Joux, A. (ed.) EUROCRYPT 2009. LNCS, vol. 5479, pp. 443–461. Springer, Heidelberg (2009). https://doi.org/10.1007/978-3-642-01001-9_26

46. Viand, A., Knabenhans, C., Hithnawi, A.: Verifiable fully homomorphic encryption. CoRR arxiv:2301.07041 (2023). https://doi.org/10.48550/arXiv.2301.07041

47. Wu, L., Perin, G., Picek, S.: I choose you: automated hyperparameter tuning for deep learning-based side-channel analysis. IEEE Trans. Emerg. Topics Comput. (2022)

48. Zaid, G., Bossuet, L., Habrard, A., Venelli, A.: Methodology for efficient CNN architectures in profiling attacks. IACR Trans. Cryptogr. Hardw. Embed. Syst. **2020**(1), 1–36 (2019). https://doi.org/10.13154/tches.v2020.i1.1-36. https://tches.iacr.org/index.php/TCHES/article/view/8391

PUF/RNG

Leakage Sources of the ICLooPUF: Analysis of a Side-Channel Protected Oscillator-Based PUF

Niklas Stein[iD] and Michael Pehl[(✉)][iD]

School of Computation, Information and Technology, Chair of Security in
Information Technology, Technical University of Munich, 80333 Munich, Germany
{niklas.stein,m.pehl}@tum.de

Abstract. In the last years, Physical Unclonable Functions (PUFs)
became a popular security primitive, which is nowadays also used in
several products. As a lightweight solution for key storage, they are frequently suggested in an environment where attackers have direct access
to the hardware. This triggered the evaluation of PUFs regarding side-
channel weaknesses and the development of corresponding countermeasures. One primitive to overcome such attacks is the Interleaved Challenge Loop PUF (ICLooPUF). While the first analyses seem to support
the resilience of this novel PUF against side-channel attacks, we identify
in our work two leakage sources: First, we show that a yet unreported
weakness of the counters used to measure the ICLooPUF period lengths
allows for an attack. Second, we show that interleaving can be considered
a modulation. As a consequence, the PUF leaks via its sidebands of the
power spectrum in the frequency domain. Theoretical analysis provides
an understanding of the root cause of the leakage; Practical experiments
show the significance of the leakage sources and the feasibility of the
attack. Potential countermeasures and the impact on the Loop PUF and
its derivatives are discussed.

Keywords: Physical Unclonable Function · Side-Channel Analysis ·
Counter Leakage · Frequency Modulation · Interleaved Challenge Loop
PUF · Loop PUF · Two-Metric Helper Data

1 Introduction

In the last two decades, Physical Unclonable Functions (PUFs) developed from
an interesting research idea to a primitive, which is nowadays in first products.
Silicon-based PUFs derive secrets from inherent process variations influencing
the chip. They measure such minuscule and unavoidable variations in, e.g., doping concentration, electron mobility, and threshold voltage, quantize the measurement, and derive a device's unique fingerprint. The resulting – due to measurement noise, environmental conditions, and aging – noisy fingerprint is then,
in most applications, further processed to a secret key or used in a challenge-
response protocol. A long list of PUF primitives has been presented, with the

© The Author(s), under exclusive license to Springer Nature Switzerland AG 2024
R. Wacquez and N. Homma (Eds.): COSADE 2024, LNCS 14595, pp. 157–176, 2024.
https://doi.org/10.1007/978-3-031-57543-3_9

most well-known ones being Ring Oscillator (RO) PUFs [20], Arbiter PUFs [6], and SRAM PUFs [8,10]. Another PUF primitive – and the ancestor of the Interleaved Challenge Loop PUF (ICLooPUF) [22] we analyze in this work – is the Loop PUF. It has been introduced in [4] as a PUF that is easy to design.

Since PUFs are used to generate secret information on a chip, they are also an interesting target for attackers. For multi-challenge PUFs like the Arbiter PUF, the main attack vector is machine learning based on the challenge-response behavior [18]. However, PUFs are also electronic circuits and, as such, exhibit operation-dependent side-channels. SRAM PUFs, e.g., have been attacked by observing the photon emission of the opened chip [9], and RO PUFs have been attacked by laser-voltage probing [13]. Most commonly, however, power and electromagnetic (EM) leakage of PUFs is exploited by Side-Channel Analysis (SCA) attacks. While attacks on other PUFs – like the one on the Arbiter PUFs in [1] – exist, for this work in particular attacks on RO PUFs, the Transient Effect Ring Oscillator (TERO) PUF [3], and the Loop PUF are of relevance.

SCA of RO PUFs: While not only power and EM SCA attacks exist for RO PUFs, these two side channels are the most dominant ones researched in literature. The leakage behavior of ROs has been studied first in [16], showing that for an overlapping comparison[1] and sequential measurement of RO pairs all secret PUF bits are revealed by an SCA. While this attack can be mitigated by a better bit derivation strategy, later research has shown that the counters counting RO periods for frequency measurement and the routing to the counters leak most, and the counters might be resolvable with localized EM measurements [15]. Thus, it was suggested to hide the corresponding leakage by placing the counters in an interleaved way or by placing them at least close enough that they cannot be distinguished. However, [19] has shown that even spatially closely placed counters on an Application-Specific Integrated Circuit (ASIC) can be resolved with localized EM SCA. As an alternative, random shuffling of counters for measurements has been suggested in [15] and solves the counter leakage problem. But the path from the ROs through a multiplexer to the counter might still be resolvable.

To mount the described analyses, the aforementioned works used time-domain power and EM measurements of the targeted PUF device and observed the power spectrum in the frequency domain after Fast Fourier Transform (FFT). Due to the long measurement time used for RO based PUFs, a good resolution of different frequencies of ROs is achieved, resulting in good prediction accuracy for observed frequencies, and, thus, for the secret.

SCA of the TERO PUF: Different from RO PUFs, TERO PUFs oscillate only for a short period before they ideally converge into their stable state or are stopped otherwise. The secret is derived from the number of oscillations it takes

---

[1] Overlapping comparison means that for a set of, e.g., three ROs with frequencies f_A, f_B, f_C, bits are derived as the signs of the differences $f_A - f_B$ and $f_B - f_C$; I.e., f_B is used twice.

until the TEROs stops. It was initially assumed that this construction is hard to attack via SCA. However, the parallel works in [24] and [17] have shown that revealing the secret from a TERO PUF is feasible. Relevant to this work is the method to achieve this: [24] used for this purpose a Short-Time Fourier Transform (STFT). With this method, it was not possible to resolve the frequency accurately. However, the amplitude of the power spectrum in a specific frequency band revealed how long the oscillators were running. We use a similar method in this work for parts of the ICLooPUF analysis.

SCA of the Loop PUF: The Loop PUF was analyzed with power and EM SCA, too [21]. Since it is an oscillator PUF with low frequency – due to many delay stages; cf. Section 2 for some details – it is no surprise that it can be attacked just as it was the case for RO PUFs. Thus, temporal masking has been suggested in [21] to protect the secret sign bit of the frequency difference. However, since the Loop PUF provides a digitized analog response in the form of a counter value – just like RO and TERO PUFs – it would be beneficial to combine it with more efficient quantization mechanisms that result either in higher reliability, as it is the case with the Two Metric Helper Data Scheme (TMHD) scheme [5], or in the derivation of more entropy per measurement, which can be achieved with equiprobable quantization introduced to the PUF context in [7, 12] or Lehmer-Gray encoding used in [14]. All these methods share the property that they not only exploit the sign of a difference as the secret but also consider the magnitude of a value to derive secret information. As a consequence, it is not sufficient to protect the sign bit but protection of the magnitude must be achieved. [23] reached this goal by using a significant amount of random bits. To reduce this demand for randomness and to protect the Loop PUF in a more lightweight manner, the ICLooPUF was suggested in [22] as a highly side-channel protected PUF primitive. The first analyses of this primitive, which we discuss in more detail in Sect. 2, did not reveal any obvious weakness. However, our more detailed analysis of the PUF shows that the design has leakage sources, too.

Contribution: The main contribution of this publication is the more in-depth analysis of the ICLooPUF primitive. In this, we demonstrate the following achievements:

- We theoretically motivate two yet unknown leakage sources for the ICLooPUF: An up/down sampling counter running with constant frequency and the amplitude of the sidebands in the power spectrum. To theoretically motivate the leakage in the sidebands, we provide an improved model for the power consumption of the ICLooPUF.
- We demonstrate with a practical attack on an ICLooPUF implemented on Field Programmable Gate Array (FPGA) that the leakage is indeed exploitable. The experiments show that the counter-related leakage is the most critical effect, while the amplitudes of the sidebands in the frequency spectrum correlate with the secret but exploitation would require a large number of traces and significant computational power.

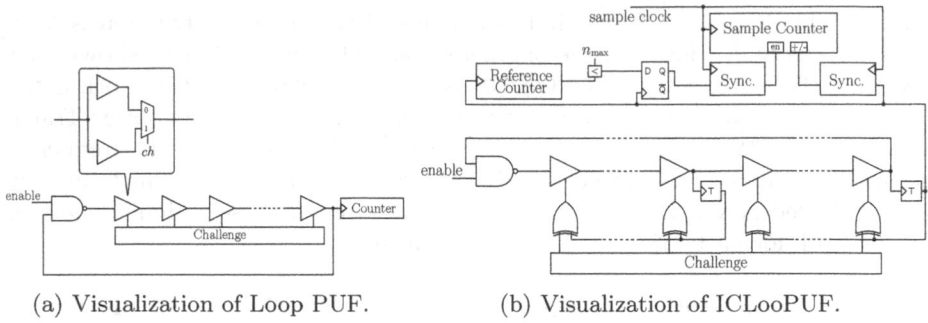

(a) Visualization of Loop PUF.   (b) Visualization of ICLooPUF.

Fig. 1. Loop PUF and ICLooPUF design.

– We analyze for the counter-based leakage different options for mitigation, showing that a good solution would go hand in hand with a significant area overhead for the design.

Structure: The rest of this work is structured as follows: Sect. 2 Introduces the ICLooPUF as an advancement of the Loop PUF and the target of our research. The leakage sources are discussed on a theoretical basis in Sect. 3. Sections 4 to 6 provide practical experiments for the counter leakage and the leakage via the sidebands. We discuss the findings of this paper in Sect. 7. Section 8 draws conclusion of this work.

2   The Interleaved Challenge Loop PUF

The ICLooPUF [22] has been introduced as an advancement of the Loop PUF [4] with improved side-channel resistance. It was, in particular, designed to allow for applying amplitude-based quantization schemes such as the TMHD scheme [5]. As an offspring of the Loop PUF, it is a PUF with challenge-response behavior but dedicated to key storage scenarios. As visualized in Fig. 1, Loop PUF as well as ICLooPUF consist of a chain of N_{ch} delay elements; For each delay element, shown in the upper part of Fig. 1a, a challenge bit selects either the upper or the lower path through it. Given the inverting feedback, which also contains an enable for the PUF, and neglecting the XORs for the ICLooPUF in Fig. 1b, both PUFs oscillate – when enabled – with a challenge-specific frequency. This frequency is unique for every challenge, every chip, and every position on a chip since the precise delay of the delay elements depends on local process variations.

Like for the Loop PUF, the challenges for the ICLooPUF are constructed as and limited to Hadamard codewords. This is, there are N_{ch} possible challenges with a mutual Hamming Distance (HD) and a Hamming Weight (HW) of $N_{ch}/2$. Using challenges with a HW of $N_{ch}/2$ cancels any imbalance in the delay stages, as long as they are equally designed since always the same number of upper and lower paths are traversed by the signal. Using challenges with a HD of $N_{ch}/2$

ensures that the challenges are well spread over the challenge space, helping to reach a high level of entropy per bit.

To derive a secret bit from the Loop PUF or the ICLooPUF, the delay of the chain of delay elements under challenge **ch** and complementary challenge ¬**ch** – i.e., the bitwise inverted challenge – are compared. By this approach, all elements in the ring are changed so that well-distinguishable delays can be expected.

For the *Loop PUF*, in Fig. 1a, the delay of the delay chain is measured by observing the oscillation frequency of the PUF. I.e., the output of the oscillator based PUF is fed into a counter, counting rising (or falling) edges. The counter value after a fixed time, which is measured with a second system-clock-driven counter, is proportional to the frequency. The simplest method to derive a secret bit from the Loop PUF is to build the difference of the two counter values generated for some pair **ch** and ¬**ch** and to take the sign bit as a secret. However, it has been shown in [21, 25] that the oscillation frequency of the Loop PUF is well-observable in the spectrum when power or EM measurements are taken for a device, and that even remote observation of the Loop PUF with a Time-to-Digital Converter (TDC) is possible. A temporal masking strategy has been suggested in [21] to protect against this weakness. However, it is only effective for protecting the sign bit. [23] discussed that for more efficient methods exploiting the magnitude – like the TMHD scheme, equiprobable quantization, and Lehmer-Gray encoding – temporal masking is not effective. Thus, a strategy based on challenge permutation was suggested in the same work, which annihilates the attack vector but comes at the cost of requiring a large number of random bits.

The goal of the *ICLooPUF design* was to provide an effective countermeasure against SCA that does not require randomness. The idea is to mix the frequencies of the PUF for challenge and complementary challenge in a way so that the attacker can only observe the mixed frequency and cannot compute back to the individual frequencies. Assuming an ideal realization of this concept, sign-based as well as magnitude-based bit-derivation schemes cannot be attacked anymore using SCA on the frequency of the PUF. The concept for the realization of the improvement is as follows: In the lower part of figure Fig. 1b, the measurement part of the PUF is shown, which is modified – compared to the Loop PUF – by the insertion of Toggle Flip Flops (TFFs). If a rising edge traverses the delay chain, it triggers a toggle of the TFFs. Since the output of each TFF is XORed with the challenge bits to the left, the challenge is inverted, i.e., the complementary challenge is applied until the next rising edge reaches the TFF. Please note that at first glance, more flip-flops are switched with each rising edge, causing an increased Signal-to-Noise Ratio (SNR) for an attacker mounting an SCA. However, **ch** and ¬**ch** are applied in turns for always only one period, so that [22] claims that the individual frequencies cannot be resolved by an attacker.

The protection mechanism causes, however, that the measurement used for the Loop PUF cannot be used any longer. Thus, while the Loop PUF was measured in the frequency domain, the ICLooPUF is measured in the time domain as shown in the upper part of Fig. 1b. For this purpose, a pre-defined number n_{max} of oscillations of the ICLooPUF is taken. By oversampling with a *sampling clock*, which runs on a fixed frequency, the period length of the ICLooPUF is approximated. A *sample counter*, implemented as an up-/down-counter is used, which is incremented with each rising edge of the sampling clock for one period of the ICLooPUF (e.g., for the period, where **ch** is applied) and decremented with each rising edge of the sampling clock for the next period of the ICLooPUF (where, e.g., ¬**ch** is applied). The number of increments and decrements corresponds to the period length of the ICLooPUF measured under **ch** and ¬**ch**. Applying the process of alternatingly up- and down-counting for many periods helps to remove noise effects and to receive a sufficiently precise measurement of the delay difference of the ICLooPUF under **ch** and ¬**ch**. It is worth noting that in the block diagram in Fig. 1b, several synchronization steps are needed since the PUF and the sample clock constitute two different clock domains. More details on the ICLooPUF can be found in [22].

As a result of first experiments [22] has shown that it seems indeed harder to attack the ICLooPUF when compared to the Loop PUF. As a consequence, it should be possible to combine the ICLooPUF with bit-derivation schemes such as the TMHD, making the design a highly reliable alternative to other PUF constructions. This claim of high reliability was substantiated in [22] with measurements over temperature and voltage variations. To motivate the claim of high SCA resilience, power measurements were taken and a model was presented to show that an attacker is not able to resolve the two frequencies (or delays) of the ICLooPUF under **ch** and ¬**ch**. In this work, however, we provide a refined model that shows that there is indeed leakage observable by an attacker. Furthermore, we focus on the up-/down-counter in the system and show a yet unexplored weakness in this regard.

3   Theoretical Analysis of Leakage Sources

In this section, we analyze the ICLooPUF regarding potential leakage sources. We identify two attack vectors, namely leakage of the sample counter and via the sidebands of the frequency spectrum.

3.1   Counter Leakage

In most oscillator-base PUF designs, two separate counters plus a reference counter are used, and defense strategies are concerned with preventing localized leakage of the two counters counting RO periods. The reason is that these counters are the most relevant leakage points in such designs [15]. If it is possible to resolve these counters – as it has been done, e.g., in [19] – the attacker can measure the frequency of individual oscillators and derive the secret from this observation, just as the device can do it.

In the classical Loop PUF design, a single counter, counting the number of oscillations of the Loop PUF, and a reference counter are used. Like for other oscillator-based designs, the reference counter does not reveal secret information, and only the counter for the oscillator periods within a fixed time must be protected.

In the ICLooPUF design, again, two counters are involved: A reference counter ensures a sufficient number of periods of the oscillator to get a stable response. From an attacker perspective, this counter is related to the oscillation frequency and is relevant regarding the leakage discussed in Sect. 3.2. The counter value, however, is no secret information. In addition, the TFFs in the feedback path cause similar leakage, which might dominate.

The second counter involved in the ICLooPUF design is the sample counter. This counter is implemented as an up/down counter that is driven by a fixed clock. At the end of each measurement of the ICLooPUF under **ch** and ¬**ch**, it contains the secret information generated by the PUF and is thus another target for an attack.

Different from the leakage caused by the oscillation counters at the oscillator output, the exploitable information for the sample counter cannot be found in its (constant) frequency. However, the straightforward binary counter used in the original ICLooPUF design obviously suffers from HD leakage: The values that the counter can take are mapped to words from a binary codebook. The bits of these words are stored in Flip-Flops, which adapts the new value with a rising edge. If a bit value stays the same in the new word, the power consumption is negligible. If it changes, the charge of the wire capacities changes and the connected logic gates toggle as well, resulting in a measurable spike in the power. This is for a binary counter, in particular, critical if many bits flip, which is, for instance, the case when passing with a two's complement up-/down-counter from positive to negative values or vice versa. We show in Sect. 5 that this leakage is indeed exploitable and discuss possible solutions like replacing the counter with alternative implementations.

3.2 Amplituded Spectrum Used for SCA

Most Side-Channel Attacks on cryptographic functions operate on the time domain, trying to exploit data-dependent power consumption or runtime of certain operations. In contrast to this, attacks on oscillating PUFs usually exploit leakage in the frequency domain. For this, the ith captured trace $s_i(t)$ is multiplied by a window function $w(t)$ and transformed into the frequency domain using the Discrete Fourier Transform (DFT). In this domain, usually, the power spectrum is analyzed. Multiple traces are normally taken and transformed and the result is averaged in the frequency domain to increase the SNR and to make the identification of peaks in the spectrum easier. The amplitude spectrum we operate on in the following is therefore computed as

$$|S(f)| = \frac{1}{N_{rep}} \sum_{i=0}^{N_{rep}-1} |\mathcal{F}(s_i(t) \cdot w(t))|,$$

with $\mathcal{F}(\bullet)$ representing the transform into the frequency domain and N_{rep} the repetions of the same measurement.

Related methods are the STFT and the Welch estimator. They split each trace into highly overlapping segments; the window function is individually applied to each segment. For the STFT, these segments are interpreted as time points, creating a time-frequency representation. Averaging is only possible across traces if the signal is lined up correctly. For the Welch estimation, the average over all segments and all traces is used for the amplitude spectrum. This allows for a better and smoother estimate of long traces in the presence of temporal variances.

3.3   Improved Spectral Model of the ICLooPUF

Like [22] we model the power consumption of an RO as a sinusoidal wave. The electrical current in this model is given as $I(t) = sin(2\pi \cdot f \cdot t) + I_{const}$ with oscillation frequency f.

For the ICLooPUF, the ring alternately oscillates with two different frequencies, f_{ch} for the non-inverted challenge and $f_{\neg ch}$ for the inverted challenge. The initial publication of the ICLooPUF [22] modeled the power consumption with a piecewise-defined function, interleaving one sine period of f_{ch} with a duration of $T_{ch} = 1/f_{ch}$ and one sine period of $f_{\neg ch}$.

$$s(t) = \begin{cases} sin(2\pi \cdot f_{ch} \cdot t) & \text{if } t \mod (T_{ch} + T_{\neg ch}) \leq T_{ch} \\ sin(2\pi \cdot f_{\neg ch} \cdot t) & \text{if } t \mod (T_{ch} + T_{\neg ch}) > T_{ch} \end{cases}$$

When counting the zero-crossings in the output signal against a timer, this results in a mean frequency of $f_\mu = 2/(T_{ch}+T_{\neg ch})$. [22] assumed that the design is secure, since the difference $T_{ch} - T_{\neg ch}$ cannot be predicted from f_μ. However, the Fourier transform of this function is again a piecewise-defined function, so this model turned out to be not adequate to predict leakage in the spectrum.

To improve the model and to account for the differentiability at the switching point between the two frequencies, we formulate the signal as a continuous modulated sine wave with an instantaneous frequency $f(t)$:

$$f(t) = \begin{cases} f_{ch} & \text{if } t \mod (T_{ch} + T_{\neg ch}) < T_{ch} \\ f_{\neg ch} & \text{if } t \mod (T_{ch} + T_{\neg ch}) > T_{ch} \end{cases}$$

The approximation of this signal by a Fourier Series of a rectangular wave with a duty cycle d is:

$$f(t) = f_\mu + f_\Delta \cdot \sum_{n=0}^{\infty} a_n \cdot \cos(2\pi n f_{mod} t) \tag{1}$$

with the peak frequency deviation

$$f_\Delta = \frac{f_{ch} - f_{\neg ch}}{2},$$

the baseband frequency of the temporal deviation

$$f_{mod} = \frac{1}{T_{ch} + T_{\neg ch}} = \frac{f_{ch} \cdot f_{\neg ch}}{f_{ch} + f_{\neg ch}},$$

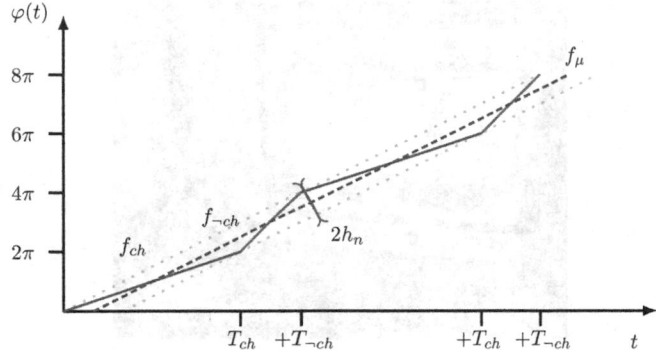

Fig. 2. Instantanious phase of the signal: the modulation causes a temporal deviation of $\pm h_n$ from the mean frequency.

the duty cycle of the rectangular function accounting for the different duration of the sections

$$d = \frac{T_{\mathbf{ch}}}{T_{\mathbf{ch}} + T_{\neg\mathbf{ch}}} = \frac{f_{\neg\mathbf{ch}}}{f_{\mathbf{ch}} + f_{\neg\mathbf{ch}}},$$

and the coefficients of the Fourier Series

$$a_0 = (2d - 1)$$

$$a_{n>0} = \frac{4}{\pi n} \cdot \sin(\pi n d).$$

The domain of the sine function is the instantaneous phase, the integral over the instantaneous frequency:

$$\varphi(t) = 2\pi \cdot \int_0^t f(\tau)d\tau. \tag{2}$$

Figure 2 visualizes the development of $\varphi(t)$ of the ICLooPUF over time; depending on the currently applied challenge the phase changes faster or slower. By inserting Eq. (1) in Eq. (2), the instantanious frequency of the ICLooPUF is given by:

$$\varphi(t) = 2\pi \cdot \int_0^t f_\mu + f_\Delta \cdot a_0 + f_\Delta \cdot \sum_{n=1}^{\infty}(a_n \cdot \cos(2\pi n f_{mod}\tau)))d\tau$$

$$= 2\pi f_\mu t + 2\pi f_\Delta(2d-1)t + 2\pi f_\Delta \int_0^t \sum_{n=1}^{\infty}(\frac{4}{\pi n} \cdot \sin(\pi n d) \cdot \cos(2\pi n f_{mod}\tau))d\tau$$

$$= 2\pi f_\mu t + 2\pi f_\Delta(2d-1)t + \frac{f_\Delta}{f_{mod}} \cdot \sum_{n=1}^{\infty}(\frac{2}{\pi^2 n^2} \cdot \sin(\pi n d) \cdot \sin(2\pi n f_{mod}t)).$$

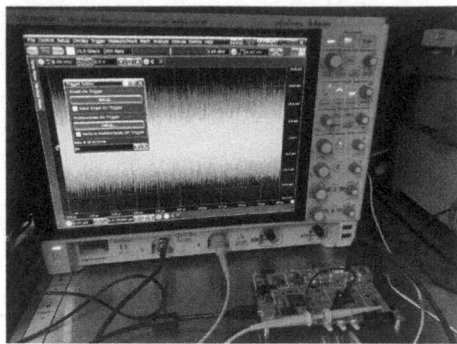

Fig. 3. Setup for Side-Channel analysis: FPGA target board and digital storage oscilloscope showing a typical trace (mainly noise is visible without processing).

As the signal modulated onto the mean frequency has a non-zero mean for $T_{ch} \neq T_{\neg ch}$, this model results in the harmonic instead of the arithmetic mean as the carrier frequency f_T. It tends slightly towards the lower component:

$$f_T = f_\mu + f_\Delta \cdot (2d - 1) = \frac{2 \cdot f_{ch} \cdot f_{\neg ch}}{f_{ch} + f_{\neg ch}}.$$

The amplitude factors can be united to form a modulation coefficient h for each term of the series:

$$h_n = \frac{f_\Delta}{f_{mod}} \cdot \frac{2}{\pi^2 n^2} \cdot \sin(\pi n d).$$

This coefficient describes the amplitude of the deviation from the mean in the instantanious phase, as shown in Fig. 2. Their magnitude decreases quadratically with rising n, so even a low number of terms will approximate the waveform well. For $n = 1$, this results in the standard formula for a frequency-modulated signal with a sinusoidal baseband:

$$s(t) \approx sin(2\pi f_T t + h_1 \sin(2\pi f_{mod} t)).$$

The Fourier spectrum of such a function is given by the Bessel functions of the first kind. It consists of the carrier frequency f_T with an amplitude of $J_0(h)$ and the first sidebands at $f_T \pm f_{mod}$ with an amplitude of $J_1(h)$. Further sidebands are placed at the higher harmonics with rapidly decreasing energy. As $h \ll 1$, the carrier contains the majority of the power, the sidebands will increase in power with rising h. In other words, since h_n contains via f_Δ information about $f_{ch} - f_{\neg ch}$ and, thus, about the secret $T_{ch} - T_{\neg ch}$, we can expect from the model a correlation of the amplitude of the sidebands and the secret. We show in Sect. 6 that such leakage is observable in practice.

4   Experimental Setup

Before diving into the experimental validation of the leakage sources, we introduce in this section the used setup. The side channel measurement setup uses

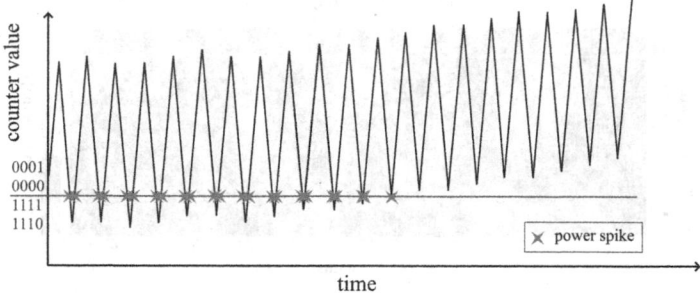

Fig. 4. Visualization of the development of counter values stored in the sample counter over time.

NewAE's ChipWhisperer CW305 target board. The ICLooPUF is implemented on the Artix 7 (XC7A100T-2FTG256) FPGA on that board. The design strategy on FPGA follows the one described in [22], with the XORs in the ICLooPUF design in Fig. 1b replaced by multiplexers and the delay elements realized through Lookup Tables (LUTs). The resulting design behaves similarly to an ASIC implementation but oscillates at a lower speed. The power consumption is measured over a shunt resistor, which forms a voltage divider with the FPGA core. The resistor has a very low value of $0.1\,\Omega$ in order not to influence the functionality of the chip, so an additional $20\,\mathrm{dB}$ amplifier is used to measure the voltage drop. This voltage is then captured by a Digital Storage Oscilloscope for evaluation on a computer. For the experiments published in [22], a PicoScope 6000 was used. It has a rather low sampling rate of at most $2.5\,\mathrm{GSa/s}$ and sampling resolution of 8 bits, but it can capture a large number of traces in a short time. This is well-suited for most SCA applications. In contrast, our experiments used the high-end Keysight DSO-S 254A. It can capture $20\,\mathrm{GSa/s}$ at 10-bit resolution. As the oscillator runtime is fixed by the design, the higher sampling rate allows for capturing more samples in a single trace rather than more traces. The FPGA has background noise much stronger than the oscillator signal; this determines the necessary voltage capture range to avoid clipping. The higher sample resolution at this range reduces the quantization noise, greatly improving the ability to isolate weaker components. This setup can be seen in Fig. 3.

5   Leakage-Evaluation of Counters and Countermeasures

In this section, we experimentally validate the existence of counter-related leakage and suggest corresponding design improvements.

5.1   Analysis of Counter-Related Leakage

The original design utilizes a binary two's complement up-/down-counter. In the FPGA design of the ICLooPUF, it is implemented using the corresponding resources on the Xilinx FPGA, including the fast carry chain and N_{FF} Flip

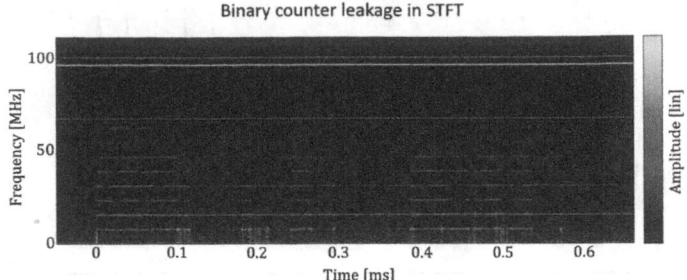

Fig. 5. STFT spectrum of a single trace, taken from an unstable challenge. The high SNR is only possible because the high-resolution setup, in combination with the higher power consumption of the ICLooPUF.

Flops (FFs). As the FPGA supports this structure as a primitive, it can reach a high sampling frequency of f_s =400 MHz, which is generated by an on-board Phase-Locked Loop (PLL).

As described in Sect. 3.1, the Hamming Distance of two subsequent values stored to the counter FFs depends on the carry-over. The maximum distance of N_{FF} occurs when transitioning between 0 (all-zeros) and -1 (all-ones). Particularly notable is the distribution of this Hamming Distance: the values next to a high-bit carry-over only use much lower carry-overs.

The ICLooPUF decides via the period lengths under **ch** and ¬**ch** how many times the counter counts upwards and downwards, resulting ultimately in a metric for the difference of the period lengths and thus in the secret information: During $T_{\mathbf{ch}}$ the counter counts upwards with each clock cycle of f_s, during $T_{\neg\mathbf{ch}}$ it counts downwards. This results in roughly $T_{\mathbf{ch}} \cdot f_s$ upward pulses followed by $T_{\neg\mathbf{ch}} \cdot f_s$ downward pulses. The precise number of up and down counts also depends on phase jitter and clock alignment. This observation allows for modeling the value of the counter as a highly autocorrelated and slightly biased random walk visualized in Fig. 4. Over a long time, its mean slowly drifts away from the start position depending on the secret, and the deviation from zero can become much larger than f_μ/f_s with $f_\mu = 2/(T_{\mathbf{ch}}+T_{\neg}\mathbf{ch})$ as before.

Combining the knowledge on counter leakage with the knowledge of the expected signal sequence of the ICLooPUF results in exploitable information, as shown in Fig. 4. Visible in the figure is a single measurement of the ICLooPUF under one pair of **ch** and ¬**ch**. The waterfall plot shows the amplitude of the frequency spectrum derived from power measurements over time generated with an STFT. The continuous horizontal lines starting left of time point 0 are related to frequencies on the FPGA that are not linked to the experiment. The continuous lines starting at time point zero (at approx. 16 MHz and – less pronounced – at approx. 32 MHz) correspond to the oscillation frequency of the ICLooPUF and the first harmonic. The counter-related information is visible as interrupted horizontal lines at half of the oscillation frequency and the corresponding harmonics.

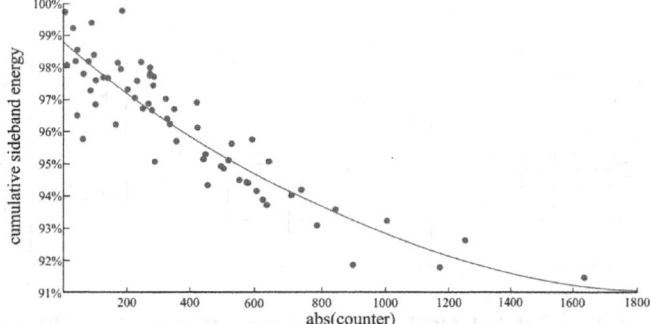

Fig. 6. Correlation of the area-integrated energy with the absolute counter value on a single 64-challenge instance. 100% refers to the highest observed measurement, 0% to absolute zero. (10 measurements at 10 GSa/s each)

Recall that the counter follows a shape as sketched in Fig. 4. I.e., the counter passes the same value – e.g. the binary all-zero state – many times from both directions until the secret-dependent mean drifts away far enough. Passing through a high-bit carry-over periodically consumes a significant amount of energy, while the energy consumption for other counter-state transitions is negligible. It follows that the lower the drift, the longer the counter value stays in the range with high energy consumption visible as the interrupted lines in Fig. 5: The figure shows the case of two similar ICLooPUF period lengths under **ch** and ¬**ch** and the implementation uses a zero-initialized 16-bit counter. The counter needs about 0.1 ms to leave the initial value, and due to noise it later re-enters it several times. On a more stable challenge, the leakage occurs for a much shorter time and the high-leakage domain around zero is not re-entered.

The observable leakage from the power side channel results in the question if this leakage is exploitable. For this purpose, we correlate the cumulative energy of all frequency bins from 5–50 MHz with the observed counter values, which an attacker tries to predict and which we read out in the experiment for verification purposes. Figure 6 visualizes that the measurement shall indeed allow for entropy reduction: The duration the counter remains in the high-leakage domain is proportional to the energy in the spectrum. Therefore, similar period lengths under **ch** and ¬**ch** result in higher cumulative band energy than distinct ones, so that the band energy is correlated with the absolute counter values. This effect is already well visible for averaging over only ten repetitions of the measurement.

It is worth noting that the sign bit is not revealed by this attack. I.e., the leakage is of particular relevance for amplitude-based quantization approaches like the TMHD scheme, previously analyzed in [23]. We sketch an attack on this scheme in the following: The TMHD scheme cuts the with a Gaussian distribution approximated probability density function of the ICLooPUF counter values into octiles. The outer two quantiles and the inner two quantiles are mapped to the same binary value. Counting from left to the right, differences contained

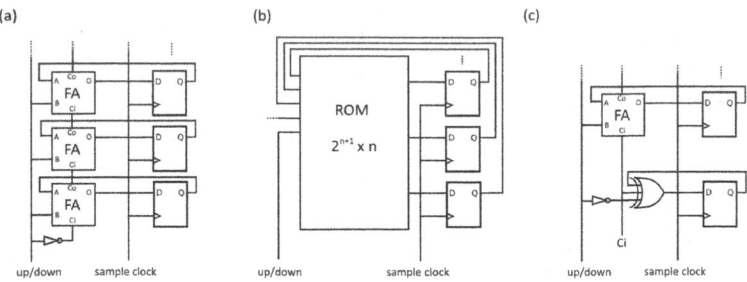

Fig. 7. Different hardware implementations of counters: (a) binary two's complement, (b) state machine Gray code counter, (c) dual rail counter.

in the 1st, 4th, 5th, and 8th octile can be considered as being very stable since they are separated from each other by the 2nd/3rd and 6th/7th octile. In Fig. 6 these correspond to the leftmost and rightmost 25% of the counter values. An attacker only observes the spectrum, i.e., the y-axis in the plot. They might conclude that the upper and lower 25% correspond to the respective left and right counter values. Following this approach, we reveal for our experiment already 23 bits correctly, which corresponds to an entropy reduction of roughly 30%. A practical attacker can do even better: Since the dependence of measurement and helper data of the TMHD scheme is known, the attacker can make guesses for all bits, exploit the correction capabilities of the TMHD scheme, and make probabilistic statements about the likelihood that a guess is correct. Subsequent error correction in the PUF scenario can be used to further reduce entropy.

5.2   Mitigation Strategies for Counter-Related Leakage

Since the direct implementation of a straight-forward up-/down-counter in [22] leaks information about the amplitude and the ICLooPUF is dedicated to protecting this case, it is worth investigating how the leakage can be prevented. We discuss the following three concepts: (i) A randomization approach, (ii) the use of a dual-rail concept, and (iii) the usage of low-leakage counters. Please note that multiplexing with each period of the ICLooPUF between two separate counters that only count in one direction would avoid leakage. But the alternating enable of the two counters might be observable and – just as counters of classical RO PUFs – such a construction would be vulnerable against localized attacks.

Randomization Approach. A naive approach to overcome the attack is to initialize the counter with a random seed. While indeed the counter might not immediately leak, it will likely pass through a state where a large number of bits changes while converging towards the final difference.[2] Thus, exploitable leakage

---

[2] This is not necessarily the transition from 0 to −1 in two's complement; Also transitions to, e.g., a sufficiently large power of 2 show the same leakage effect. On our data set it can be observed down to 2^7.

is still observable. While energy consumption depends on the concrete hamming distance for the critical counter transition where many bits flip, the duration of this leakage only depends on the difference between the period lengths and possible noise effects. Thus, it is still possible to exploit the leakage by measuring the duration.

Dual-Rail Concepts. The second approach we discuss is to hide Hamming Weight leakage with a dual-rail logic. Such a construction has the potential to balance the power consumption of the counter, which would at least make an attack much harder. However, a perfect dual-rail implementation is hard to achieve and not at all feasible on FPGA [11]. We focus, therefore, on a hiding strategy visualized in Fig. 7, where the leakage of the Flip-Flops is compensated by another circuit. For this, each stage of the adder chain is paired with a second Flip-Flops which toggles when and only when the data bit does not change in this step. While the data bits follow the same coding as before, these 'dummy' bits follow a code with the complementary HD, together resulting in a code with constant (maximum) HD for each transition. The concept is efficient to implement on the used FPGA. However, while it indeed reduces the SNR, the leakage identified for the counters is still observable on large data sets. This is presumably caused by the carry chain's energy consumption, which cannot be compensated. The alternative to this is counters directly operating on equidistant codes, which are discussed next.

Low-Leakage Counters. Many different counter implementations operate on equidistant codes. The One-Hot counter, e.g., is commonly used in state machines. But like some others, it is impractical to be used in the case of counting towards large numbers since the area grows linearly with the maximum counter value. Polynomial counters like an LFSR can be used as up/down counters, too, but they are not equidistant and suffer from the same potential leakage properties as the binary counter. The remaining choice is the implementation of a *Gray code counter*, which is both compact and equidistant. It rearranges the codewords of a binary counter so that subsequent codewords have a HD of one. A drawback of this counter is, however, that the logic necessary to build a synchronous up/down counter suffers from long combinatorial paths. Alternatively, it can be implemented using ROM – e.g., the ROM256 primitives of Xilinx FPGAs – as a Look-up-table. This allows for small counters of 7 bits to reach the same clock speed as a binary counter.

This structure was the only solution found in this research that did not show any counter leakage. Unfortunately, while of acceptable size on FPGA,[3] the implementation as a look-up table in ROM has a significant area cost on an ASIC. For an n-bit counter approx. $2^{n+1} \cdot n$ transistors plus address decoders are needed in the masked ROM. Taking the maximum counter value observed for the difference for our FPGA implementation as a reference, at least $n = 10$ bits

---

[3] A seven-bit counter can be implemented, e.g., in seven slizes.

would be needed to cover the required number range, which results in an area cost no longer competitive with other PUF designs. Please note that it is not possible to chain equidistant counters, e.g., add a One-Hot counter as a prescaler to the gray counter. This would cause periods with an observable overflow from this prescaler to the Gray code counter and vice versa; This results in observable leakage since the two counters have different power profiles. Sharing the counter across several ICLooPUFs to reduce costs is possible but would prevent parallel measurement, increasing the already long evaluation time per bit.

Another issue to be mentioned comes with the application of localized EM attacks. No study of localized attack resistance was part of the measurement campaigns. Nevertheless, from a theoretical perspective, a counter using the common binary-reflected Gray code would be potentially attackable with a localized attack: It still consists of more and less significant bits. When only the more significant ones can be observed, this would result in the same leakage as before. Thus well-balanced Gray codes – as they are introduced, e.g., in [2] – seem advantageous.

6   Exploitation of Modulation Effect

The frequency-modulated model predicts two types of leakage which were not identified in the initial evaluation of [22]. First, the mean frequency should vary slightly depending on f_Δ in case $T_{ch} + T_{\neg ch} = const$. However, with the observed values on the test device of $f_\mu \approx 16\,\mathrm{MHz}$ and $f_\Delta < 10\,\mathrm{KHz}$, the expected difference between the harmonic and arithmetic mean is less than $6.25\,\mathrm{Hz}$. This is below any obtainable accuracy and was, thus, practically neither observed by the initial evaluation of the ICLooPUF in [22] nor by our more advanced one.

Secondly, the model predicts the existence of sidebands, especially at the frequencies of $0.5 \cdot f_T$ and $1.5 \cdot f_T$, with f_Δ-dependent magnitude. By simulation, these sidebands would be expected to be $-40\,\mathrm{dB}$ below the main band for the highest counter values. Our practical evaluation revealed, however, that the power of the sidebands is actually several dB stronger. Unlike in the formula, the modulation coefficient can, e.g., also be subject to temporal noise. This averages out in the counter value but not in the power spectrum. Also, the modeled mechanism is not the only effect in the ICLooPUF capable of inducing sidebands. The ring itself was observed to resonate at half and double of f_T, leaving only $1.5 \cdot f_T$ as a good point for detecting correlations.

Figure 8 shows the correlation of the absolute value of the up-/down-counter with the sideband at $1.5 \cdot f_T$ A correlation of sideband and counter value is visible, although it is much less pronounced than the correlation with the counter leakage in Fig. 6: For the sidebands and our data set, a Pearson correlation coefficient of 78% was reached.

The attack strategy would be the same as sketched for the counter leakage. However, the results indicate that this second attack vector via the sidebands is much harder to exploit than the counter leakage above: First of all, the leakage is only observable after implementing the low-leakage Gray counter discussed

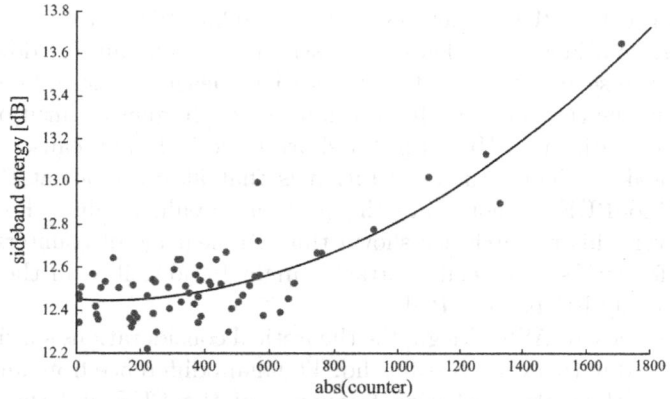

Fig. 8. Correlation of the energy in the first sideband with the absolute counter value on a single 64-challenge instance. (20 measurements at 20 GSa/s each)

above. As the binary counter leakage appears in the same frequency bands but with significantly more power, its negative correlation supersedes this weakly positive one. In addition, to reach the high SNR necessary to achieve the results, a large data set was necessary and different from the analysis in [22] with an FFT, the more robust Welch estimate was needed. Each trace consists of 128 MSa at 20 GSa/s. This allows for capturing the entire time of a challenge evaluation with 2^{17} oscillations. The evaluation of the 1280 traces on a workstation with an Intel Xeon E5-1650 @ 3.50 GHz and 128 GB RAM took with the Welch estimate about 30 h. With this significant effort, only large and sufficiently distinct counter values are reliably distinguishable, as it is visible in Fig. 8.

It is important to note that the power spectrum does not leak the signum of the counter value. No correlation was found in this regard across all frequencies, despite the, compared to [22], much more precise measurement for our data set. However, the model suggests that such leakage exists in the form of a phase shift between the bands. This is impossible to evaluate with the power estimator methods used here but further research in this regard is needed.

7   Discussion of Results and Impact

The analyses in this work have revealed HD leakage of counters and variations of the sidebands as relevant leakage sources for the ICLooPUF. Exploitation of the leakage will become harder if multiple ICLooPUFs run in parallel. However, if the PUFs run on different mean frequencies – which we observed on FPGA – they can still be distinguished, and localized EM measurement can be used to attack such designs. Our results show that the counter leakage is much more relevant and can only be prevented by careful design of the counter. Nevertheless, it is worth discussing both aspects (i) what the impact to other PUF structures is and (ii) if the attack vectors can be expected to be exploitable also in ASIC designs.

Regarding other PUF structures, only the ICLooPUF and the Loop PUF with temporal masking were identified as structures using an up-/down-counter for deriving the secret and only the ICLooPUF measures the difference of the delay chain in the time domain. In addition, only a frequent transition between counter states with large HD within a short period of time causes significant exploitable leakage. Thus, the expectation is that at the moment PUFs other than the ICLooPUF do not share the particular vulnerability shown in this work. However, this research has shown that HD leakage of counters is indeed exploitable for PUFs, and related attacks might be identified in the future for other – especially RO-based – PUFs.

When it comes for ASIC design, the theoretical considerations survive and the model described in this work is still valid. The main difference from an attacker's perspective is, thus, the oscillation frequency of the PUF and the degrees of freedom for a designer. A higher oscillation frequency for the ICLooPUF likely means a shorter measurement time, i.e., lower oversampling and shorter traces. To partly counter the effect, the expectation is that more traces are needed to receive similar results as shown in this work, which also increases the computation time. As a consequence, the attacks shown in this work are not expected to become infeasible but are possibly too expensive for attacks on lightweight solutions. In addition, implementing low-leakage counters in an ASIC design can be expected to be much more feasible than on an FPGA due to the higher flexibility in the design.

It should also be highlighted that the analyses carried out in this work were not able to exploit the leakage in order to reveal the sign bit of the counter value. While further research might be needed, since the new model in this work suggests leakage in this regard, from a practical perspective this can be considered still a benefit of the ICLooPUF, since it seems to practically protect the sign bit without relying on any randomness. Already with the results in this work it can be stated that the ICLooPUF provides a much higher protection level than, e.g., the classical Loop PUF, which was without additional protection mechanisms fully broken with only very few traces [21].

8   Conclusion

The analyses in this work have shown two yet unreported side-channel vulnerabilities of the ICLooPUF, a novel PUF primitive introduced to overcome side-channel weaknesses. They show that the sample counter needed for the PUF requires careful design to prevent significant leakage. In addition, a new model for the PUF revealed the sidebands as a relevant leakage source, although the experiments show that this leakage is hard to exploit. After the analyses, only the sign bit remains fully protected. However, the developed model indicates leakage via the phase, and additional research is needed to obtain confidence that this is practically not exploitable. Nevertheless, the overall results also show that the ICLooPUF is much harder to attack than the classical Loop PUF and seems a valid starting point for further improvements towards side-channel resistant PUFs.

Acknowledgments. This work was funded by the the German Federal Ministry of Education and Research in the project APRIORI (grant no. 16KIS1389K).

Disclosure of Interests. The authors have no competing interests to declare that are relevant to the content of this article.

References

1. Aghaie, A., Moradi, A.: TI-PUF: toward side-channel resistant physical unclonable functions. IEEE Trans. Inf. Forensics Secur. **15**, 3470–3481 (2020). https://doi.org/10.1109/TIFS.2020.2986887
2. Bhat, G.S., Savage, C.D.: Balanced gray codes. Electron. J. Combinat. (E-JC) (1996). https://doi.org/10.37236/1249
3. Bossuet, L., Ngo, X.T., Cherif, Z., Fischer, V.: A PUF based on a transient effect ring oscillator and insensitive to locking phenomenon. IEEE Trans. Emerg. Top. Comput. **2**(1), 30–36 (2014). https://doi.org/10.1109/TETC.2013.2287182
4. Cherif, Z., Danger, J.L., Guilley, S., Bossuet, L.: An easy-to-design PUF based on a single oscillator: the loop PUF. In: 2012 15th Euromicro Conference on Digital System Design, pp. 156–162 (2012). https://doi.org/10.1109/DSD.2012.22
5. Danger, J.L., Guilley, S., Schaub, A.: Two-metric helper data for highly robust and secure delay PUFs. In: 2019 IEEE 8th International Workshop on Advances in Sensors and Interfaces (IWASI), pp. 184–188 (2019). https://doi.org/10.1109/IWASI.2019.8791249
6. Gassend, B.: Physical Random Functions. Master's thesis, Massachusetts Institute of Technology (2003)
7. de Groot, J.A., Skoric, B., de Vreede, N., Linnartz, J.M.G.: Quantization in zero leakage helper data schemes. EURASIP J. Adv. Signal Process. **2016**, 54 (2016). https://doi.org/10.1186/s13634-016-0353-z
8. Guajardo, J., Kumar, S.S., Schrijen, G.-J., Tuyls, P.: FPGA intrinsic PUFs and their use for IP protection. In: Paillier, P., Verbauwhede, I. (eds.) CHES 2007. LNCS, vol. 4727, pp. 63–80. Springer, Heidelberg (2007). https://doi.org/10.1007/978-3-540-74735-2_5
9. Helfmeier, C., Nedospasov, D., Boit, C., Jean-Pierre, S.: Cloning physically unclonable functions. In: Proceedings of the IEEE International Symposium of Hardware-Oriented Security and Trust. IEEE (2013)
10. Holcomb, D.E., Burleson, W., Fu, K.: Initial SRAM state as a fingerprint and source of true random numbers for RFID tags. In: Proceedings of the Conference on RFID Security (2007)
11. Immler, V., Specht, R., Unterstein, F.: Your rails cannot hide from localized em: how dual-rail logic fails on fpgas (2017). https://doi.org/10.1007/978-3-319-66787-4_20
12. Immler, V., Uppund, K.: New insights to key derivation for tamper-evident physical unclonable functions. IACR Trans. Cryptogr. Hardw. Embed. Syst. 30–65 (2019)
13. Lohrke, H., Tajik, S., Boit, C., Seifert, J.-P.: No place to hide: contactless probing of secret data on FPGAs. In: Gierlichs, B., Poschmann, A.Y. (eds.) CHES 2016. LNCS, vol. 9813, pp. 147–167. Springer, Heidelberg (2016). https://doi.org/10.1007/978-3-662-53140-2_8

14. Maes, R., Van Herrewege, A., Verbauwhede, I.: PUFKY: a fully functional PUF-based cryptographic key generator. In: Prouff, E., Schaumont, P. (eds.) CHES 2012. LNCS, vol. 7428, pp. 302–319. Springer, Heidelberg (2012). https://doi.org/10.1007/978-3-642-33027-8_18

15. Merli, D., Heyszl, J., Heinz, B., Schuster, D., Stumpf, F., Sigl, G.: Localized Electromagnetic Analysis of RO PUFs. In: Proceedings of the IEEE Int. Symposium of Hardware-Oriented Security and Trust. IEEE (Jun 2013)

16. Merli, D., Schuster, D., Stumpf, F., Sigl, G.: Semi-invasive EM attack on FPGA RO PUFs and countermeasures. In: 6th Workshop on Embedded Systems Security (WESS'2011). ACM, Taipei (2011)

17. Mureddu, U., Colombier, B., Bochard, N., Bossuet, L., Fischer, V.: Transient effect ring oscillators leak too. In: 2019 IEEE Computer Society Annual Symposium on VLSI, ISVLSI 2019, Miami, FL, USA, 15–17 July 2019, pp. 37–42. IEEE (2019). https://doi.org/10.1109/ISVLSI.2019.00016

18. Rührmair, U., Sehnke, F., Sölter, J., Dror, G., Devadas, S., Schmidhuber, J.: Modeling attacks on physical unclonable functions. In: Proceedings of the 17th ACM Conference on Computer and Communications Security, CCS 2010, pp. 237–249. ACM, New York (2010). https://doi.org/10.1145/1866307.1866335

19. Shiozaki, M., Fujino, T.: Simple electromagnetic analysis attacks based on geometric leak on an ASIC implementation of ring-oscillator PUF. In: Proceedings of the 3rd ACM Workshop on Attacks and Solutions in Hardware Security Workshop, ASHES 2019, pp. 13–21. Association for Computing Machinery, New York (2019). https://doi.org/10.1145/3338508.3359569

20. Suh, G.E., Devadas, S.: Physical unclonable functions for device authentication and secret key generation. In: ACM/IEEE Design Automation Conference (DAC), pp. 9–14 (2007)

21. Tebelmann, L., Danger, J.-L., Pehl, M.: Self-secured PUF: protecting the loop PUF by masking. In: Bertoni, G.M., Regazzoni, F. (eds.) COSADE 2020. LNCS, vol. 12244, pp. 293–314. Springer, Cham (2021). https://doi.org/10.1007/978-3-030-68773-1_14

22. Tebelmann, L., Danger, J., Pehl, M.: Interleaved challenge loop PUF: a highly side-channel protected oscillator-based PUF. IEEE Trans. Circ. Syst. I: Regular Papers 69(12), 5121–5134 (2022). https://doi.org/10.1109/TCSI.2022.3208325

23. Tebelmann, L., Kühne, U., Danger, J.-L., Pehl, M.: Analysis and protection of the two-metric helper data scheme. In: Bhasin, S., De Santis, F. (eds.) COSADE 2021. LNCS, vol. 12910, pp. 279–302. Springer, Cham (2021). https://doi.org/10.1007/978-3-030-89915-8_13

24. Tebelmann, L., Pehl, M., Immler, V.: Side-channel analysis of the TERO PUF. In: Polian, I., Stöttinger, M. (eds.) COSADE 2019. LNCS, vol. 11421, pp. 43–60. Springer, Cham (2019). https://doi.org/10.1007/978-3-030-16350-1_4

25. Tebelmann, L., Wettermann, M., Pehl, M.: On-chip side-channel analysis of the loop PUF. In: Proceedings of the 2022 Workshop on Attacks and Solutions in Hardware Security, ASHES 2022, pp. 55 –63. Association for Computing Machinery, New York (2022). https://doi.org/10.1145/3560834.3563827

Impact of Process Mismatch and Device Aging on SR-Latch Based True Random Number Generators

Javad Bahrami[1], Mohammad Ebrahimabadi[1(✉)], Sylvain Guilley[2,3],
Jean-Luc Danger[3], and Naghmeh Karimi[1]

[1] University of Maryland Baltimore County, Baltimore, MD, USA
e127@umbc.edu
[2] Secure-IC S.A.S., Cesson-Sévigné, France
[3] LTCI, Télécom Paris, Institut Polytechnique de Paris, Palaiseau, France

Abstract. The True Random Number Generator (TRNG) is an inescapable primitive for security and cryptographic functions. A common TRNG architecture in digital devices exploits the noise jitter accumulation with ring oscillators. The Set-Reset latch (SR-latch) TRNG is another type which exploits the state of latches around metastability. In this TRNG the dynamic noise is extracted by analysing the convergence state of the related latch. The advantage is its very high throughput as it runs at (or near) the clock frequency. However, it is not so popular as there is no assurance that the quality of the randomness will exist in real silicon. This notably comes from the fact that there is a lack of a proven stochastic model against the quality of the process, and about its unknown behavior evolution over time (when aged). This makes the evaluation methods, like BSI AIS-31 or NIST SP 800-90B, difficult to succeed. To fill the gap, in this paper, we propose a closed form of the average entropy of the SR-latch based TRNG taking into account the process mismatch and allowing the designer to know precisely the number of SR-latches required for an optimal entropy. This is highly crucial to avoid low entropy if not enough latches are integrated, yet meanwhile preventing high overhead by not including more latches than needed. Moreover, the impact of device aging is deeply studied by simulation over 7 years. Interestingly, the results show that the aging has no significant impact on the entropy. This makes the SR-latch based TRNG a good candidate, for main TRNG or as a second entropy source.

Keywords: SR-latch based TRNG · stochastic model · regulatory standards · number of instances for a given entropy goal · impact of aging · self-rejuvenation of SR-latch TRNG

1 Introduction

Context. The generation of random numbers is essential to execute cryptographic protocols. More precisely there is a strong requirement to use a "true"

© The Author(s), under exclusive license to Springer Nature Switzerland AG 2024
R. Wacquez and N. Homma (Eds.): COSADE 2024, LNCS 14595, pp. 177–196, 2024.
https://doi.org/10.1007/978-3-031-57543-3_10

random number generator (TRNG) which exploits physical sources and is nondeterministic, contrary to "pseudo" random number generators which are derived from mathematical sequences. For instance, initialization vectors of AES operating modes, HMAC keys, ECDSA nonces, Crystals Kyber noise, masking of protected implementations, etc. all need to be provided by TRNGs. Hence, TRNGs in CMOS digital devices have been put forward.

Ring-Oscillator based TRNGs (RO-TRNG [1]) have been studied for a while and their security level is well known [2]. As they rely on the accumulation of jitter at each ring oscillation, their throughput is limited to a few dozen of Mb/s. Moreover, leveraging only one type of TRNG exposes the risk of *single point of failures* (SPOFs) which can wreck havoc the entire system, for lack or loss of entropy (see e.g., [3,4]).

Our Subject-Matter: The SR-Latch Based TRNG. To fill the gap, in this paper we tackle another type of TRNG entropy source relying on a bistable element: the so-called Set-Reset latch (SR-latch). Contrary to the Ring Oscillator which exploits the phase noise of a free-running combinational loop, the bistable latch exploits the amplitude noise when it is near its metastable state, i.e., between the two stable states '0' and '1' where a small dynamic noise forces the latch to go to a stable state. Thus, the latch plays both the role of *amplifier* and *extractor* of the physical noise to the digital domain. Such an entropy source is particularly fast as it can run at a very high speed rate. This type of entropy source is already used in the Intel's Ivy bridge [5] which is a full custom and analog technology. However, it requires a lot of care at the design stage as starting in a metastable state is hardly possible and a smart feedback loop is necessary to remain metastable. More importantly, it is not portable to any CMOS digital technology.

Problematic. In CMOS devices, an approach to use SR-latch based TRNG is to use a set of latches as proposed in [6–9]. However, this fully digital approach is not without risk, as there is no proven assurance that the entropy will be satisfactory in silicon, which is sensitive to process mismatch. Moreover, the impact of device aging has to be known to make sure the entropy is not going down over time [10]. Our first approach to assess the SR-latch TRNG was initiated in [11], yet that research provided neither a formal and in-depth study in investigating the number of latches needed for the SR-Latch TRNG nor a thorough analysis of the impact of aging on this type of TRNG. To fill the gap, this paper aims at formalizing and validating the TRNG relying on SR-latches against the process mismatch and device aging.

Our Contributions. More precisely the contributions of this paper are:

1. Proof of the scholastic model of the SR-latch TRNG to formalize the average entropy against the process mismatch;
2. Study of the impact of device aging on the SR-latch based TRNGs;
3. Demonstration that the mean entropy of a batch of SR-latch based TRNGs is not significantly impacted when aging.

Outline. The rest of this paper is organized as follows. After presenting the background in Sect. 2, Sect. 3 formalizes the proof expressing the stochastic model of entropy against the mismatch. Section 4 deals with the impact of aging on the targeted TRNGs and Sect. 5 discusses the experimental results. Finally, Sect. 6 concludes the paper and draws future directions of this research.

2   Research Background

2.1   SR-Latch Based TRNG

TRNGs in digital devices leverage clock jitter noise or the noise around metastable states for generating random numbers. While oscillator-based TRNGs (e.g., RO-based or self-timed rings [12]) are robust, metastable-state based TRNGs offer speed advantages. However, benefiting from metastable states is more tricky as it requires analog and custom cell design [5,13]. To tackle such a problem in a fully digital environment, deploying SR-latches has been proposed in the literature [6].

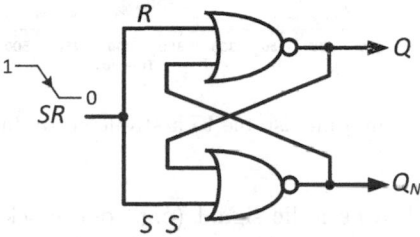

Fig. 1. An SR-latch realized via cross-coupled NOR gates.

Figure 1 depicts a NOR-based SR-latch TRNG. The Set (S) and Reset (R) inputs are both derived from the same SR signal. With perfectly balanced NOR gates, the latch enters a metastable state at around $V_{dd}/2$ voltage when SR goes to zero. Then the dynamic environmental noise pushes the latch to a stable state V_{dd} (logic '1') or logic '0', hence creating an entropy extractor from the physical noise to the digital world. Figure 2 depicts the simulations of this latch for $V_{dd} = 1.2$ V and a temperature of 25 °C. The simulation is a *transient noise analysis* for 100 cycles with a noise of min/max frequency equal to 10 kHz/20 GHz. The simulation engine is Spectre, running on the placed-and-routed netlists where parasitics had been extracted by Innovus, both tools being commercialized by Cadence. As shown, the propagation time between SR and Q or Q_N depends on the noise magnitude when SR goes to '0'. A long propagation time should correspond to a state very near metastability. Being around the metastable state provides an optimal entropy for a small level of noise. To characterize this propagation time according to the metastability level, we consider a perfect SR-latch with two separated S and R inputs having a small time difference. This difference expresses the dynamic noise, but it can also come from a bias due to the process mismatch, which is bad for entropy as it is static. Figure 3 shows the relationship between the propagation time and this S-R time difference. As shown in this figure when there is no time difference between S and R signals, the propagation time is very high due to the metastability, yet the propagation time decreases when there is a time difference between the S and R signals.

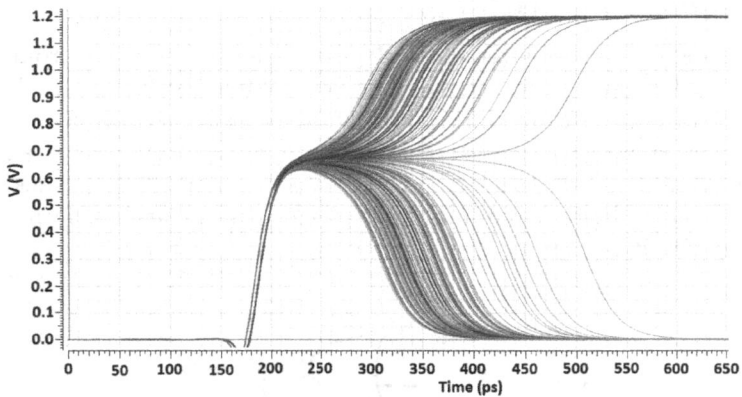

Fig. 2. Transition from a metastable to a stable state due to input noise.

By feeding SR with a periodic signal (e.g., one clock) this design yields a random bit every clock cycle, combining speed and compactness; thus efficient in terms of Power-Performance-Area (PPA).

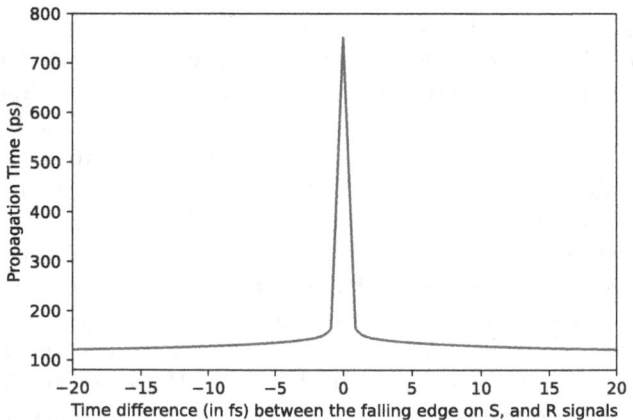

Fig. 3. Evolution of propagation time in one SR-latch based on the time difference between the falling edges on S and R signals.

The SR-latch can serve as a TRNG thanks to the dynamic noise. One first precondition is however that the routing is symmetric, if not *geometrically* at least *from the timing standpoint*. This could be achieved thanks to either *manual placement-and-routing* or *timing constraints* (e.g., SDC files). SDC constraints for balancing paths are described in [14]. The idea is to leverage a "Local Clock Set" (LCS) methodology where the SR source signal is defined as a virtual clock and S and R are set at leaves. The SDC constraint ensures that source-to-destination delays are equal, up to a bounded skew. In particular, the two NOR gates interfaces shall be plugged alike, namely input A (resp. B) receiving R (resp. Q_N) in the upper gate shall receive S (resp. Q) in the lower gate. A second precondition for the SR-latch to behave as a TRNG is that both NOR gates should be balanced, which is rarely the case as the 2 NORs are impacted by local process mismatch. Hence, the latch becomes deterministic, resembling a Physically Unclonable Function (PUF [15]). Accordingly, if multiple latches are XORed as shown in Fig. 4, we can expect that statistically a few latches will be sufficiently near metastability to provide a good entropy. This paper aims to size theoretically the number of required latches according to the mismatch and the noise level.

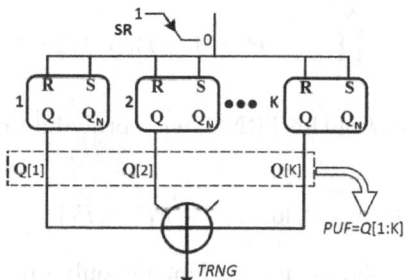

Fig. 4. The PUF-TRNG circuitry composing of a set of SR-latches.

2.2   Long-Lasting Randomness Provision

To ensure that SR-latch based TRNGs are promising for industrial applications we need to investigate their functionality over the course of usage. Indeed as the electrical specifications of transistors and in turn their delay and power consumption change over time due to device-aging [16], it is highly crucial to investigate whether a TRNG delivers high entropy even after aging or not.

In this paper, we focus on the impact of Bias Temperature Instability (BTI) and Hot Carrier Injection (HCI) [17] which are the most prominent aging mechanisms [18]. BTI includes NBTI and PBTI mechanisms (referring to negative and positive BTIs respectively) which affect PMOS and NMOS transistors respectively; resulting in the increase of their threshold voltage (Vth) when a transistor is ON. When OFF, the transistor experiences a partial recovery from the BTI stress as a result of which the aging-induced increase of its Vth partially decreases. HCI affects NMOS transistors when they experience a switching in their gate input.

This results in the change of Vth and the current passes through the transistor. Such changes increase the delay of the underlying gate during the course of usage.

3 Impact of Mismatch on the SR-Latch Based TRNG Architecture

In this section, we focus on the SR-latch based TRNGs realized via cross-coupled NOR gates unless otherwise mentioned. The NAND-based structures follow the same discussions and thus are not discussed here to prevent redundancy.

In a SR-latch based TRNG with multiple latches, each latch i has a probability of p_i to be at '1' after SR goes from '1' to '0':

$$p_i = \mathbb{P}[latch_i = 1].$$

The probability p_i has to be as close as possible to the metastable state corresponding to $p_i = 1/2$. We define the bias $\varepsilon_i = p_i - 1/2$. By applying the *piling-up lemma* [19], the probabilities $P_0 = \mathbb{P}[TRNG = 0]$ and $P_1 = \mathbb{P}[TRNG = 1]$ of the $TRNG$ composed by XORing N latches are equal to:

$$P_0 = 1/2 + 2^{N-1} \prod_{i=1}^{N} \varepsilon_i, \quad P_1 = 1 - P_0 = 1/2 - 2^{N-1} \prod_{i=1}^{N} \varepsilon_i. \tag{1}$$

The Shannon entropy H of the TRNG, with probabilities P_0 and P_1, is given by:

$$H = -P_0 \log(P_0) - P_1 \log(P_1). \tag{2}$$

The entropy equation shows that it depends only on the magnitude of the final bias $|\epsilon| = |\prod_{i=1}^{N} \varepsilon_i|$ as $H_\epsilon = H_{-\epsilon}$. The constant ϵ must be as close to zero as possible to achieve a probability near $1/2$ and an optimal entropy of 1 Shannon bit. Hence, only one latch being in a metastable state (i.e., $\varepsilon_i = 0$) is enough to have an optimal entropy.

The probability p_i highly depends on the internal process mismatch between identical elements of the microelectronics process. The mismatch arises from factors such as transistor channel width/length change owing to its atomic scale [20], or doping density in the active area, where the discrete number of dopants can depend from transistor to transistor [21].

The mismatch between two NOR gates of the SR-latch i can be modeled by a delay offset Δ_{M_i} of S against R with a perfectly balanced SR-latch. For a given latch i, its output is equiprobable (i.e. $p_i = 1/2$) if the mismatch Δ_{M_i} is exactly equal to zero. Without noise, as shown in Fig. 5a, there is no chance to get this condition. With noise, the p_i of some latches with small Δ_{M_i} can be closer to $1/2$; thus giving rise to the TRNG's randomness, as shown in Fig. 5b. In fully digital technology, if we consider a TRNG built by XORing multiple latches, we could think some of them could be sufficiently close to metastability to build a good TRNG. We consider that every latch has a static process mismatch Δ_{M_i} which follows a normal distribution: $\Delta_{M_i} \sim \mathcal{N}(0, \Sigma^2)$.

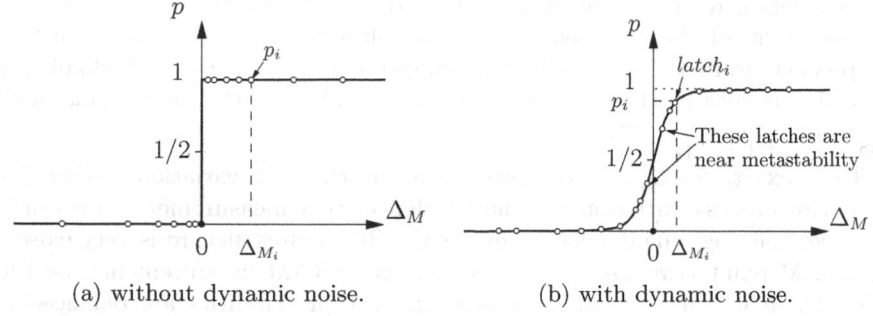

(a) without dynamic noise.   (b) with dynamic noise.

Fig. 5. The latches can produce entropy if $0 < p_i < 1 \implies \Delta_{M_i} = 0$ with noise.

The TRNG can be generated as there is a physical random source of dynamic noise Z considered as Gaussian: $Z \sim \mathcal{N}(0, \sigma^2)$. As expressed in Eqs. 1 and 2, the TRNG's randomness depends on the small values of the bias $\varepsilon_i = p_i - 1/2$.

To get a closed form of the entropy, let us first define the "Mismatch to Noise Ratio" MNR as being:

$$\text{MNR} = \frac{\Sigma}{\sigma} . \tag{3}$$

Intuitively, the smaller MNR, the larger the entropy.

The blue curve in Fig. 6 represents the distribution ΔM of all the ΔM_i, where ΔM_i is the process mismatch of latch i. The orange curve depicts the distribution of the measurement of ΔM_i where the Gaussian noise Z is added to ΔM_i. In this figure, the probability p_i of the latch i at '1' corresponds to the hatched area of Fig. 6.

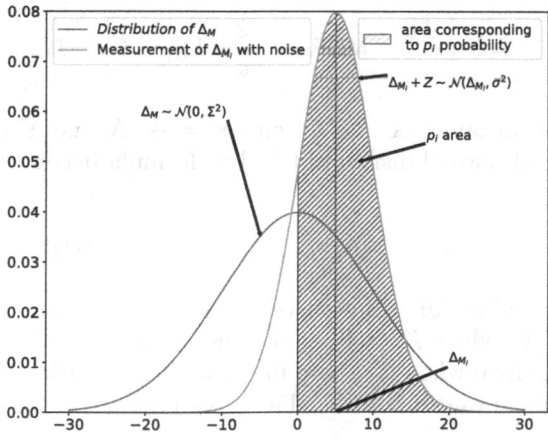

Fig. 6. Graphical representation of the probability p_i. (Color figure online)

As mentioned earlier, the entropy depends on the bias magnitude $|\prod_{i=1}^{N} \varepsilon_i|$. A closed form of the mean entropy can be obtained if we consider each latch independent from the others. This assumption is realistic since technological dispersion is very local as shown in [20,21]. In this case the mean value of the bias $|\widehat{\prod_{i=1}^{N} \varepsilon_i}| = \prod_{i=1}^{N} \widehat{|\varepsilon_i|}$.

To be exact, [20,21] focus on process-mismatch (local variation) rather than the entire process variation and noise. Hence, real measurements are crucial for understanding true dependencies. As the SR-latch structure is very close to the SRAM point (two inverters vs two gates), SRAM measurements used for PUF [22] show that the bias is limited and the probabilities are balanced for SRAM.

Lemma 1. *The mean bias* $\widehat{|\varepsilon_i|} = \widehat{|p_i - 1/2|}$ *according to* MNR *is given by:*

$$\widehat{|\varepsilon_i|} = \frac{1}{\pi} \arctan{(\text{MNR})}. \tag{4}$$

Proof.

$$\varepsilon_i = p_i - 1/2$$

$$\implies |\varepsilon_i| = \begin{cases} p_i - 1/2 & \text{if } p_i > 1/2 \\ 1/2 - p_i & \text{otherwise.} \end{cases}$$

As p_i is equally distributed around $1/2$, the mean value $\widehat{|\varepsilon_i|}$ of ε_i can be expressed as:

$$\begin{aligned} \widehat{|\varepsilon_i|} &= \widehat{p_i} - 1/2, p_i > 1/2 \\ &= \mathbb{P}\left[(\Delta_{M_i} + Z) > 0, \Delta_{M_i} > 0\right] - 1/2 \\ &= \mathbb{P}\left[\Delta_{M_i} > -Z, \Delta_{M_i} > 0\right] - 1/2 \\ &= \mathbb{P}\left[\frac{\Delta_{M_i}}{\Sigma} \cdot \text{MNR} > -\frac{Z}{\sigma}, \Delta_{M_i} > 0\right] - 1/2. \end{aligned}$$

If we consider the variables $X = \frac{\Delta_{M_i}}{\Sigma}$ and $Y = \frac{Z}{\sigma}$, X and Y are independent and follow standard normal distributions. The formula becomes:

$$\widehat{|\varepsilon_i|} = \mathbb{P}[X \cdot \text{MNR} > -Y, X > 0] - 1/2 = \mathbb{P}[Y > -X \cdot \text{MNR}, X > 0] - 1/2.$$

Since the probability distribution of (X, Y) is isotropic, the value $\mathbb{P}[Y > -X \cdot \text{MNR}, X > 0]$ when $X > 0$ equals the proportion of the grey area on Fig. 7 on the half circle when X, Y are in polar representation. This proportion is $(\theta + \pi/2)/\pi$, where $\tan(\theta) = \text{MNR}$. Thus, we have:

$$\widehat{|\varepsilon_i|} = \frac{1}{\pi} \arctan{(\text{MNR})}.$$

$\square$

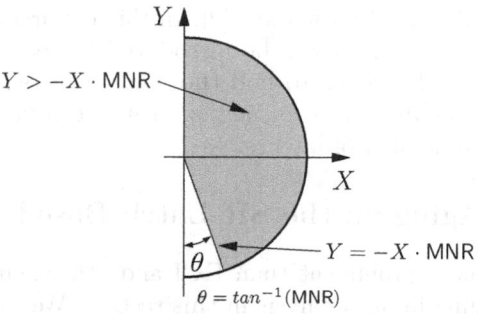

Fig. 7. Polar representation of X and Y.

The mean probabilities $\widehat{P_0}$ and $\widehat{P_1}$ are given by Eq. 5, with $s = sign(\prod_{i=1}^{N} \varepsilon_i)$:

$$\widehat{P_0} = 1/2 + (-1)^s \cdot 2^{N-1} \left(\frac{1}{\pi} \arctan(\text{MNR})\right)^N, \quad \widehat{P_1} = 1 - \widehat{P_0}. \tag{5}$$

The mean entropy $\widehat{H}$ is deduced from these formulas and illustrated in Figure 8 according to the number of latches and the MNR parameter.

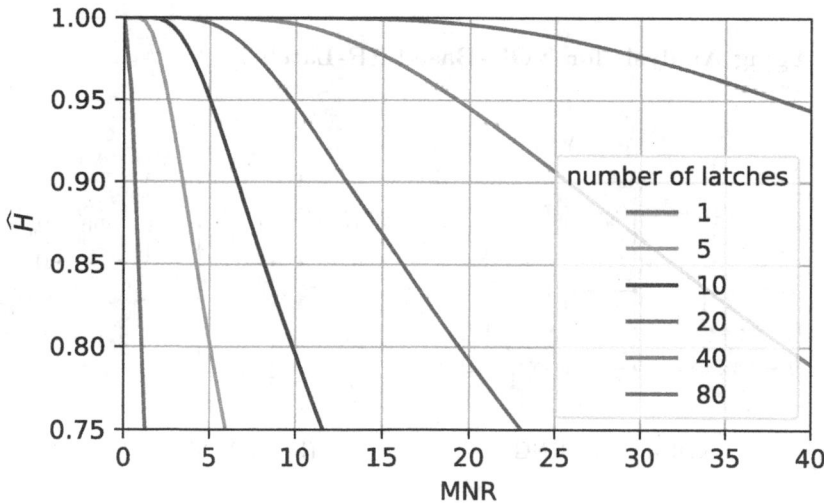

Fig. 8. Mean Entropy $\widehat{H}$ according to Mismatch to Noise Ratio (MNR) for different number of latches.

In the study presented in [9] about SR-latch in FD-SOI 28 nm technology, the MNR was estimated at 7. For such MNR value, Fig. 8 indicates that at least 40 SR-latches are necessary to have an average entropy of 1 bit. More precisely, with 40 SR-latches, the entropy is greater than 0.997 bit, which is the threshold value mandated by the AIS-31 standard [2]. In this research, we characterize Σ by the sweeping method, which will be introduced in Sect. 5.2. Meanwhile we add artificial noise to SR signals to find the number of required latches based on Fig. 8. Note that the impact of routing/parasitics can be modeled by adding safety margins in the number of latches.

4   Impact of Aging on the SR-Latch Based TRNG

As BTI impact is more prominent than HCI and other aging mechanisms, we focus on the BTI aging in our analysis in this section. We can simplify the conditions in which the BTI aging occurs with the following rules which correspond to the conduction of the transistor:

- A PMOS is degraded (in terms of stress resulting in the increase of its threshold voltage and in turn its delay) by NBTI aging when gate = '0', source = '1' (and thus drain = '1');
- An NMOS is degraded by PBTI aging (in terms of stress) when its gate = '1', source = '0' (and thus the drain = 0).

In this section, we discuss the impact of aging on both NOR- and NAND-based TRNGs for the sake of completeness, yet as both structures behave similarly, for the sake of space, we focus only on the NOR-based structures in Sect. 5 where we present the experimental results.

4.1   Aging Analysis for NOR-Based SR-Latch

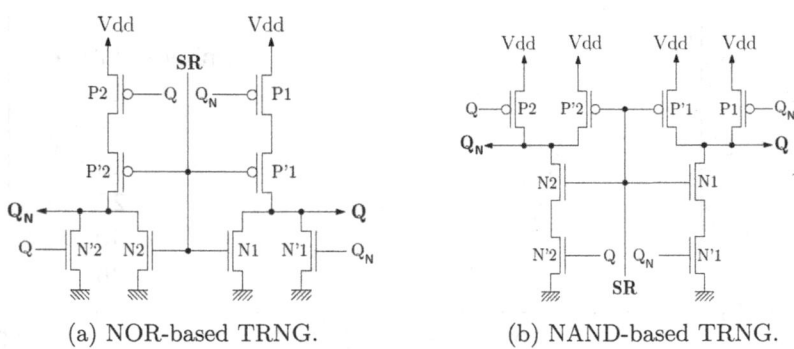

(a) NOR-based TRNG.   (b) NAND-based TRNG.

Fig. 9. Structures of the NOR and NAND SR-latch based TRNGs.

Here we focus on the TRNG structure realized with NOR-based SR-latches shown in Fig. 9a. In the initial phase SR is '1' and so the output of each NOR becomes '0'. Without loss of generality, let's assume that the output Q_N changes faster than Q (due to mismatch). In this case when SR goes from '1' to '0', the output Q_N rises faster than Q and toggles to '1', whereas Q stays at '0'. Therefore in such a situation the transistors' aging would be as below:

- When SR = 1 ⟹ N1, N2, P1, P2 get aged;
- When SR = 0 ⟹ N'1, P2, P'2 get aged;
- N'2 and P'1 do not get aged.

The above discussion shows that P2 almost ages twice more than P1. Also P'2 ages more than P'1. This should slow down Q_N. *This analysis shows that aging can have a positive impact towards metastability on this latch as Q_N changes slower than Q due to aging (referring to the above discussion) while it was faster initially.*

To support our analysis, we have conducted HSpice simulations and extracted the aging impacts in terms of the evolution of Vth over 7 years of usage (with the steps of 2 months) for the NOR-based SR-latch in Fig. 9a. The results depicted in Fig. 10 follow our above discussion. For example, as shown the change of Vth in P2 increases is almost twice more than P'2. Also please note that NBTI impact (in PMOS transistors) is almost twice of PBTI impact in NMOS transistors.

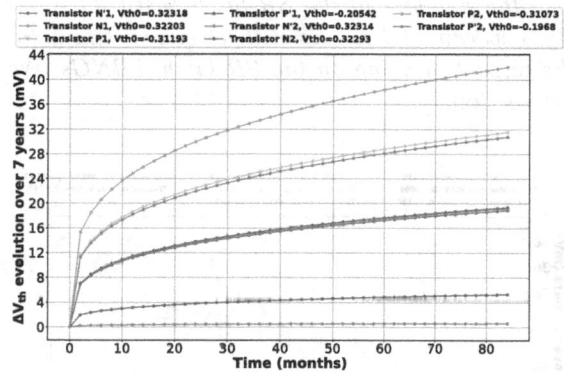

Fig. 10. Threshold voltage (Vth) evolution with aging for the NOR-based SR-latch. Vth0 denotes the initial threshold (before aging) for each transistor.

4.2 Aging Analysis in NAND-Based SR-Latch

Similar to the NOR-based SR-latch discussed earlier, in this section we analyze the aging impact in the NAND-based structure shown in Fig. 9b. In this structure, initially we give '0' to SR and so the output of each NAND would be '1'. Without loss of generality, here we assume that the output Q is changed faster than Q_N when going from the initial to final phase, i.e., when SR goes from '0' to '1', the output Q will fall faster than Q_N and thus Q toggles to '0', whereas Q_N stays at '1' and loses the race. Therefore in such situation the transistors aging would be as follows:

- When SR = 0 ⟹ N'1, N'2, P'1, P'2 get aged;
- When SR = 1 ⟹ N'1, N1, P2 get aged;
- N2 and P1 do not get aged.

The above discussion shows that N'1 ages almost twice more than N'2 and N1 while N2 does not age much (unless for HCI). Thus the change of Q gets slow over the course of usage (aging) although it was faster initially compared to Q_N. *This again confirms that aging can positively affect the TRNG over time and results in metastability and thus higher randomness.*

Our HSpice simulation result for the NAND-based Latch is shown in Fig. 11 which again follows our above discussion. For example as shown N'1 ages twice more than N1. Note that in Fig. 10 and Fig. 11 the graphs depicting the ΔVth have overlap for some transistors and may not be seen clearly (e.g., N1 and N'1 in Fig. 10). Also it is noteworthy to mention that NBTI effect (as expected) is more than PBTI thus the PMOS transistors observe more change in their threshold voltage than the NMOS counterparts in similar situations (i.e., being ON for the same amount of time).

In sum, the above analysis and the extracted results can lead to the conclusion that aging can move the SR-latch based TRNG towards more metastability for both NOR and NAND based circuits. Albeit there are some high-order effects which make the analysis of the SR-latch based TRNGs not straightforward. Accordingly, experimental results with electrical simulation are necessary to better learn the impact of aging on the SR-latch TRNGs. We will show such results in the next section.

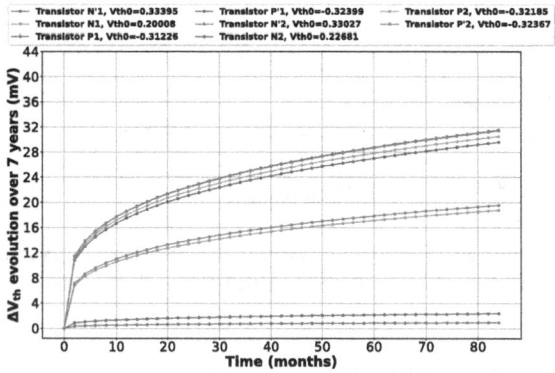

Fig. 11. Threshold voltage (Vth) evolution with aging for the NAND-based SR-latch. Vth0 denotes the initial threshold (before aging) for each transistor.

5   Experimental Results and Discussions

5.1   Experimental Setup

We implemented the TRNGs at the transistor level using a 45nm open-source NANGATE library [23]. Our Initial netlist includes 1024 SR-latches in parallel (recall Fig. 4). To mimic the real-silicon behavior, we considered process mismatch through Monte-Carlo simulations with Gaussian distributions: transistor gate length L: $3\sigma = 10\%$, threshold voltage V_{th}: $3\sigma = 30\%$, and gate-oxide thickness t_{OX}: $3\sigma = 3\%$. This allows us to derive the delay offset of the mismatch Δ_M through the sweeping process that will be discussed in the next section. Moreover to resemble real silicon, we also added a white noise to the input of each latch with $\mu = 0$ and $\sigma = 1.029$ ps.

In our implementation of the SR-latch based TRNG, while the Q_N outputs of all latches are left floating, the Q outputs are XORed to build the final single bit of randomness. Also, We added buffers on SR signals to include the inputs' slope (between 81.43V/ps and 99.65V/ps for the smallest and largest buffers, respectively) however this did not highly affect TRNG's metastability. We used Synopsys HSpice for the simulations, and the HSpice built-in MOSRA Level 3 model [24] to evaluate aging effects for 7 years of device operation in different time steps from minutes (30 min) to months (6 months). We considered BTI and HCI for aging simulations, however we just discussed NBTI for the 1st-order analysis in our discussion. The simulations were conducted for the temperature of 85°C, $V_{dd} = 1.2$ V.

5.2   Experimental Results

A. Impact of Aging on the Propagation Time of the TRNG: The first set of results relates to the propagation time of the latches composing a TRNG considering their metastability status. Indeed, as discussed in Sect. 2, propagation time significantly increases when approaching metastability as shown in Fig. 3. To measure the propagation time of each underlying latch, we applied a falling edge signal to both R and S of the latch and kept the SR (the signal feeding both S and R) value '0' till either Q or Q_N get stable at '1'. The propagation time is defined as the time difference from when the SR signal crosses 0.8 V until the absolute value of $Q - Q_N$ exceeds 0.8 V. To analyze the results, we categorized the latches into 2 sets based on their outcome. In the first set, the outputs of latches stay at the same value, e.g, $(Q, Q_N) = (1, 0)$ when SR goes to 0 without aging and stay at $(1, 0)$ after aging. For the second set, the output toggles with aging: $(Q, Q_N) = (1, 0) \Rightarrow (Q, Q_N) = (0, 1)$ and vice-versa.

SR-Latches Keeping the Same State: Figures 12a and 12b illustrate the histogram of propagation time for latches keeping the state $Q = 1$ in both new and 7 years-aged latches. As depicted, aging increases the propagation time; with averages of 81.63 ps for new latches and 98.87 ps for aged latches. A similar observation can be made for latches staying with state $Q_N = 1$ in Figs. 12c and 12d, with the average propagation time increasing from 82.4 ps to 99.35 ps. This implies that for this first set of latches which keep the same state for both fresh and aged devices, there is a trend to go towards metastability, thus corroborating the analysis in Sect. 4. This should improve the quality of the TRNG over time. To investigate the aging impacts on the SR-latch in more detail, the evolution of the propagation time when the SR-latches are aged is shown for different aging steps. Figure 13a and Fig. 13b depict the cases for two sample latches (among the 1024 latches we simulated) whose output stays at $Q = 1$ before and during the

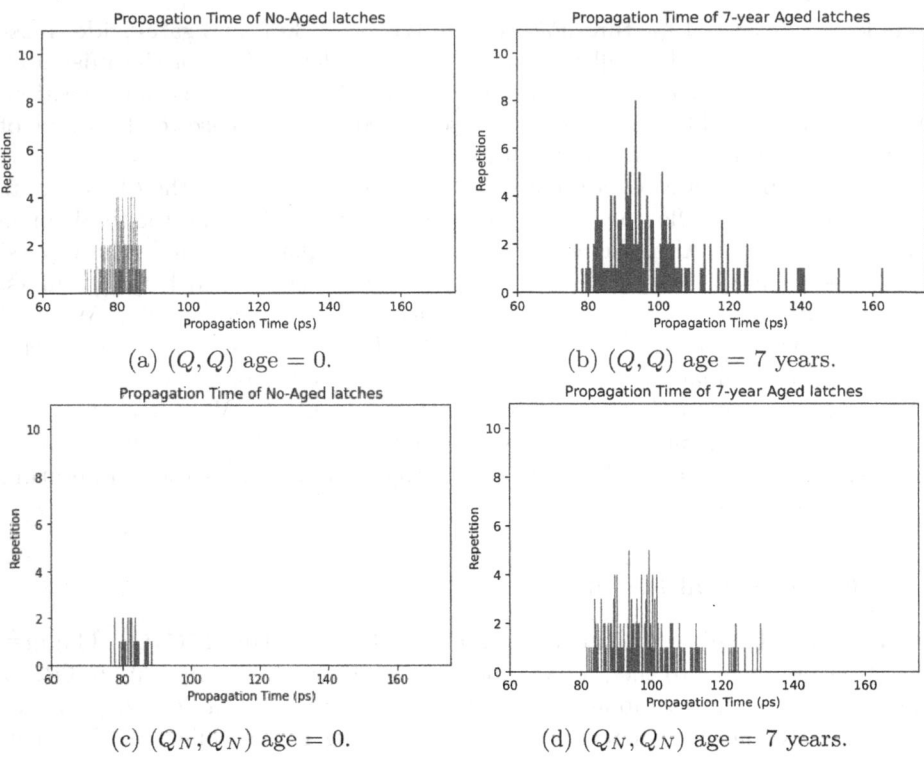

(a) (Q, Q) age $= 0$.

(b) (Q, Q) age $= 7$ years.

(c) (Q_N, Q_N) age $= 0$.

(d) (Q_N, Q_N) age $= 7$ years.

Fig. 12. Distribution of the propagation time of the SR-latch when the fresh and aged devices have the same state.

course of aging. We can notice that the propagation time increases monotonically but not at the same rate. We observe the same effect for latches whose output stays at $Q_N = 1$ as shown in Fig. 14a and Fig. 14b. This monotonic evolution of the propagation time is not the same for all the latches but all go toward the metastable state, thus involving a better entropy.

SR-Latches with State Toggling: For this second set of latches, the outputs change state with aging. If the no-aged SR-latch outputs $(Q, Q_N) = (1, 0)$ after SR goes to 0, when it changes to $(0, 1)$ after a certain amount of age. The propagation time starts to increase, as expected according to the analysis of Sect. 4, but decreases once the state goes beyond metastability, involving a toggling of the output. This is illustrated in Fig. 15 where we can observe the toggling on their output in a different port after some time of aging. As shown, the propagation time increases first but after such toggling at time t it starts decreasing. For example, for the first sampled latch in Fig. 15a such toggling occurs after $t = 180$ min $(= 6 \times 30)$ of aging. For the other samples, as shown in Fig. 15b-15c-15d, the toggling occurs at a different point of time (42 months, 150 min and 50 days) due to the process mismatch. It is interesting to note that the mismatch

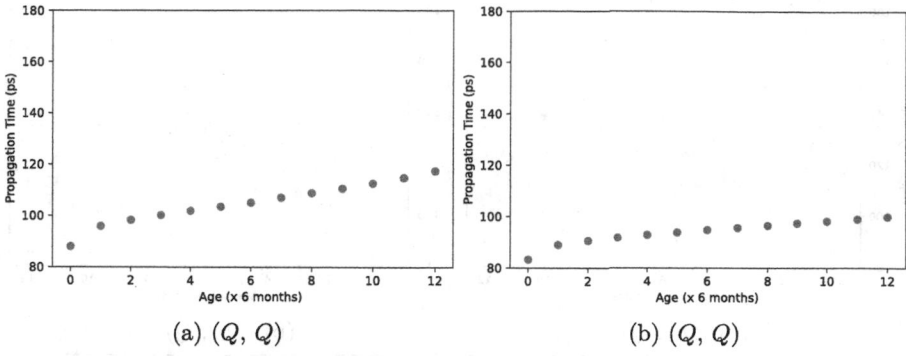

(a) (Q, Q) (b) (Q, Q)

Fig. 13. Evolution of propagation time with aging for 2 sample latches keeping the state $Q = 1$.

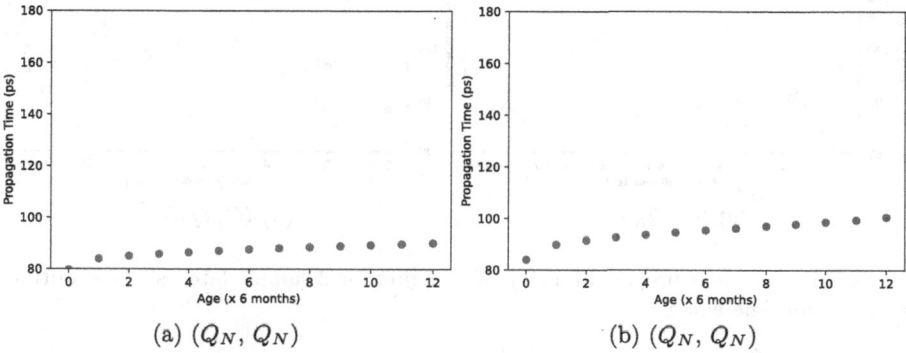

(a) (Q_N, Q_N) (b) (Q_N, Q_N)

Fig. 14. Evolution of propagation time with aging for 2 sample latches keeping the state $Q_N = 1$.

for this set of latches, expressed in the time difference between the S and R signals, is small, below 1 ps, while in other cases such difference is higher than 1.11 ps.

The takeaway from these observations is that the reasoning of Sect. 4 applies and the latches go toward the metastable state and contribute to the increase of the propagation time. However, for the set of latches that are near metastability and thus their output toggle due to the course of aging, the propagation time decreases after toggling, meaning that their state goes away from metastability. This could decrease the entropy of the SR-latch TRNG for these cases.

B. Process Mismatch Characterization and Entropy Assessment. This set of results extracts process mismatch impact in terms of their effect on the transient response time of TRNGs. This evaluation is essential in assessing the MNR value (recall Eq. 3) and in turn deciding about the number of latches to be inserted in the TRNG design for fabrication.

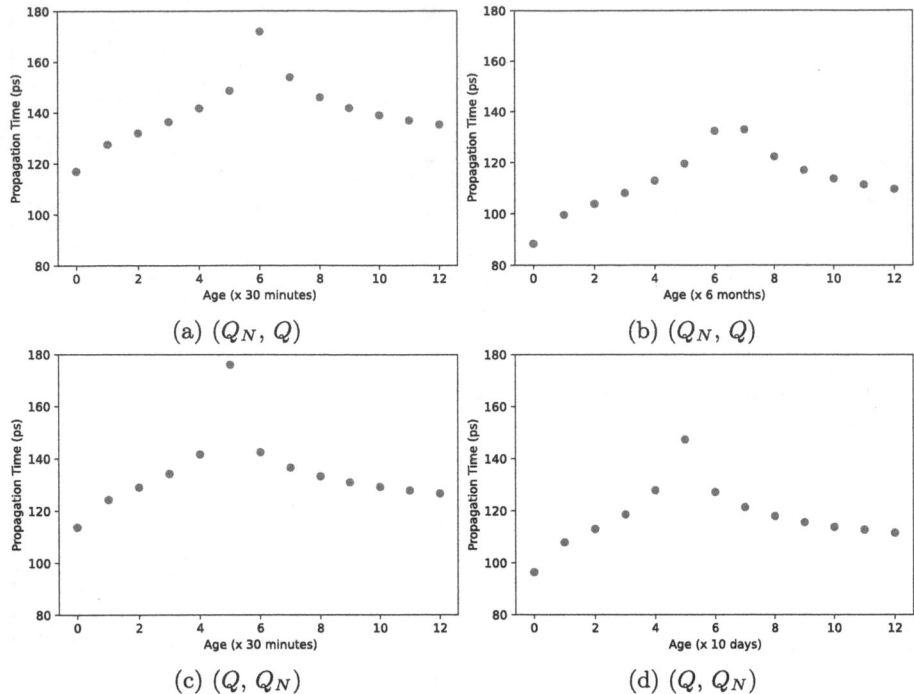

Fig. 15. Evolution of propagation time with aging for 2 sample latches whose outputs toggle during the aging.

In this experiment we do not add any noise to be able to see the sole impact of process mismatch among different latches and even among the 2 NOR gates resided in each latch. To do so, we inject a transition (fall in case of NOR-based latch) in S signal and then sweep the R signal such that it observes a transition in a different time. Then we measure the time difference between the transitions on S and R that results in toggling the latch output (*the time that the latch goes to its final state and exits the metastable state*). This time (referred to as ΔM_i for each latch i in Sect. 3) is changed from one latch to another due to process mismatch and manifests the impact of process mismatch in the randomness of the TRNG. In our experiments, the sweeping step is 80 fs.

Figures 16a and 16b show the distribution of the extracted ΔM_i for the NOR-based TRNGs when they are new (age = 0) or 7-year old. In this experiment, we initially inserted 1024 latches to find the MNR value and then decide about the number of latches based on Fig. 8. As expected the distributions follow a Gaussian model. When fresh (age:0), the results exhibit a mean of -0.1173 ps and a standard deviation of 1.0294 ps while the mean and standard deviation of the 7-year aged TRNGs is -0.0655 ps and 0.6396 ps, respectively. As shown through the course of aging, the standard deviation of the distribution of ΔM_i decreases. The takeaway point from these observations is that the SR-Latch

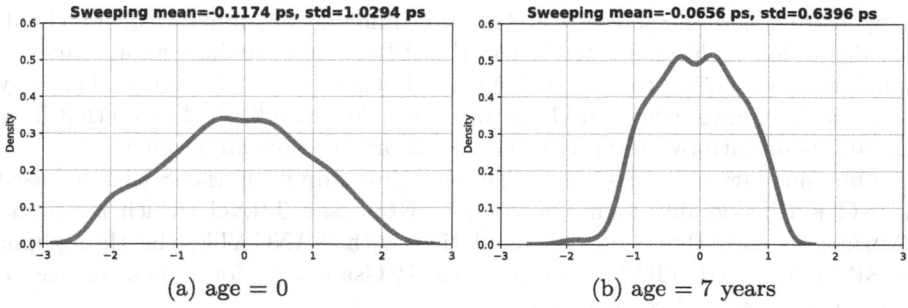

Fig. 16. Distribution of the ΔM_i for the targeted NOR-based TRNGs when they are new (age = 0) or 7-year old.

based TRNG becomes more metastable over time; thus its randomness increases over the course of usage. This confirms that SR-latch based TRNGs remain qualified (if not getting better) over time. In practice, the effect of temperature on the entropy of the TRNG is insignificant as temperature affects all NOR gates (or NAND gates) similarly.

In the next step, we conducted simulations to get the mean entropy for MNR = 10 and MNR = 20. As the standard deviation of the process mismatch is at $\Sigma = 1.0294$ ps in Fig. 16a), we used respectively a Gaussian noise with $\sigma = 100$ fs and 50 fs at the input of the S signal. The entropy is calculated using Eq. 2 for a number of latches $\in \{20, 40, 80\}$. As shown in Table 1, the average entropy greatly increases with the number of latches and is slightly increased with aging but not monotonically as discussed in the next section. This is comparable with the theoretical analysis of the mean entropy in Fig. 8, especially when the number of latches increases, involving a lower statistical bias.

Table 1. Aging-induced evolution of the mean Entropy for MNR = 10 (left) and MNR = 20 (right) when we have 20, 40, and 80 latches.

year \ #latches	20	40	80	year \ #latches	20	40	80
0	0.833	0.985	0.997	0	0.580	0.876	0.943
2	0.927	0.995	0.999	2	0.700	0.918	0.995
4	0.960	0.999	1	4	0.731	0.923	0.994
6	0.940	0.995	1	6	0.721	0.913	0.999

5.3 Discussion

Here we analyze the results presented and interpret the experimental results presented earlier. Furthermore, we comment more generally on our contributions.

It is known that, in general, aging increases the variability, on individual gates. However, given the symmetrical structure of SR-latches, such variability happens to contribute to fix their structural imbalance (rooted in local technology dispersion). This is due to the fact that SR-latches are differential elements, which react according to the relative delay between S and R inputs; this delay decreases in average when variability increases. As a result, SR-latches that have initially poor entropy are likely to become more entropic after aging.

Our simulation results show that the throughput of the SR-latch based TRNG is considerably high compared to RO-based TRNG (which is around 3Mb/s per [25]). Based on our simulation with NANGATE, the throughput of SR-latch based TRNG changes from 12 Gsample/s for a new device to 10 Gsample/s after 7 years of aging.

It is also probable that some SR-latches that are well balanced at birth go further from their tiny balance after aging. However, in general, this situation is rare because only a minority of SR-latches happen to be fabricated well balanced. All in all, the mean of the entropy should slightly increase with aging.

Notice that metastability, in that a signal is not resolved, is not the phenomenon we leverage as an entropy source. Still metastability is correlated to the fact that an SR-latch is behaving randomly. In practice, anyway, the output of an SR-latch is re-sampled, resolving the metastability. Hence, we insist that in terms of the stochastic model, the entropy arises from the difference between S and R input signals.

Regarding the industrial interest in SR-latch TRNGs, one should note that they nicely complement other TRNGs designs, such as ring-oscillator TRNGs. Notice that some TRNGs have been found to fail [26]. It is thus a safe practice to implement two instances of TRNGs with different rationales. This is even mandated by regional regulations such as OSCCA GM/T-0078 in China.

Eventually, let us comment on the PPA. Our findings in Sect. 5.2 is that 80 SR-latches are required for the technology we considered, which means roughly 160 gate equivalent (GE). Such size of entropy source is very small, compared to RO-TRNG (recall that the seminal paper on the RO-TRNG [1] contender suggests 114 RO, each comprised of dozens of GE). This low overhead makes SR-latch based TRNGs even more appealing; on top of its better or at least same entropy (not less) when aged.

6   Conclusion

The study in this paper allows to better control and understand the behavior of SR-latch TRNG against the process mismatch and aging. This type of TRNG provides very high throughput compared to RO-based but is not well mastered in digital technology. The presented work paves the way towards a better comprehension of the SR-latch allowing the TRNG designer to use it in a trusted manner. The impact of mismatch has notably been formally expressed to size the number of latches according to the required entropy and the environmental noise. It is also shown that the aging provides a slight improvement towards the metastability of latches, hence a better entropy of the TRNG. Future works are to confirm these results on real devices with different process mismatch and noise levels. Another important work is to formally analyze the second order impact of aging, i.e. when the latches toggle and move away from metastability.

Acknowledgements. Secure-IC acknowledges partial funding from the European Union's Horizon Europe research and innovation program through ALLEGRO project, under grant agreement No. 101070009. This research is also supported in part by the National Science Foundation CAREER Award under Grant NSF CNS-1943224.

References

1. Sunar, B., Martin, W.J., Stinson, D.R.: A provably secure true random number generator with built-in tolerance to active attacks. IEEE Trans. Comput. **56**(1), 109–119 (2007)
2. Peter, M., Schindler, W.: A Proposal for Functionality Classes for Random Number Generators, Version 2.0 (2022). https://www.bsi.bund.de/SharedDocs/Downloads/EN/BSI/Certification/Interpretations/AIS_31_Functionality_classes_for_random_number_generators_e.pdf?__blob=publicationFile&v=5
3. Markettos, A.T., Moore, S.W.: The frequency injection attack on ring-oscillator-based true random number generators. In: Cryptographic Hardware and Embedded Systems (CHES), vol. 5747, pp. 317–331 (2009)
4. Martin, H., Martin-Holgado, P., Peris-Lopez, P., Morilla, Y., Entrena, L.: On the entropy of oscillator-based true random number generators under ionizing radiation. Entropy **20**(7), 513 (2018)
5. Hamburg, M., Kocher, P., Marson, M.E.: Analysis of Intel's Ivy Bridge digital random number generator (2012). http://www.cryptography.com/public/pdf/Intel_TRNG_Report_20120312.pdf
6. Danger, J.-L., Guilley, S., Hoogvorst, P.: High speed true random number generator based on open loop structures in FPGAs. Microelectron. J. **40**(11), 1650–1656 (2009)
7. Lozach, F., Ben-Romdhane, M., Graba, T., Danger, J.-L.: FPGA design of an open-loop true random number generator. In: Euromicro Conference on Digital System Design (DSD), pp. 615–622 (2013)
8. Ben-Romdhane, M., Graba, T., Danger, J.-L., Mathieu, Y.: Design methodology of an ASIC TRNG based on an open-loop delay chain. In: New Circuits and Systems Conference (NEWCAS), pp. 1–4 (2013)
9. Danger, J.-L., et al.: Analysis of mixed PUF-TRNG circuit based on SR-latches in FD-SOI technology. In: Euromicro Conference on Digital System Design (DSD), pp. 508–515 (2018)
10. Fischer, V.: A closer look at security in random number generators design. In: Constructive Side-Channel Analysis and Secure Design (COSADE), pp. 167–182 (2012)
11. Bahrami, J., Ebrahimabadi, M., Danger, J., Guilley, S., Karimi, N.: Special session: security verification & testing for SR-latch TRNGs. In: VLSI Test Symposium (VTS), pp. 1–10 (2023)
12. Cherkaoui, A., Fischer, V., Fesquet, L., Aubert, A.: A very high speed true random number generator with entropy assessment. In: Cryptographic Hardware and Embedded Systems (CHES), vol. 8086, pp. 179–196 (2013)
13. Kinniment, D., Chester, E.: Design of an on-chip random number generator using metastability. In: European Solid-State Circuits Conference, pp. 595–598 (2002)

14. Gimenez, G., Cherkaoui, A., Cogniard, G., Fesquet, L.: Static timing analysis of asynchronous bundled-data circuits. In: International Symposium on Asynchronous Circuits and Systems (ASYNC), pp. 110–118 (2018)
15. Maes, R.: Physically Unclonable Functions - Constructions, Properties and Applications. Springer, Heidelberg (2013). https://doi.org/10.1007/978-3-642-41395-7
16. Anik, M.T.H., Reefat, H.I., Danger, J.-L., Guilley, S., Karimi, N.: Aging-induced failure prognosis via digital sensors. In: ACM Great Lakes Symposium on VLSI (GLSVLSI), pp. 703–708 (2023)
17. Oboril, F., et al.: Extratime: modeling and analysis of wearout due to transistor aging at microarchitecture-level. In: DSN, pp. 1–12 (2012)
18. Huang, K., Anik, M.T.H., Zhang, X., Karimi, N.: Real-time IC aging prediction via on-chip sensors. In: 2021 IEEE Computer Society Annual Symposium on VLSI (ISVLSI), pp. 13–18 (2021)
19. Matsui, M.: Linear cryptanalysis method for DES cipher. In: Helleseth, T. (ed.) EUROCRYPT 1993. LNCS, vol. 765, pp. 386–397. Springer, Heidelberg (1993). https://doi.org/10.1007/3-540-48285-7_33
20. Asenov, A., Kaya, S., Davies, J.H.: Intrinsic threshold voltage fluctuations in decanano mosfets due to local oxide thickness variations. IEEE Trans. Electron Devices 49(1), 112–119 (2002)
21. Asenov, A., Slavcheva, G., Brown, A.R., Davies, J.H., Saini, S.: Increase in the random dopant induced threshold fluctuations and lowering in sub-100 nm MOSFETs due to quantum effects: A 3-D density-gradient simulation study. IEEE Trans. Electron Devices 48(4), 722–729 (2001)
22. Maes, R., Tuyls, P., Verbauwhede, I.: A soft decision helper data algorithm for SRAM PUFs. In: International Symposium on Information Theory, pp. 2101–2105 (2009)
23. Nangate 45 nm open cell library. http://www.nangate.com
24. Synopsys: HSPICE User Guide: Basic Simulation and Analysis (2016)
25. Petura, O., Mureddu, U., Bochard, N., Fischer, V., Bossuet, L.: A survey of AIS-20/31 compliant TRNG cores suitable for FPGA devices. In: International Conference on Field Programmable Logic and Applications (FPL), pp. 1–10 (2016)
26. Bernstein, D.J., et al.: Factoring RSA keys from certified smart cards: coppersmith in the wild. In: ASIACRYPT, pp. 341–360 (2013)

Lightweight Leakage-Resilient PRNG from TBCs Using Superposition

Mustafa Khairallah[1], Srinivasan Yadhunathan[1], and Shivam Bhasin[2]([✉])

[1] Seagate Research Group, Singapore, Singapore
{mustafa.khairallah,srinivasan.yadhunathan}@seagate.com
[2] Nanyang Technological University, Singapore, Singapore
sbhasin@ntu.edu.sg

Abstract. In this paper, we propose a leakage-resilient pseudo-random number generator (PRNG) design that leverages the rekeying techniques of the PSV-Enc encryption scheme and the superposition property of the Superposition-Tweak-Key (STK) framework. The random seed of the PRNG is divided into two parts; one part is used as an ephemeral key that changes every two calls to a tweakable block cipher (TBC), and the other part is used as a static long-term key. Using the superposition property, we show that it is possible to eliminate observable leakage by only masking the static key. Thus, our proposal itself can be seen as a superposition of masking and rekeying. We show that our observations can be used to design an unpredictable-with-leakage PRNG as long as the static key is protected, and the ephemeral key cannot be attacked with 2 traces. Our construction enjoys better theoretical security arguments than PSV-Enc; better Time-Data trade-off and leakage assumptions, using the recently popularized unpredictability with leakage. We verify our proposal by performing Test Vector Leakage Assessment (TVLA) on an STK-based TBC (Deoxys-TBC) operated with a fixed key and a dynamic random tweak. Our results show that while the protection of the static key is non-trivial, it only requires $\approx 10\%$ overhead for first-order protection in the most conservative setting, unlike traditional masking that may require significant overheads of 300% or more.

Keywords: Leakage Resilience · PRNG · TBC · Levelled Implementations · Unpredictability · TVLA · STK · PSV-Enc

1 Introduction

For more than 25 years, side-channel analysis has been at the forefront of cryptology in general, and symmetric key cryptography in particular. While in classical cryptography the adversary is assumed to interact with the cryptographic scheme in a black-box way, respecting a set of pre-imposed rules and limitations, side-channel analysis is concerned with adversaries that can observe the device's behaviour in action (also known as grey-box model) and make inferences based on physical measurements, such as timing, power or electromagnetic measurements. One of the most famous examples of this paradigm is the

© The Author(s), under exclusive license to Springer Nature Switzerland AG 2024
R. Wacquez and N. Homma (Eds.): COSADE 2024, LNCS 14595, pp. 197–217, 2024.
https://doi.org/10.1007/978-3-031-57543-3_11

Differential Power Analysis (DPA) proposed in [KJJ99]. Protecting implementations against side channel attacks has been a goal for designers for more than 25 years. The most widespread countermeasure against DPA-like attacks is circuit masking [ISW03], where all the secret and sensitive variables are encoded using a secret-sharing scheme, and the circuit/software is adjusted to compute the function over the new representation. This task is far from trivial, as the designers must make sure that the secret is never unveiled in plain during any step of the computation. Several models having been proposed over the years to capture this goal, most notably the probing model [ISW03], which represents the implementation as a circuit and makes sure that for any adversary that can observe d wires during any one execution, cannot deduce any sensitive variables, d is known as the security order of the implementation. It was later shown that the probing model does not capture the full reality, as combining shares of the secret may happen in other ways than unveiling the secret in temporary variables (represented by wires). Different types of *glitches* have been shown to leak the secret even if the scheme is secure in the probing model [NRR06], which led to new security models and many masking schemes attempting to address these issues [CS20]. These countermeasures may increase the cost of computations by several orders of magnitude, due to multiple reasons. The cost of masking non-linear functions grows quadratically with d. Besides, protecting against glitches requires synchronizing temporary variables in sophisticated ways that slow down the operation and may require large amounts of random bits.

For these reasons, a new design paradigm emerged known as leakage-resilient cryptography [DP08,BBC+20]. In this approach, a cryptographic mode of operation is designed such that it may be costly as a black-box design, compared to classical methods, but is easier to protect against side-channel analysis. The main approach towards this goal is the so-called *levelled implementations*, where the algorithm is divided into two parts: one part uses a long-term secret key, is heavily protected against side-channel analysis, and the other part uses only temporary secrets that acts as moving targets for the adversary. This makes DPA significantly harder as it requires many traces with the same secret. If the heavily protected part is protected against DPA, the adversary can only target the other part, and since it does not expose long-term secrets, DPA is not possible. This leaves the adversary with Simple Power Analysis (SPA). SPA refers to attacks that use low trace counts, typically single trace. Besides, SPA is sometimes used as an umbrella-term that includes all attacks that require a small number of traces with the same key, but can have extensive modelling/profiling phases, where the adversary can collect traces from the implementation with their own key. Template attacks with small number of traces fall into this category. These (profiled/non-profiled single trace) attacks are much harder to mount, and are easier to protect against compared to DPA. For software, a cheaper countermeasure such as shuffling can be used [VCMKS12], while in hardware if the implementation includes many parallel functionalities, such attacks maybe unfeasible due to inherent noise (or cost effective noise sources could be easily deployed).

Another related countermeasure is fresh rekeying, initially proposed by Medwed *et al.* [MSGR10a] and improved through various methods (see Sect. 2). This type of countermeasure assumes the existence of a easier to protect rekeying function that takes the secret key and a public rekeying parameter and uses it to generate temporary keys that are only used a small number of times. This rekeying function needs to be easier to protect against DPA than a classical cryptographic mode targeting the same security goal. It can be a leakage-resilient PRF, such as the GGM scheme [GGM85] or more recently the LR4 scheme [UHIM23]. It has also been shown that it can be a weaker function such as Galois Field Multiplication [MSGR10a]. Mennink [Men20] formalized the requirement using Universal Hash Functions (UHFs), where depending on the rekeying scheme, the rekeying function needs to satisfy a combinatorial security goal.

This Work: One of the early symmetric key encryption modes that target levelled implementations is the PSV-Enc scheme proposed in [PSV15]. The scheme requires a heavily protected key-derivation function that takes as input a key and a nonce (or random IV) and generates an initial subkey K_0 that is used in the scheme depicted in Fig. 1. The PSV-Enc scheme is based on the 2-PRG construction [SPY13] and in this paper, we will focus on using it as a Pseudo-Random Number Generator (PRNG), where we assume that a randomness source exists that generates a uniformly random initial key K_0, and the scheme in Fig. 1 is used as a PRNG. Note that is equivalent to assessing the outcome of a single query of the original PSV-Enc, with query length q_e. Since each key is used only twice (unless a collision on the subkeys occurs), the scheme is leakage resilient as long as the underlying Block Cipher (BC) cannot be attacked with a 2-trace attack. On the other hand, PSV-Enc as a PRNG (the 2-PRG construction) experiences the following limitations:

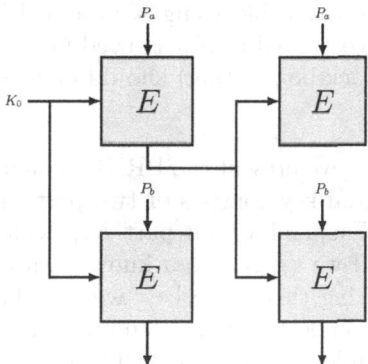

Fig. 1. Two blocks of the PRNG used in PSV-Enc.

- As a PRNG, PSV-Enc can only achieve birthday bound security, even in the black box setting. This is due to the fact that if any two subkeys collide, the output string will have a short periodic cycle, and can be easily distinguished from a random stream of bits. Besides, the PRNG suffers from a Time-Data trade-off, where the attacker can guess any of the subkeys, and their advantage is close to one when they make q_p offline guesses and observed q_e blocks, such that $q_e q_p \approx 2^n$. Both these limitations maybe addressed using a Tweakable Block Cipher (TBC), rather than a BC, by including a counter as a tweak in the TBC calls.

– A related limitation is that the BC calls in PSV-Enc do not (and should not) share a common secret key, making its analysis in the black-box setting rely on easier ideal cipher model or multi-key analysis of the BC. In terms of leakage resilience, this makes it harder to use the unpredictability with leakage assumption, recently introduced in [BGPS21]. This limitation, unlike the previous one, cannot be addressed using a TBC.

– PSV-Enc is designed such that the subkey size is equal to the block size n. This means that if we want higher security, or larger input to the PRNG, we need to not only use a (T)BC with a larger key size, but also with a larger block size. Another possibility is to use $b + 1$ calls per iteration to generate a (bn)-bit subkey. However, this increases the cost by a factor of $(b + 1)/2$ and requires a stronger assumption that the BC is secure against $(b + 1)$-trace attacks.

This presents us with a set of research goals to design a new leakage-resilient PRNG:

– The key size should be decoupled from the block size.
– It should be possible to use the unpredictability with leakage assumption on the underlying (T)BC to derive the unpredictability with leakage of the PRNG.
– The design should be realizable using a practical TBC with a very small performance penalty compared to if it is used in a PSV-Enc-like design.
– The design (in the black-box setting) should only permit much safer Time-Data trade-offs.

To address these goals, we present the PRNG design in Fig. 2. It is similar to PSV-Enc except that initial key consists of two parts: an n-bit part K_0, which is similar to K_0 in PSV-Enc, and a k-bit part K_m, which is used as a static key to an underlying TBC. If we set K_m to a known constant, the two designs are similar. However, by having this static key, we are able to model the TBC as a standard Tweakable Pseudo-Random Permutation (TPRP) in the black-box model and an unpredictable-with-leakage TBC. Besides, we are able to improve the security against Time-Data trade-offs and decouple the size of the input from the block-size of the TBC, allowing using TBCs with smaller block sizes.

On the other hand, when the reader sees Fig. 2, alarm bells should be ringing: *how can this design be implemented without using a heavily protected TBC?* The answer is *superposition*. Superposition is a concept introduced in the Superposition-Tweak-Key (STK) framework in [JNP14], where the tweak and the key are seen as a (cn)-bit string called the tweakey for a small constant c

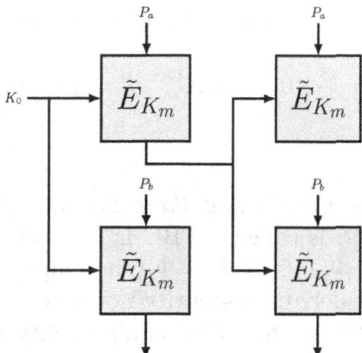

Fig. 2. The proposed PRNG with STK-based TBCs.

(typically 2 or 3), and c linear transformations are applied in parallel on each c-bit section of the tweakey to generate c n-bit sub-tweakeys for each round of the TBC. Then, these c values are bitwise-XORed to generate the round subkey. Consider a case where one n-bit section of the tweakey is uniformly random (with n-bit entropy), then the round keys are also randomly selected with n-bit entropy. Thus, when a static secret key is added to the random tweak, the information from the secret key is perfectly hidden. This means that we do not need heavy protection of the bulk of TBC, specially the costly SBox operation. What remains is to protect the part of the key schedule that operates on the static key against DPA. This is the main goal of the experiments performed in Sect. 4. Several TBCs follow the STK framework, such as Deoxys-TBC [JNPS21] and Skinny [BJK+16]. In the rest of the paper, we will focus on Deoxys-TBC as a proof-of-concept.

It worth noting that this is not the first design that uses a static key in a function that is not heavily protected and claims leakage resilience. ISAP [DEM+17] uses a similar concept for its rekeying function, which uses a static secret key but relies on the properties of the underlying Sponge function with a very small (1-bit) rate to ensure it is hard to perform DPA. Our proposal can be seen in the same category, where we rely on the superposition property of the underlying TBC to make a similar claim.

2 Preliminaries

Pseudo-Random Number Generators (PRNGs). A PRNG is a function $G :$ $\{0,1\}^\lambda \times \mathbb{N} \rightarrow \{0,1\}^{\lambda+l}$ that takes as input a short λ-bit input and a natural number l and returns a $\lambda + l$-bit output. Its security ensures that if the input selected uniformly at random from $\{0,1\}^\lambda$, its output is indistinguishable from a string selected uniformly at random from $\{0,1\}^{\lambda+l}$. In other words, let **A** be an adversary that requests a $(\lambda + l)$-bit string and outputs 0 or 1. Let $ be an oracle that when queried with any input returns a string sampled uniformly from

$\{0,1\}^{\lambda+l}$. Then, we say G is a secure PRNG if for any adversary,

$$\mathbf{Adv}_G^{\mathrm{prng}}(\mathbf{A}) \stackrel{\mathrm{def}}{=} |\Pr[r \stackrel{\$}{\leftarrow} \{0,1\}^{\lambda} : \mathbf{A}^{G(r,l)} \Rightarrow 1] - \Pr[\mathbf{A}^{\$(l)} \Rightarrow 1]| \leq \epsilon_{\mathrm{prng}}$$

where ϵ_{prng} is negligible.

Tweakable Block Ciphers (TBC) and their Security Models. A function $\tilde{E} : \mathcal{K} \times \mathcal{T} \times \{0,1\}^n \rightarrow \{0,1\}^n$ is called a TBC is for each pair $(K,T) \in \mathcal{K} \times \mathcal{T}$, $\tilde{E}$ acts a permutation over $\{0,1\}^n$. If $\mathcal{T} = \Phi$ (the empty set), then $\tilde{E}$ is simply a block cipher. The most widely used security notion of TBCs, commonly referred to as the standard model, is the indistinguishability from tweakable random permutations; given a key K selected uniformly at random, then for each $T \in \mathcal{T}$, $\tilde{E}$ is indistinguishable from a random permutation. In this case, we say $\tilde{E}$ behaves as a TPRP. Let $\tilde{\Pi}$ be a family of $|\mathcal{T}|$ permutations selected uniformly at random and indexed by $T \in \mathcal{T}$, then for an adversary $\mathbf{A}$,

$$\mathbf{Adv}_{\tilde{E}}^{\mathrm{tprp}}(\mathbf{A}) \stackrel{\mathrm{def}}{=} |\Pr[K \stackrel{\$}{\leftarrow} \mathcal{K} : \mathbf{A}^{\tilde{E}(K,\cdot,\cdot)} \Rightarrow 1] - \Pr[\mathbf{A}^{\tilde{\Pi}} \Rightarrow 1]|.$$

and for all adversaries that can make q queries and run in time at most t,

$$\mathbf{Adv}_{\tilde{E}}^{\mathrm{tprp}}(q,t) \stackrel{\mathrm{def}}{=} \max_{\mathbf{A}} \mathbf{Adv}_{\tilde{E}}^{\mathrm{tprp}}(\mathbf{A}).$$

Another security notion of TBCs is the ideal cipher model (ICM). The ICM states that a TBC $\tilde{E}$ behaves as a random permutation for all possible key-tweak pairs.

Rekeying: A rekeying scheme (in our context, inspired by [Men20]) is a scheme that uses a (T)BC and targets the protection of the secret key against side-channel attacks by separating encryption into two functionalities: a subkey generation function that takes as input the master key and a public parameter R to generates a subkey S. A block encryption function takes the subkey S and encrypts the message. The subkey generation function does not need to be cryptographically strong but needs to be protected against side-channel analysis like differential power analysis (DPA). The block encryption needs to provide TPRP security but only needs to be protected against simple power analysis (SPA). This concept was introduced in the context of block ciphers by Medwed *et al.* [MSGR10a] and has since been one of the bedrocks of leakage-resilient symmetric key cryptography [DEMM14, DKM+16, BKP+18, BGP+19, GIK+22]. It has been adopted in some industrial applications [nxp]. A few years ago, Mennink [Men20] showed that in terms of its syntax and security goal, a rekeying scheme is not different from a TBC. What matters is how it is designed and how efficient it is to implement it in a secure fashion against side-channel attacks.

The Superposition Tweakay (STK) Construction: Jean et al. [JNP14] introduced the tweakey framework for designing adhoc TBC and its variant, the STK construction, specifically for AES-like designs. It was used to design the Deoxys-TBC [JNPS21]. Let $\tilde{E} : \{0,1\}^k \times \{0,1\}^t \times \{0,1\}^n \rightarrow \{0,1\}^n$ be a TBC, such that $(k+t)$ is a multiple of n, i.e. $(k+t) = cn$ where c is a small constant integer. A tweakey is constructed by concatenating the key and tweak, i.e. $T_K = K \| T$. T_K is divided into c blocks of n bits, each. During each round of the cipher, the c blocks are XORed together to generate the round key, then the round function is applied. Simultaneously, d parallel linear transforms are applied in parallel to the c blocks of the key. A single round of a TBC built using the STK framework is described in Algorithm 5.

3   An Unpredictable PRNG from Unpredictable TBCs

Consider a rekeying scheme $\tilde{R} : \{0,1\}^k \times \{0,1\}^t \times \{0,1\}^n \to \{0,1\}^n$, where $k = \lambda$ and $q_e = \lceil l/n \rceil$, $t \geq log_2(q_e + 1)$. Then, we can define a PRNG as in Algorithm 1. It is easy to see that if $\tilde{R}$ is a secure TPRP, each loop calls the function with a unique tweak. Hence, for any adversary **A** against the PRNG that runs in time at most t, there is a TPRP adversary **B** that makes q_e queries and runs in time $O(t + q_e)$, such that

$$\epsilon_{\mathrm{prng}} \leq \mathbf{Adv}_{\tilde{R}}^{\mathrm{tprp}}(\mathbf{B}).$$

By observing that the rekeying scheme is used in counter-in-tweak mode (the tweak is a counter), this opens up different possibilities for building efficient designs. A popular design paradigm has started with the PSV-Enc proposed in [PSV15]. The design is depicted in Fig. 1. The design makes calls to an ideal cipher. During each iteration, a call is made to the ideal cipher to *"increment"* the ephemeral key, while a second call is made (with a different constant TBC plaintext) to generate a block of the output. In practice, the initial key is generated from a master secret key using a key generation function. However, this is beyond the scope of the PRNG itself. This design has inspired many leakage-resilient designs, such as TEDT [BGP+19] and Romulus-T [GIK+22]. On the other hand, it suffers from two limitations:

1. It forces $\lambda \leq n$, where n is the block size of the TBC.
2. It can only achieve birthday bound security, due to collisions between the TBC keys and the possibility of the adversary to guess one of these keys. While this can be easily captured from an analysis of PSV-Enc as a PRNG. It is also captured in the analysis in [PSV15, Lemma (4)], where the security of PSV-Enc used for l-block encryption is $l \times \epsilon_1$ where ϵ_1 is the advantage of performing l single block encryptions. The single-block encryption security is related to a term denoted as ϵ_{2-sim} in [PSV15, Lemma (2)] which is (in simple terms) the security of the BC against adversaries that can observe 2 traces per key. This is capped (from ideal cipher security with random keys) to

$$\frac{\sigma^2}{2^n} + \frac{\sigma q_p}{2^n},$$

where σ is the number of keys used and q_p is the number of offline queries made to the ideal cipher. In the PRNG setting we are concerned with, we generate one message with q blocks. Thus, applying the bound in [PSV15] would only lead to less than birthday bound security. However, in the black-box setting, a dedicated analysis may reclaim birthday bound security but not more.

The designs of TEDT and Romulus-T aim to solve the second limitation by achieving beyond birthday bound security, using extra counters and nonce. However, this requires extra assumptions, such as nonce-respecting adversaries or limited nonce-misuse, and is outside the scope and syntax of PRNGs. On the other hand, the first limitation is inherent in the design strategy. We can, conceptually, use $\lambda > n$ if the TBC supports $k > n$. However, this would require generating $k + n$ bits in each iteration, which would increase the number of calls to the TBC per iteration to at least 3 calls, which would also mean a stronger security model.

Another difference between our set-up and the set-up from [PSV15] and follow-up works is that in [PSV15] a full query either leaks or does not leak, but in our set-up, there is only one long query, and we are looking at the unpredictability of the next block, given the leakage from all the previous blocks have been observed.

This leads to an interesting research question:

> *Can we design a PSV-like PRNG with only two calls per block that takes more than n-bit input and does not suffer from a significant Time-Data trade-off security degradation like PSV-Enc?*

In Fig. 2, we propose a variant of PSV-Enc, which instead of using a cipher with n-bit key, it uses a TBC with n-bit tweak and k-bit key. The construction is a natural extension of PSV-Enc, where the ideal cipher is replaced by a TPRP. However, the interesting challenge is how to implement it without heavily protecting it, while maintaining some form of leakage-resilience. In this case, we can view the PRNG construction as having $\lambda = (n + k)$, where a k-bit part is fixed for all blocks, while an n-bit part is ephemeral in the same manner as PSV-Enc. Of course, this is not leakage-resilient in general except when the TBC is heavily protected, since K_m is fixed, which goes against the motivation of PSV-Enc. However, we will show that the synergy between Fig. 2 and the STK design paradigm allows for a very efficient solution that does not require heavy protection of the TBC.

In the remainder of this section, we will focus on the black-box security of the proposed PRNG.

Algorithm 1. A framework for building PRNGs from rekeying schemes.	**Algorithm 2 .** Our proposed PRNG from TBCs.
1: $K \xleftarrow{\$} \{0,1\}^{\lambda}$ 2: $X \leftarrow \varepsilon$ 3: **for** $i \in \{1,\dots q\}$ **do** 4: $\quad C \leftarrow \tilde{R}(K, i, 0^n)$ 5: $\quad X \leftarrow X \| C$ 6: **end for** 7: **return** X	1: $(K_m, K_0) \xleftarrow{\$} \{0,1\}^k \times \{0,1\}^n$ 2: $X \leftarrow \varepsilon$ 3: **for** $i \in \{1,\dots q\}$ **do** 4: $\quad C \leftarrow \tilde{E}_{K_m}^{K_{i-1}}(P_b)$ 5: $\quad K_i \leftarrow \tilde{E}_{K_m}^{K_{i-1}}(P_a)$ 6: $\quad X \leftarrow X \| C$ 7: **end for** 8: **return** X

Theorem 1. *Let* $\tilde{E} : \{0,1\}^k \times \{0,1\}^n \times \{0,1\}^n \to \{0,1\}^n$ *be a TBC and let* $G : \{0,1\}^{k+n} \to (\{0,1\}^n)^*$ *be the PRNG given in Algorithm 2. Then, for any adversary* **A** *against* G *that generates* q *blocks and runs in time* t, *there exists an adversary* **B** *against* $\tilde{E}$, *such that,*

$$\mathbf{Adv}_G^{\mathrm{prng}}(\mathbf{A}) \leq \mathbf{Adv}_{\tilde{E}}^{\mathrm{tprp}}(\mathbf{B}) + \frac{q^2 + q}{2^n},$$

where **B** *makes* $2q$ *TBC calls and runs in time* $t' = O(t + q)$.

Proof. In the first step of the proof, we replace $\tilde{E}$ with an ideal TBC $\tilde{\Pi}$, we call this Game 1, where E_1 is the event that the adversary wins according to the PRNG game definition in Sect. 2. Then, we define Game 2 as the game that terminates if for an index $i > 0$, with tweak K_i, there exists an index $0 \leq j < i$, such that $K_i = K_j$. E_2 that the adversary wins according to the PRNG game definition in Sect. 2. Using the hybrid argument,

$$|\Pr[E_2] - \Pr[E_1]| \leq \sum_{i=1}^{q} \frac{i}{2^n} \leq \frac{q^2}{2^n}.$$

Next, we define Game 3 where we replace $\tilde{\Pi}$ with a random function $\tilde{F}$ with the same domain and range. In this case, we can see that each tweak K_i used at most twice, and Games 2 and 3 can only be distinguished if for any index i, $\tilde{F}(K_i, P_a) = \tilde{F}(K_i, P_b)$, which can happen with probability $1/2^n$. Thus,

$$|\Pr[E_3] - \Pr[E_2]| \leq \sum_{i=1}^{q} \frac{1}{2^n} = \frac{q}{2^n}.$$

Finally, Game 3 is indistinguishable from an ideal PRNG. Thus,

$$\Pr[E_3] = 0.$$

The bound follows from adding the transition probabilities.

3.1 Unpredictability of the Next Block: A Leakage Resiliency Target for PRNGs

Unpredictability as a leakage resiliency target for TBCs was discussed in [BGPS21]. The adversary observes a certain number of evaluations of the TBC with chosen plaintexts with their corresponding leakages[1], then wins if they can predict the outcome of a new evaluation of the TBC that has not been observed before. Unpredictability as a target for leakage-resilient symmetric-key cryptography is a well-established topic that dates earlier than [BGPS21], and has been discussed in multiple works [DS09,DJS19]. We follow the definition of [BGPS21] since it is the most mature for TBCs. In this section, we recall the definition of unpredictability with leakage given in [BGPS21], and propose the unpredictability of the next block as a security goal for PRNGs. Then, we show that if $\tilde{E}$ is unpredictable with leakage, then our PRNG achieves unpredictability of the next block. The definition below is adapted from [BGPS21], removing the inverse function and adapting notation.

Definition 1. *A TBC $\tilde{E} : \{0,1\}^k \times \{0,1\}^n \times \{0,1\}^n \to \{0,1\}^n$ with a leakage function $\mathsf{L_{Eval}}$ is $(q_l, q_c, t, \epsilon_{\mathrm{upl1}})$-unpredictable with forward leakage if for any (q_l, q_c, t)-adversary $\mathbf{A}$, we have*

$$\mathbf{Adv}^{\mathrm{upl1}}_{\tilde{E}}(\mathbf{A}) \le \epsilon_{\mathrm{upl1}},$$

where the UPL1 game is defined in Algorithm 3, and $\mathbf{A}$ makes at most q_c construction queries with leakage, such that each tweak is repeated at most twice, and q_l modelling queries with leakage to the modelling oracle L.

Berti *et al.* [BGPS21] define modelling queries as queries made to the TBC with chosen plaintext and chosen key to model the leakage function. They are meant to capture attacks such as template attacks. They are similar to primitive queries in the ideal cipher model.

Algorithm 3. TBC Unpredictability with Leakage Game

```
 1: Initialize :                7: Enc(M, T) :              16: Finalize :
 2: K ←$ {0,1}^k               8: if T[T] = 2 then         17: (M, T, C) ← A^{L,Enc}
 3: L ← φ                       9:     return ⊥             18: if (M, T, C) ∈ L then
 4: for X ∈ {0,1}^n do         10: end if                  19:     return 0
 5:     T[X] ← 0               11: T[T] ← T[T] + 1          20: else if C = Ẽ_K^T(M) then
 6: end for                    12: C ← Ẽ_K^T(M)            21:     return 1
                               13: l_e ← L_{Eval}(M, T; K)  22: else
                               14: L ← L ∪ {(M, T, C)}      23:     return 0
                               15: return (C, l_e)          24: end if
```

---

[1] [BGPS21] discusses strong unpredictability, which also allows chosen ciphertext queries. However, this is not needed for our construction.

As discussed earlier and studied in [Men20], a rekeying scheme is nothing but a TBC with special implementation properties. Thus, consider a rekeying scheme that is $(q_l, q_e, t, \epsilon_{\text{upl1}})$-unpredictable as the building block of Algorithm 1. Algorithm 4 describes a security game where an adversary $\mathbf{A}$ makes a single query to the PRNG in Algorithm 1 with output $k + ln$, observing the output string and the associated leakage, and tries to guess the next n bits. It is easy to see that if the rekeying scheme is $(q_l, q_e, t', \epsilon_{\text{upl1}})$-unpredictable, then the PRNG is $(q_l, q, t, \epsilon_{\text{upl1}})$-next-block-unpredictable, where $t' = O(t + q)$.

Algorithm 4. PRNG Unpredictability of the Next Block with Leakage Game

1: Initialize :	3: PRNG(q) :	11: Finalize :
2: $K \xleftarrow{\$} \{0,1\}^k$	4: $X \leftarrow \varepsilon$	12: $C \leftarrow \mathbf{A}^{\text{L,PRNG}}$
	5: $l_p \leftarrow \phi$	13: if $C = \tilde{R}(K, q+1, 0^n)$
	6: for $i \in \{1, \ldots, q\}$ do	then
	7: $\quad X \leftarrow X \| \tilde{R}(K, i, 0^n)$	14: $\quad$ return 1
	8: $\quad l_p \leftarrow l_p \cup \{L_R(K, i, 0^n)\}$	15: else
	9: end for	16: $\quad$ return 0
	10: return (X, l_p)	17: end if

Definition 2. *We say the PRNG G in Algorithm 1 with associated leakage function is $(q_l, q, t, \epsilon_{\text{prng-upl1}})$-unpredictable if for any (q_l, q_e, t)-adversary $\mathbf{A}$, we have*

$$\mathbf{Adv}_G^{\text{prng-upl1}}(\mathbf{A}) \leq \epsilon_{\text{prng-upl1}},$$

where $\mathbf{Adv}_G^{\text{prng-upl1}}(\mathbf{A})$ is the advantage that for any $0 \leq i \leq q$, $\mathbf{A}$ observes the first in bits and predicts the next n bits.

Theorem 2. *Given a rekeying scheme $\tilde{R}$ that is $(q_l, q_e, t', \epsilon_{\text{upl1}})$-unpredictable, a PRNG that is defined according to Algorithm 1 is $(q_l, q_e, t, q_e\epsilon_{\text{upl1}})$-unpredictable where $t' = O(t + q_e)$.*

Proof. The proof follows from simple hybrid argument where the adversary calls Finalize in Algorithm 4 after observing each block and the associated leakage, and wins if the function returns 1 at any call. Since the rekeying scheme is $(q_l, q_e, t', \epsilon_{\text{upl1}})$-unpredictable, then at any time Finalize is called, the advantage is at most ϵ_{upl1}, the function is called at most q_e times. $t' = O(t + q_e)$ since the time taken an adversary against the rekeying scheme is bounded by at most the time needed by the adversary against the PRNG in addition to a constant overhead per query. ∎

Theorem 3. *Let $\tilde{E} : \{0,1\}^k \times \{0,1\}^n \times \{0,1\}^n \to \{0,1\}^n$ be a TBC and let $G : \{0,1\}^{k+n} \to (\{0,1\}^n)^*$ be the PRNG given in Algorithm 2. If $\tilde{E}$ is $(q_l, 2q_e, t', \epsilon_{\text{upl1}})$-unpredictable, G is $(q_l, q_e, t, \epsilon_{\text{prng-upl1}})$-unpredictable, where*

$$\epsilon_{\text{prng-upl1}} \leq q_e\epsilon_{\text{upl1}} + \frac{q_e^2}{2^n}$$

and $t' = O(t + q_e)$.

Proof. First, we define a hybrid game that terminates if for an index $i > 0$, with tweak K_i, there exists an index $0 \leq j < i$, such that $K_i = K_j$. This is analyzed in Game 2 of the proof of Theorem 1. Otherwise, we notice that the TBC is never called with the same tweak twice. Using the hybrid argument in Theorem 2, we get the full bound.

Theorem 3 can be understood as follows: if $\tilde{E}$ is secure against key recovery, with K_m as the key, and secure against 2-trace attacks trying to leak any K_i, then the PRNG remains unpredictable (up to birthday bound). The rest of the paper is dedicated to reaching a lightweight realization of Algorithm 2 when $q_l = 0$, *i.e.* for non-profiled attacks. This is done as a proof of concept, since the protection against profiled attacks with low number of traces, such as SPA and template attacks, are usually cheaper than non-profiled attacks. For instance, Simple Power Analysis (SPA) and template attacks may be made harder using cheaper countermeasures such as hiding and shuffling. That being said, we note that both our proposed design and PSV-Enc equally require protection against template and SPA-like attacks.

Comparison to PSV-Enc: Algorithm 2 can clearly be more costly than PSV-Enc. For instance, it has a static key that needs to be protected. For a general TBC, this means heavy protection of the full TBC. Luckily, as we shall see in Sect. 4, the cost of protecting the static key in STK TBCs is minimal. On the other hand, PSV-Enc suffers from the security bound $q_e q_p / 2^n$, since its black-box security is in the ideal cipher model and the adversary can guess one of the keys by making q_p queries to the primitive and q_e queries to PSV-Enc, such that $q_p q_e \approx 2^n$. It also restricts the key size to n, making it harder to use TBCs with small block but large tweakey. For instance, consider Algorithm 2 with a TBC with 128-bit tweakey and 64-bit block, and an adversary that successfully guesses the static part of the key K_m, the adversary can recover one of the ephemeral keys with $q_p q_e \approx 2^{64}$. Since the probability of guessing K_m is 2^{-64}, the adversary needs $q_p q_e \approx 2^{128}$ and $q_p \geq 2^{64}$ to get a close to 1 advantage of guessing a full key. If q_e is limited to 2^{32} blocks, then q_p can go up to 2^{96}. These attacks are captured in Theorem 1 by the computational term of the TPRP security. On the other hand, PSV-Enc with a 64-bit cipher would only tolerate $q_p \approx 2^{32}$ in this case, which is far from secure.

Based on this, while we focus our proof-of-concept in the rest of the paper on Deoxys-TBC, we believe our proposed scheme has much broader design space, and can be used with TBCs such as Skinny-64-128 or Skinny-64-192.

3.2   Comparison to BBB Secure PSV-Enc-like Encryption

As discussed earlier, TEDT and Romulus-T aim to make PSV-Enc-like constructions BBB secure using large tweaks. In particular, TEDT replaces the constants P_a and P_b with two counters. This prevents the formation of short periodic cycles, in case two of the keys collide. It also includes a random tweak T: Since TEDT is an Authenticated Encryption with Associated Data (AEAD) scheme, T

is the authentication tag generated using a PRF MAC. However, in our PRNG set-up, this tag does not affect the security as it is can be treated as a public constant. Romulus-T goes a step further where the counters are included as part of the tweak, which improves the security bounds slightly. These ideas do not help at least one of the aspects of the problem we are trying to solve. Namely, it is still not possible to use the unpredicatbility with leakage assumption proposed in [BGPS21], since this assumption requires a secret TPRP-style TBC, and not an ideal cipher which these schemes use. One the other hand, these ideas can be used in conjunction with our proposal. In such a combined construction, the TBC has larger tweak space and the tweak is appended by a public counter and two public constants. This makes sure that even if two keys collide, all the tweakeys are unique. This improves the black-box security to

$$\epsilon_{\text{prng}} \leq \mathbf{Adv}_{\tilde{E}}^{\text{tprp}}(2q_e, t).$$

However, when it comes to unpredictability with leakage, things are more subtle. If we want to maintain that the adversary can only observe two traces for the same ephemeral key, key collisions still affect the security. However, we could relax the assumption to n traces instead of two, and rely on bounding the probability of getting a multi-collision of size $> n$. This would again remove the birthday-bound term, but make the unpredictability assumption stronger and the analysis more involved. Since our goal is to introduce the possibility of using unpredictability assumptions with a static key to build leakage-resilient PRNGs, we leave a dedicated analysis of its BBB security with leakage as future-work.

We also note that the techniques proposed by Chen *et al.* [CLMP21] can be used to generalize the PSV-Enc/2-PRG construction to have higher security using a block cipher with $2n$-bit key and n-bit blocks, and 3 calls to the block cipher per output block. However, this approach is less efficient than ours as it requires three calls to the block cipher, while we only need two. One may argue that these calls are to a block cipher and not a TBC, which makes them cheaper, but this is not necessarily true in practice, as the difference in cost between a BC with $2n$-bit key and a TBC with n-bit key and n-bit tweak is minimal, and does not offset the cost of a full extra call. For instance, AES-256 requires 16 AES rounds, while Deoxys-128-256 requires 14 AES rounds and the total size of the key and tweak is $2n$ bits. In many cases, the same TBC is used as the block cipher, which makes such approach significantly more expensive than ours. Besides, the approach of Chen *et al.* still does not satisfy our goal of using the unpredictability assumption.

4 Lightweight Realization of Algorithm 2 Using the STK Framework

Consider an instance of the STK framework with n-bit block and $(2n)$-bit tweakey. A single round of the construction is described in Algorithm 5. L_0 and L_1 are two different linear transforms that satisfy certain security properties of the STK construction. What we observe is that if one of the tweakey components, say T_1, is fixed, and the other component T_0 is selected uniformly at random, then the round key K_{r_i} has a uniform distribution, and the same applies for the output S. However, during one execution, the round keys are not independent (since T_0 is used in all the rounds up to a linear transformation). If the TBC consists of r rounds, then T_0 (up to different linear transformations) is used r times. It is a common assumption that if the implementation is protected against SPA with a small number of traces, and T_0 is used only in a small number of calls, then it cannot be recovered by an adversary. Hence, the only target for SCA in Algorithm 5 is T_1, which needs to be masked.

Algorithm 5. A single round of the STK framework.

1: $T_0, T_1 \xleftarrow{n} T$
2: $T_0 \leftarrow L_0(T_0)$
3: $T_1 \leftarrow L_1(T_1)$
4: $K_{r_i} \leftarrow T_0 \oplus T_1$
5: $S \leftarrow R_{r_i}(S) \oplus K_{r_i}$

Algorithm 6. A secure implementation single round of the STK framework.

1: $T_0, A_1, B_1 \xleftarrow{n} T$
2: $T_0 \leftarrow L_0(T_0)$
3: $A_1 \leftarrow L_1(A_1)$
4: $B_1 \leftarrow L_1(B_1)$
5: $K_{r_i} \leftarrow T_0 \oplus A_1$
6: $K_{r_i} \leftarrow K_{r_i} \oplus B_1$
7: $S \leftarrow R_{r_i}(S) \oplus K_{r_i}$

Algorithm 6 adopts this idea. During a call to the TBC, we consider $|T| = 3n$, and divide it into 3 components (or shares). Each of the three components appears indistinguishable from a block selected uniformly at random, except that at lines 3 and 4, $A_1 \oplus B_1 = T_1$. K_{r_i} in line 6 is an unmasked version of the round key. However, since A_1 is first added to T_0, which is sampled uniformly, then the adversary observing K_{r_i} gains no more information than the adversary observing T_0.

4.1   Application to Deoxys-TBC with Unprotected Round Function

Theoretically while we show that the key unmasking is done securely, in practice, similar to masking schemes, it does require careful implementation on the device. In the following section, we describe a series of experiments that applies this design strategy in practice. These experiments are conducted on modified versions of the reference implementation of the Deoxys-TBC [JNPS21].

Measurement Setup. Our measurement setup to validate the secure unmasking of the round key consists of the Chipwhisperer CW308 UFO platform, with STM32F303 as the target board. The STM32F303RCT6 is an ARM Cortex-M4 CPU with 256KB flash, 48KB SRAM and 72MHz operating frequency. The device is programmed with a C implementation of Deoxys-TBC, compiled with arm-none-eabi-gcc compiler using -O3 optimization level. In the software implementation the entire round subtweakeys are computed upfront and stored, and the cipher round functions are called later, as seen in the power trace from Fig. 3. The clock and communication to the target is handled by the Chipwhisperer Husky device. The target runs at 44 MHz and the power measurement of

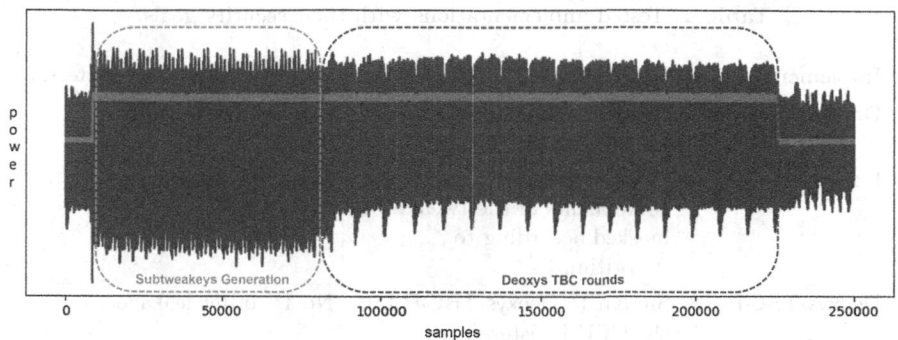

Fig. 3. Deoxys-TBC power trace showing subtweakey generation and cipher rounds.

the device is captured using the LeCroy WavePro 404 oscilloscope at a sampling frequency of 250MS/s. We employed the Test Vector Leakage Assessment (TVLA) method [GJJR11] to validate the leakages during key unmasking.

Deoxys TBC Designs We analyzed four different implementations of the Deoxys-TBC. They are summarized in the Table 1 along with the expected security goals and the experimental results. For the unprotected Deoxys-TBC instance (Deoxys-TBC-ORIG) with 384-bit tweakey, we used the reference C implementation [JNPS21]. As discussed in Sect. 3, the first 128 bits of the tweakey component is the static key K_m while the second 128 bits is the ephemeral key K_i. The third component is not used and is set to 0, but it can be dedicated to the counter in a higher level construction. In other words, the 384-bit key is assigned as: $K_m \| K_i \| 0^{128}$. For the protected Deoxys-TBC instance (Deoxys-TBC-P) with 384-bit tweakey the first 128 bits of the tweakey are masked, the second 128-bit component is selected uniformly at random. If the masked key is $K_m^a \| K_m^b$, then the protected implementation takes $K_m^a \| K_m^b \| K_i \| 0^{128}$.

We performed two types of TVLA:

- Plaintext TVLA: We fix K_m and acquire traces using fixed vs. random plaintext. In our construction, the plaintext is a public constant, so plaintext leakage bears little value to our analysis. However, this was done to verify the soundness of our approach: when one of the tweakey components is changing randomly, the round function should not leak.
- Key TVLA: In this case, we fix the plaintext and acquire two sets of traces, one with K_m fixed to a single value and one with K_m changing randomly. This is done to make sure that the key schedule does not experience 1st order leakage and that we can detect glitches and micro-architectural leakage.

We have also performed TVLA without changing K_i to make sure that our set-up can detect leaky implementations.

With the protected Deoxys-TBC-P design, during the key TVLA, we observed leakages in multiple rounds of the round key generation function. To understand

Table 1. Tested implementations with their security goals.

Implementation	Description	Security Goal	Result
Deoxys-TBC-ORIG	Reference implementation provided with [JNPS21]	Leakage in the key schedule	PASS
Deoxys-TBC-P	One of the 128-bit components of the tweakey is masked according to Algorithm 6	No 1st order leakage	FAIL
Deoxys-TBC-P-RP	Similar to Deoxys-TBC-P but the CPU registers are randomly pre-charged	No 1st order leakage	PASS
Deoxys-TBC-P-SH	Similar to Deoxys-TBC-P but the operations used to compute the round keys are randomly shuffled	No 1st order leakage	PASS

the root-cause we generated the assembly code for the roundkey generation function. After analyzing it we concluded that the observed leakages were potentially due to micro-architectural and transient glitches that invalidate our assumptions on masking. This shows that, similar to any masking schemes, it does require some care when implementing the design on a device, as there could be leakages due to transient glitches from platform architecture and compiler optimizations. To address these micro-architectural leakages for the current platform, we improved the Deoxys-TBC-P design by pre-charging the CPU user registers with random values before each round of the tweak key generation (Deoxys-TBC-P-RP). This pre-charging had a 4.01% overhead for the round key generation and 1.24% increase for the overall cipher. Similarly, we also tested a secure design where the sub-parts of the tweaks that is XOR-ed during the secure unmasking are handled in a random shuffled order (Deoxys-TBC-P-SH). This countermeasure resulted in a 34.82% overhead for the round key generation and 10.62% overhead for the overall cipher. This shuffling Deoxys-TBC-P-SH design, while comparatively slower, should be secure and should eliminate any potential micro-architectural leakages, similar to the one discussed above, on any platform. We used an LFSR to generate the randomness for the Deoxys-TBC-P-RP and Deoxys-TBC-P-SH designs. This is done as an example, and in a real-world implementation a secure random source should be used. It is expected that a practical system would have its own randomness source.

Experimental Results. Figure 4 shows the plaintext TVLA leakage for the Deoxys-TBC-ORIG implementation with 1,000 traces, when the tweak is fixed. And Fig. 5 shows the plaintext TVLA leakage with 1 million traces, when the tweak is selected uniformly at random. Using a random tweak with the unprotected design eliminates the observed plaintext TVLA leakages from the cipher rounds. Similarly, Fig. 6 shows the key TVLA leakage for the Deoxys-TBC-ORIG implementation with a fixed tweak for 1,000 traces. As expected, the unprotected design shows TVLA leakages with t-values over the 4.5 bounds, in the round key generation.

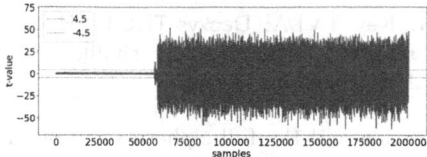

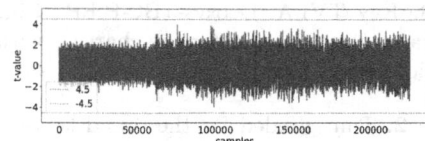

Fig. 4. Plaintext TVLA: Deoxys-TBC-ORIG with fixed tweak, 1000 traces.

Fig. 5. Plaintext TVLA: Deoxys-TBC-ORIG with random tweak, 1 million traces.

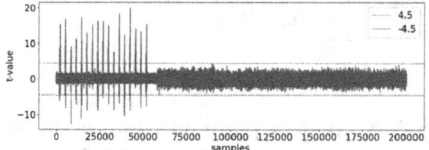

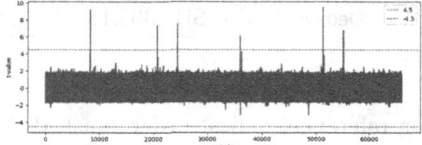

Fig. 6. Key TVLA: Deoxys-TBC-ORIG with random tweak, 1000 traces.

Fig. 7. Key TVLA: Deoxys-TBC-P sub-tweakey generation with random tweak, 10000 traces.

For the protected Deoxys-TBC-P design as discussed in Algorithm 6 and in Sect. 4, the masked key gets securely unmasked during the subtweakey generation. When the design is used with a random tweak, it is expected be secure against a key TVLA, but we observed leakage in the roundkey generation as shown in the Fig. 7. By generating and analyzing the assembly instructions of this implementations, we attributed the leakage to transient glitches and microarchitectural leakage, which understandably are more probable during our secure unmasking operation. We studied the register pre-charging (Deoxys-TBC-P-RP) and shuffled order XOR (Deoxys-TBC-P-SH) designs to eliminate such platform dependent leakages. Figure 8 and Fig. 9 shows the key TVLA with a random tweak for the Deoxys-TBC-P-RP and Deoxys-TBC-P-SH designs, respectively. Both the protected designs show no leakage and are secure against the key TVLA with 1 million traces.

Table 2 summarises the total time taken by the target for the round key generation and the full cipher operation, at 44MHz, for all the four implementations discussed in the Sect. 4.1. It is to be noted that for Deoxys-TBC-P-RP and Deoxys-TBC-P-SH implementations, the time measured is inclusive of randomness generation required for register pre-charging and for creating the shuffle buffer.

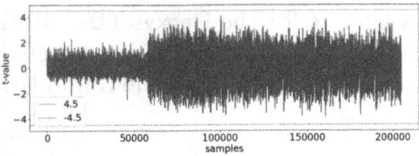

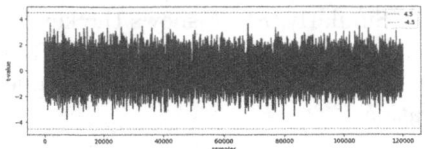

Fig. 8. Key TVLA: Deoxys-TBC-P-RP with random tweak, register pre-charge, 1 million traces.

Fig. 9. Key TVLA: Deoxys-TBC-P-SH with random tweak, secure shuffled operations, 1 million traces.

Table 2. Time needed for the round key generation and the full cipher execution of different implementations.

Algorithm	Roundkey generation (μs)	Deoxys-TBC (μs)
Deoxys-TBC-ORIG	213.71	798.96
Deoxys-TBC-P	263.42	850.11
Deoxys-TBC-P-RP	273.99	860.68
Deoxys-TBC-P-SH	355.15	940.41

For reference, a first-order masked AES-128 [ans] implementation requires 1375.38 μs on the same platform. It is to be noted that the Deoxys-TBC-ORIG implementation used for the work is the reference implementation without any modifications and hence it can be optimized further.

5   Conclusions

In this paper, we studied a new PRNG construction inspired by the PSV-Enc construction and leveraging the superposition property of STK-based ciphers. We have provided theoretical analysis of our construction both as a black-box PRNG and as an unpredictable-with-leakage PRNG, based on the unpredictability-with-leakage assumption for TBCs, popularized in [BGPS21]. We have also provided experimental proof-of-concept results using TVLA on Deoxys-TBC showing that the cost of eliminating first-order observable leakage in our proposal ranges from $\approx 1 - 10\%$.

Applications. The proposed PRNG can be used in any setting where a leakage-resilient PRNG is needed and that the protocol can maintain a $2k + n$-bit state, where $2k$ bits are the masked static key K_m and n bits are the ephemeral key K_i. It was shown in [IKMP20] that STK-based TBCs allow maintaining a static key at no additional (storage) cost beyond the implementation of the TBC itself, due to the properties of the tweakey schedule. Note that we require k to be a multiple of n so that the security arguments on the STK framework hold and that the mask is refreshed after each TBC call. Two notable applications come to mind:

- Stream ciphers: we can use our construction to build a leakage-resilient stream cipher with (K_m, K_0) as the initial key. We note that using a leakage-resilient PRNG as a stream cipher requires care of decryption leakage and/or authentication, as discussed in details in [BGP+19, BBC+20].
- Subkey generation: we can use our construction as a stateful subkey generation function in a bigger scheme. For example, it can be used as the rekeying function in the rekeying-based ΘCB mode proposed by Mennink in [Men20].

Future Work. Several natural follow-up research directions can arise from our work:

- Evaluating our PRNG with a small-block TBC, *e.g.*, Skinny-64-192.
- Evaluating the cost of implementing this PRNG in hardware. While our software experiments show that the cost of implementation is extremely cheap (5%–18% overhead), it also shows that it is not trivial. Hardware may present a new set of challenges that we may need to study.
- Designing a complete AEAD scheme using our PRNG as an underlying primitive, either as the encryption part using levelled implementations, or as the subkey generation function for a rekeying-based AEAD.
- Security analysis of our scheme combined with tweak counters and nonce using the unpredictability with leakage assumption, or another BBB-secure variant.

Acknowledgements. We would like to thank the anonymous reviewers for their insightful comments. We would like to also thank Thomas Peyrin (NTU) for sharing the reference implementation of Deoxys-TBC that allowed us to perform our experiments. We acknowledge the generous support of Seagate Technology towards this study.

References

[ans] Masked AES-128 implementation in C for the STM32F3/STM32F4 platforms. https://github.com/ANSSI-FR/SecAESSTM32/tree/3b9ed68a45 76255636634ec539079476cd5bbc92

[BBC+20] Bellizia, D., et al.: Mode-level vs. implementation-level physical security in symmetric cryptography: a practical guide through the leakage-resistance jungle. In: Micciancio, D., Ristenpart, T. (eds.) CRYPTO 2020. LNCS, vol. 12170, pp. 369–400. Springer, Cham (2020). https://doi.org/10.1007/978-3-030-56784-2_13

[BGP+19] Berti, F., Guo, C., Pereira, O., Peters, T., Standaert, F.-X.: TEDT, a leakage-resist AEAD mode for high physical security applications. IACR Trans. Cryptogr. Hardw. Embed. Syst. (1), 256–320 (2020)

[BGPS21] Berti, F., Guo, C., Peters, T., Standaert, F.-X.: Efficient leakage-resilient macs without idealized assumptions. In: Tibouchi, M., Wang, H. (eds.) ASIACRYPT 2021. LNCS, vol. 13091, pp. 95–123. Springer, Cham (2021). https://doi.org/10.1007/978-3-030-92075-3_4

[BJK+16] Beierle, C., et al.: The skinny family of block ciphers and its low-latency variant mantis. In: Robshaw, M., Katz, J. (eds.) CRYPTO 2016. LNCS, vol. 9815, pp. 123–153. Springer, Heidelberg (2016). https://doi.org/10.1007/978-3-662-53008-5_5

[BKP+18] Berti, F., Koeune, F., Pereira, O., Peters, T., Standaert, F.-X.: Ciphertext integrity with misuse and leakage: definition and efficient constructions with symmetric primitives. In: Proceedings of the 2018 on Asia Conference on Computer and Communications Security, pp. 37–50 (2018)

[CLMP21] Chen, Y.L., Luykx, A., Mennink, B., Preneel, B.: Systematic security analysis of stream encryption with key erasure. IEEE Trans. Inf. Theory **67**(11), 7518–7534 (2021)

[CS20] Cassiers, G., Standaert, F.-X.: Trivially and efficiently composing masked gadgets with probe isolating non-interference. IEEE Trans. Inf. Forensics Secur. **15**, 2542–2555 (2020)

[DEM+17] Dobraunig, C., Eichlseder, M., Mangard, S., Mendel, F., Unterluggauer, T.: ISAP–towards side-channel secure authenticated encryption. IACR Trans. Symmetric Cryptol. 80–105 (2017)

[DEMM14] Dobraunig, C., Eichlseder, M., Mangard, S., Mendel, F.: On the security of fresh re-keying to counteract side-channel and fault attacks. In: Joye, M., Moradi, A. (eds.) CARDIS 2014. LNCS, vol. 8968, pp. 233–244. Springer, Cham (2014). https://doi.org/10.1007/978-3-319-16763-3_14

[DJS19] Degabriele, J.P., Janson, C., Struck, P.: Sponges resist leakage: the case of authenticated encryption. In: Galbraith, S., Moriai, S. (eds.) ASIACRYPT 2019. LNCS, vol. 11922, pp. 209–240. Springer, Cham (2019). https://doi.org/10.1007/978-3-030-34621-8_8

[DKM+16] Dobraunig, C., Koeune, F., Mangard, S., Mendel, F., Standaert, F.-X.: Towards fresh and hybrid re-keying schemes with beyond birthday security. In: Homma, N., Medwed, M. (eds.) CARDIS 2015. LNCS, vol. 9514, pp. 225–241. Springer, Cham (2016). https://doi.org/10.1007/978-3-319-31271-2_14

[DP08] Dziembowski, S., Pietrzak, K.: Leakage-resilient cryptography. In: 2008 49th Annual IEEE Symposium on Foundations of Computer Science, pp. 293–302. IEEE (2008)

[DS09] Dodis, Y., Steinberger, J.: Message authentication codes from unpredictable block ciphers. In: Halevi, S. (ed.) CRYPTO 2009. LNCS, vol. 5677, pp. 267–285. Springer, Heidelberg (2009). https://doi.org/10.1007/978-3-642-03356-8_16

[GGM85] Goldreich, O., Goldwasser, S., Micali, S.: On the cryptographic applications of random functions. In: Blakley, G.R., Chaum, D. (eds.) CRYPTO 1984. LNCS, vol. 196, pp. 276–288. Springer, Heidelberg (1985). https://doi.org/10.1007/3-540-39568-7_22

[GIK+22] Guo, C., Iwata, T., Khairallah, M., Minematsu, K., Peyrin, T.: Security proof for romulus-t (2022)

[GJJR11] Goodwill, G., Jun, B., Jaffe, J., Rohatgi, P.: A testing methodology for side channel resistance (2011)

[IKMP20] Iwata, T., Khairallah, M., Minematsu, K., Peyrin, T.: Duel of the titans: the romulus and remus families of lightweight AEAD algorithms. IACR Trans. Symmetric Cryptol. **2020**(1), 43–120 (2020)

[ISW03] Ishai, Y., Sahai, A., Wagner, D.: Private circuits: securing hardware against probing attacks. In: Boneh, D. (ed.) CRYPTO 2003. LNCS, vol. 2729, pp. 463–481. Springer, Heidelberg (2003). https://doi.org/10.1007/978-3-540-45146-4_27

[JNP14] Jean, J., Nikolić, I., Peyrin, T.: Tweaks and keys for block ciphers: the tweakey framework. In: Sarkar, P., Iwata, T. (eds.) ASIACRYPT 2014.

LNCS, vol. 8874, pp. 274–288. Springer, Heidelberg (2014). https://doi. org/10.1007/978-3-662-45608-8_15

[JNPS21] Jean, J., Nikolic, I., Peyrin, T., Seurin, Y.: The deoxys AEAD family. J. Cryptol. **34**(3), 31 (2021)

[KJJ99] Kocher, P., Jaffe, J., Jun, B.: Differential power analysis. In: Wiener, M. (ed.) CRYPTO 1999. LNCS, vol. 1666, pp. 388–397. Springer, Heidelberg (1999). https://doi.org/10.1007/3-540-48405-1_25

[Men20] Mennink, B.: Beyond birthday bound secure fresh rekeying: application to authenticated encryption. In: Moriai, S., Wang, H. (eds.) ASIACRYPT 2020. LNCS, vol. 12491, pp. 630–661. Springer, Cham (2020). https://doi. org/10.1007/978-3-030-64837-4_21

[MSGR10a] Medwed, M., Standaert, F.-X., Großschädl, J., Regazzoni, F.: Fresh re-keying: security against side-channel and fault attacks for low-cost devices. In: Bernstein, D.J., Lange, T. (eds.) AFRICACRYPT 2010. LNCS, vol. 6055, pp. 279–296. Springer, Heidelberg (2010). https://doi. org/10.1007/978-3-642-12678-9_17

[NRR06] Nikova, S., Rechberger, C., Rijmen, V.: Threshold implementations against side-channel attacks and glitches. In: Ning, P., Qing, S., Li, N. (eds.) ICICS 2006. LNCS, vol. 4307, pp. 529–545. Springer, Heidelberg (2006). https://doi.org/10.1007/11935308_38

[nxp] Leakage resilient primitive (LRP) specification. https://www.nxp.com/ docs/en/application-note/AN12304.pdf

[PSV15] Pereira, O., Standaert, F.X., Vivek, S.: Leakage-resilient authentication and encryption from symmetric cryptographic primitives. In: Proceedings of the 22nd ACM SIGSAC Conference on Computer and Communications Security, pp. 96–108 (2015)

[SPY13] Standaert, F.-X., Pereira, O., Yu, Yu.: Leakage-resilient symmetric cryptography under empirically verifiable assumptions. In: Canetti, R., Garay, J.A. (eds.) CRYPTO 2013. LNCS, vol. 8042, pp. 335–352. Springer, Heidelberg (2013). https://doi.org/10.1007/978-3-642-40041-4_19

[UHIM23] Ueno, R., Homma, N., Inoue, A., Minematsu, K.: Fallen Sanctuary: A Higher-Order and Leakage-Resilient Rekeying Scheme. Cryptology ePrint Archive (2023)

[VCMKS12] Veyrat-Charvillon, N., Medwed, M., Kerckhof, S., Standaert, F.-X.: Shuffling against side-channel attacks: a comprehensive study with cautionary note. In: Wang, X., Sako, K. (eds.) ASIACRYPT 2012. LNCS, vol. 7658, pp. 740–757. Springer, Heidelberg (2012). https://doi.org/10.1007/978-3-642-34961-4_44

Cryptographic Implementations

The Impact of Hash Primitives and Communication Overhead for Hardware-Accelerated SPHINCS+

Patrick Karl[1]([✉])[iD], Jonas Schupp[1][iD], and Georg Sigl[1,2][iD]

[1] TUM School of Computation, Information and Technology, Technical University of Munich, Munich, Germany
{patrick.karl,jonas.schupp,sigl}@tum.de
[2] Fraunhofer Institute for Applied and Integrated Security, Garching, Germany

Abstract. SPHINCS+ is a signature scheme included in the first NIST post-quantum standard, that bases its security on the underlying hash primitive. As most of the runtime of SPHINCS+ is caused by the evaluation of several hash- and pseudo-random functions, instantiated via the hash primitive, offloading this computation to dedicated hardware accelerators is a natural step. In this work, we evaluate different architectures for hardware acceleration of such a hash primitive with respect to its use-case and evaluate them in the context of SPHINCS+. We attach hardware accelerators for different hash primitives (SHAKE256 and Ascon-Xof for both, full and round-reduced versions) to CPU interfaces having different transfer speeds. We show, that for most use-cases, data transfer determines the overall performance if accelerators are equipped with FIFOs and that reducing the number of rounds in the permutation does not necessarily lead to significant performance improvements when using hardware acceleration.

Keywords: SPHINCS+ · PQC · post-quantum cryptography · hardware acceleration · Ascon

1 Introduction

Post-Quantum Cryptography (PQC) describes cryptographic algorithms that provide security in the presence of large-scale quantum computers. In 2016, the National Institute of Standards and Technology (NIST) started a public standardization process to analyze and evaluate quantum-secure algorithms for public-key encryption and key-exchange, as well as digital signatures. Recently, NIST selected a first set of algorithms to be standardized, one key encapsulation algorithm and three digital signature schemes [14]. In general, most PQC algorithms spend a substantial amount of computation time to hash data to a fix-sized digest or to generate pseudo-randomness that is required for computation. One of the quantum-secure signature schemes selected by NIST for standardization is SPHINCS+ [2], a hash-based PQC framework that can be instantiated

© The Author(s), under exclusive license to Springer Nature Switzerland AG 2024
R. Wacquez and N. Homma (Eds.): COSADE 2024, LNCS 14595, pp. 221–239, 2024.
https://doi.org/10.1007/978-3-031-57543-3_12

with different hash primitives. It's security solely relies on the security of the selected hash function that is extensively applied during key and signature generation as well as during signature verification. One of the proposed instances uses the SHA-3. For this choice, the algorithm spends more than 95% of its runtime inside the hash function when running on a commonly used microcontroller [12]. Moreover, using the SHA-3 functions for hashing and generation of pseudo-randomness is a usual choice also for other PQC algorithms. Thus, hardware acceleration for the underlying hash primitive is a natural step to improve the performance and energy consumption of PQC schemes, and in particular SPHINCS+.

Related Work. Previous works investigated hardware implementations for SPHINCS+, but mostly focused on co-processors that compute the entire signature. For instance, the work in [1] presents a standalone, high-throughput co-processor using SHAKE256. In [3], another co-processor with area efficiency as primary design goal is presented using SHA-2 as hash primitive. These standalone designs yield high performance, but lack flexibility – they speed-up a single algorithm, but their re-use for other schemes is limited. Hardware/software co-designs provide a trade-off between performance and flexibility by offloading only computationally intensive operations to dedicated hardware, but run the main algorithm in software. The work in [18] investigates the use of SPHINCS+ in the context of secure boot within a hardware-software co-design, and extends the platform's SHA-2 core to improve the performance for hash-based signatures in general. To the best of our knowledge, no hardware/software co-design evaluating SPHINCS+ using the SHA-3 standard has been presented so far.

Contribution. To close this gap, we explore different design architectures for hardware accelerators and evaluate the advantages and disadvantages of these options with respect to resource cost and performance. For that, we use a publicly available 32-bit micro-controller platform based on the open-source RISC-V Instruction Set Architecture (ISA) and include dedicated hardware extensions. We show that the choice for the most performant design option is application dependent. We use SPHINCS+ as a case study and provide performance metrics for the resulting hardware/software co-design. Furthermore, we replace the SHAKE256 primitive with other alternatives like TurboSHAKE256 [4], a round-reduced SHAKE256 version, and functions from the Ascon [6] suite, the winner of the NIST Lightweight Cryptography (LWC) competition. Instantiating Ascon in the SPHINCS+ framework has been submitted to NIST's additional call for signature schemes[1] under the name of Ascon-Sign[2]. To summarize, our contributions are as follows:

- Design-space exploration and benchmark of hash-accelerator architectures on a 32-bit RISC-V platform, considering the corresponding requirements of data transfer.

---

[1] https://csrc.nist.gov/Projects/pqc-dig-sig/standardization.

[2] https://csrc.nist.gov/Projects/pqc-dig-sig/round-1-additional-signatures.

- A practical analysis of the hidden (performance) cost of hash accelerators on a 32-bit platform and it's implications for SPHINCS+.
- Performance evaluation for SPHINCS+ using hardware-acceleration for different primitives, i.e. SHAKE256, TurboSHAKE256, Ascon-Xof and Ascon-Xofa.

Organization. Section 2 provides a brief overview of the SPHINCS+ signature scheme, the SHA-3 standard and our evaluation setup. In Sect. 3 we explain different architectures for the investigated hardware accelerators and their parameterization and cost. A performance analysis of these architectures and their application to SPHINCS+ is conducted in Sect. 4. Section 5 investigates the usage of cryptographic primitives for SPHINCS+ that are not part of the NIST submission and discuss their implications on performance and further optimization strategies. Finally, Sect. 6 concludes this work.

2 Preliminaries

2.1 The SPHINCS+ Framework

SPHINCS+ [2] is a stateless hash-based PQC signature scheme that has been selected by NIST as a winner of their first PQC standardization effort [14]. It uses different families of hash- and pseudo-random functions and solely relies on their (second-) preimage resistance. The core idea of SPHINCS+ is to combine several layers of Merkle trees with Winternitz One-Time Signature (WOTS+) [11] key pairs on its leafs. In the last layer of the resulting so-called hypertree, a Few-Time Signature (FTS) scheme called Forest Of Random Subsets (FORS) [2] is employed. In a simplified view, the signature of SPHINCS+ consists of the FORS signature and a series of WOTS+ signatures on the selected path through the hypertree. A verifier can then verify the signatures on the selected path and re-compute and verify the root node of the hypertree. For details, we refer to the original work in [2].

In the construction of the trees within SPHINCS+, the following pseudo-random and message-digest functions are used, where $\mathbb{B}$ denotes the set of bytes:

$$\boldsymbol{PRF} : \mathbb{B}^n \times \mathbb{B}^{32} \to \mathbb{B}^n$$
$$\boldsymbol{PRF_{msg}} : \mathbb{B}^n \times \mathbb{B}^n \times \mathbb{B}^* \to \mathbb{B}^n$$
$$\boldsymbol{H_{msg}} : \mathbb{B}^n \times \mathbb{B}^n \times \mathbb{B}^n \times \mathbb{B}^* \to \mathbb{B}^m$$

Furthermore, a hash function $\boldsymbol{T_l}$ with its two special cases $\boldsymbol{F} = \boldsymbol{T_1}$ and $\boldsymbol{H} = \boldsymbol{T_2}$ is defined as follows:

$$\boldsymbol{T_l} : \mathbb{B}^n \times \mathbb{B}^{32} \times \mathbb{B}^{ln} \to \mathbb{B}^n$$

The parameter $n \in \{16, 24, 32\}$ defines the output length (in bytes) of all the functions being used except for H_{msg}, that outputs an m-byte string. Likewise, the size of n determines the NIST security levels I, III and V. In this work, we consider parameter sets using the XOF SHAKE256 from the SHA-3 standard [15] as the underlying primitive, as specified in the SPHINCS+ NIST submission[3]. Therefore, we briefly explain its concept in Sect. 2.2.

2.2   Keccak and the SHA-3 Standard

SHAKE256 is based on the Keccak primitive and consists of a 1,600-bit state on which the permutation function `keccak-f1600` is applied for 24 rounds. For all the functions defined in the SHA-3 standard [15], Keccak is used in a sponge construction. In the sponge mode, the 1,600-bit state is divided into a rate r and a capacity c and is initialized with zeroes. The input data is split into several blocks b_i of size r, that are consecutively absorbed into the state. Between the absorption of two blocks, the permutation function is applied. After absorbing all blocks, the output blocks b_o (of size r) are squeezed and if more than one block is requested, the state is permuted again after each output block.

SHA-3 defines several hash functions with fixed output lengths and two XOF functions with outputs of arbitrary length, i.e. SHAKE128 and SHAKE256.

2.3   Evaluation Platform

As a baseline platform for the evaluation in this work, we use the PULPino microcontroller platform[4] that instantiates the cv32e40p, a 4-stage pipelined 32-bit RISC-V core supporting the *RV32IMC* and optional F instruction set [10]. The open-source character of RISC-V and the PULPino microcontroller enables to integrate arbitrary hardware extensions and accelerators. We evaluate our experiments on a Zynq UltraScale+ FPGA (xczu9eg-ffvb1156-2) using Vivado 2020.2 as synthesis tool. On this platform, the PULPino baseline implementation consumes 16,038 Look-Up Tables (LUTs) and 10,050 Flip-Flops (FFs) after synthesis and runs at a frequency of 150 MHz. It is noteworthy, that none of the hardware extensions investigated in this work lead to a decrease in frequency and thus, the reduction in cycle counts directly translates to performance gains in terms of latency. Software is compiled with the PULP compiler[5] with -O3.

3   Accelerator Architectures

Figure 1 shows the schematic of the PULPino microcontroller and different accelerator options. The accelerator architectures that are investigated in this work

---

[3] https://csrc.nist.gov/Projects/post-quantum-cryptography/post-quantum-cryptography-standardization/round-3-submissions.

[4] https://github.com/pulp-platform/pulpino.

[5] https://github.com/pulp-platform/pulp-riscv-gnu-toolchain.

are colored blue. In general, a designer has different options to integrate custom logic, that mainly differs in the interfacing logic. For instance, one can integrate custom functionality *tightly* into the processor and extend the ISA with corresponding instructions. One can also connect a co-processor *loosely* to the system bus. Finally, the last option is to connect the co-processor to the Load-Store Unit (LSU) before bridging onto the system bus. For evaluation, we implemented the investigated hash cores in SystemVerilog and integrated them in the different architectures as described in the following sections. The hash cores themselves have a 32-bit interface, automatically perform the padding in hardware and compute one round of the corresponding permutation per clock cycle. The correct functionality of the cores has been verified both in simulation and on the FPGA by comparing the computed outputs against software reference implementations.

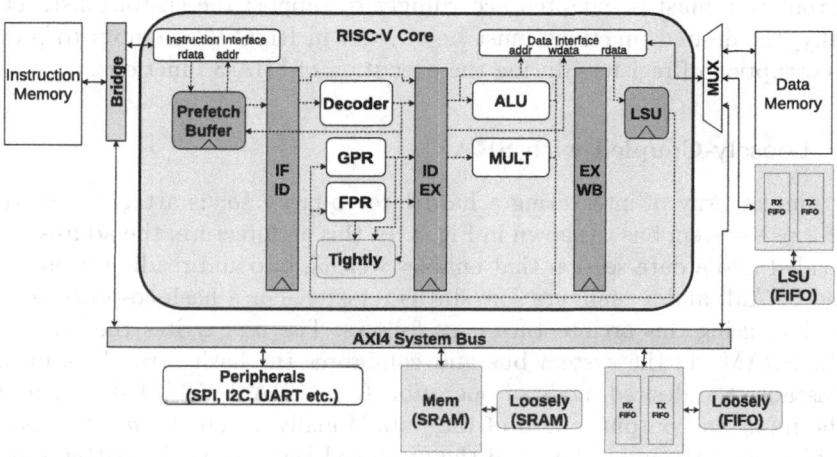

Fig. 1. Extended PULPino with accelerator architectures (blue). (Color figure online)

3.1 Tightly-Coupled into Register Set

In [9], the SHA-3 round function `keccak-f1600` has been integrated tightly-coupled into the register set of a RISC-V microcontroller. A fixed selection of registers that stores the entire Keccak state is chosen at design time and the logic of the round function is implemented in hardware – hardwired to the specific selection of registers. This concept is depicted in Fig. 2. The advantage of this strategy is, that it prevents load-store overheads that are required for loosely-coupled solutions connected to a system bus. It also provides a flexible solution that can be re-used for any function relying on the Keccak permutation, because only the round function itself is implemented in hardware. Consequently, different functions (e.g., SHA-3 hash functions SHA3-256, SHA3-384, SHA3-512, SHAKE128 or SHAKE256) are run in software and only their costly permutation routine is replaced by a single custom RISC-V instruction per round.

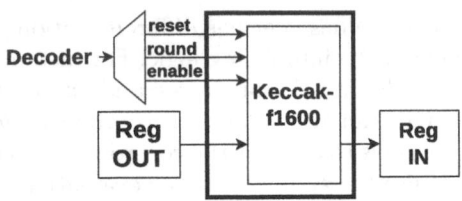

Fig. 2. Tightly-coupled architecture as proposed in [9].

A drawback, however, is that for 32-bit platforms, it requires the presence of both the General-Purpose Registers (GPRs) and the Floating-Point Registers (FPRs) to store the entire 1,600-bit Keccak state. Besides that, the compilation toolchain must be adapted accordingly to support the custom instruction. Finally, the desired functions must be written in RISC-V assembly to prevent any corruption of registers during the execution of SHA-3 functions.

3.2   Loosely-Coupled with SRAM

The simplest way of integrating a hardware co-processor is attaching it to the platforms's system bus as shown in Fig. 3. In this architecture, the address space is divided into a data section that enables writing into and reading from a dedicated SRAM, and a configuration/status register. For a hash co-processor, the procedure using this architecture is as follows: The user writes the input data to the SRAM via the system bus and configures the hash core. This includes for instance the desired mode of operation (e.g., SHA-3-256, SHAKE256, etc.) or the input and output length of the data. Finally, a signal *start* triggers the core to process the input data and the produced hash output is written into the SRAM. Afterwards, the produced data can be read again via the AXI4 interface. The advantage of this approach is the easy integration into the platform and its accessibility in software – software drivers can be written in generic C for instance. The drawback is, that the core starts the computation after the data is fully written into the memory and the produced digest is read after the computation is finished. As we show in Sect. 4, this has a severe impact on performance for large data sizes. Nevertheless, it is notable that the additional SRAM memory is not only usable by the accelerator but can also be used by the RISC-V core when the accelerator is idle.

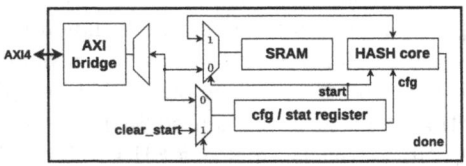

Fig. 3. Loosely-coupled architecture using SRAM.

3.3   Loosely-Coupled with FIFOs

Using First-In-First-Outs (FIFOs) as depicted in Fig. 4 instead of a dedicated SRAM enables to hide the computation inside the hash core in the data transfer. A (from software perspective) write-only *RX FIFO* buffers the input data and a read-only *TX FIFO* buffers the output data. This enables the co-processor to start absorbing the input data as soon as the first chunk is written into the *RX FIFO*. The output data produced by the hash core is written into the *TX FIFO* and the microcontroller can immediately start reading the output. This also reduces the complexity in the module, as no control bits are required anymore. How to properly dimension the FIFOs depends on the underlying hash function (the number of permutation rounds), as during permutation, no input data can be absorbed and no output data is produced. This is further analyzed in Sect. 3.5.

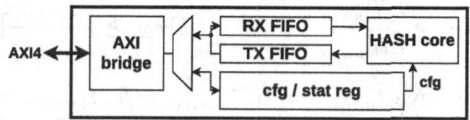

Fig. 4. Loosely-coupled architecture using FIFOs.

3.4   LSU-Coupled Using FIFOs

Although the usage of FIFOs benefits the performance in general, writing and reading the data via the AXI4 system bus can still pose a notable overhead due to the bus latency. Therefore, the last design option is to integrate the co-processor closer to the RISC-V core and to connect it directly to the core's LSU, as shown in Fig. 5. This yields two advantages: First, the latency caused by the system bus is reduced as no bridging is required anymore – it only requires multiplexing between the accelerator's and the remaining address space. Second, the co-processor does not require a complex AXI4 interface anymore which reduces the area cost. The drawback of this approach is, however, the increased integration complexity. Connecting the module to the LSU requires slightly more knowledge of the microcontroller implementation than knowing a standard interface as e.g. AXI4.

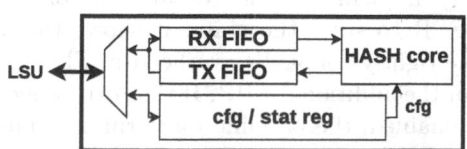

Fig. 5. LSU-coupled architecture using FIFOs.

3.5   FIFO Dimensions

For the architectures discussed in Sect. 3.3 and Sect. 3.4 the FIFOs sizes influence the resource cost as well as the accelerator's performance. Both FIFOs have a width of 32-bit to comply with the word width of the RISC-V core. The *RX FIFOs* should be large enough to buffer incoming data while the hash core is permuting without running full, so that the data transfer is not blocked. That is, the FIFO's depth (D_{RX}) depends on the number of permutation rounds T_{perm} of the hash function and the bus latency $t_{bus,wr}$ to perform a write operation. For the *TX FIFO*, it is desirable that whenever the microcontroller wants to read data, the FIFO is not empty. However, it should be able to store enough data that the hash core can finish the next permutation while the FIFO is still being read without running empty. As a consequence, the required depths (in 32-bit words) of the FIFOs are as follows:

$$D_{RX} \geq \lceil \frac{T_{perm}}{t_{bus,wr}} \rceil \qquad\qquad D_{TX} \geq \lceil \frac{T_{perm}}{t_{bus,rd}} \rceil \qquad\qquad (1)$$

In our design, we have $t_{axi,wr} = 6$, $t_{axi,rd} = 7$, $t_{lsu,wr} = 2$ and $t_{lsu,rd} = 3$, until the data is inside the corresponding FIFO or read from it. With $T_{perm} = 24$ for SHAKE256, we end up with FIFO depths of $D_{RX} = D_{TX} = 4$ for the loosely-coupled case and $D_{RX} = 16$ and $D_{TX} = 8$ for the LSU-coupled version. Note, that although for the LSU-coupled version, $D_{RX} = 12$ would meet the requirements, we slightly increased it to stick to a power-of-two. Due to the small size of the FIFOs, they are inferred as distributed memory (LUTRAM) which has a minimum depth of 32 and thus, the power-of-two ceiling does not increase area cost.

3.6   Resource Overhead

A comparison of the different architectures with respect to resource overhead compared with the plain PULPino design is given in Table 1. To provide a meaningful comparison, we synthesized the whole platform with the different accelerator architectures and only stated their additional overhead. For a discussion on the Ascon cost we refer to Sect. 5.1. Only stating the resource consumption for the architectures as depicted previously would omit the cost of additional circuitry like bus connections within PULPino's crossbar or the connection to the LSU.

The results highlight the advantage of the tightly-coupled approach: Because this architecture only implements the round function in hardware but reuses the GPR and FPR to store the state, it shows the least overhead. It is worth noting that the tightly-coupled's overhead in FFs mainly stems from the $32 \times 32 = 1,024$-bit of the additional FPR. If the corresponding RV32F floating-point extensions are enabled, the baseline platform consumes 20,209 LUTs and 11,535 FFs. Then the additional overhead for the tightly-coupled SHA-3 accelerator is only about 2,419 additional LUTs for the Keccak round function and the corresponding instruction. The loosely- and LSU-coupled architectures require more logic resources due to bus interfaces, control logic and the local memory in terms of FIFOs or SRAM. The SRAM overhead for the loosely-coupled version is omitted for two reasons. First, the accelerator's SRAM can later be re-used for normal operation of the RISC-V core and thus, does not need to be accelerator-specific. Second, the SRAM size depends on the specific application – it needs to be big enough to store the maximum amount of input or output data. Nevertheless, a single Xilinx BRAM of our FPGA with the size of 4 kB is sufficient for all our experiments. For SPHINCS+, the minimum required SRAM size would be either defined by the amount of input bytes of the function T_2 (as described in Sect. 2.1), or by the function H_{msg} that hashes a message of arbitrary length. Thus, the minimum size is determined by the maximum length of the inputs for T_2 and H_{msg}. In contrast to that, the FIFO dimensions are application independent. Application independent in the sense that the FIFO dimensions do not depend on the amount of input or output data, but only on the small amount of data that needs to be buffered while the hash core is permuting.

Table 1. Resource overhead including the hash core. Maximum frequency of 150 MHz is not affected by accelerators.

Architecture	SHA-3		Ascon	
	LUTs	FFs	LUTs	FFs
baseline no FPU	14,334 (100%)	8,720 (100%)	14,334 (100%)	8,720 (100%)
loosely-cpld + SRAM	+8,516 (+59.4%)	+2,477 (+28.4%)	+1,803 (+12.6%)	+1,159 (+13.3%)
loosely-cpld + FIFOs	+8,760 (+61.1%)	+2,438 (+28.0%)	+1,777 (+12.4%)	+1,130 (+13.0%)
lsu-cpld	+8,154 (+56.9%)	+1,881 (+21.6%)	+960 (+6.70%)	+523 (+6.01%)
tightly-cpld	+4,597 (+32.1%)	+1,061 (+12.3%)	+662 (+4.62%)	+19 (+0.22%)

4 Performance Evaluation

4.1 Architecture Benchmark

In the following, we compare the performance of the architectures described above. For the benchmark, we consider two scenarios:

In the **Hash** scenario, we benchmark the performance for a fixed output length and vary the input length that is absorbed. Concretely, we set the output length to 32 B and vary the input lengths up to 4 kB. This reflects a use case, where an arbitrarily sized input is hashed to a fix-sized digest.

In the **Cryptographically Secure Pseudo-Random Number Generator (CSPRNG)** scenario, the input length is fixed to 16 B and the output length varies up to 4 kB. This scenario typically occurs in PQC schemes when a small seed is extended to provide pseudo-random data that is, for instance, used to sample variables. For both scenarios we consider SHAKE256, that can be used for arbitrary input and output lengths and is used within SPHINCS+.

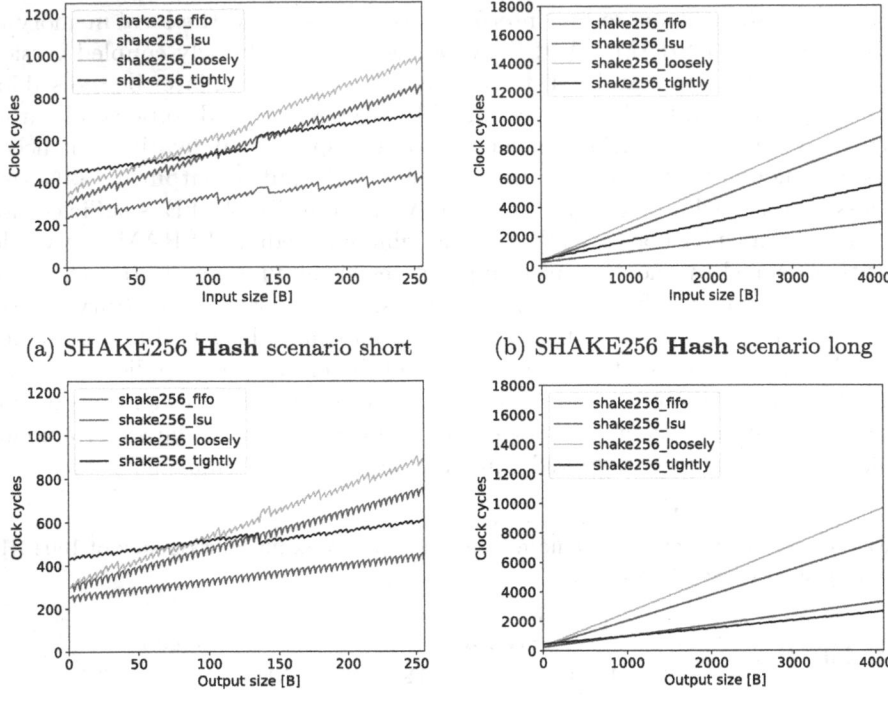

(a) SHAKE256 **Hash** scenario short   (b) SHAKE256 **Hash** scenario long

(c) SHAKE256 **CSPRNG** scenario short   (d) SHAKE256 **CSPRNG** scenario long

Fig. 6. Performance evaluation of the SHAKE256 accelerators in the **Hash** (Figs. 6a and 6b) and **CSPRNG** (Figs. 6c and 6d) scenario.

The results for both scenarios are shown in Fig. 6. The LSU- and tightly-coupled versions perform best depending on the scenario and amount of data to be processed. To explain this, the data transfer has to be considered. In both cases, the input data is first loaded from memory into the register set and after computation, the hash output is written back to memory. Yet, the computation is different depending on the architecture: In the tightly-coupled case, input blocks b_i must first be loaded into some free GPR registers. For the parts of the state's rate that lie within the FPR, the corresponding state word must be moved to the GPR, then absorption (xor) is performed, and afterwards, the updated word is written back to the FPR. This requires 3 instructions for the rate part in the FPR (in our implementation 16 regs × 3 instr), whereas the rate part in the GPR can be absorbed within one single xor instruction (18 regs × 1 instr). Therefore, the absorption takes 66 clock cycles per input block, as for SHAKE256, the rate consists of 34 words of 4 B each. After absorption of each input block b_i and squeezing of output blocks b_o, the state must be permuted for T_{perm} cycles. Thus, the computation can be modeled as:

$$t_{tightly} = b_i(66 + T_{perm}) + b_o T_{perm} + t_{sw} \tag{2}$$

where t_{sw} denotes a software overhead e.g., for calling functions. It should be noted that the absorption of the last input block might take less than 66 cycles if it is only partially filled.

For the LSU-coupled and loosely-coupled architectures, the input data must be written to and the output data read from the accelerator. However, when using FIFOs, the absorption, squeezing and subsequent permutations are hidden in the data transfer assuming the FIFOs do not run full or empty. With this assumption, the behavior of the architectures can be modelled as follows:

$$t_{loosely,sram} = t_{store} + (b_i + b_o)T_{perm} + t_{load} + t_{hw} \tag{3}$$

$$t_{loosely,fifo} = t_{store} + t_{load} + t_{hw} \tag{4}$$

$$t_{lsu} = t_{store} + t_{load} + t_{hw} \tag{5}$$

The variables t_{store} and t_{load} denote the cycles to write data to and read data from the accelerator, t_{hw} the constant overhead of the hardware drivers.

Implications for Hash Scenario. For the hash scenario, the t_{load} as well as b_o is negligible, as only a fixed, typically small amount of data is read back from the hash core. For the LSU-coupled approach, Eq. (5) yields $t_{lsu} = t_{store} + t_{hw}$. In fact, as the co-processor is connected directly to the LSU, writing to the co-processor only takes a single cycle and thus, $t_{store} \approx \frac{d_{in}}{4}$ is equal to the amount of input data words where d_{in} is the input data in bytes. If we neglect the terms t_{sw} and t_{hw}, Eq. (2) yields $t_{tightly} \approx b_i(66 + T_{perm}) = \lceil \frac{d_{in}}{34 \times 4} \rceil \times (66 + T_{perm}) \approx d_{in}\frac{90}{136} > \frac{d_{in}}{4}$, such that $t_{tightly} > t_{lsu}$, which confirms the observations of Figs. 6a and 6b.

For both loosely-coupled scenarios, t_{load} and t_{store} is larger than in the LSU-coupled case. In fact, in our design writing takes 6 instead of 1 clock cycle, hence $t_{loosely,fifo} > t_{lsu}$ according to Eqs. (4) and (5). Furthermore, as the loosely-coupled solution using a SRAM interface cannot hide the absorption and squeezing phase, it is clear that $t_{loosely,sram} > t_{loosely,fifo} > t_{lsu}$. Nevertheless, as the data transfer time for small data sizes is negligible, the computational overhead of the tightly-coupled approach exceeds the loosely-coupled variants.

Implications for CSPRNG Scenario. If a small seed is absorbed (typically smaller than one block of the Keccak primitive), we can neglect the impact of the terms containing b_i, as the absorption phase is negligible. In the LSU-coupled case, we can neglect t_{store} for the same reason. Hence, we end up with $t_{tightly} \approx b_o T_{perm} + t_{sw} = \lfloor \frac{d_{out}}{34 \times 4} \rfloor 24 + t_{sw} \approx d_{out}\frac{3}{17} + t_{sw}$ and $t_{lsu} \approx t_{load} + t_{hw} = 2\frac{d_{out}}{4} + t_{hw} = \frac{d_{out}}{2} + t_{hw}$, where d_{out} denotes the number of output bytes and loading from the LSU-coupled accelerator requires 2 cycles. As $\frac{3}{17} < \frac{1}{2}$ the tightly-coupled architecture will be faster as soon as the lower computational effort for sufficient amounts of data compensates that $t_{sw} > t_{hw}$. In our experiments this point is reached when squeezing about 952 B of output data. Concerning the two loosely-coupled approaches, the same consideration as for the hash scenario holds, i.e. the larger penalty for data transfers dominates the smaller initial overhead compared to the tightly-coupled approach from a certain amount of data on.

4.2 Application to SPHINCS+

The results in Sect. 4.1 have shown, that either the tightly-coupled or the LSU-coupled approach shows the best performance. Therefore, we restrict our evaluations for SPHINCS+ to these architectures and only present results for the *simple* versions of SPHINCS+ that are considered by NIST [13]. We consider message sizes of 59 B as in the pqm4 benchmarks [12] and take the C reference code of the NIST submission as baseline. In the following, all cycle counts are averaged over 50 iterations and the numbers are given in kilo clock cycles.

A comparison of the cycle counts for both architectures is given in Table 2 for the *fast* (-f) variant and Table 3 for the *small* variant (-s) of all NIST security levels. For comparison, the numbers of the software implementation that does not use hardware acceleration are included. The LSU-coupled architecture shows advantages compared to the tightly-coupled alternatives. These results are in line with the results observed in the benchmark in Fig. 6. As discussed in Sect. 2.1, the main hash computations within SPHINCS+ have rather short outputs of only n-byte (remember that $n \in \{16, 24, 32\}$), the LSU-coupled architecture is expected to be faster, as also the previous benchmark showed an advantage of the LSU-coupled version for all input sizes. Compared to the software reference, the LSU-coupled architecture yields speed-up factors between ×81 and ×84 for NIST level I (`128f-simple` and `128s-simple`).

5 Deviation from the SPHINCS+ NIST Submission

In this section, we evaluate deviations from the official NIST submission of SPHINCS+. More specifically, we investigate the use of the Ascon suite [6] and evaluate the changes also for round-reduced versions for Ascon and SHAKE256.

5.1 Ascon Primitive

As mentioned previously, SPHINCS+ is a framework that can be instantiated with different primitives for hash functions and pseudo-random number generation. Recently, NIST selected Ascon [6], that also features hash- and XOF functions, as the winner of the LWC competition [17].

Just as Keccak, Ascon is based on the sponge construction but consists only of a 320-bit state and a round function that is applied for 12 rounds. Due to its smaller state and less numbers of rounds, performance gains could be expected. Yet, it has a rate of $r = 64$-bit (or 2 words, compared to SHAKE256's 34 words), such that it requires more permutations when large amounts of data are processed. Furthermore, due to the smaller state, Ascon only provides a (second-)preimage resistance of 128-bit and thus, reaches only NIST security level I if instantiated within SPHINCS+. For evaluation we developed a small hash core that fits into the architectures described previously. Moreover, we implemented a tightly-coupled approach as presented in [16]. In the following, we perform the same analysis as for the SHAKE256 use-case before.

Table 2. Kilo cycles for SPHINCS+ fast variant.

Architecture	Keygen	Sign	Verify
128f-simple			
shake256_sw	145,119	3,602,835	201,209
shake256_lsu	1,725	42,598	2,458
shake256_tightly	2,902	71,921	4,091
192f-simple			
shake256_sw	213,034	5,806,444	294,981
shake256_lsu	2,639	72,134	3,725
shake256_tightly	4,530	123,534	6,327
256f-simple			
shake256_sw	563,213	11,625,520	300,496
shake256_lsu	8,663	179,501	4,804
shake256_tightly	13,528	280,112	7,384

Table 3. Kilo cycles for SPHINCS+ small variant.

Architecture	Keygen	Sign	Verify
128s-simple			
shake256_sw	9,28,8740	70,607,335	69,400
shake256_lsu	109,770	837,742	852
shake256_tightly	184,914	1,410,992	1,419
192s-simple			
shake256_sw	13,577,843	121,983,442	100,193
shake256_lsu	168,459	1,538,599	1,301
shake256_tightly	289,052	2,617,293	2,183
256s-simple			
shake256_sw	8,974,362	106,785,700	146,674
shake256_lsu	137,921	1,666,663	2,369
shake256_tightly	216,045	2,596,080	3,655

FIFO Dimensions. Following Eq. (1), the FIFO depths D_{RX} and D_{TX} of the loosely-coupled architecture are set to $D_{RX} = D_{TX} = 2$, as Ascon permutes for $T_{perm} = 12$ rounds. For the LSU-coupled version, the same dimensions apply although the rationale is different: With a write-delay of only 2 cycles, the micro-controller can provide up to 6 data words while Ascon is permuting. As the rate of Ascon is only 64-bit, i.e. 2 words, data is provided faster than it is processed by the hash core. Thus, setting $D_{RX} = 2$ is sufficient to constantly provide data to the hash core. The same applies for D_{TX}: Data is read faster than the hash core can produce and thus, $D_{TX} = 2$ is sufficient such that the hash core can output a full block and continue permuting the state immediately. As such, the permutation of the Ascon state is the actual bottleneck in the computation.

Resource Overhead. Table 1 shows the overhead for the Ascon primitive. Compared to the SHA-3 core, it shows reductions in both, the LUT and FF count, mostly due to the smaller state. In particular for the tightly-coupled architecture, this overhead is almost neglectable. Compared with the tightly-coupled SHA-3 version, the reduction in FFs mainly stems from the fact that for the 320-bit Ascon state, no FPR set is required, as it fits well into the 32×32 bit GPR set.

Architecture Benchmark. Figures 7a and 7b show the architecture benchmark using Ascon-Xof. For the CSPRNG scenario (Fig. 7b), the loosely-coupled version with FIFOs is similiarly fast as the LSU-coupled architecture (same slope, only a small offset). This indicates that the Ascon core is the actual bottleneck, but not the bus latency. However, this is not the case for the hash scenario (Fig. 7a), because the data transmission partially hides the computation in the absorption phase. For small amounts of data, the tightly-coupled version is competitive but the arithmetic overhead for a tightly-coupled option poses a notable drawback in both scenarios when the amount of data increases.

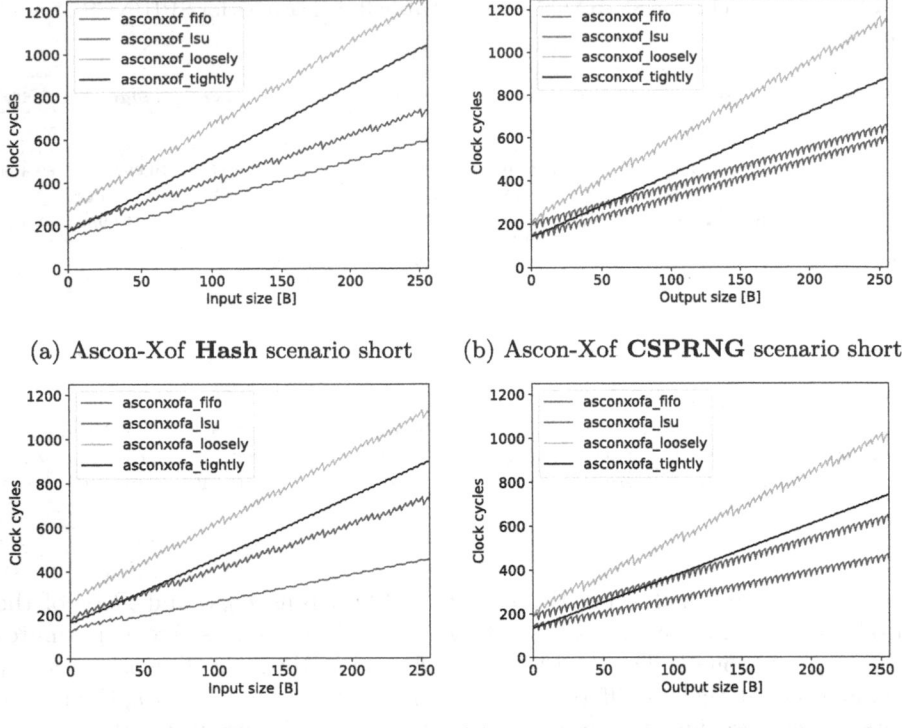

(a) Ascon-Xof **Hash** scenario short   (b) Ascon-Xof **CSPRNG** scenario short

(c) Ascon-Xofa **Hash** scenario short   (d) Ascon-Xofa **CSPRNG** scenario short

Fig. 7. Architecture benchmarking with functions from the Ascon suite.

Application to SPHINCS+. In Tables 4 and 5 we provide the cycle counts using Ascon-Xof for SPHINCS+. It can be seen, that the gap between the two Ascon accelerator architectures is smaller than for the SHAKE256 variants in Tables 2 and 3. While the LSU-coupled versions of SHAKE256 and Ascon are roughly in the same ballpark, the tightly-coupled Ascon-Xof design yields better results than its SHAKE256 counterpart, as it does not require the FPR. Compared to the software reference implementation, the LSU-coupled architecture yields speed-up factors between ×64 and ×65. Furthermore, a comparison shows that using Ascon-Xof over SHAKE256 already yields a speed-up of about 22.5% for signature generation for the plain software comparison.

Table 4. Kilo cycles for SPHINCS+-128f-simple.

Architecture	Keygen	Sign	Verify
asconxof_sw	11,2543	2,793,036	159,128
asconxof_lsu	1,733	42,868	2,475
asconxof_tightly	2,298	56,896	3,282

Table 5. Kilo cycles for SPHINCS+-128 s-simple.

Architecture	Keygen	Sign	Verify
asconxof_sw	7,203,739	54,787,744	55,470
asconxof_lsu	110,308	843,462	864
asconxof_tightly	146,232	1,116,889	1,147

5.2 Round-Reduced Versions

Ascon-Xofa is a round-reduced version of Ascon-Xof that is also part of the Ascon cipher suite. Compared to Ascon-Xof, the first permutation and the permutation after absorbing the last input block remain at 12 rounds, all others are reduced to 8 rounds when using Ascon-Xofa. Reducing the number of rounds within a permutation has also been discussed in the context of the Keccak primitive. There has been a lot of cryptanalysis on the Keccak primitive over the years, but the Keccak primitive has shown to provide a huge security margin. As a result, reducing the number of rounds from 24 to 12 has been formalized under the name of TurboSHAKE256 [4]. In the following, we evaluate the advantages of the round-reduced versions for Ascon-Xof and SHAKE256 and perform the architecture benchmark as well as the impact on SPHINCS+.

FIFO Dimensions and Resource Overhead. For TurboSHAKE256, halving the number of rounds per permutation also enables to halve the FIFO dimensions of the accelerator. For the Ascon-Xofa variant, however, the *RX FIFO* in the loosely-coupled case must be slightly increased to $D_{RX} = 4$.

Architecture Benchmark. For the architecture benchmark, our results for TurboSHAKE256 look similar as the ones shown in Fig. 6, with only minor offsets, which underlines the dominant impact of the data transfer. As dicussed previously, due to the high rate of the Keccak primitive in general, the data transfer poses more of a bottleneck than the actual round permutation, which is mostly hidden. For Ascon-Xofa, this case is slightly different. As already mentioned, the Ascon core is a bottleneck due to its lower rate. This is visible in Fig. 7b, where the slope of the loosely-coupled FIFO version and the LSU-coupled architecture are equal. Yet, Fig. 7d shows that this changes for Ascon-Xofa. The cycle counts are reduced and the slope of the LSU- and loosely-coupled FIFO version are different, as the computation within the core is blocking the data transfer less. In addition to that, Fig. 7c also shows that both the loosely-coupled FIFO version and the LSU-coupled version benefit from the round-reduction in the hash scenario as well.

Application to SPHINCS+. Tables 6 and 7 list the corresponding cycle counts for the round-reduced versions in the context of SPHINCS+. As expected, it shows performance gains for all cases, It is notable, however, that the reduction for the round-reduced version Ascon-Xofa is larger than for TurboSHAKE256 (abbreviated as t_shake256) when taking hardware acceleration into account. This is due to the obervation made previously, where the computation inside the hash core posed a bottleneck. Reducing the rounds speeds up this computation and thus, resolves this issue. As a consequence, the Ascon-Xofa design yields the highest performance when instantiated in SPHINCS+ using the LSU-coupled architecture. Compared to the software implementations, the LSU-coupled architecture yields speed-up factors of between ×49 and ×51 for TurboSHAKE256 and between ×52 and ×53 for Ascon-Xofa for NIST security level I.

Table 6. Kilo cycles for SPHINCS+ fast variant.

Architecture	Keygen	Sign	Verify
128f-simple			
t_shake256_sw	85,584	2,124,535	118,879
t_shake256_lsu	1,684	41,594	2,401
t_shake256_tightly	2,848	70,574	4,014
asconxofa_sw	82,716	20,529,62	116,680
asconxofa_lsu	1,571	38,851	2,242
asconxofa_tightly	2,136	52,884	3,049
192f-simple			
t_shake256_sw	126,040	3,435,129	175,154
t_shake256_lsu	2,574	70,332	3,650
t_shake256_tightly	4,450	121,346	6,242
256f-simple			
t_shake256_sw	333,873	6,892,927	178,042
t_shake256_lsu	8,508	176,300	4,722
t_shake256_tightly	13,319	275,794	7,272

Table 7. Kilo cycles for SPHINCS+ small variant.

Architecture	Keygen	Sign	Verify
128s-simple			
t_shake256_sw	5,477,698	41,640,940	40,760
t_shake256_lsu	106,892	815,862	828
t_shake256_tightly	181,436	1,384,566	1,388
asconxofa_sw	5,294,278	40,266,442	40,881
asconxofa_lsu	99,944	764,591	788
asconxofa_tightly	135,874	1,038,107	1,073
192s-simple			
t_shake256_sw	8,009,407	71,976,146	59,307
t_shake256_lsu	164,690	1,504,662	1,278
t_shake256_tightly	283,971	2,571,655	2,153
256s-simple			
t_shake256_sw	5,304,720	63,1475,85	86,923
t_shake256_lsu	135,171	1,6337,96	2,331
t_shake256_tightly	212,696	2,556,251	3,610

5.3   Discussion on Round-Reduced Versions for SPHINCS+

Comparing the above results shows a direct performance gain for the round-reduced versions when looking at the pure software implementations. When taking hardware acceleration into account, the performance gain is not as significant as could be expected. To visualize that, Fig. 8 depicts these savings for the pure software versions as well as the LSU- and tightly-coupled versions at the example of the 128f-simple variant of SPHINCS+. In the case of the SHA-3 functions (Fig. 8a), the software implementations benefit the most from the round-reduction. As the permutation function is the main effort in software computation, reducing the rounds by 50% has a similar strong impact on the overall performance. However, when employing hardware acceleration, the benefit of round-reduction is almost negligible, as the main effort in the computation is not the permutation anymore, but rather the data transfer and in the case of

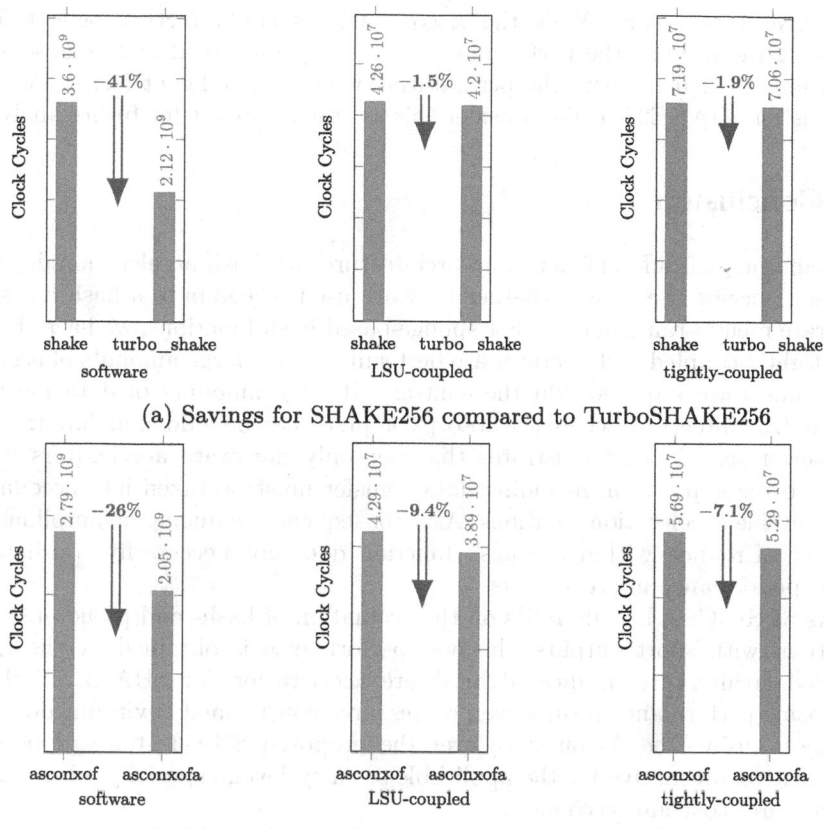

(a) Savings for SHAKE256 compared to TurboSHAKE256

(b) Savings for Ascon-Xof compared to Ascon-Xofa

Fig. 8. Relative savings for SPHINCS+ signature generation (128f-simple) when using round-reduced versions of the primitives.

the tightly-coupled version, the remaining instructions required for absorption, byte counters, stack operations etc.

When looking at the case for Ascon (Fig. 8b), the round-reduction also benefits the hardware-accelerated versions. This can be explained by the observation made previously, that due to Ascon's smaller rate, it must permute more often and partially slows down the data transfer speed in the LSU-coupled case. In the tightly-coupled case, the overall software driver requires less instructions and thus, the permutation itself makes up a larger part of the overall computational effort compared to the SHAKE256 version. As a consequence, the tightly-coupled Ascon variant benefits more from a round-reduction (relatively speaking) then the SHAKE256 variant.

Taking these observations into account implies that additional design changes like unrolling of multiple rounds (i.e. computing multiple rounds in a single clock cycle) would not yield a significant performance improvement for SHAKE256 hardware acceleration. While the Ascon variants could further benefit from unrolling the rounds, the performance gain is expected to decrease as soon as the point is reached where the permutation is not a significant factor anymore (as it is for SHAKE256). We consider this as starting point for future analysis.

6   Conclusion

The efficiency of different hardware architectures for hash acceleration depends on their specific use-case – whether they are used to compute a hash digest or generate pseudo-random data. For sponge-based hash functions, we have shown, that tightly-coupled architectures are best suited when large amounts of pseudo-randomness are required. On the contrary, if large amounts of data must be digested, architectures where the absorption phase can be hidden in data transfer are better suited. This illustrates that not only hardware accelerators itself, but also the application including data transfer must be taken into account to find suitable acceleration solutions. As a consequence, reducing or unrolling the number of rounds within the hash function does not necessarily translate to direct performance improvements.

As SPHINCS+ heavily relies on the evaluation of hash- and pseudo-random functions with short outputs, the best performance is obtained by the LSU-coupled architecture. Dedicated hardware acceleration for SHAKE256 shows promising performance results even on resource constrained environments. Furthermore, using the Ascon suite over the proposed SHA-3 standard poses a competitive alternative for the applicable security level, especially when taking the resource cost into account.

For future work, we consider extending the analysis to other PQC schemes like CRYSTALS-Kyber [5], CRYSTALS-Dilithium [7] or Falcon [8]. Although the input and output sizes of the hash- and CSPRNG functions used in these schemes most likely fall in a range where the LSU-coupled architecture is the fastest solution, a detailed investigation is necessary to quantify the results.

Acknowledgments. The authors acknowledge the financial support by the Federal Ministry of Education and Research of Germany in the programme of "Souverän. Digital. Vernetzt.". Joint project 6G-life, project identification number: 16KISK002.

References

1. Amiet, D., Leuenberger, L., Curiger, A., Zbinden, P.: FPGA-based SPHINCS+ implementations: mind the glitch. In: 23rd Euromicro Conference on Digital System Design, DSD 2020, Kranj, Slovenia, 26–28 August 2020, pp. 229–237. IEEE (2020). https://doi.org/10.1109/DSD51259.2020.00046
2. Bernstein, D.J., Hülsing, A., Kölbl, S., Niederhagen, R., Rijneveld, J., Schwabe, P.: The SPHINCS+ signature framework. In: Proceedings of the 2019 ACM SIGSAC Conference on Computer and Communications Security. ACM (2019). https://doi.org/10.1145/3319535.3363229

3. Berthet, Q., Upegui, A., Gantel, L., Duc, A., Traverso, G.: An area-efficient SPHINCS+ post-quantum signature coprocessor. In: IEEE International Parallel and Distributed Processing Symposium Workshops, IPDPS Workshops 2021, Portland, OR, USA, 17–21 June 2021, pp. 180–187. IEEE (2021). https://doi.org/10.1109/IPDPSW52791.2021.00034

4. Bertoni, G., et al.: TurboSHAKE. IACR Cryptology ePrint Archive, p. 342 (2023). https://eprint.iacr.org/2023/342

5. Bos, J., et al.: CRYSTALS-KYBER: a CCA-secure module-lattice-based KEM. In: 2018 IEEE European Symposium on Security and Privacy (EuroS&P), pp. 353–367. IEEE (2018)

6. Dobraunig, C., Eichlseder, M., Mendel, F., Schläffer, M.: Ascon v1.2 (2021). https://ascon.iaik.tugraz.at/specification.html

7. Ducas, L., et al.: CRYSTALS-Dilithium: a lattice-based digital signature scheme. IACR Trans. Cryptogr. Hardw. Embed. Syst. **2018**(1), 238–268 (2018)

8. Fouque, P.A., et al.: Falcon: Fast-Fourier lattice-based compact signatures over NTRU. Submission to the NIST's post-quantum cryptography standardization process **36** (2018). https://falcon-sign.info/falcon.pdf

9. Fritzmann, T., Sigl, G., Sepúlveda, J.: RISQ-V: tightly coupled RISC-V accelerators for post-quantum cryptography. IACR Trans. Cryptogr. Hardw. Embed. Syst. **2020**(4), 239–280 (2020). https://doi.org/10.13154/tches.v2020.i4.239-280

10. Gautschi, M., et al.: Near-threshold RISC-V core with DSP extensions for scalable IoT endpoint devices. IEEE Trans. Very Large Scale Integr. Syst. **25**(10), 2700–2713 (2017). https://doi.org/10.1109/TVLSI.2017.2654506

11. Hülsing, A.: W-OTS+ - shorter signatures for hash-based signature schemes. In: Youssef, A., Nitaj, A., Hassanien, A.E. (eds.) AFRICACRYPT 2013. LNCS, vol. 7918, pp. 173–188. Springer, Heidelberg (2013). https://doi.org/10.1007/978-3-642-38553-7_10

12. Kannwischer, M.J., Rijneveld, J., Schwabe, P., Stoffelen, K.: PQM4: Post-quantum crypto library for the ARM Cortex-M4. As of commit 918f379. https://github.com/mupq/pqm4

13. Moody, D.: NIST PQC: looking into the future (2022). https://csrc.nist.gov/Presentations/2022/nist-pqc-looking-into-the-future

14. NIST: Status report on the third round of the NIST post-quantum cryptography stadardization process (2022). https://doi.org/10.6028/NIST.IR.8413-upd1

15. National Institute of Standards and Technology: SHA-3 standard: permutation-based hash and extendable-output functions. Technical report (2015). https://doi.org/10.6028/nist.fips.202

16. Steinegger, S., Primas, R.: A fast and compact RISC-V accelerator for ascon and friends. In: Liardet, P., Mentens, N. (eds.) CARDIS 2020. LNCS, vol. 12609, pp. 53–67. Springer, Cham (2020). https://doi.org/10.1007/978-3-030-68487-7_4

17. Turan, M.S.: Status report on the final round of the NIST lightweight cryptography standardization process (2023). https://doi.org/10.6028/nist.ir.8454

18. Wagner, A., Oberhansl, F., Schink, M.: To be, or not to be stateful: post-quantum secure boot using hash-based signatures. In: Chang, C., Rührmair, U., Mukhopadhyay, D., Forte, D. (eds.) Proceedings of the 2022 Workshop on Attacks and Solutions in Hardware Security, ASHES 2022, Los Angeles, CA, USA, 11 November 2022, pp. 85–94. ACM (2022). https://doi.org/10.1145/3560834.3563831

HaMAYO: A Fault-Tolerant Reconfigurable Hardware Implementation of the MAYO Signature Scheme

Oussama Sayari[1(✉)], Soundes Marzougui[1,2(✉)], Thomas Aulbach[3(✉)],
Juliane Krämer[3], and Jean-Pierre Seifert[1,4]

[1] Technical University of Berlin, Berlin, Germany
oussama_sayari@yahoo.fr, jean-pierre.seifert@tu-berlin.de
[2] STMicroelectronics, Diegem, Belgium
soundes.marzougui@st.com
[3] University of Regensburg, Regensburg, Germany
{thomas.aulbach,juliane.kraemer}@ur.de
[4] Fraunhofer Institute SIT, Darmstadt, Germany

Abstract. MAYO is a topical modification of the established multivariate signature scheme UOV. Signer and Verifier locally enlarge the public key map, such that the dimension of the oil space and therefore, the parameter sizes in general, can be reduced. This significantly reduces the public key size while maintaining the appealing properties of UOV, like short signatures and fast verification. Therefore, MAYO is considered as an attractive candidate in the NIST call for additional digital signatures and might be an adequate solution for real-world deployment in resource-constrained devices.

When emerging to hardware implementation of multivariate schemes and specifically MAYO, different challenges are faced, namely resource utilization, which scales up with higher parameter sets. To accommodate this, we introduce a configurable hardware implementation designed for integration across various FPGA architectures. Our approach features adaptable configurations aligned with NIST-defined security levels and incorporates resources optimization modules. Our implementation is specifically tested on the Zynq ZedBoard with the Zynq-7020 SoC, with performance evaluations and comparisons made against previous hardware implementations of multivariate schemes.

Furthermore, we conducted a security analysis of the MAYO implementation highlighting potential physical attacks and implemented lightweight countermeasures.

Keywords: MAYO · Multivariate Cryptography · Post-Quantum Cryptography · Digital Signature · Hardware Implementation · Physical Security

1 Introduction

As quantum computing continues to advance, it is anticipated that quantum attacks can break many of the computational problems that classical

© The Author(s), under exclusive license to Springer Nature Switzerland AG 2024
R. Wacquez and N. Homma (Eds.): COSADE 2024, LNCS 14595, pp. 240–259, 2024.
https://doi.org/10.1007/978-3-031-57543-3_13

cryptography relies on, such as factorization and discrete logarithms used in RSA and ECDSA, respectively. To address this, researchers have proposed new mathematical assumptions and computational problems that are difficult to solve with quantum computers, resulting in the field of post-quantum cryptography. These new assumptions are grouped into different families, such as lattice-based, code-based, hash-based, and multivariate cryptography.

Multivariate schemes mainly rely on the difficulty of solving large systems of multivariate quadratic equations, known as the MQ Problem. As such, the signature scheme Rainbow [DS05] was a finalist in the third round of the NIST post-quantum cryptography (PQC) Standardization Process. Rainbow is a two-layered version of the UOV signature scheme [KPG99]. Hence, multivariate signature schemes based on the oil and vinegar principle received a lot of attention. They offer very short signatures and efficient verification, since the signature is mainly the solution to a system of multivariate quadratic equations, and verifying boils down to evaluating the polynomials at the presumed solution. Still, during the third round, Beullens developed an algebraic attack on Rainbow [Beu22a], targeting the layer structure that differentiates Rainbow from UOV. This led to the elimination of Rainbow from the ongoing process since it lost all its alleged advantages over the base scheme UOV.

Since mainly lattice-based signatures remained in the competition, NIST called for the submission of additional post-quantum digital signature schemes to enhance the given variety of signatures by prioritizing those that are not reliant on structured lattices, have short signatures and fast verification. The majority of the multivariate schemes submitted to this process are based on the oil and vinegar principle.

MAYO, introduced in [Beu22b], is one of them. It uses the same trapdoor - a secret oil space that is annihilated by the public key map - but is developed such that the signer and the verifier locally enlarge the public key matrices. Therefore, the dimension of the oil space can be reduced. That also allows to reduce other parameters like the number of variables in the quadratic equations since certain algebraic attacks get harder with a smaller oil space [KS06]. In total, this leads to significantly smaller public keys in MAYO, while keeping good performance numbers and signature sizes. For instance, with parameters targeting the first security level of the NIST process, the public key size of MAYO is 1,168 bytes, the secret key is 24 bytes, and the signature size is 321 bytes [BCC+23]. These results make the MAYO signature scheme even more compact than state-of-the-art lattice-based signature schemes such as Falcon and Dilithium [PQD23].

Contribution. In this paper, we present an open source pure hardware implementation of the multivariate signature scheme MAYO. Our main target was a trade-off between SRAM/BRAM Consumption and FPGA Slides. In a second part, we investigated the physical security of MAYO implementation against side-channel analysis and fault-injection attacks. We, moreover, suggest lightweight countermeasures and implement them.

The contribution is summarized as follows:

- We manually settle a pure hardware implementation of MAYO. Our implementation is reconfigurable and can be easily integrated with different FPGA architectures and for different security levels.
- Certain functionalities used within key generation and signing are optimized, with a focus on low memory consumption.
- We present a new approach for the Gaussian solver and compare it to the well-known GSMITH approach of Rupp et al. in [REBG11].
- We considered threats emerging from possible fault injection and side channel analysis attacks, and cover them by employing low cost countermeasures.

The source code is available upon request.

Deployed Parameter Set. When we started with the hardware implementation, there was only one proof of concept implementation available on https://github.com/WardBeullens/MAYO and it used the parameter set ($n = 62, m = 60, o = 6, k = 10, q = 31$) (see also [Beu22b, Section 8]). Thus, we also deployed these parameters in our work. In the meantime, the parameters were updated and as a main difference, MAYO also works over a field with even characteristic now, i.e., $q = 16$. This allows for higher efficiency and further implementation tricks, since now one field element occupies 4 bits instead of 5, and consequently, 2 field elements can be stored in one byte. The other parameters were also updated, but with minor impact. Thus, our work is one of the very few implementations of a multivariate schemes that utilizes a finite field with odd characteristic.

Related Work. At the time of writing this paper, there is a scarcity of complete hardware designs for post-quantum cryptographic schemes [ZZW+21,XL21, FG18,HZ18]. However, given that the NIST PQC reached the fourth round and started the call for additional digital signature schemes, it is expected that more dedicated hardware designs will emerge. These designs would be instrumental in showcasing the strength and inherent properties of specific protocols [NIS23a].

Multivariate schemes necessitate the development of comprehensive and extensive implementation designs to address the challenging gaps due to the schemes' large key sizes [DS05,KPG99]. These key sizes often pose challenges for devices with limited resources, as they may struggle to accommodate the storage requirements of these schemes. Moreover, multivariate schemes commonly involve memory and time-consuming blocks, with the Gaussian solver being a well-known performance bottleneck [REBG11]. Despite the above-mentioned challenges, there have been a few published hardware implementations that have reported results for multivariate schemes [TYD+11,HZ18,FG18].

In [FG18], Ferozpuri and Gaj present a high-speed FPGA implementation of Rainbow. Their hardware implementation uses a parameterized system solver where the execution time is proportional to the system dimension, i.e., it can solve an n-by-n system in n clock cycles. Moreover, their work reduces the number of required multipliers by almost half, speeds up execution as compared to the previous state-of-the-art work, and implements Rainbow for higher security levels.

In [TYD+11], Tang et al. present another high-speed hardware implementation of Rainbow. The authors targeted similar functionalities for optimization as in [FG18], i.e., the Gaussian solver and the multipliers. They developed a new parallel hardware design for the Gaussian elimination and designed a novel multiplier to speed up the multiplication of three elements over a finite field. With Rainbow being broken [Beu22a], all its previously published software and hardware implementations needs to be revised and transferred to secure schemes for practical use. To address this issue, MAYO is seen as a viable alternative, showcasing improved performance results.

Simultaneous Work. During the preparation of this paper, hardware implementations of UOV [BCH+23] and MAYO [HSMR23] were published in 2023. The latter already features the updated parameter set of MAYO ($n = 66, m = 64, o = 8, k = 9, q = 16$), where m is chosen to be a multiple of 32 and q is a power of 2 to facilitate further implementation optimizations.

2 Preliminaries

The MAYO signature scheme [Beu22b] is a special modification of the UOV signature scheme [KPG99] and belongs to the field of multivariate cryptography. Herein, the main object is the multivariate quadratic map $\mathcal{P} : \mathbb{F}_q^n \to \mathbb{F}_q^m$ with m components and n variables. In more detail, it is a sequence $p_1(\mathbf{x}), \ldots, p_m(\mathbf{x})$ of m quadratic polynomials in n variables $\mathbf{x} = (x_1, \ldots, x_n)$, with coefficients in a finite field $\mathbb{F}_q$. Very abbreviated, multivariate cryptography is based on the hardness of finding a preimage $\mathbf{s} \in \mathbb{F}_q^n$ of a target vector $\mathbf{t} \in \mathbb{F}_q^m$ under a given multivariate quadratic map $\mathcal{P}$, i.e., solving a multivariate system of quadratic equations. This task is often referred to as the MQ problem. One way that allows the signer to compute a signature $\mathbf{s}$ is to install a secret trapdoor into the public map $\mathcal{P}$.

2.1 The Trapdoor in UOV

In UOV, the trapdoor information is a basis of a secret linear subspace $\mathcal{O} \subset \mathbb{F}_q^n$ of dimension $\dim(\mathcal{O}) = m$, the so-called oil space [Beu21]. The multivariate quadratic map $\mathcal{P} : \mathbb{F}_q^n \to \mathbb{F}_q^m$ is then chosen in a way that it vanishes on this oil space, i.e., $\mathcal{P}(\mathbf{o}) = \mathbf{0}_m$ for all $\mathbf{o} \in \mathcal{O}$. For the multivariate quadratic polynomials $p_i(\mathbf{x})$, which constitute the map $\mathcal{P}$ via $\mathcal{P}(\mathbf{x}) = p_1(\mathbf{x}), \ldots, p_m(\mathbf{x})$, one can define their *polar form* or *differential* as

$$p_i'(\mathbf{x}, \mathbf{y}) := p_i(\mathbf{x} + \mathbf{y}) - p_i(\mathbf{x}) - p_i(\mathbf{y}) + p_i(\mathbf{0}).$$

Since we commonly work with homogeneous polynomials, the term $p_i(\mathbf{0})$ will be omitted in the following. Similarly, we can define the polar form of $\mathcal{P}$ as

$$\mathcal{P}'(\mathbf{x}, \mathbf{y}) = p_1'(\mathbf{x}, \mathbf{y}), \ldots, p_m'(\mathbf{x}, \mathbf{y}).$$

As shown in [Beu21, Theorem 1], the map $\mathcal{P}' : \mathbb{F}_q^n \times \mathbb{F}_q^n \to \mathbb{F}_q^m$ is a symmetric and bilinear map. Furthermore, if one has knowledge of the secret oil space, it can be used to efficiently find preimages $\mathbf{x} \in \mathbb{F}_q^n$ of a given target $\mathbf{t} \in \mathbb{F}_q^m$ such that $\mathcal{P}(\mathbf{x}) = \mathbf{t}$. To do so, one can randomly pick a vinegar vector $\mathbf{v} \in \mathbb{F}_q^n$ and solve the system $P(\mathbf{v} + \mathbf{o}) = \mathbf{t}$ for $\mathbf{o} \in \mathcal{O}$. This is possible since in

$$\mathbf{t} = \mathcal{P}(\mathbf{v} + \mathbf{o}) = \mathcal{P}(\mathbf{v}) + \mathcal{P}(\mathbf{o}) + \mathcal{P}'(\mathbf{v}, \mathbf{o}) \tag{1}$$

the term $\mathcal{P}(\mathbf{v})$ is constant and $\mathcal{P}(\mathbf{o})$ vanishes, so whenever the linear map $\mathcal{P}'(\mathbf{v}, \cdot)$ is non-singular, the system has a unique solution $\mathbf{o} \in \mathcal{O}$, which can be computed efficiently. This happens with probability roughly $\frac{q-1}{q}$. If this is not the case, one can simply pick a new value for $\mathbf{v}$ and try again. Without a description of the oil space $\mathcal{O}$, the term $\mathcal{P}(\mathbf{o})$ implies that Eq. 1 constitutes a system of quadratic equations, which remains hard to solve.

Building a signature scheme directly from this setting has one big disadvantage. The oil space needs to be as large as the image space of the multivariate quadratic map $\mathcal{P}$, i.e., dim $\mathcal{O} = m$. To counter the Kipnis-Shamir attack [KS06], the parameter n needs to be sufficiently larger than m, with $n \approx 2,5m$ being used in all currently considered implementations. The parameter m itself needs to be of a certain size as well, to provide security against direct attacks or the intersection attack [Beu21]. This leads to key pairs of enormous size, which is considered the main drawback of multivariate signatures. Recently, Beullens developed the signature scheme MAYO to tackle this problem.

2.2   Description of MAYO

The essential modification is the downsizing of the dimension of the oil space to dim $\mathcal{O} = o < m$. Actually, this oil space is now too small to sample signatures, since the system $\mathcal{P}(\mathbf{v} + \mathbf{o}) = \mathbf{t}$ given in Eq. 1 consists consequently of m linear equations in o variables and is unlikely to have any solutions. Thus, the approach taken in [Beu22b] is to stretch the public key map into a larger whipped map $\mathcal{P}^* : \mathbb{F}_q^{kn} \to \mathbb{F}_q^m$, such that it accepts k input vectors $\mathbf{x} \in \mathbb{F}_q^n$. This is realized by defining

$$\mathcal{P}^*(\mathbf{x}_1, ..., \mathbf{x}_k) := \sum_{i=1}^{k} \mathbf{E}_{ii} \mathcal{P}(\mathbf{x}_i) + \sum_{1 \leq i < j \leq k} \mathbf{E}_{ij}(\mathcal{P}'(\mathbf{x}_i, \mathbf{x}_j)), \tag{2}$$

where the matrices $\mathbf{E}_{ij} \in \mathbb{F}_q^{m \times m}$ are fixed system parameters with the property that all their non-trivial linear combinations have rank m.

It is easy to see that $\mathcal{P}^*$ vanishes on the subspace $\mathcal{O}^k = \{(\mathbf{o}_1, \ldots, \mathbf{o}_k)|$ with $\mathbf{o}_i \in \mathcal{O}$ for all $i \in [k]\}$ of dimension ko. By choosing the parameters such that $ko \geq m$, the k copies of the oil space are large enough to construct preimages of a target vector $\mathbf{t} \in \mathbb{F}_q^m$ under the whipped map $\mathcal{P}^*$. In more detail, the signer randomly samples $(\mathbf{v}_1, \ldots, \mathbf{v}_k) \in \mathbb{F}_q^{kn}$, and then solves

$$\mathcal{P}^*(\mathbf{v}_1 + \mathbf{o}_1, ..., \mathbf{v}_k + \mathbf{o}_k) = \mathbf{t} \tag{3}$$

for $(\mathbf{o}_1, ...\mathbf{o}_k) \in \mathcal{O}^k$. Observe from Eq. 2 that this system remains linear in the presence of the linear emulsifier maps $\mathbf{E}_{ij} \in \mathbb{F}_q^{m \times m}$. Thus, the signer can efficiently compute a preimage $\{\mathbf{s}_i = \mathbf{v}_i + \mathbf{o}_i\}_{i \in [k]}$ of $\mathbf{t}$. Similar to UOV, the verifier just needs to check if the given $\{\mathbf{s}_i\}_{i \in [k]}$ satisfy Eq. 3.

Remark 1. Please note that both, the signer and the verifier, only locally whip up the public key map $\mathcal{P}$ to $\mathcal{P}^*$, so this modification comes with no additional cost in terms of key sizes. However, it entails additional computations during signing and verification. Furthermore, it increases signature size, since now a k-tuple of vectors in $\mathbb{F}_q^n$ constitute the signature. These negative effects are cushioned by the ability to reduce parameter sizes while maintaining the security level.

2.3   The Implemented MAYO Functionalities

The above descriptions remain rather high-level and abstract. Here we show more details about the main functionalities that need to be implemented, e.g., evaluations of (parts of) the public key map $\mathcal{P}$ via vector-matrix multiplications and finding solutions to the generated linear system via Gaussian elimination. Due to the page limit we do not present all the algorithms we implemented here, but refer to the MAYO specification [BCC+23, Section 2], specifically to the algorithms *MAYO.CompactKeyGen()*, *MAYO.ExpandSK(csk)* and *MAYO.Sign(esk,M)*. The latter will also play a major role in our security discussion in Sect. 4, so it is presented in Algorithm 1 below. The first few lines are used to sort the bit string of the expanded secret key to the respective matrices (line 1–5) and to derive a target vector $\mathbf{t} \in \mathbb{F}_q^m$ and salt (line 7–11). The main part of the signing process can be described by generating random variables (line 15–19), inserting the vinegar variables $\mathbf{v}_i$ into $\mathcal{P}$ to set up a linear system (line 21–35), solving the system (line 37–40) and adding the solution to the vinegar variables (line 42–45).

3   Hardware Design

In this section, we present the hardware design of our implementation. Our primary goal is to provide a reconfigurable hardware code that can be easily integrated with different FPGA architectures and for different security levels.

Although MAYO has keys of reduced size compared to other multivariate alternatives, it still necessities a large amount of internal memory to execute the key-generation and signing phase [Beu22b] in the order of several dozen KB. This is partially attributed to the fact that the keys are stored as seeds. During the signing the seed is expanded into large matrices, e.g., for the parameter set $(n, m, o, k, q) = (66, 64, 8, 9, 16)$, the public key of 1168B is expanded into 70KB.

For implementation and testing of our hardware design, we opted for the target board Zynq ZedBoard with the Zynq-7020 SoC [Xil23], which has 85K Logic Cells and 4.9MB Block RAM serving as an upper bound for the memory consumption.

Algorithm 1. MAYO.Sign(esk,M) [BCC+23]

Input: Expanded secret key $esk \in \mathcal{B}^{\text{esk bytes}}$, Message $M \in \mathcal{B}^*$
Output: Signature $sig \in \mathcal{B}^{\text{sig bytes}}$

1: // Decode esk
2:    $seed_{sk} \leftarrow esk[0 : \text{sk\_seed\_bytes}]$
3:    $\mathbf{O} \leftarrow \text{Decode}_O(esk[\text{sk\_seed\_bytes} : \text{sk\_seed\_bytes} + \text{O\_bytes}])$
4:    $\{\mathbf{P}_i^{(1)}\}_{i \in [m]} \leftarrow \text{Decode}_{P^{(1)}}(esk[\text{sk\_seed\_bytes} + \text{O\_bytes}] : \text{sk\_seed\_bytes} + \text{O\_bytes} + \text{P1\_bytes}])$
5:    $\{\mathbf{L}_i\}_{i \in [m]} \leftarrow \text{Decode}_L(esk[\text{sk\_seed\_bytes} + \text{O\_bytes}] + \text{P1\_bytes} : \text{esk\_bytes}])$
6:
7: // Hash message and derive salt and $\mathbf{t}$
8:    $M_{digest} \leftarrow \text{SHAKE256}(M, \text{digest\_bytes})$
9:    $\mathrm{R} \leftarrow \mathbf{0}_{R_{bytes}}$
10:   $salt \leftarrow \text{SHAKE256}(M_{digest} \parallel R \parallel seed_{sk}, \text{salt\_bytes})$
11:   $\mathbf{t} \leftarrow \text{Decode}_{vec}(m, \text{SHAKE256}(M_{digest} \parallel salt, \lceil (m \log(q))/8 \rceil))$
12:
13: // Attempt to find a preimage for $\mathbf{t}$
14: **for** ctr from 0 to 255 **do**
15:    # Derive $\mathbf{v}_i$ and r
16:    $V \leftarrow \text{SHAKE256}(M_{digest} \parallel salt \parallel seed_{sk} \parallel ctr, k \cdot v_{bytes} + \lceil ko \log(q)/8 \rceil)$
17:    **for** i from 0 to $k - 1$ **do**
18:      $\mathbf{v}_i \leftarrow \text{Decode}_{vec}(n - o, V[i \cdot v_{bytes} : (i + 1) \cdot v_{bytes}])$
19:    $\mathbf{r} \leftarrow \text{Decode}_{vec}(ko, V[k \cdot v_{bytes} : k \cdot v_{bytes} + \lceil ko \log(q)/8 \rceil])$
20:
21:    // Build linear system $Ax = y$.
22:    $\mathbf{A} \leftarrow \mathbf{0}_{m \times ko} \in \mathbb{F}_q^{m \times ko}$
23:    $\mathbf{y} \leftarrow \mathbf{t}, \ell \leftarrow 0$
24:    **for** i from 0 to $k - 1$ **do**
25:      $\mathbf{M}_i \leftarrow \mathbf{0}_{m \times o} \in \mathbb{F}_q^{m \times o}$
26:      **for** j from 0 to $m - 1$ **do**
27:        $\mathbf{M}_i[j, :] \leftarrow \mathbf{v}_i^{\mathsf{T}} \mathbf{L}_j$
28:      **for** j from $k - 1$ to i **do**
29:        $\mathbf{u} \leftarrow \{\mathbf{v}_i^{\mathsf{T}} \mathbf{P}_a^{(1)} \mathbf{v}_i\}_{a \in [m]}$ **if** $i = j$
30:        $\mathbf{u} \leftarrow \{\mathbf{v}_i^{\mathsf{T}} \mathbf{P}_a^{(1)} \mathbf{v}_j + \mathbf{v}_j^{\mathsf{T}} \mathbf{P}_a \mathbf{v}_i\}_{a \in [m]}$ **if** $i \neq j$
31:        $\mathbf{y} \leftarrow \mathbf{y} - \mathbf{E}^{\ell} \mathbf{u}$
32:        $\mathbf{A}[:, i \cdot o : (i + 1) \cdot o] \leftarrow \mathbf{A}[:, i \cdot o : (i + 1) \cdot o] + \mathbf{E}^{\ell} \mathbf{M}_j$
33:        **if** $i \neq j$ **then**
34:          $\mathbf{A}[:, j \cdot o : (j + 1) \cdot o] \leftarrow \mathbf{A}[:, j \cdot o : (j + 1) \cdot o] + \mathbf{E}^{\ell} \mathbf{M}_i$
35:        $\ell \leftarrow \ell + 1$
36:
37:    // Try to solve the system
38:    $\mathbf{x} \leftarrow \text{SampleSolution}(\mathbf{A}, \mathbf{y}, \mathbf{r})$
39:    **if** $\mathbf{x} \neq \perp$ **then**
40:      **break**
41:
42: // Finish and output the signature
43: $\mathbf{s} \leftarrow \mathbf{0}_{kn}$
44: **for** i from 0 to $k - 1$ **do**
45:    $\mathbf{s}[i \cdot n : (i + 1) \cdot n] \leftarrow (\mathbf{v}_i + \mathbf{O}\mathbf{x}[i \cdot o : (i + 1) \cdot o] \parallel \mathbf{x}[i \cdot o : (i + 1) \cdot o])$
     return $sig = \text{Decode}_{vec}(s) \parallel salt$

The majority of the system architecture of our hardware design is described in VHDL, while a few modules are implemented using Verilog.

It is essential for the architecture to be encapsulated as an Intellectual Property (IP), to ensure design reuse. We developed Keygen and Sign IPs intended for use on an end-user device in diverse applications such as the authentication of bank transactions. It remains paramount that these two IPs guarantee compliance with the device's memory constraints, especially regarding time and memory utilization. In contrast, we expect that the verification process takes place within an environment boasting ample resources such as a dedicated server, where security measures are not as critical as those required for IPs operating directly on confidential data, i.e., Keygen and Sign.

It is possible to utilize one of the IPs on the target chip. Both cores are independent and capable of coexisting on the Programmable Logic operating at respectable frequencies.

The CPU-Peripheral communications between the built IPs are handled through AXI4-FULL, AXI-Lite, and interrupts. The provided firmware takes care of the AXI transactions, thanks to the Zynq hybrid architecture. Incidentally, the design focuses on maintaining high transfer bit-rates by extensively leveraging the CPU's 32-bit architecture. Frequencies and reset signals are also controlled by the hardcore and are propagated throughout the design.

Based on the proposed MAYO pseudo-code in [BCC+23], the scheme incorporates multiple helper functions that are implemented as sub-modules and arithmetic units within the hardware IPs. This approach fulfills another significant design requirement by minimizing unused module and minimizing the utilization of Flip-Flops (FFs) and Lookup Tables (LUTs). By avoiding code duplication in hardware and organizing the design into smaller, specialized modules, each capable of performing a single functionality, the overall efficiency and modularity of the design are improved.

Considering the scheme's parameter set, the memory is divided into *three* True Dual Port BRAMs, statically partitioned into $2 \times 256\text{KB}$ BRAMs to store big matrices and large vectors like the $\mathcal{P}$ system and $\mathcal{O}^k$ subspaces, and $1 \times 4\text{KB}$ BRAM designated for small scratch buffers and sensitive information such as the seed, signature, and secret key. Among these BRAMs, only one of the big BRAMs is exposed to CPU through the AXI bus. Detailed memory management and utilization is deliberated later in Sect. 3.4. As shown in Fig. 1, most modules are connected to the BRAMs accordingly.

3.1 Hash Function

Our design employs the Keccak core [BDH+22] to generate seeds and expand the message as a first step of the signing process. For the first security level, SHAKE128 was used as an extendable-output function (XOF) based on the FIPS 202 standard [NIS23c]. We note that for higher security levels, it is necessary to adjust the parameters within the Keccak core accordingly. Nonetheless, the fundamental design of the hash sub-module remains applicable and does not require significant changes.

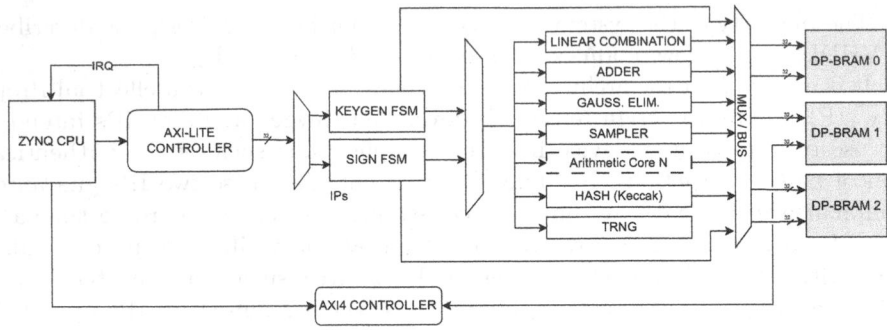

Fig. 1. Block Diagram of the MAYO Core

The Keccak implementation in [BDH+22] streams data utilizing a different format compared to the proposed MAYO hardware 32-bit format. To address this discrepancy, we developed a wrapper around the core. The reasoning behind this is that MAYO algorithm requires a hash of approximately 120KB for the key generation. The hash is eventually stored in the inner 32-bit-wide block memory.

The proposed architecture stores the input seed and output message in separate descriptor-like registers. These intermediate registers are simultaneously accessed by the hash core and BRAM. The core itself takes care of BRAM communication and indexing, simplifying the architecture's state change and its modularity.

3.2   Random Number Generator

The random number generator leverages AES-128 in CTR Cipher mode, with the flexibility to seamlessly switch to AES-256 if necessary. Tinkering with key parameters like seed and counter interval (PRNG-Based) is effortlessly accomplished within the core. To optimize FPGA Slice utilization, the core's decryption functionalities have been deprecated, given the inherent independence of CTR-mode from such operations.

3.3   Vector-Matrix Multiplication

Referring to Sect. 2.2, it is evident that matrix-vector multiplication proceeded by a $\mathbb{F}_q$ space reduction, is a frequently utilized operation throughout the algorithm. Hence, its optimization will improve the performance of our design.

Compared to the initial MAYO Software C implementation[1], the vector-matrix multiplication iterates through a matrix stored in a row-wise manner, as seen in the left side of Fig. 2, multiplying (using MULT operation) the content with a given series of coefficients and accumulating the results. Once this nested

---

[1] Note here that we refer to the first implementation of MAYO scheme by Ward Beullens in [Beu22b].

row/column loop concludes, another loop starts reducing the accumulated result through MOD operation. For instance, on an ARM Cortex-M3 with ARMv7-M instruction set, a single MULT operation with 8-bit operands takes around 2 to 3 clock cycles [ARM]. The reduction is done using the MOD operation that is usually translated to MULT and UDIV as Cortex-M3 lacks native modulo calculation. Consequently, the vector-matrix multiplication function could consume up to 6500 clock cycles, excluding the memory load and store operations.

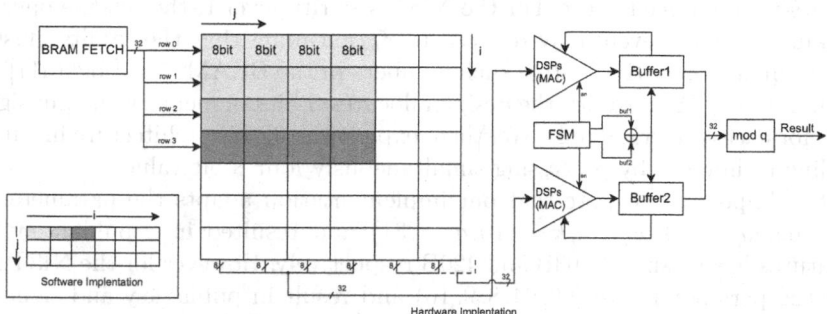

Fig. 2. Matrix-Vector multiplication architecture; on the left side the vector-matrix multiplication iterates through a matrix stored in a row-wise manner as in the software implementation. In hardware design, we reversed the indexing order, and input four bytes to each DSP which executes 4 multiplications simultaneously.

In this paper, we process the multiplications differently. Firstly, our design offers four values on each memory read operation thanks to its 32-bit wide bus and executes 4 MULT operations from one row simultaneously. Secondly, we reversed the indexing of the input matrix, as shown in Fig. 2.

As matrices are stored row-wise, each memory access returns *four* sequential cells from *one* row. Note that the matrix is stored in BRAMs and not in an FF-layered structure.

Furthermore, the input of both Digital Signal Processors (DSPs) is composed of 4 bytes. This architecture helps increase the throughput and enables the parallelization of both MULT and MOD operations.

Once the accumulated data of a block of four columns begins the final MOD operation, the subsequent block is fetched and starts with MULT operation. The first row of the Matrix **M** and the first coefficient of the Vector **V** are fetched from the BRAMs. The read port then keeps feeding the system with blocks from each consequent row noted as **M**[*rowIndex, columnBlock*], until the accumulated result is ready to be stored through a different write-only port (WriteRES).

3.4   Memory Organization

The hardware implementation of MAYO mainly relies on BRAMs to store its vectors and matrices. To ensure that both cores, namely the KeyGen and Sign, have sufficient stack-like memory, 82% (4.03 Mb) of the available on-chip BRAM is allocated for the implementation. Thereby we provide enough headroom for potential parameter modification of MAYO that might increase memory usage, e.g., when changing the security level from 1 to 5, the expanded secret key size increases from 70KB to 557KB [BCC+23].

The design aligns itself with the 32-bit ARM multi-core processor architecture and uses a 32-bit data bus width. This approach simplifies data processing within each sub-module. In the case of MAYO, the values are usually stored in a 5 bits-wide reduced space. For the NIST security level 1, the scheme operates on values that are eventually reduced to $\mathbb{F}_q$, meaning that the results must be less or equal to $q = 31$. To store such numbers in the BRAM, $5 = \lceil \log_2(31) \rceil$ bits are mandatory. As a result, the design allocates 8 bits of memory (i.e., unsigned char) for each numerical unit. We, then, exploit the 32-bit architecture in various pipeline techniques by processing simultaneously four 8-bit values.

It is important to note that our implementation adapts the parameter set $(n = 62, m = 60, o = 6, k = 10, q = 31)$ and resulted in a public key and signatures have a size of 803B and 420B respectively. However for the NIST first level the parameters are $(66, 64, 8, 9, 16)$ and result in public key and signature size of 926B and 387B.

There exist different variants of the MAYO first security level where the public key size is increased at the expense of smaller signature. Precisely, these variants increase the n which is the number of variables in the multivariate quadratic polynomials in the public key at the expense of decreasing k which is the whipping parameter. This results in bigger public key size and smaller signature size as the whipping parameters are directly connected to the calculation of the signature.

In addition, the q does not have significant impact on the sizes of the public key and the signature itself but more on the stack-like memory during the key generation and the singing processes. On the other hand, if $q = 16$, one byte can be used to pack two elements as all elements are in $\mathbf{F}_{16}$. However, this is not the case for our implementation.

It is important to note, that not *all* the allocated memory is utilized for the first security level. In fact, only roughly 70% (2.8 Mb) of the allocated BRAM of the Zynq device is filled with data. The rest is left empty, but deemed necessary due to ARM's 32-bit memory alignment rules. The content of the BRAM cells is pre-allocated and statically organized since the sizes of most elements are pre-defined. In other words, all vectors and matrices' addresses are provided in a VHDL file to create a mapping. This file is then included in all sub-modules for better consistency. To eliminate dependency on vendor-specific SDKs, a set of Python scripts takes charge of memory template generation. These scripts meticulously analyze the VHDL file, dynamically determining the required depth of BRAMs. This approach not only fosters platform independence but also enhances adaptability by allowing seamless adjustments to memory configurations based on the specifics of the VHDL code. The result is a more agile and versatile solution for memory management within the FPGA design, especially for various parameter sets.

The memory is partitioned into *three* dual port BRAMs, offering enhanced performance and flexibility. This configuration allows, for instance, efficient reading from one port while dedicating the other port for writing. Some sub-modules, such as vector-matrix multiplication, or vector addition, tend to utilize three ports for dual read and final write operations, therefore allowing better opportunities for parallelism within the sub-module.

Small buffers and vectors that are not meant to be accessed exclusively by programmable hardware are found in the smaller BRAM. The big BRAMs are indeed also shared with the CPU through AXI bus to stream input information such as the message and secret key to the MAYO core itself. Furthermore, since the key generation and the signing are not designed to operate synchronously but rather consecutively, multiple arrays and vector spaces overlap if one of their lifetimes expires. This approach helps the system avoid unnecessary increases in memory fingerprints.

3.5   Gaussian Elimination

Solving a System of Linear Equations (SLE) is evidently one of the primordial computations for the MAYO algorithm to generate a valid message signature as explained in Sect. 2.2. Several publications deal with hardware implementation of Gaussian elimination for various cryptographic applications, primarily focusing on $\mathbb{F}_2$. Among them, GSMITH [REBG11] has been widely recognized for efficiently handling $\mathbb{F}_{2^k}$ equations. Unfortunately, GSMITH's architecture only conforms with small and medium-sized matrices, whereas MAYO's SLE $m \times m$ shaped matrix is larger. This quadratic shape depends on the NIST security level. Not only would the proposed GSMITH architecture utilize costly resources, but also hinder the overall architecture's performance and increase the needed Look-up Tables (LUTs) when targeting $\mathbb{F}_{31}$. GSMITH describes, in fact, a systolic network composed of various types of tiny processors capable of specific Gaussian steps and propagating its values. Yet, since the source code was not open-sourced, we had to redesign GSMITH. The final architecture, however, fails to meet our resource requirements, depleting the Zynq's FFs and LUTs, due to the internal registers required in each GSMITH processor and its interconnection with the proposed BRAM. When considering the other needed arithmetic cores, we concluded it was unfeasible to fit GSMITH for the first security level.

To overcome this issue, we developed a state machine that fetches values directly from BRAM as the matrix is stored externally rather than within the core's FFs. Additionally, it was mandatory to allocate sufficient memory to accumulate every cell in the matrix. In other words, during the first step of the Gaussian elimination, multiplying rows with scalars may surpass the existing 8-bit limit. Hence, the targeted matrix is initially unpacked into 16-bit wide values with added padding, meaning that every row in the BRAM now contains two instead of four values.

Moreover, to speed up the mod-inverse, which calculates the needed value to transform the pivot element into 1 throughout the first scale step, prefilled Read-Only Memory (ROM) with end results of this operation is utilized instead of performing the actual calculations on run-time. These optimizations contribute to the overall effectiveness of the MAYO core in solving an SLE. Although GSMITH might offer superior performance, this core certainly consumes less memory resources. Our architecture is theoretically compatible with other configuration sets, with a marginal difference in resource utilization. For instance, n, m, o control the SLE size which should affect BRAM consumption, while q modifies the LUT consumption, cell width, and the unpacking operation. The solver should support up to $\mathbb{F}_{2^8}$ and for smaller q values, unpacking the matrix might become unnecessary, as the result could still fit inside the original 8-bit vector.

3.6   Optimizations and Firmware

Besides resource utilization, the goal of our design is to achieve a reasonable time area trade-off. Therefore, we designed the sub-modules in a way that they share the same access to one of the BRAM ports. Nevertheless, the usage of each port, whether for reading, writing, or both differs. The core responsible for the vectors addition, for example, features multiple modes depending on the location of the input vectors in different BRAMs. It efficiently utilizes all available ports to leverage data throughput and synchronize the addition process accordingly.

Another notable design optimization lies in the polynomial reduction sub-module where multiple arrays of scratch buffers are used to minimize memory interactions. Hence, the core is provided only with new values which are stored as final results.

Various functionalities of MAYO are divided into separate modules, each described individually. That said, each module still has access to header-like files that declare the security level parameters, the memory space allocations, utility functions required to fetch offsets or even ROM secret keys specifically intended for non-debugging purposes. Numerous bit vectors are built upon these constants. The code's style guide itself heavily discourages simple number inclusion, but instead, it is expected to utilize these pre-defined macro-like lines to improve code readability and ensure that the overall architecture can fit different configuration sets, i.e., different security levels.

In addition to the hardware implementation, the utilization of the MAYO core necessitates the development of accompanying firmware. This firmware serves as the interface between the hardware core and the software MAYO application, setting AXI/AXI-Lite transactions up. The existing C Bit-fields feature Control and Status Registers that can enable debug mode, interrupts, and supply the ARM CPU with the end of executions information besides the interrupt signal.

4 Mitigation of Physical Attack Vectors in MAYO

In Sect. 2.2, we stated that the secret key is solely given by the secret linear oil space O. Thus, an attacker is able to forge signatures, as soon as she recovered O. Even more, the description of the reconciliation attack in [Beu22b, Section 4.1] shows that it is enough to know a single vector $o_1 \in O$, to recover the remaining space O in polynomial time, since the first vector o_1 implies m linear equations via $\mathcal{P}'(o_1, o_2)$ on the entries of o_2. Consequently, we need to solve m quadratic equations in $n - m - o$ variables. Since in MAYO $n < m + o$ holds, the remaining basis vectors of O can be obtained just by solving linear equations.

Moreover, the randomly generated vinegar variables can also be used to recover the secret key. Recall, that a given MAYO signature has the form $s = (s_1, \ldots, s_k) = (v_1 + o_1, \ldots, v_k + o_k)$, so the knowledge of one of the v_i's together with the corresponding s_i leads the attacker to a vector of the oil space and thus, to the full secret key.

In the following, we show different scenarios where the attacker uses fault injection or side-channel attacks to reveal either a vinegar or an oil vector.

4.1 Fault Injection

The attacks suggested in the following are first-order fault injection attacks and assume an attacker to be able to skip one specific instruction during the signing process. The resulting faulted signature is used to recover the secret key.

Skip Sampling of Vinegar Values (Re-using). The main idea here is to insert an instruction skip during the sampling of the vinegar variables. In Algorithm 1, this corresponds to a jump over line 18, for one (or more) of the $i \in 1, \ldots, k$. This fault injection attack forces the same vinegar variable $v_i \in \mathbb{F}_q^n$ to be used for two consecutive signatures of different messages m and m'. We subtract the obtained correct (not faulted) signature s and the faulted signature s' and receive $s - s' = (s_1 - s'_1, \ldots, s_k - s'_k)$. Observe that for the entry i, where $v_i = v'_i$ holds, we have

$$s_i - s'_i = v_i + o_i - v'_i - o'_i = o_i - o'_i.$$

Since O forms a subspace, we know $o_i - o'_i \in O$ and thus, we found a vector in the secret subspace.

It has already been shown that UOV [KPG99] and Rainbow [DS05] are vulnerable to this kind of attack [AKKM22], so this can be seen as an extension of the approach to MAYO, which also works with vinegar and oil variables. Note, that the attack leads to valid signatures, and therefore, cannot be mitigated by a signature check.

Implemented Countermeasure. To mitigate this attack we shuffle the vinegar variables $v_i \in \mathbb{F}_q^n$ at the end of the signing algorithm. This is more secure than zeroing the respective variables since $v_i = 0$ could also lead to the leakage of oil variables in the next signing procedure. Thus, it is advisable to permute the entries of the used variables instead, rendering them unknown to an attacker and ensuring $v_i \neq v_i'$.

Skip Addition of Oil Values. An attack vector that follows a similar reasoning, is to skip the addition of the oil variable o_i at the end of the signing process (see line 45 in Algorithm 1) for one (or more) $i \in 1, \ldots, k$. If the fault is injected correctly, this modifies the resulting signature to $s' = (v_1+o_1, \ldots, v_i, \ldots, v_k+o_k)$. First, we see that s' is not a valid signature anymore, since $\mathcal{P}(s') \neq t$ with very high probability. Let s be the valid signature corresponding to the same message, then we can compute

$$s_i - s_i' = v_i + o_i - v_i' = o_i \in O.$$

Note that the signing is deterministic and the randomness that is used to generate the vinegar variable depends solely on the given message, which we have chosen to be identical. Therefore, $v_i = v_i'$. Again, we found a vector of the secret oilspace $o_i \in O$ and recover the remaining space with the reconciliation attack in negligible time.

Implemented Countermeasure. To avoid this attack we need to guarantee, that the vinegar and oil variables are really added, and neither of them are part of the signature by skipping their addition or the assignment of their values. Since the faulted signature is not valid anymore, one option is to verify the generated signature. However, this comes with a considerable performance overhead. Therefore, we rather chose to implement a check, that monitors if the entries of the computed signature s_i are different from the earlier generated vinegar variables v_i.

4.2 Side Channel Analysis

In this section, we focus on the leakage of the vector-matrix multiplication function. This function is called multiple times during key generation, secret key expansion and signing. It multiplies a secret vector by a known matrix (part of the public key), as shown in line 29 and 30 of Algorithm 1, as well as in line 16 of the algorithm MAYO.CompactKeyGen() and in line 17 of MAYO:ExpandSK(csk), for which we refer to [BCC+23, Section 2.1.5]. In MAYO, or more general, in UOV-based signature schemes, this is repeated for a considerable amount of public key matrices $P_i^{(1)}$.

An attacker is able to measure the power traces of the multiplication $(v_i)_j \cdot (P_a^{(1)})_{j,\cdot}$ for several $a \in [m]$, perform a profiling or a correlation attack, and predict the value $(v_i)_j$ which is supposed to remain unknown. This attack strategy was demonstrated in [ACK+23] ,where the authors attack an implementation of UOV, that incorporates similar operations as the one mentioned above. Again, the recovered values of v_i lead to efficient key recovery.

Implemented Countermeasure. In order to execute the SCA successfully, the attacker needs to know both, the value of the cofactor in $P_a^{(1)}$ and at which point in time the target $(v_i)_j$ is multiplied with this value. Thus, our approach to mitigate this attack, is to rearrange the order in which the multiplications are executed. In previous implementations optimized for efficiency a vinegar variable $(v_i)_j$ is picked and multiplied consecutively to the corresponding entry in all $P_a^{(1)}$ for $a \in \{1, \ldots, m\}$. This way, there is a certain interval in the power trace, that contains m multiplications of the sensitive value $(v_i)_j$ with public values. We treat the $P_a^{(1)}$ individually, and thus, the entry $(v_i)_j$ is only multiplied with $(P_a^{(1)})_j$. before we move on to the next multiplication $(v_i)_{j+1} \cdot (P_a^{(1)})_{j+1,\cdot}$. Consequently, on a 32-bit architecture, where at least 4 field elements are treated at once (even 8 if we move to the updated parameters $q = 16$), this massively increases the failure probability of a correlation attack, since the power trace is now related to 4 different secret field elements $((v_i)_j, (v_i)_{j+1}, (v_i)_{j+2}, (v_i)_{j+3})$ at once, and not only to the same secret element $(v_i)_j$ as previously. However, more advanced analysis methods that employ machine learning for the selection of point of interest might still pose a threat to this approach. This could require a vast amount of profiling traces and we leave a concrete analysis thereof as future work.

5 Results, Comparison, and Discussion

In Table 1, we show the resource consumption of the whole design and submodules for the first security level defined by the NIST PQC standardization process [NIS23b]. The parameters defining MAYO are q (the size of the finite field), n (the number of variables in the multivariate quadratic polynomials in the public key), m (the number of multivariate quadratic polynomials in the public key), o (the dimension of the oil space), and k (the whipping parameter, satisfying $ko \geq m$). For our results, these parameters are set to $q = 31$, $n = 62$, $m = 60$, $o = 6$, and $k = 10$.

Our design stands out as the most optimized among the current implementations of multivariate schemes concerning resource utilization. The proposed design effectively utilizes roughly 31% of the total logic resources available on the Zynq board, specifically accounting for 13K Flip-Flops (FFs) and 21K Look-Up Tables (LUTs). These resources are distributed among different sub-modules.

The dominance of the Keccak core is evident as it commands the majority of FPGA slices, enveloping nearly third of the entire design. This dominance arises from its expansive internal buffer and its' interwoven XOR network, crucial for generating the output hash. Additionally, the RNG Core, integrating AES-128, significantly contributes to resource consumption. Remarkably, the combined impact of these cores results in approximately 40% (9K LUTs) of the design's overall slice usage, underscoring the notion that the MAYO core in isolation represents a minimalist design.

Our Gaussian elimination proves an improvement in the memory utilization as compared to the previous work [REBG11]. In [REBG11], the FPGA implementation on Xilinx Spartan-3 XC3S1500 (300 MHz) consumes 7,384 and 2,574 LUTs and FFs, respectively, for a number of equations equal to 50. In our implementation on a Zynq Z-7020 (100MHz), for a number of equations equal to 60, the consumption in LUTs and FFs is 1,822 and 413, respectively.

Table 1. Resource utilization of our hardware design on Zynq 7020 at a frequency of 100 MHz.

	Resource Utilization		
Submodules	LUTs	FFs	DSP
Keccak (Hash)	6759	4453	0
RNG	2354	3208	0
Vector-Matrix multiplication	1035	528	8
Oil Space Sampling	176	289	0
Gaussian Elimination	1822	413	3
Vector Addition	485	300	0
Vector Negation	176	93	0
Vinegar Sampling	245/686*	277/614*	0
BRAMs Port management	448	0	0
FSM Signing	2871	1057	0
Combined Architectures	21000	13005	11

* Secure implementation

Table 2. Comparison of our results with related work

Implementation	Platform	LUT	FF	DSP	BR
Our	Z-7020 @ 100MHz	21,000	13,005	11	129
[HSMR23]	KC705 @ 100MHz	91,266	42,113	2	45
[HSMR23]	AU280 @ 225MHz	89,014	42,066	2	45
[BCH+23]	Artix-7 @ 90.8MHz	32,422	23,262	2	48

Implementation	Platform	Key Generation cylcles	Signing cycles
Our	Z-7020 @ 100MHz	996K	2,867K
[HSMR23]	KC705 @ 100MHz	12K	42K
[BCH+23]	Artix-7 @ 90.8MHz	11,072K	843K

We present in Table 1 the resource utilization of our implementation. While the implementation by [HSMR23] is highly optimized for efficiency, our implementation shows better performance in the direction of LUT and FF usage, as showed in Table 2. We use 4.3× less LUTs and 3.2× less FFs while our BRAM utilization is 2.8× more, we believe that this is due to the parameter set we follow specifically the choice of q = 31. This also has a significant impact on the execution time, since we could not rely on optimized modules, but had to build some of them from scratch like the method for solving SLEs (see Sect. 3.5 for more details). Tuning our implementation to the new parameter set so that each two elements can be packed in one byte for example will result in reducing considerably the BRs utilization and execution time.

When compared to the implementation from [BCH+23] corresponding to a hardware implementation of the variant of ov-Ip with $n = 112$, $m = 44$, and F_{256}, our implementation shows less consumption of LUTs. This is mainly due to the fact that their implementation LUTs utilization increases with higher q [BCH+23]. For example, for F_{256}, the LUT is 8-in-8-out and requires 40 LUTs in the synthesis, while for F_{16}, it requires 2 LUTs [BCH+23]. Our results show reduced LUTs and FFs which lead to faster logic operations, potentially resulting in improved clock speeds and reduced latency, especially for the key generation. The integration of 8 DSPs for vector-matrix multiplication shows potential for heightened parallel processing capabilities within the system architecture.

Our primary goal revolved around achieving an efficient usage of memory utilization and taking a first step towards physical security. Furthermore, our parameters choice proved the adaptability of the MAYO scheme for deployment in resource-constrained devices *even* in case the field is extended to $q = 31$ instead of 16. In fact, our implementation offers a commendable trade-off, showcasing an adept combination of efficient resource utilization and operational speed. Furthermore, the implementation of the proposed countermeasures had hardly any impact on resource utilization as shown in Table 1. The increase in clock cycles that originates from the countermeasures lies in the order of hundreds and can be disregarded when considering the overall costs.

6 Conclusion

The implementation of multivariate signature schemes has faced challenges due to their large key sizes, impeding them from deployment on resource-constrained embedded devices. In response, the MAYO scheme was developed as a new modification of the mature UOV signature scheme. MAYO has successfully addressed the issue of large key sizes and can now be seen as one of the prominent candidates of NIST's call for additional digital signatures in regard of performance, key, and signature size. In this paper, we introduced a reconfigurable hardware implementation of MAYO, optimized to reduce the memory consumption during the key generation and the signing processes. Our implementation serves as evidence of MAYO's practicality for real-world deployment especially when deployed in resource-constraints devices. In fact, our design highlights the necessity of time area trade off. Moreover, we discussed a set of new security challenges brought by the deployment of MAYO in embedded systems, particularly in terms of defending against fault injection and side-channel attacks and suggest lightweight countermeasures.

Acknowledgments. The authors acknowledge the financial support by the Federal Ministry of Education and Research of Germany in the programme of the project Full Lifecycle Post-Quantum PKI - FLOQI (ID 16KIS1074). Furthermore, this work was funded by the Deutsche Forschungsgemeinschaft (DFG, German Research Foundation) - project number 505500359. Moreover, we would like to thank Amir Moradi for his valuable input which greatly improved the paper.

References

[ACK+23] Aulbach, T., Campos, F., Krämer, J., Samardjiska, S., Stöttinger, M.: Separating oil and vinegar with a single trace: side-channel assisted Kipnis-Shamir attack on UOV. IACR Trans. Cryptogr. Hardw. Embed. Syst. 221–245 (2023)

[AKKM22] Aulbach, T., Kovats, T., Krämer, J., Marzougui, S.: Recovering rainbow's secret key with a first-order fault attack. In: Batina, L., Daemen, J. (eds.) AFRICACRYPT 2022. LNCS, vol. 13503, pp. 348–368. Springer, Cham (2022). https://doi.org/10.1007/978-3-031-17433-9_15

[ARM] ARM. Armv7-m architecture reference manual. https://developer.arm.com/documentation/ddi0403/d/Application-Level-Architecture/The-ARMv7-M-Instruction-Set

[BCC+23] Beullens, W., Campos, F., Celi, S., Hess, B., Kannwischer, M.: MAYO-algorithm specifications. MAYO team (2023). https://pqmayo.org/assets/specs/mayo.pdf

[BCH+23] Beullens, W., et al.: Modern Parameters and Implementations. Cryptology ePrint Archive (2023)

[BDH+22] Bertoni, G., Daemen, J., Hoffert, S., Peeters, M., Van Assche, G., Van Keer, R.: Keccak open-source hardware implementation (2022). https://keccak.team/index.html

[Beu21] Beullens, W.: Improved cryptanalysis of UOV and Rainbow. In: Canteaut, A., Standaert, F.X. (eds.) EUROCRYPT 2021. LNCS, vol. 12696, pp. 348–373. Springer, Cham (2021). https://doi.org/10.1007/978-3-030-77870-5_13

[Beu22a] Beullens, W.: Breaking rainbow takes a weekend on a laptop. In: Dodis, Y., Shrimpton, T. (eds.) CRYPTO 2022. LNCS, vol. 13508, pp. 464–479. Springer, Cham (2022). https://doi.org/10.1007/978-3-031-15979-4_16

[Beu22b] Beullens, W.: MAYO: practical post-quantum signatures from oil-and-vinegar maps. In: Altawy, R., Hülsing, A. (eds.) SAC 2021. LNCS, vol. 13203, pp. 355–376. Springer, Cham (2022). https://doi.org/10.1007/978-3-030-99277-4_17

[DS05] Ding, J., Schmidt, D.: Rainbow, a new multivariate polynomial signature scheme. In: Ioannidis, J., Keromytis, A., Yung, M. (eds.) ACNS 2005. LNCS, vol. 3531, pp. 164–175. Springer, Heidelberg (2005). https://doi.org/10.1007/11496137_12

[FG18] Ferozpuri, A., Gaj, K.: High-speed FPGA implementation of the NIST round 1 rainbow signature scheme. In: 2018 International Conference on ReConFigurable Computing and FPGAs (ReConFig), pp. 1–8 (2018)

[HSMR23] Hirner, F., Streibl, M., Mert, A.C., Roy, S.S.: A hardware implementation of mayo signature scheme. IACR Cryptology ePrint Archive 2023:1267 (2023)

[HZ18] Yi, H., Nie, Z.: High-speed hardware architecture for implementations of multivariate signature generations on FPGAs. EURASIP J. Wirel. Commun. Netw. 1687–1499 (2018)

[KPG99] Kipnis, A., Patarin, J., Goubin, L.: Unbalanced oil and vinegar signature schemes. In: Stern, J. (ed.) EUROCRYPT 1999. LNCS, vol. 1592, pp. 206–222. Springer, Heidelberg (1999). https://doi.org/10.1007/3-540-48910-X_15

[KS06] Kipnis, A., Shamir, A.: Cryptanalysis of the oil and vinegar signature scheme. In: Krawczyk, H. (ed.) CRYPTO 1998. LNCS, vol. 1462, pp. 257–266. Springer, Heidelberg (2006). https://doi.org/10.1007/BFb0055733

[NIS23a] NIST. NIST post-quantum cryptography standardization (2023). https://csrc.nist.gov/Projects/post-quantum-cryptography/workshops-and-timeline

[NIS23b] NIST. NIST post-quantum cryptography standardization: evaluation criteria (2023). https://csrc.nist.gov/projects/post-quantum-cryptography/post-quantum-cryptography-standardization/evaluation-criteria/security-(evaluation-criteria)

[NIS23c] NIST. SHA-3 standard: permutation-based hash and extendable-output functions (2023). https://csrc.nist.gov/publications/detail/fips/202/final

[PQD23] PQDB post-quantum data base (2023). https://www.pqdb.info/

[REBG11] Rupp, A., Eisenbarth, T., Bogdanov, A., Grieb, O.: Hardware SLE solvers: efficient building blocks for cryptographic and cryptanalytic applications. Integration **44**(4), 290–304 (2011)

[TYD+11] Tang, S., Yi, H., Ding, J., Chen, H., Chen, G.: High-speed hardware implementation of rainbow signature on FPGAs. In: Yang, B.Y. (ed.) PQCrypto 2011. LNCS, vol. 7071, pp. 228–243. Springer, Heidelberg (2011). https://doi.org/10.1007/978-3-642-25405-5_15

[Xil23] AMD Xilinx. Zynq-7000 SoCs with Hardware and Software Programmability (2023). https://www.xilinx.com/products/silicon-devices/soc/zynq-7000.html

[XL21] Xing, Y., Li, S.: A compact hardware implementation of CCA-secure key exchange mechanism CRYSTALS-KYBER on FPGA. IACR Trans. Cryptogr. Hardw. Embed. Syst. **2021**(2), 328–356 (2021)

[ZZW+21] Zhao, C., et al.: A compact and high-performance hardware architecture for CRYSTALS-Dilithium. IACR Trans. Cryptogr. Hardw. Embed. Syst. **2022**(1), 270–295 (2021)

Combining Loop Shuffling and Code PolyMorphism for Enhanced AES Side-Channel Security

Nicolas Belleville[1]($\boxtimes$) and Loïc Masure[2]

[1] Univ. Grenoble Alpes, CEA, List, F-38000 Grenoble, France, 17 avenue des martyrs, 38054 Grenoble CEDEX 9, France
nicolas.belleville@cea.fr
[2] LIRMM, Univ. Montpellier, CNRS, Montpellier, France
loic.masure@lirmm.fr

Abstract. Combining countermeasures against side-channel attacks represents a promising approach to defend against powerful attackers. Existing works on this topic show that the hope for a significant increase of security is sometimes fulfilled, although not always. In this paper, we consider the combination of two hiding countermeasures, namely loop shuffling and code polymorphism. We study the combination on a custom implementation of AES, tailored to ease shuffling while providing a balance between performance and RAM usage. Our experimental study exploits real-world traces and simulated noiseless traces. On real-world traces, we show that code polymorphism effectively mitigates leakage stemming from the permutation variable employed for loop shuffling, and that both countermeasures resist surprisingly well to a deep learning attack that showed great success against code polymorphism in a former work. On simulated traces, we show that combining the countermeasures complicates both a simple CPA and a deep learning attack. As is, the combination of these countermeasures seems beneficial and should be particularly relevant in any context where loop shuffling benefits vanish due to the leakage of its permutation variables.

Keywords: side-channel attacks · countermeasures · hiding · loop shuffling · code polymorphism · aes · deep learning

1 Introduction

Side-channel attacks threaten the security of embedded systems and IoT devices. In particular, they are famous for how easily they break unprotected cryptography implementations. As the confidentiality of cryptographic keys is critical for the whole security of such systems, there is a strong need for countermeasures.

Two classes of countermeasures have emerged from this need: masking countermeasures and hiding countermeasures [19]. Masking countermeasures rely on the idea of secret-sharing, applied to all sensitive variables manipulated by the

© The Author(s), under exclusive license to Springer Nature Switzerland AG 2024
R. Wacquez and N. Homma (Eds.): COSADE 2024, LNCS 14595, pp. 260–280, 2024.
https://doi.org/10.1007/978-3-031-57543-3_14

implementation. Hiding countermeasures leverage various techniques in order to lower the signal-to-noise ratio, but usually do not involve a modification of variables manipulated by the implementation. Despite the large number of countermeasures developed along the years, side-channel analysis remains an active area of research.

While many hiding countermeasures have been explored and attacked, they have been studied mostly in isolation: the interest of their combination in general is still an open question. We notice in particular that code polymorphism and loop shuffling seem complementary from a theoretical point of view, as they operate on different scales: loop shuffling shuffles large sequences of instructions without modifying them, while code polymorphism acts by inserting, replacing, and shuffling instructions without being able to shuffle very large sequences. Moreover, attacks against loop shuffling frequently exploit leakage of the permutation used, and we believe that code polymorphism could help hiding this leakage. In this paper, we ask whether these remarks translate into a security gain in practice, i.e., whether code polymorphism and loop shuffling actually benefit from each other. As such, we propose to combine both countermeasures to protect an AES implementation.

Contributions

- We study this combination on a custom implementation of AES that features an execution-time faster than by-the-book 8-bit implementations while having a lower memory usage than T-table implementations.
- We pinpoint the interest of having dynamic code transformations in order to make loop iterations length less consistent, and propose the use of dynamic variants in code polymorphism as a response.
- We show that code polymorphism effectively hides the leakage of loop shuffling parameters.
- We consider both real-world traces as well as simulated noiseless traces to study the countermeasures' response to CPA and to a deep learning attack, and notice (1) how both countermeasures resist surprisingly well to the deep learning attack in the real-world setting, either alone or combined, (2) how combining the countermeasures increases the difficulty of both the CPA and the deep learning attack in the simulation setting.
- We release the dataset used for deep learning along with our paper, to allow future work to continue comparing the security of the different implementations considered.

2   Background and Related Work

2.1   Loop Shuffling

Loop shuffling consists in executing independent loop iterations in a random order. Different strategies can be used for this purpose: (1) using a random start index [28], (2) performing a random walk [23], (3) generating a random permutation [28].

In the random start index strategy, one random number is drawn and the loop iterations are executed starting from this number. The ith iteration index is given by $i + s$ mod b, where s is the random start index and b is the loop bound. This strategy has a low randomness cost, at the price of a low number of achievable permutations. For a loop iterating 2^k times, this strategy only gives 2^k variants.

The random walk strategy extends the random start index strategy by using a more complex formula for iterating, while still using few random numbers. For instance, a random increment can be drawn as long as it is co-prime with the number of loop iterations. The ith iteration index is given by $i \cdot c + s$ mod b, where c is the random increment, s is the random start index and b is the loop bound. This strategy keeps a low randomness cost, while increasing notably the number of achievable permutations. For a loop iterating 2^k times, this strategy gives $2^k \cdot 2^{(k-1)}$ variants, as all odd numbers can be used as increments.

Finally, the random permutation strategy consists in drawing a random permutation among all possible ones, e.g. using Fisher-Yates algorithm. While this strategy is costly in terms of randomness in general, it is the only one that reaches the maximum number of variants. For a loop iterating 2^k times, this strategy gives $2^k!$ variants.

2.2 Code Polymorphism

Code polymorphism consists in varying the sensitive code from one execution to another. Its effectiveness relies on several principles: (1) introduce temporal desynchronisation between the attacker's traces, (2) modify the leakage profile, (3) increase noise.

The countermeasure was first proposed by Amarilli et al. [5], using a program graph that guides a dynamic rewriting process to shuffle independent operations. In the same vein, Luo et al. [17] proposed later on a method to detect the independence between statements and to automatically shuffle them, this time without any rewriting. Malagón et al. [18] proposed to generate several versions of a same function using slightly varying compiler optimisation options, and to randomly choose between them at runtime. Meanwhile, Agosta et al. [3] proposed the use of dynamic code morphing engine to make the code vary using various code transformations. Couroussé et al. [9,14] later on followed a similar idea, using dynamic code generators. Agosta et al. [4] also proposed the use of switch statements generated statically in the code and controlled dynamically by random variables in order to avoid any dynamic code modification. Finally, Antognazza et al. [6] proposed a hardware approach to morph the code without any software change and with a smaller execution time overhead.

In this paper, we follow and extend the method proposed by Belleville et al. [9], based on dynamic code generation, that we present in more details below. Figure 1 presents the application flow of the countermeasure when using this approach. The countermeasure is automatically applied at compilation time on

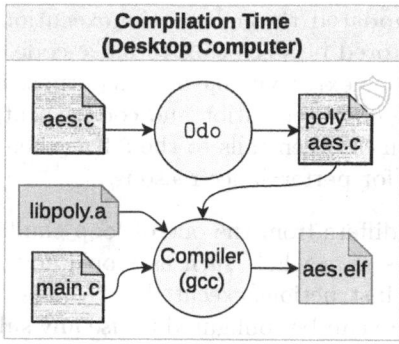 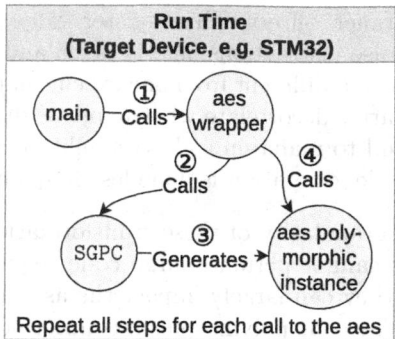

Fig. 1. Compilation flow and runtime code execution for a polymorphic AES, similar to [9]. Odo is a compiler that automatically applies code polymorphism. SGPC is a runtime generator of polymorphic code.

any function labelled as sensitive by the developer. The source-to-source compiler Odo is in charge of transforming the code for this purpose. Odo replaces any labelled function by a wrapper and a specialized generator of polymorphic code (SGPC), whose behaviour will be explained later on. Then, the C file obtained is built along with a library (libpoly.a) using any standard compiler into an elf file. At run time, the wrapper intercepts any call to the labelled function. The wrapper calls the SGPC to generate the new code in memory, and then calls the generated code (a.k.a. the **polymorphic instance**). At every call, the **polymorphic instance** is different from one another as the SGPC generates the code applying various code transformations guided by randomness. The SGPC has inherent knowledge of a reference assembly code, and generates variants of that code. It supports the following code transformations:

- *Random register permutation*: the SGPC draws a random permutation among the general purpose registers (except registers used for argument passing). For instance, the SGPC could emit an instruction using R11 instead of R5. The change is global for all instructions to preserve the program semantics.
- *Instruction shuffling*: the SGPC randomly chooses the order of instructions that are independent of each other.
- *Semantic variants*: for some instructions, the SGPC knows several semantically equivalent sequences of instructions. The SGPC randomly chooses one of them. As an example, a xor can be replaced by a sequence of an **and**, an **or**, and a xor: $a \oplus b = (a \wedge b) \oplus (a \vee b)$.
- *Noise instructions*: the SGPC inserts a random number of useless instructions in between useful instructions. The noise instructions are randomly chosen among various frequently-used instructions.
- *Dynamic noise*: the SGPC sometimes inserts a sequence of contiguous noise instructions preceded by a branch instruction that will randomly jump inside the sequence during the execution of the polymorphic instance. A register is reserved to hold random data that is used at runtime to determine the

branch offsets. This register value is updated throughout the execution by noise instructions, and is saved and restored between calls to make code execution different from one execution to the next. Dynamic noise's purpose is to partly decorrelate what happens during code generation and code execution, and to maintain code variability even in between calls to the SGPC when the code generation is done less frequently for performance reasons.

The granularity of these transformations differs from the one of loop shuffling: they cannot permute large code sequences as a whole such as loop iterations, but they can largely impact the assembly instructions executed.

The code polymorphism countermeasure can be configured to use any subset of these code transformations, and some code transformations have an unlimited number of possible configurations: for noise instructions, the probability distribution used to decide how many noise instructions to insert can be tuned. For the rest of this paper, we will consider all transformations are enabled and code is regenerated before every execution. Also, we will use this probability law to determine how many noise instructions are inserted in between useful instructions:

$$P[X = 0] = \frac{7}{8} + \frac{1}{64}$$

$$\forall i \in [1, 7], P[X = i] = \frac{1}{64}$$

2.3   Attacks Against Loop Shuffling and Code Polymorphism

To the best of our knowledge, most attacks against shuffling rely on template attacks [13,27,28], although some recent work uses neural networks [22]. The proposed attacks either sequentially exploit leakages from the permutation and the secret-related intermediate variables, or jointly exploit their leakages.

Attacks against code-polymorphism attempt to limit the effects of desynchronization through various ways: (1) pattern extraction using correlation to extract SBox related code [2], (2) re-alignment techniques combined with CPA or with template attacks [21], and (3) use of shift-invariant deep neural networks like convolutional neural networks [21]. The latter deep neural network approach stands out for its efficiency: once trained, about 10–20 traces were enough to find all key bytes on the considered AES implementation on a low-noise platform, while several hundreds of thousands of traces were needed with re-aligned CPA or template attacks. From this work, we additionally note that the trace amplitude changes when executing code in flash (before polymorphic instance) and in RAM (the polymorphic instances). It is probable that clear patterns visible during polymorphic instance execution are due to data flash access to the SBox [20, Fig. 7.10, p. 121]. They are the only flash accesses performed as instruction fetch loads the polymorphic instance code from RAM. Such flaw could have been implicitly leveraged by the trained model.

3 Countermeasures Combination

Approaches combining countermeasures share a common goal, and so does our paper: find whether combining the countermeasures improves significantly security. Rivain et al. first showed that masking and shuffling could be advantageously combined [25]. This idea was extended by Azouaoui et al. that compared the various possibilities of shuffling enabled by higher-order masking, and showed as a result that the security gain from shuffling could be amplified [7]. With affine masking, Fumaroli et al. combined multiplicative masking and Boolean masking and suggested this combination leads to much improved resistance to higher-order attacks [15]. Affine masking was latter on combined with shuffling [10,11]. Finally, Udvarhelyi et al. examined the combination of rekeying with masking and shuffling for ISAP cipher and showed that such combination hardly leads to any significant security improvement on low noise platforms [27].

4 Approach

Our main idea is to combine loop shuffling with code polymorphism in order to strengthen security. This approach builds onto the difference between both countermeasures. On the one hand, code polymorphism introduces desynchronization and alters leakage at instruction level. On the other hand, it is not able to reorder large code blocks such as loop iterations, while loop shuffling enables this possibility. As a result, the desynchronization obtained from the combination of both countermeasures is expected be much stronger. In addition, the fine-grain effect provided by code-polymorphism should prevent any easy recovering of loop shuffling parameters. For this study, we choose AES as a benchmark, and develop a custom implementation for this purpose.

4.1 AES Implementation

We propose in this paper an AES implementation with less memory usage than T-tables implementations, while being faster than an 8bits by-the-book implementation. Our AES implementation exploits the following principles:

- Round functions are combined to avoid useless (and leaky) reads and writes of the state bytes in memory.
- The AES state is duplicated: during each round, we have different arrays for input state and output state, which enables the combination of all round functions, shiftRows included.
- We leverage parallelism as much as possible by doing computations in 32-bit words for mixColumns and addRoundKey.
- The key schedule is precomputed.
- SBox is stored in RAM: (1) RAM access are faster than flash accesses, (2) flash memory accesses induce clearly visible leakage when executing polymorphic instances as code is stored in RAM, (3) memory usage of our AES implementation is limited and having the SBox in RAM is not prohibitive.

The AES function first calls addRoundKey, that is performed word by word, then calls the combined round function SR_SB_MC_ARK, presented in Listing 1, once for each round, except for the last round where a similar function is called, without the mixColumns steps. The combined round function first performs the shiftRows and subBytes on state bytes, then packs all bytes from a column into a 32-bit word, and performs mixColumns and addRoundKey on 32-bit words.

4.2 Loop Shuffling

The loop shuffling countermeasure consists in executing loop iterations in a random order. As explained in Sect. 2.1, loop shuffling can be implemented through the use of random start index, random walks, or random permutations. The random permutations strategy gives the largest amount of possibilities, at the cost of being more costly to implement in general.

As we iterate on columns, the opportunities of loop shuffling are reduced compared to a loop iterating on all bytes of the state. In order to maximise as much as possible the countermeasure impact, despite the low number of iterations, we decided to use a random permutation strategy, and to randomly shuffle as well the memory accesses and computations done for each of the 4 bytes used within the loop. This shuffles the use of the 4 bytes within the shiftRows and subBytes steps, while the mixColumns and addRoundKey still operates on the 4 bytes at once, packed in a 32bits word.

Such strategy gives $4! \times (4!)^4 = 331,776$ different possibilities when the whole loop is considered, as we make a first permutation choice for the loop iterations, and we then choose again how to shuffle the bytes 4 times (once per iteration).

Random Permutation Generation. Random permutation generation is costly in general but the restricted number of iterations and bytes to shuffle gives an opportunity to have a much faster permutation generation. We propose to tabulate all $4! = 24$ possible permutations. Such a table makes permutation generation very simple: a random number in $[0, 24[$ is drawn, and the corresponding permutation in the table is chosen.

We generate the random number in $[0, 24[$ as follows: we draw a random number on 32bits, discard the 2 most significant bits, and consider the remaining bits as a fixed point decimal value in the range $[0, 8[$, with 3 bits encoding the integer part and 27 bits encoding the decimal part. Multiplying this value by 3, which can be done in one instruction by adding the value with a shifted version of itself in ARM-Thumb2, gives us a fixed point decimal value in the range $[0, 24[$, with 5 bits encoding the integer part and 27 bits encoding the decimal part. Keeping 5 most significant bits then gives us an integer in $[0, 24[$. Such technique allows a good trade-off between speed and statistical uniformity, as all possible resulting integers probabilities can differ only by approximately $2^{-27} \approx 10^{-8}$. It also avoids the use of a costly modulo.

The table storing permutations encodes permutations as bytes. Each byte contains 4 2-bits integers, that give the list of 4 permuted values. More formally, for any permutation $p =\{a,b,c,d\}$ of 2-bits integers, the encoding used

```
1   #define ROR(in, a) (((in) >> (a)) ^ ((in) << (32 - (a))))
2
3   // gives shiftRows input index from an output index.
4   // shiftRows would map state[input_SR(i)] to state[i]
5   uint32_t input_SR(uint32_t dest) {
6     return (dest + ((dest & 3) << 2)) & 15;
7   }
8
9   void SR_SB_MC_ARK(const uint8_t state_in[16],
10    uint32_t state_out[4], const uint32_t key[4]) {
11    for(int column = 0; column < 4; column++) {
12      int i = column << 2;
13      // perform shiftRows (sr) and subBytes (sb)
14      uint8_t byte_sr_sb_0 = sbox[state_in[input_SR(i)]];
15      uint8_t byte_sr_sb_1 = sbox[state_in[input_SR(i+1)]];
16      uint8_t byte_sr_sb_2 = sbox[state_in[input_SR(i+2)]];
17      uint8_t byte_sr_sb_3 = sbox[state_in[input_SR(i+3)]];
18      // pack all bytes together
19      uint32_t column = byte_sr_sb_0 ^ byte_sr_sb_1<<8
20                      ^ byte_sr_sb_2<<16 ^ byte_sr_sb_3<<24;
21
22      //------- mixColumns parallel computation --------
23      // serial mixColumns would compute each byte with:
24      // out_0 = in1 ^ in2 ^ in3 ^ xtime(in0 ^ in1);
25      // in0 corresponds to byte_sr_sb_0, etc...
26      // This parallel implementation follows the same formula.
27      // We call xor3 the result of in1 ^ in2 ^ in3,
28      // xor2 the result of in0 ^ in1, and xt_xor2 the
29      // result of xtime(in0 ^ in1).
30      uint32_t xor2 = column ^ ROR(column, 8);
31      uint32_t xor3 = ROR(xor2 ^ ROR(column, 16), 8);
32      //------- xtime parallel computation --------
33      // first we keep only the MSB of each byte
34      uint32_t msbs = xor_two_bytes & 0x80808080;
35      // MSB>>7 == 0 if no reduction is needed, 1 otherwise.
36      uint32_t reduc_bool = msbs >> 7;
37      // adding 0x1F gives 0x1F if no reduction is needed,
38      // 0x20 otherwise. Then the NOT gives 0b11011111 if a
39      // reduction is needed, and 0b11100000 otherwise.
40      uint32_t reduc_mask = ~(reduc_bool + 0x1F1F1F1F);
41      // AND with 0x1B to get 0x1B if a reduction is needed
42      uint32_t reducer = reduc_mask & 0x1B1B1B1B;
43      // shift left least significant bits and reduce
44      uint32_t xt_xor2 = ((xor2 & 0x7F7F7F7F) << 1) ^ reducer;
45
46      uint32_t mixcolumn_result = xor3 ^ xt_xor2;
47      // perform addRoundKey on 32bits and store back result
48      state_out[column] = mixcolumn_result ^ key[column];
49    }
50  }
51
```

Listing 1. Implementation of AES round function that performs subBytes, shiftRows, mixColumns and addRoundKey in one loop.

```
1  uint8_t perm[24] = {0x1b, 0x1e, 0x27, 0x2d, 0x36, 0x39,
2    0x4b, 0x4e, 0x63, 0x6c, 0x72, 0x78, 0x87, 0x8d, 0x93,
3    0x9c, 0xb1, 0xb4, 0xc6, 0xc9, 0xd2, 0xd8, 0xe1, 0xe4};
4
```

Listing 2. Table containing byte encodings of all possible permutations between numbers strictly lower than 4. Each permutation of 4 2-bits values is encoded in one byte consisting of the concatenation of the 4 values.

is: $(a<<6) \char`\^ (b<<4) \char`\^ (c<<2) \char`\^ d$. Listing 2 shows the obtained permutation table. Once one permutation byte is drawn from the table, the index of each iteration is obtained by extracting successively the 4 2-bits values composing the encoding.

Impact on AES Implementation. The AES implementation with shuffling closely follows the implementation described in Sect. 4.1. In particular, all the `mixColumns` parallel computation remains unchanged. Compared to Listing 1, the following changes are done to enable shuffling:

- The loop on columns (line 11) iterates following a randomly drawn index permutation.
- Input state indexes (`i`, `i+1` etc., lines 14 to 17) are shuffled using a randomly drawn permutation. A new permutation is drawn at each loop iteration.
- The packed column representation (`column`, line 11) is computed by shifting each byte according to its line index: a byte corresponding to a line index j is shifted left by $8 * j$.

4.3   Code Polymorphism

The code polymorphism countermeasure is implemented as proposed in [9]. This approach is presented in Sect. 2.2.

We propose to adapt the countermeasure in order to better hide loop iterations. Indeed, dynamic noise set apart, the code executed remains the same during consecutive loop iterations. Such constant behaviour could be used to construct attacks that work across loop iterations, as all samples from different iterations would be vertically aligned. Such attacks on loops have been demonstrated to recover masks during masked table precomputation [26], and could maybe translate to column permutation index recovery.

In order to have different behaviour during loop iterations, random branches are needed. Dynamic noise can fulfil this goal. While it was proposed to decorrelate what happens during generation and execution and to lower code generation frequency, the random branches it creates do decorrelate loop iterations. Dynamic noise works thanks to a reserved register that holds a random data at runtime, which is updated by some noise instructions, as explained in Sect. 2.2.

We extend the use of random branches to semantic variants, and propose the use of dynamic variants in combination of dynamic noise. As explained in

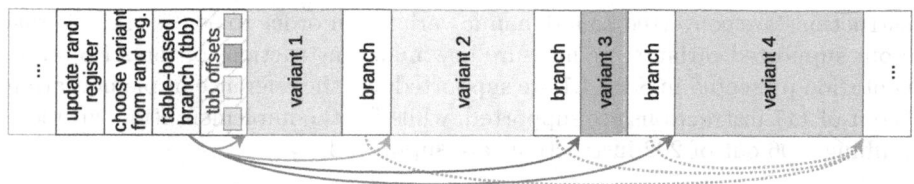

Fig. 2. Code structure of a dynamic variant. First, the random register is value is updated. Then, the variant to execute is randomly chosen. Then, the tbb instruction branches to the selected variant. Finally, after the variant is executed, the execution continues with the code right after the dynamic variant sequence.

Sect. 2.2, the use of semantic variants consists in randomly choosing during code generation a variant among several code sequences that all are semantically equivalent. When using dynamic variants, the code generator no longer chooses a variant, but instead generates a switch-case containing all variants. Such approach is inspired by the MEET approach, that leverages such mechanism to implement code polymorphism without code generation [4].

Both dynamic noise and dynamic variants are implemented using the table-based branch ARM-Thumb2 instruction (tbb). This instruction consists in a PC-relative branch whose offset is stored in a table. Having different offsets in the table and accessing the table at random indexes results in an efficient random switch-case implementation. Concerning dynamic noise, the use of this instruction lowers the overhead compared to [9].

Figure 2 shows how a dynamic variant is structured. The dynamic variant is implemented by having a preamble responsible from selecting randomly a variant, then a tbb instruction ("table-based branch" in Fig. 2) that jumps to different offsets ("tbb offsets" in Fig. 2) depending on the random variable value, then the supported variants ("variant 1–4" in Fig. 2). Branch instructions are inserted between variants to continue execution after one variant is executed.

As in dynamic noise, the switch-case used for dynamic variants is controlled by the random register, allowing the random choice of a variant during execution. The random register value may not change sufficiently along the execution depending on the noise instructions inserted. In particular, if several dynamic variants are inserted consecutively, the probability of absence of noise instruction updating the random register in between can be high. To solve this issue, we propose to update the register value before any dynamic variant ("update rand register" in Fig. 2). We use the following formula: `r=r+ROR(r,7)`. While it is not a pseudo random number generator (PRNG) with good statistical properties, one instruction is sufficient to implement it in ARM-Thumb2 assembly, hence its choice. The only fixed point is 0, and the rotate right allows making most-significant bits impact the least-significant bits of the next random numbers. This choice is motivated by use of the least-significant bits in dynamic variants.

Dynamic variants require developing several instruction sequences semantically equivalent, which can be difficult for some instructions. As such, not all instructions are converted to a dynamic variant. In order to assess the coverage of our supported variants, we measure how many instructions of the AES implementation presented in Sect. 4.1 are supported: for the reference implementation, 75 out of 117 instructions are supported, while for the implementation with loop shuffling, 106 out of 202 instructions are supported.

5   Experimental Results

This section aims at evaluating how the combination of countermeasures behaves compared to implementations featuring only one countermeasure.

5.1   Experimental Setup

We use a STM32 Nucleo-144 development board featuring a STM32F756ZG with an ARM Cortex-M7 core. We capture electromagnetic emission using a Langer RF-B 3–2 electromagnetic probe, a Langer preamplifier PA 303 and a picoscope 5244B. The sampling resolution is set to 8bits, and the sampling frequency is set to 500 Msamples/s. The STM32F7 CPU frequency is set to 166.666 MHz to capture exactly 3 samples per clock cycle to ease traces analysis. A trigger is placed right before the call to the AES polymorphic instance to ease synchronisation (right before step 4 of Fig. 1).

The electromagnetic probe is manually placed at a position where instructions boundaries and shapes are clearly visible on the oscilloscope measurements. This setup is validated by performing a non-specific t-test on the unprotected AES implementation, with 50k traces in each class. We obtain a maximal tvalue of 223.90, indicating strong leakage, hence a good probe placement.

Unprotected AES C code is compiled with `Odo` with the following options: `-O2 -target thumb-none-eabi -mcpu=cortex-m7`. C code is compiled using `arm-none-eabi-gcc`, with the following options: `-O2 -Wno-unused-function -mcpu=cortex-m7 -mthumb -static`. Memory usage is measured using `arm-noneeabi-size` on a minimally working elf file.

5.2   Performance, Table Size and Code Size

Our evaluation starts by validating the interest of our custom AES implementation compared to an 8-bits and a T-table implementation. Then, the impact of the countermeasures is studied.

Comparison of Our AES Implementation w.r.t. 8bits and T-Table. We compare the execution time, table size, and code size for unprotected AES implementations. We use: (1) an 8-bits by-the-book implementation, (2) a T-table implementation from Mbed TLS library [1], (3) our implementation (Sect. 4.1). All implementations have constant tables in RAM to improve performance, and have the key schedule precomputed. Table 1 presents the results, with execution time averaged over 1000 executions. Our implementation is 1.88× slower than T-table implementation, while being 3.64× faster than 8-bits implementation. Meanwhile, its tables' size is only 16 bytes larger than 8-bits implementation, but is 3840 bytes smaller than T-table implementation. In addition, our implementation has the lowest code size. All in all, our implementation represents a performance vs. size trade-off well positioned w.r.t other implementations considered.

Table 1. Comparison of execution time, table size, and code size for 3 unprotected AES implementations. We measure .text section to get code size.

Implementations (unprotected)	Execution time in clock cycles	Tables size in bytes		Code size in bytes
		SBox/T-tables	State(s)	
8-bits (by the book)	13834	256	16	564
T-table (Mbed TLS)	2017	4096	32	960
Ours (Sect. 4.1)	3800	256	32	536

Countermeasures Overhead. We pursue our experiments by measuring the impact of countermeasures on execution time and code size. Table 2 presents the measurements obtained. Execution time is averaged over 1000 executions. Both countermeasures have a significant overhead, reaching a 4.28× increase of execution time and 20.77× increase of size when combined. The large size increase is mainly due to code polymorphism that embeds the code generator and related functions in .text section and allocates a large buffer for the polymorphic instances in .bss. We note that even with such a large increase, the flash and RAM size in absolute remain low enough for many embedded systems, even for the implementation with combined countermeasures.

5.3 Security Evaluation on STM32F7 Traces

While each countermeasure's effect on security has already been studied, the effect of their combination is unknown. We ask whether the security obtained with combined countermeasures is higher than the security obtained with either countermeasure taken alone. As code polymorphism is slightly modified compared to previous work, we start by highlighting the effect of this modification. Then, we study how code polymorphism hides leakage of the loop shuffling permutation index. Finally, we assess how countermeasures resist to CPA with integration, and to the deep-learning attack from [21], that previously showed great success against code polymorphism.

Table 2. Execution time and size of our AES implementation presented in Sect. 4.1 with each countermeasure configuration considered.

Configuration	Execution time		Size in bytes				
	Clock cycles	Overhead	.text	.data	.bss	Total	Overhead
Unprotected	2710	baseline	536	512	788	1836	baseline
Loop shuffling	3925	×1.45	884	540	788	2212	×1.20
Code polymorphism	9128	×3.37	23008	1364	7748	32120	×17.49
All countermeasures	11620	×4.29	27120	1392	9620	38132	×20.77

Impact of Dynamic Transformations on Loop Iterations. First, the interest of dynamic transformations put forward in this paper needs to be checked. As their goal is to induce variations in loop iterations, we inspect loop patterns in side-channel traces. For this purpose, a favourable setting is used: traces are averaged over 1000 executions. Randomness seeds are reset to ensure identical PRNG outputs for all the 1000 executions, and thus the identical code paths. In addition, traces undergo a moving average of 3 samples to further aid visualisation of repeating patterns. Figure 3 shows cropped parts of the resulting traces, for the different AES configuration we consider. Without dynamic transformation, we notice loop patterns whose size is constant, except for the first iteration with code polymorphism, which is a bit longer than the others. This may be due to cache misses. As expected, the implementation with code polymorphism with dynamic transformations enabled exhibits iterations with consistently varying size. Variance of iteration size could be further increased by choosing longer variants or longer dynamic noise sequences.

Impact of Code Polymorphism on Loop Shuffling Security. Template attacks are frequently the attack of choice against loop shuffling, as explained in Sect. 2.3. Such attack starts with a point-of-interest extraction. We ask whether code polymorphism could harden such step, hiding the points of interest. To check this hypothesis, we perform a non-specific t-test targeting all permutation variables. For this purpose, we use a PRNG dedicated to the random permutation choice, whose seed is initialised in a fixed-vs.-random way. We collect 50k traces for both classes. Figure 4 shows the results of the t-tests, with and without code polymorphism. Without code polymorphism, strong leakage is visible: the t-value is above the 4.5 threshold for numerous samples, and reaches values as high as 79.30. With code polymorphism, the t-value is well contained in the $[-4.5, 4.5]$ range. As a result, no point of interest stands out from the analysed traces. As such, template attacks against the permutation index seem impractical.

Resistance of Considered Implementations Against a CPA with Integration. We first attack all implementations using a CPA with integration [25]. Integration is beneficial even for the unprotected implementation due to inherent jitter caused by our target platform. We determined an integration win-

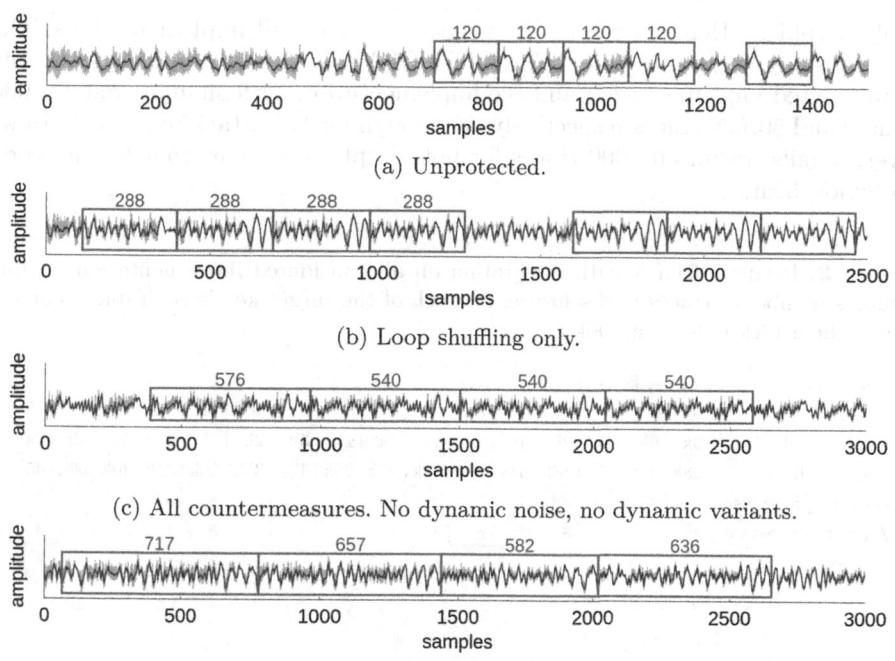

(a) Unprotected.

(b) Loop shuffling only.

(c) All countermeasures. No dynamic noise, no dynamic variants.

(d) All countermeasures. Dynamic noise and dynamic variants enabled.

Fig. 3. Electromagnetic traces obtained for different AES. The figure shows in grey in the background an average trace obtained by averaging 1000 executions with identical PRNG seed. The figure shows in blue the average trace post-processed using a moving average with a window of 3 samples. Repeating patterns are framed in rectangles, and their length in samples is indicated in red. (Color figure online)

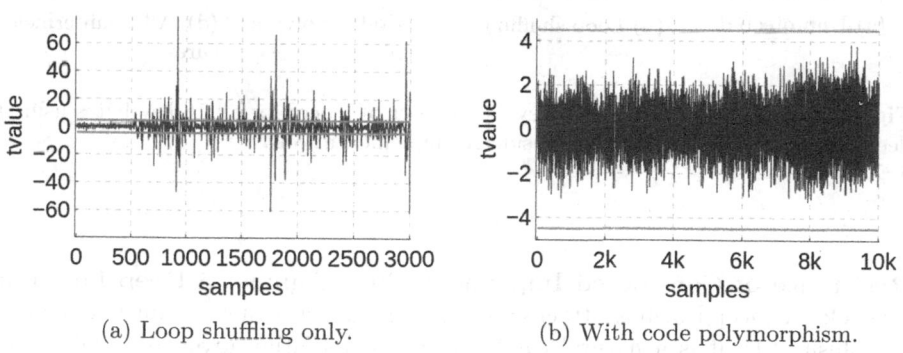

(a) Loop shuffling only.

(b) With code polymorphism.

Fig. 4. Non specific t-tests (50k vs. 50k traces) targeting leakage from the permutation variable used to shuffle loops, with code polymorphism disabled (left) or enabled (right). Red lines indicate the 4.5 leakage detection threshold. (Color figure online)

dow of 24 samples was appropriate for this purpose. Changing the size of the integration window did not lead to any improvement, even in presence of code polymorphism. Hence, we kept the window of 24 for all implementations. The CPA results are presented in Table 3. The CPA easily finds all key bytes to the unprotected implementation and the implementation with shuffling only: 6, 000 traces and 50, 000 traces respectively are enough for the attack to succeed. However, it fails within 500, 000 traces for both implementations that feature code polymorphism.

Table 3. Results of CPA with integration on all considered implementations. Table reports number of traces to disclosure, for each of the target key byte. Table reports ✗ when the attack fails with 500k traces.

Configuration	Target key byte															
	0	1	2	3	4	5	6	7	8	9	10	11	12	13	14	15
Unprotected	3k	6k	1k	2k	3k	2k	4k	1k	2k	3k	2k	4k	4k	3k	4k	2k
Loop shuffling	28k	32k	35k	18k	38k	28k	42k	45k	20k	18k	35k	20k	35k	40k	50k	45k
Code polymorphism	✗	✗	✗	✗	✗	✗	✗	✗	✗	✗	✗	✗	✗	✗	✗	✗
All countermeasures	✗	✗	✗	✗	✗	✗	✗	✗	✗	✗	✗	✗	✗	✗	✗	✗

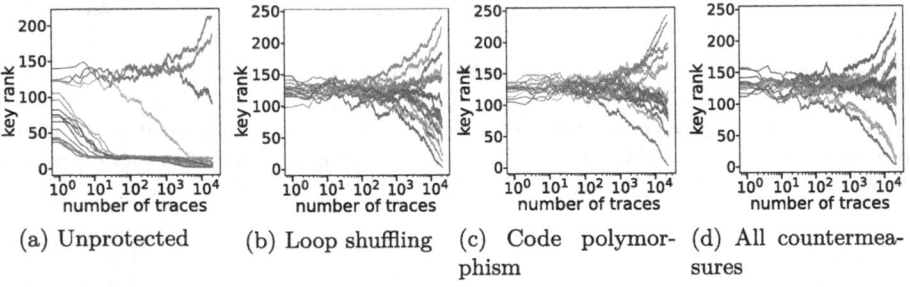

(a) Unprotected   (b) Loop shuffling   (c) Code polymorphism   (d) All countermeasures

Fig. 5. Average rank of the right key vs. number of traces for all 16 key bytes using a deep learning attack against all considered implementations.

Resistance of Considered Implementations Against a Deep Learning Attack. As deep learning attacks are state-of-the-art attacks against code polymorphism [21], it is a natural candidate for a potential adversary against the enhanced version of code polymorphism combined with loop shuffling considered in this paper. As the target platform used in this paper slightly differs from the one used in [21], the neural network parameters require some modifications. Indeed, our clock frequency is much faster than the one of the STM32F3 used in [21], resulting in a lower number of samples per clock cycle (from 50 in [21] to 3 here). Accordingly, we remove the first layer that was specifically designed to handle the large number of samples per clock cycle. Apart from that, we keep the same hyper-parameters as in [21]: the filter size and the pooling size are respectively $w = 11, p = 5$, the number of convolution filters per layer is $k_0 = 10$ at the first layer, and doubles at every layer. Given the size of the traces, the number of convolutional layers is set to 3. The network is trained with the Adam optimiser [16] during 100 epochs on the Pytorch framework [24], with batch size equal to 32 traces. Given that a data-set of 100,000 traces has been measured, we split it into 80,000 training traces, and 20,000 validation traces. Hence, there are $80,000/32 = 2500$ iterations per epoch. Once the training is finished, we run a key recovery attack by plugging the model's predictions into a maximum likelihood distinguisher. More precisely, we compute the cumulative sum of the log probabilities returned by the trained model for each trace from the validation set. Based on the cumulative scores, we may compute the rank of the right key. We repeat the procedure 50 times, by shuffling the order of the validation traces. This re-sampling (a.k.a. bootstrapping) method allows avoiding sampling 50 new validation datasets of 20,000 traces each, although at the cost of a biased measure of the guessing entropy when the considered number of attack traces becomes close to the size of the validation set.

Figure 5 presents the attack results for all considered implementations. First, we notice that for 12 out of the 16 target bytes, the attacks succeeds in lowering the average rank of the right key significantly enough for a key enumeration, within 40 traces for the baseline (unprotected) implementation. Considering other implementations, none of them depicts a convincing key recovery. The curve diverging towards different key ranks on the right side of Figs. 5b, 5c and 5d may be due to the bias induced by the re-sampling method. This suggests anyway that 20,000 traces were not sufficient to observe the guessing entropy converging towards 0 with confidence. It is worth noticing the failed attack against loop shuffling alone, especially as we could succeed a CPA with integration to find all key bytes. We note some much more complex trained models have been shown efficient against shuffling [22]. Nevertheless, the latter models were not specifically designed against code polymorphism, hence we kept a neural network architecture close to the one of [21] as a baseline. Studying much heavier architectures that have been shown efficient against shuffling on polymorphic implementations remains an open problem, and is left for further works.

Likewise, code polymorphism seems to exhibit a better resistance than in [21]. This may be due to the difference of platform and implementation, including the storage of the SBox in RAM to avoid loads from flash. Finally, the combination of both countermeasures shows similar trend. Overall, these experiments are not sufficient to prove the security of the enhanced code polymorphism combined with loop shuffling with overwhelmingly high confidence. Yet, they provide significant empirical evidences that the baseline attacks from [21] may not straightforwardly apply, and that a successful adversary, should it exist, would be much more involved. In order to challenge this conjecture, we release our dataset along with the paper: https://zenodo.org/records/10650737.

5.4   Security Evaluation on Simulated Noiseless Traces

As our security evaluation on real-world traces is insufficient to compare security of combined countermeasures w.r.t. code polymorphism alone, we pursue our security evaluation by simulating a perfect noiseless setting to ease attacks.

Traces Simulation. Our simulation framework builds upon QEMU simulator [8]. We instruct QEMU to execute the program by steps of 1 assembly instruction. For each assembly instruction executed, our simulation framework outputs 2 samples: one that sums the Hamming Weights of the input operands before the instruction, and one that contains the Hamming Weight of the output operand after the instruction. No noise is added to the samples. We use this framework to simulate traces for all the considered countermeasure configurations.

Table 4. Results of CPA on simulated noiseless traces for all considered implementations. Table reports number of traces to disclosure, for each of the target key byte. Traces are simulated using the Hamming Weight model on registers used by each executed assembly instruction.

Config.	Target key byte															
	0	1	2	3	4	5	6	7	8	9	10	11	12	13	14	15
Unprotect.	8	9	9	8	8	8	8	11	8	8	8	10	12	7	8	8
Loop shuf.	1165	921	707	713	1030	1186	1268	615	1104	1060	838	1047	891	604	234	1280
Code poly.	41k	41k	47k	61k	29k	25k	35k	55k	39k	42k	25k	85k	23k	24k	25k	50k
All	595k	215k	752k	369k	>1M	767k	998k	744k	>1M	592k	703k	747k	848k	588k	763k	735k

Resistance of Considered Implementations Against a CPA on Simulated Noiseless Traces. We perform a CPA [12] on the simulated traces. We note such setting is particularly favourable, as the employed Hamming weight model for simulation is the same as the one employed for the leakage estimation of the CPA. The results are presented in Table 4. As expected, we notice that the attack is much faster than in the real-world setting. The attack succeeds on all configurations. The added value of combined countermeasure is clearly visible, as the CPA requires in average 17× more traces for the implementation with combined countermeasures compared to the implementation with code polymorphism alone.

Resistance of Considered Implementations Against a Deep Learning Attack on Simulated Noiseless Traces. In order to consolidate the CPA results on simulation, we also re-trained our deep learning models on the noiseless simulated traces. The training procedure remains the same, in particular we used the same number of training and attack traces as in Fig. 5. The results are given in Fig. 6, which depicts the average rank of the right key byte with respect to the number of attack traces. We can see on the one hand in particular on Figs. 6a and 6b that the deep-learning attack succeeds in recovering the right key within a few traces. On the other hand, on Fig. 6c the key-rank curves are much slower to converge towards 0 (in a few hundreds of traces), and converge only for a few bytes, meaning that the attack did not always succeed. More interestingly, Fig. 6d shows that no key recovery has been successful within 20,000 attack traces after a profiling step. This empirically confirms the relevance of combining both shuffling and code polymorphism.

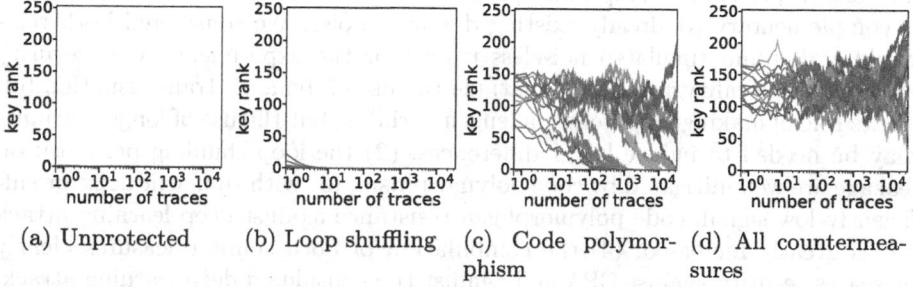

(a) Unprotected   (b) Loop shuffling   (c) Code polymor-   (d) All countermea-
                                         phism   sures

Fig. 6. Average rank of the right key vs. number of traces for all 16 key bytes using a deep learning attack against all considered implementations, on simulated traces.

6   Conclusion

In this paper, we investigated the combination of two hiding countermeasures, namely loop shuffling and code polymorphism, to protect an AES implementation. Considering loop shuffling, we extended the countermeasure by shuffling as well the memory accesses within the loop, and we selected a random permutation among all possible ones using simple computation tricks to extend the number of possibilities w.r.t. classical random start index and random walk approaches. Considering code polymorphism, we stressed the interest of dynamic transformations in presence of loops, and proposed the use of dynamic variants, which is complementary to already existing dynamic noise. We considered both real-world traces and simulated noiseless traces for the experiments. Our security experimental evaluation showed that: (1) the use of dynamic transformation fulfils its role of making loop iteration length variable, but the use of longer variants may be needed to induce larger differences, (2) the loop shuffling permutation leakage are well mitigated by code polymorphism, (3) with sufficient noise or sufficiently low signal, code polymorphism resistance against deep learning attack seems greatly increased, (4) the combination of both countermeasures clearly increases security against CPA and against the considered deep learning attack, as shown in the noiseless simulated setting.

Such combination is thus worthy, especially in contexts where loop shuffling's main flaw is due to the leakage of its permutation variables. In particular, an interesting future work could be the combination with masking countermeasure, along several axes: (1) exploiting shuffling opportunities offered by masking as in [7], (2) better secure masked table computation, as shuffling alone was shown insufficient in this regard [26].

Acknowledgement. This work was partially funded as part of the TANGO project, which has received funding from the European Union's Horizon Europe Research and Innovation Programme under the grant agreement No. 101070052. The authors would like to thank Damien Couroussé for his helpful comments, and Simon Baissat-Chavent for the development of the trace simulator used in this paper.

References

1. Mbed TLS library. https://www.trustedfirmware.org/projects/mbed-tls/
2. Abdellatif, K.M., Couroussé, D., Potin, O., Jaillon, P.: Filtering-based CPA: a successful side-channel attack against desynchronization countermeasures. In: Proceedings of the Fourth Workshop on Cryptography and Security in Computing Systems, CS2 2017, pp. 29–32. Association for Computing Machinery (2017)
3. Agosta, G., Barenghi, A., Pelosi, G.: A code morphing methodology to automate power analysis countermeasures. In: DAC, pp. 77–82 (2012)
4. Agosta, G., Barenghi, A., Pelosi, G., Scandale, M.: The MEET approach: securing cryptographic embedded software against side channel attacks. IEEE TCAD **34**(8), 1320–1333 (2015)

5. Amarilli, A., Müller, S., Naccache, D., Page, D., Rauzy, P., Tunstall, M.: Can code polymorphism limit information leakage? In: Ardagna, C.A., Zhou, J. (eds.) WISTP 2011. LNCS, vol. 6633, pp. 1–21. Springer, Heidelberg (2011). https://doi.org/10.1007/978-3-642-21040-2_1

6. Antognazza, F., Barenghi, A., Pelosi, G.: Metis: An integrated morphing engine CPU to protect against side channel attacks. IEEE Access 9, 69210–69225 (2021). https://doi.org/10.1109/ACCESS.2021.3077977

7. Azouaoui, M., Bronchain, O., Grosso, V., Papagiannopoulos, K., Standaert, F.X.: Bitslice masking and improved shuffling: how and when to mix them in software? IACR Trans. Cryptogr. Hardw. Embed. Syst. 2022(2), 140–165 (2022)

8. Bellard, F.: Qemu, a fast and portable dynamic translator. In: Proceedings of the Annual Conference on USENIX Annual Technical Conference, ATEC 2005, p. 41. USENIX Association (2005)

9. Belleville, N., Couroussé, D., Heydemann, K., Charles, H.P.: Automated software protection for the masses against side-channel attacks. In: TACO. ACM (2018)

10. Benadjila, R., Khati, L., Prouff, E., Thillard, A.: ANSSI-FR/secaesstm32: Bibliothèque C et assembleur permettant le chiffrement/déchiffrement AES-128 de messages pour des composants grand public (famille STM32F3/STM32F4). https://github.com/ANSSI-FR/SecAESSTM32

11. Benadjila, R., Lomné, V., Prouff, E., Roche, T.: ANSSI-FR/secaes-atmega8515: Secure aes128 for atmega8515. https://github.com/ANSSI-FR/secAES-ATmega8515/blob/master/src/Version2/maskedAES128enc.S

12. Brier, E., Clavier, C., Olivier, F.: Correlation power analysis with a leakage model. In: Joye, M., Quisquater, J.-J. (eds.) CHES 2004. LNCS, vol. 3156, pp. 16–29. Springer, Heidelberg (2004). https://doi.org/10.1007/978-3-540-28632-5_2

13. Bronchain, O., Standaert, F.X.: Side-channel countermeasures' dissection and the limits of closed source security evaluations. IACR Trans. Cryptogr. Hardw. Embed. Syst. 2020(2), 1–25 (2020)

14. Couroussé, D., Barry, T., Robisson, B., Jaillon, P., Potin, O., Lanet, J.-L.: Runtime code polymorphism as a protection against side channel attacks. In: Foresti, S., Lopez, J. (eds.) WISTP 2016. LNCS, vol. 9895, pp. 136–152. Springer, Cham (2016). https://doi.org/10.1007/978-3-319-45931-8_9

15. Fumaroli, G., Martinelli, A., Prouff, E., Rivain, M.: Affine masking against higher-order side channel analysis. In: Biryukov, A., Gong, G., Stinson, D.R. (eds.) SAC 2010. LNCS, vol. 6544, pp. 262–280. Springer, Heidelberg (2011). https://doi.org/10.1007/978-3-642-19574-7_18

16. Kingma, D.P., Ba, J.: Adam: a method for stochastic optimization. In: 3rd International Conference on Learning Representations, ICLR 2015, San Diego, CA, USA, 7–9 May 2015, Conference Track Proceedings (2015). https://arxiv.org/abs/1412.6980

17. Luo, P., Zhang, L., Fei, Y., Ding, A.A.: Towards secure cryptographic software implementation against side-channel power analysis attacks. In: 2015 IEEE 26th International Conference on Application-specific Systems, Architectures and Processors (ASAP), pp. 144–148 (2015).https://doi.org/10.1109/ASAP.2015.7245722

18. Malagón, P., De Goyeneche, J.M., Zapater, M., Moya, J.M., Banković, Z.: Compiler optimizations as a countermeasure against side-channel analysis in msp430-based devices. Sensors 12(6), 7994–8012 (2012)

19. Mangard, S., Oswald, E., Popp, T.: Power Analysis Attacks - Revealing the Secrets of Smart Cards. Springer, Heidelberg (2007). https://doi.org/10.1007/978-0-387-38162-6

20. Masure, L.: Towards a better comprehension of deep learning for side-channel analysis. (Vers une meilleure compréhension de l'apprentissage profond appliqué aux attaques par observations). Ph.D. thesis, Sorbonne University, Paris, France (2020). https://tel.archives-ouvertes.fr/tel-03651269

21. Masure, L., et al.: Deep learning side-channel analysis on large-scale traces. In: ESORICS (2020)

22. Masure, L., Strullu, R.: Side-channel analysis against ANSSI's protected AES implementation on ARM: end-to-end attacks with multi-task learning. J. Cryptogr. Eng. **13**(2), 129–147 (2023)

23. Naccache, D., Nguyên, P.Q., Tunstall, M., Whelan, C.: Experimenting with faults, lattices and the DSA. In: Vaudenay, S. (ed.) PKC 2005. LNCS, vol. 3386, pp. 16–28. Springer, Heidelberg (2005). https://doi.org/10.1007/978-3-540-30580-4_3

24. Paszke, A., et al.: PyTorch: an imperative style, high-performance deep learning library. In: Advances in Neural Information Processing Systems 32: Annual Conference on Neural Information Processing Systems 2019, NeurIPS 2019, Vancouver, BC, Canada, 8–14 December 2019, pp. 8024–8035 (2019)

25. Rivain, M., Prouff, E., Doget, J.: Higher-order masking and shuffling for software implementations of block ciphers. In: Clavier, C., Gaj, K. (eds.) CHES 2009. LNCS, vol. 5747, pp. 171–188. Springer, Heidelberg (2009). https://doi.org/10.1007/978-3-642-04138-9_13

26. Tunstall, M., Whitnall, C., Oswald, E.: Masking tables—an underestimated security risk. In: Moriai, S. (ed.) FSE 2013. LNCS, vol. 8424, pp. 425–444. Springer, Heidelberg (2014). https://doi.org/10.1007/978-3-662-43933-3_22

27. Udvarhelyi, B., Bronchain, O., Standaert, F.-X.: Security analysis of deterministic re-keying with masking and shuffling: application to ISAP. In: Bhasin, S., De Santis, F. (eds.) COSADE 2021. LNCS, vol. 12910, pp. 168–183. Springer, Cham (2021). https://doi.org/10.1007/978-3-030-89915-8_8

28. Veyrat-Charvillon, N., Medwed, M., Kerckhof, S., Standaert, F.-X.: Shuffling against side-channel attacks: a comprehensive study with cautionary note. In: Wang, X., Sako, K. (eds.) ASIACRYPT 2012. LNCS, vol. 7658, pp. 740–757. Springer, Heidelberg (2012). https://doi.org/10.1007/978-3-642-34961-4_44

Author Index

© The Editor(s) (if applicable) and The Author(s), under exclusive license
to Springer Nature Switzerland AG 2024
R. Wacquez and N. Homma (Eds.): COSADE 2024, LNCS 14595, pp. 281–282, 2024.
https://doi.org/10.1007/978-3-031-57543-3

Printed in the United States
by Baker & Taylor Publisher Services

Printed in the United States
by Baker & Taylor Publisher Services